Predictive Analytics and Data Optimization

Predictive Analytics and Data Optimization

Edited by **Mick Benson**

WILLFORD PRESS

New York

Published by Willford Press,
118-35 Queens Blvd., Suite 400,
Forest Hills, NY 11375, USA
www.willfordpress.com

Predictive Analytics and Data Optimization
Edited by Mick Benson

International Standard Book Number: 978-1-68285-298-9 (Hardback)

Printed in the United States of America.

Contents

Preface

This book aims to highlight the current researches and provides a platform to further the scope of innovations in this area. This book is a product of the combined efforts of many researchers and scientists from different parts of the world. The objective of this book is to provide the readers with the latest information in the field.

Data analysis models and techniques have rapidly evolved in last few decades to unfold patterns and information from large and complex datasets. This book provides a comprehensive insight with the help of topics such as analysis and synthesis of massive datasets, modelling and dynamics of large scale information networks, data mining, etc. It strives to give a fair idea about this discipline and to help develop a better understanding of the latest advances within this field. This book, with its detailed analyses and data, will prove immensely beneficial to professionals and students involved in this area at various levels.

I would like to express my sincere thanks to the authors for their dedicated efforts in the completion of this book. I acknowledge the efforts of the publisher for providing constant support. Lastly, I would like to thank my family for their support in all academic endeavors.

Editor

Long trend dynamics in social media

Chunyan Wang[1]* and Bernardo A Huberman[2]*

*Correspondence:
chunyan@stanford.edu;
bernardo.huberman@hp.com
[1] Department of Applied Physics,
Stanford University, Stanford, CA,
USA
[2] Social Computing Lab, HP Labs,
Palo Alto, California, USA

Abstract

A main characteristic of social media is that its diverse content, copiously generated by both standard outlets and general users, constantly competes for the scarce attention of large audiences. Out of this flood of information some topics manage to get enough attention to become the most popular ones and thus to be prominently displayed as trends. Equally important, some of these trends persist long enough so as to shape part of the social agenda. How this happens is the focus of this paper. By introducing a stochastic dynamical model that takes into account the user's repeated involvement with given topics, we can predict the distribution of trend durations as well as the thresholds in popularity that lead to their emergence within social media. Detailed measurements of datasets from Twitter confirm the validity of the model and its predictions.

1 Introduction

The past decade has witnessed an explosive growth of social media, creating a competitive environment where topics compete for the attention of users [1, 2]. A main characteristic of social media is that both users and standard media outlets generate content at the same time in the form of news, videos and stories, leading to a flood of information from which it is hard for users to sort out the relevant pieces to concentrate on [3, 4]. User attention is critical for the understand of how problems in culture, decision making and opinion formation evolve [5–7]. Several studies have shown that attention allocated to on-line content is distributed in a highly skewed fashion [8–11]. While most documents receive a negligible amount of attention, a few items become extremely popular and persist as public trends for long a period of time [12–14]. Recent studies have focused on the dynamical growth of attention on different kinds of social media, including Digg [15–17], Youtube [18], Wikipedia [19–21] and Twitter [14, 22–24]. The time-scale over which content persists as a topic in these media also varies on a scale from hours to years. In the case of news and stories, content spreads on the social network until its novelty decays [15]. In information networks like Wikipedia, where a document remains alive for months and even years, popularity is governed by bursts of sudden events and is explained by the rank shift model [19].

While previous work has successfully addressed the growth and decay of news and topics in general, a remaining problem is why some of the topics stay popular for longer periods of time than others and thus contribute to the social agenda. In this paper, we focus on the dynamics of long trends and their persistence within social media. We first introduce a dynamic model of attention growth and derive the distribution of trend durations for all topics. By analyzing the resonating nature of the content within the community, we provide a threshold criterion that successfully predicts the long term persistence of social trends. The predictions of the model are then compared with measurements taken from Twitter, which as we show provides a validation of the proposed dynamics.

This paper is structured as follows. In Section 2 we describe our model for attention growth and the persistence of trends. Section 3 describes the data-set and the collection strategies used in the study, whereas Section 4 discusses the measurements made on data-sets from Twitter and compares them with the predictions of the model. Section 5 concludes with a summary of our findings and future directions.

2 Model

On-line micro-blogging and social service websites enable users to read and send text-based messages to certain topics of interest. The popularity of these topics is commonly measured by the number of postings about these topics [15, 19]. For instance on Twitter, Digg and Youtube, users post their thoughts on topics of interest in the form of tweets and comments. One special characteristic of social media that has been ignored so far is that users can contribute to the popularity of a topic more than once. We take this into account by denoting first posts on a certain topic from a certain user by the variable First Time Post (*FTP*). If the same user posts on the topic more than once, we call it a Repeated Post (*RP*). In what follows, we first look at the growth dynamics of *FTP*.

When a topic first catches people's attention, a few people may further pass it on to others in the community. If we denote the cumulative number of *FTP* mentioning the topic at time t by N_t, the growth of attention can be described by $N_t = (1 + \chi_t)N_{t-1}$, where the χ_t are assumed to be small, positive, independent and identically distributed random variables with mean μ and variance σ^2. For small χ_s, the equation can be approximated as:

$$N_t \simeq \prod_{s=1}^{t} e^{\chi_s} N_0 = e^{\sum_{s=1}^{t} \chi_s} N_0. \tag{1}$$

Taking logarithms on both sides, we obtain $\log \frac{N_t}{N_0} = \sum_{s=1}^{t} \chi_s$. Applying the central limit theorem to the sum, it follows that the cumulative count of *FTP* should obey a log-normal distribution.

We now consider the persistence of social trends. We use the variable vitality, $\phi_t = \frac{N_t}{N_{t-1}}$, as a measurement of popularity, and assume that if the vitality of a topic falls below a certain threshold θ_1, the topic stops trending. Thus

$$\log \phi_t = \log \frac{N_t}{N_{t-1}} = \log \frac{N_t}{N_0} - \log \frac{N_{t-1}}{N_0} \simeq \chi_t. \tag{2}$$

The probability of ceasing to trend at the time interval s is equal to the probability that ϕ_s is lower than a threshold value θ_1, which can be written as:

$$p = \Pr(\phi_s < \theta_1) = \Pr(\log \phi_s < \log(\theta_1))$$
$$= \Pr(\chi_s < \log(\theta_1)) = F(\log(\theta_1)), \tag{3}$$

where $F(x)$ is the cumulative distribution function of the random variable χ. We are thus able to determine the threshold value from $\theta_1 = e^{F^{-1}(p)}$ if we know the distribution of the random variable χ. Notice that if χ is independent and identically distributed, it follows that the distribution of trending durations is given by a geometric distribution with $\Pr(L = k) = (1 - p)^k p$. The expected trending duration of a topic, $E(L)$, is therefore given by

$$E(L) = \sum_0^\infty (1 - p)^k p \cdot k = \frac{1}{p} - 1 = \frac{1}{F(\log(\theta_1))} - 1. \tag{4}$$

Thus far we have only considered the impact of FTP on social trends by treating all topics as identical to each other. To account for the resonance between users and specific topics we now include the RP into the dynamics. We define the instantaneous number of FTP posted in the time interval t as FTP_t, and the repeated posts, RP, in the time interval t as RP_t. Similarly we denote the cumulative number of all posts-including both FTP and RP-as S_t. The resonance level of fans with a given topic is measured by $\mu_t = \frac{FTP_t + RP_t}{FTP_t}$, and we define the expected value of μ_t, $E(\mu_t)$ as the active-ratio a_q.

We can simplify the dynamics by assuming that μ_t is independent and uniformly distributed on the interval $[1, 2a_q - 1]$. It then follows that the increment of S_t is given by the sum of FTP_t and RP_t. We thus have

$$S_t - S_{t-1} = FTP_t + RP_t = \mu_t FTP_t = \mu_t(N_t - N_{t-1}) = \mu_t \chi_t N_{t-1}. \tag{5}$$

And also

$$\begin{aligned}
E_\mu(S_t) &= E_\mu(S_{t-1}) + a_q(N_t - N_{t-1}) \\
&= E_\mu(S_{t-2}) + a_q(N_t - N_{t-2}) = \cdots \\
&= E_\mu(S_0) + a_q(N_t - N_0) = a_q N_t.
\end{aligned} \tag{6}$$

We approximate S_{t-1} by $\mu_t N_{t-1}$. Going back to Equation 5, we have

$$S_t \simeq \mu_t(\chi_t + 1)N_{t-1} \simeq \mu_t e^{\chi_t} N_{t-1}. \tag{7}$$

From this, it follows that the dynamics of the full attention process is determined by the two independent random variables, μ and χ. Similarly to the derivation of Equation 3, the topic is assumed to stop trending if the value of either one of the random variables governing the process falls below the thresholds θ_1 and θ_2, respectively. One point worth mentioning here is that, θ_1 and θ_2 are system parameters, i.e. not dependent on the topic, but only on the studied medium. The probability of ceasing to trend, defined as $p^\star$, is now given by

$$p^\star = \Pr(\chi_t < \log(\theta_1)) \Pr(\mu_t < \theta_2) = \frac{\theta_2 - 1}{2(a_q - 1)} p, \tag{8}$$

$p = F(\log(\theta_1))$. The expected value of L_q for any topic q is given by

$$E(L_q) = \frac{2(a_q - 1)}{F(\log \theta_1)(\theta_2 - 1)} - 1. \tag{9}$$

Which states that the persistent duration of trends associated with given topics is expected to scale linearly with the topic users' active-ratio. From this result it follows that one can predict the trend duration for any topic by measuring its user active-ratio after the values of θ_1 and θ_2 are determined from empirical observations.

3 Data

To test the predictions of our dynamic model, we analyzed data from Twitter, an extremely popular social network website used by over 200 million users around the world. Its interface of allows users to post short messages, known as tweets, that can be read and retweeted by other Twitter users. Users declare the people they follow, and they get notified when there is a new post from any of these people. A user can also forward the original post of another user to his followers by the re-tweet mechanism.

In our study, the cumulative count of tweets and re-tweets that are related to a certain topic was used as a proxy for the popularity of the topic. On the front page of Twitter there is also a column named trends that presents the few keywords or sentences that are most frequently mentioned in Twitter at a given moment. The list of popular topics in the trends column is updated every few minutes as new topics become popular. We collected the topics in the trends column by performing an API query every 20 minutes. For each of the topics in the trending column, we used the Search API function to collect the full list of tweets and re-tweets related to the topic over the past 20 minutes. We also collected information about the author of the post, identified by a unique user-id, the text of the post and the time of its posting. We thus obtained a dataset of 16.32 million posts on 3361 different topics. The longest trending topic we observed had a length of 14.7 days. We found that of all the posts in our dataset, 17% belonged to the *RP* category.

4 Results

We start by analyzing the distribution of N from our data-set. We found out that N_{10} follows a log-normal distribution, as can be seen from Figure 1. The Q-Q plot in Figure 1 follows a straight line. Different values of t yield similar results. The Kolmogorov-Smirnov normality test of $\log(N_{10})$ with mean 3.5577 and standard deviation 0.3266 yields a p-value of 0.0838. At a significance level of 0.05, the test fails to reject the null hypothesis that $\log(N_{10})$ follows normal distribution, a result which is consistent with Equation 1.

We also measured the distribution of χ from $\chi_t = \frac{N_t}{N_{t-1}} - 1$. We found that $\log(\chi)$ follows a normal distribution with mean equal to -1.4522 and a standard deviation value of 0.6715,

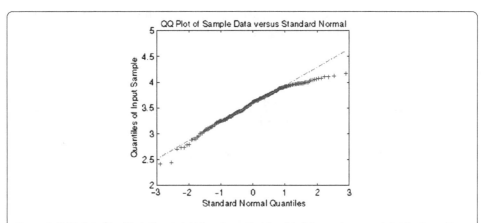

Figure 1 Q-Q plot of log(N_{10}). The straight line shows that the data follows a lognormal distribution with a slightly shorter tail.

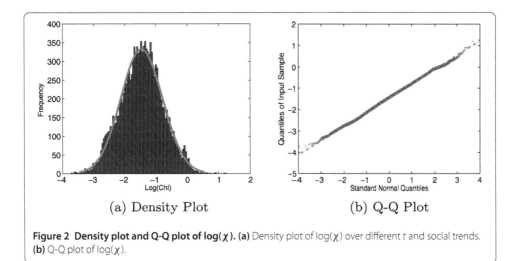

(a) Density Plot (b) Q-Q Plot

Figure 2 Density plot and Q-Q plot of log(χ). (a) Density plot of log(χ) over different t and social trends. (b) Q-Q plot of log(χ).

as shown in Figure 2. The Kolmogorov-Smirnov normality test statistic gives a high p-value of 0.5346. The mean value of χ is 0.0353, which is small for the approximations in Equation 1 and Equation 7 to be valid. We also examined the record breaking values of vitality, $\phi_t = \chi_t + 1$, which signal the behavior of the longest lasting trends. From the theory of records, if the values ϕ_t come from an independent and identical distribution, the number of records that have occurred up to time t, defined as $R_n(t)$, should scale linearly with $\log(t)$ [26, 27]. As is customary, we say that a new record has been established if the vitality of the trend at the moment is longer than all of the previous observations. As shown in Figure 3, there is a linear scaling relationship between $\log(t)$ and $R_n(t)$ for a sample topic "Kim Chul Hee". The topic kept trending for 14 days on Twitter in September 2010. Similar observations are repeated for other different topics on Twitter. One implication of this observation is that confirms the validity of our assumption that the values of $\chi_1, \chi_2, \ldots, \chi_t$ are independent and identically distributed.

Next we turn our attention to the distribution of durations of long trends. As shown in Figure 4 and Figure 5, a linear fit of trend duration as a function of density in a logarithmic scale suggests an exponential family, which is consistent with Equation 4. The red line in Figure 4 gives a linear fitting with R-square 0.9112. From the log-log scale plot in Figure 5, we observe that the distribution deviates from a power law, which is a characteristic of so-

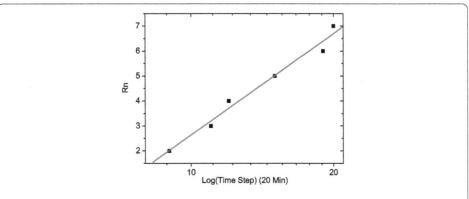

Figure 3 The linear scaling relationship between $R_n(t)$ and $\log(t)$ of topic 'Kim Chul Hee', a Korean pop star. The number of records that have occurred up to time t scales linearly with $\log(t)$.

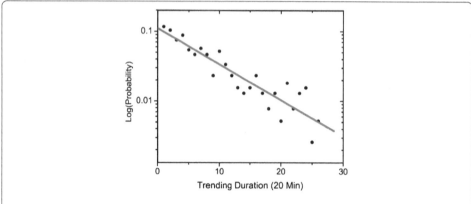

Figure 4 Semi-log plot of trending duration density. The straight line suggests an exponential family of the trending time distribution.

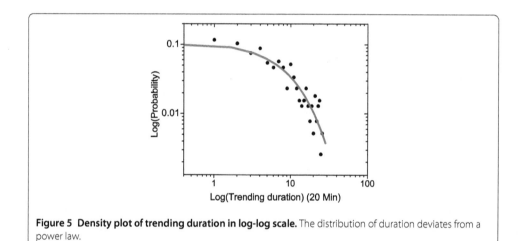

Figure 5 Density plot of trending duration in log-log scale. The distribution of duration deviates from a power law.

cial trends that originate from news on social media [25]. From the distribution of trending times, p is estimated to have a value of 0.12. Together with the measured distribution of χ and Equation 3, we can estimate the value of θ to be 1.0132.

We can also determine the expected duration of trend times stemming from the impact of active-ratio. The frequency count of active-ratios over different topics is shown in Figure 6, with a peak at $a_q = 1.2$. This observation suggests that while the ratio is centered around 1.2 for the majority of topics, there are a few topics obtain large amount of repeated attention. This observation may shadow light on existing observations about the highly skewed distribution in attention dynamic studies. As can be seen in Figure 7, the trend duration of different topics scales linearly with the active-ratio, which is consistent with the prediction of Equation 9. The R-square of the linear fitting has a value of 0.98664. From the slope of the linear fit and $\theta_1 = 1.0132$, and Equation 9 we obtain a value for $\theta_2 = 1.153$. With the value of θ_1 and θ_2, we are able to predict the expected trend duration of any given topic based on measurements of its active-ratio.

5 Discussion and conclusion

In this paper we investigated the persistence dynamics of trends in social media. By introducing a stochastic dynamic model that takes into account the user's repeated involve-

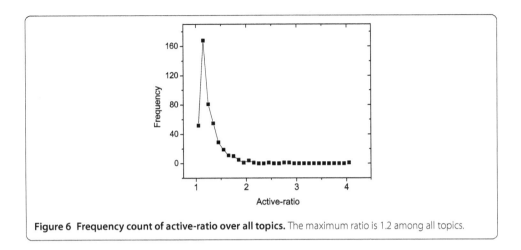

Figure 6 Frequency count of active-ratio over all topics. The maximum ratio is 1.2 among all topics.

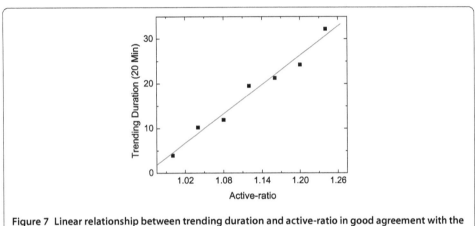

Figure 7 Linear relationship between trending duration and active-ratio in good agreement with the predictions of model.

ment with given topics, we are able to predict the distribution of trend durations as well as the thresholds in popularity that lead to the emergence of given topics as trends within social media. The predictions of our mode were confirmed by a careful analysis of a data from Twitter. Furthermore, a linear relationship between the resonance level of users with given topics, and the trending duration of a topic was derived. The proposed model provides a deeper understanding the popularity of on-line contents. Parameters θ_1 and θ_2 in our model are system specific and could be calculated from hidden algorithms when applying our model to other on-line social media websites. Possible refinements may include the effect of competition between topics, sudden burst of events, the effect of marketing campaigns and the actively censoring of specific topics [28]. In closing, we note that although the focus in this paper has been on trend dynamics that are featured on social media websites, the framework and model may be suitable to other types of content and off-line trends. The issue raised - that is, trending phenomenon under the impact of user's repeated involvement - is therefore a general one and should provide ample opportunities for future work.

Competing interests
The authors declare that they have no competing interests.

Author contributions

B.H. and C.W. designed the study and performed research. C.W. and B.H. wrote the paper. All authors read and approved the final manuscript.

Acknowledgements

We acknowledge useful discussions with S. Asur and G. Szabo. C.W. would like to thank HP Labs for financial support.

References

1. McCombs ME, Shaw DL (1993) The evolution of agenda setting research: twenty five years in the marketplace of ideas. Journal of Communication 43(2):68-84
2. Falkinger J (2008) Limited attention as a scarce resource in information-rich economies. Econ J (Lond) 118(532):1596-1620
3. Agichtein E, Castillo C, Donato D, Gionis A, Mishne G (2008) Finding high-quality content in social media. In: Proceedings of the international conference on Web search and web data mining (WSDM)
4. Kaplan AM, Haenlein M (2010) Users of the world, unite! The challenges and opportunities of Social Media. Bus Horiz 53(1):59-68
5. Zhu J-H (1992) Issue competition and attention distraction: a zero-sum theory of agenda setting. Journal Q 69:825-836
6. Wuchty S, Jones BF, Uzzi B (2007) The increasing dominance of teams in production of knowledge. Science 316(5827):1036-1039
7. Guimerà R, Uzzi B, Spiro J, Amaral LAN (2005) Team assembly mechanisms determine collaboration network structure and team performance. Science 308(5722):697-702
8. Huberman BA, Pirolli PLT, Pitkow JE, Lukose RM (1998) Strong regularities in world wide web surfing. Science 280(5360):95-97
9. Johansen A, Sornette D (2000) Download relaxation dynamics on the WWW following newspaper publication of URL. Physica A 276(1-2):338-345
10. Huberman BA (2001) The laws of the web: patterns in the ecology of information. MIT Press, Massachusetts
11. Vázquez A et al (2006) Modeling bursts and heavy tails in human dynamics. Phys Rev E 73:036127
12. Neuman WR (1990) The threshold of public attention. Public Opin Q 54:159-176
13. Klamer A, Van Dalen HP (2002) Attention and the art of scientific publishing. J Econ Methodol 9(3):289-315
14. Becker H, Naaman M, Gravano L (2011) Beyond trending topics: real-world event identification on Twitter. In: Proceedings of 15th international conference on Weblogs and Social Media (ICWSM).
15. Wu F, Huberman BA (2007) Novelty and collective attention. Proc Natl Acad Sci USA 105:17599
16. Leskovec J, Backstrom L, Kleinberg J (2009) Meme-tracking and the dynamics of the news cycle. International conference on knowledge discovery and data mining (KDD)
17. Lerman K, Hogg T (2010) Using a model of social dynamics to predict popularity of news. In: Proceedings of 19th international World Wide Web conference (WWW)
18. Crane R, Sornette D (2008) Robust dynamic classes revealed by measuring the response function of a social system. Proc Natl Acad Sci USA 105:15649
19. Ratkiewicz J, Fortunato S, Flammini A, Menczer F, Vespignani A (2010) Characterizing and modeling the dynamics of online popularity. Phys Rev Lett 105:158701
20. Capocci A, Servedio VDP, Colaiori F, Buriol LS, Donato D, Leonardi S, Caldarelli G (2006) Preferential attachment in the growth of social networks: the Internet encyclopedia Wikipedia. Phys Rev E 74:036116
21. Zlatic V, Bozicevic M, Stefancic H, Domazetl M (2006) Wikipedias: collaborative web-based encyclopedias as complex networks. Phys Rev E 74:016115
22. Jansen BJ, Zhang M, Sobel K, Chowdhury A (2009) Twitter power: tweets as electronic word of mouth. J Am Soc Inf Sci 60(11):2169-2188
23. Lee K, Palsetia D, Narayanan R, Patwary MMA, Agrawal A, Choudhary A (2011) Twitter trending topic classification. 11th IEEE international conference on data mining workshops (ICDMW)
24. Gonçalves B, Perra N, Vespignani A (2011) Modeling users' activity on Twitter networks: validation of Dunbar's number. PLoS ONE 6(8):e22656
25. Sitaram A, Huberman BA, Szabo G, Wang C (2011) Trends in Social Media: persistence and decay. In: Proceedings of 15th international conference on Weblogs and Social Media (ICWSM)
26. Redner S, Petersen MR (2006) Role of global warming on the statistics of record-breaking temperatures. Phys Rev E 74:061114
27. Krug J (2007) Records in a changing world. J Stat Mech. doi:10.1088/1742-5468/2007/07/P07001 07001
28. Sydell L (2011) How Twitter's trending algorithm picks its topics. http://www.npr.org/2011/12/07/143013503/how-twitters-trending-algorithm-picks-its-topics

Word usage mirrors community structure in the online social network Twitter

John Bryden[1], Sebastian Funk[2,3]* and Vincent AA Jansen[1]

*Correspondence:
sf7@princeton.edu
[2]Department of Ecology and
Evolutionary Biology, Princeton
University, Princeton, NJ 08544, USA
[3]London School of Hygiene &
Tropical Medicine, Keppel Street,
London, WC1E 7HT, UK
Full list of author information is
available at the end of the article

Abstract

Background: Language has functions that transcend the transmission of information and varies with social context. To find out how language and social network structure interlink, we studied communication on Twitter, a broadly-used online messaging service.

Results: We show that the network emerging from user communication can be structured into a hierarchy of communities, and that the frequencies of words used within those communities closely replicate this pattern. Consequently, communities can be characterised by their most significantly used words. The words used by an individual user, in turn, can be used to predict the community of which that user is a member.

Conclusions: This indicates a relationship between human language and social networks, and suggests that the study of online communication offers vast potential for understanding the fabric of human society. Our approach can be used for enriching community detection with word analysis, which provides the ability to automate the classification of communities in social networks and identify emerging social groups.

Background

The complexity and depth of our language is a unique and defining feature of humans. Language permeates our daily lives as we use it to convey information from simple messages to opinions and complex arguments. In addition, it has a number of functions that transcend the transmission of information, with a range of social implications. Sociolinguistic studies have shown how varieties of a language can be strongly associated with established social or cultural groups [1–5]. In general, these studies have tended to concentrate on small, distinct and relatively stable communities such as gangs [6, 7] or inner-city working communities [8].

In the study of complex networks, the term *communities* is used to denote parts of the network that are more strongly linked within themselves than to the rest of the network, a phenomenon that has been observed in many human social networks [9]. In this sense, communities are an emergent property of network structure. Much work has gone into developing methods to detect such groups from topological analysis [10], and the extent to which this is possible has been termed *modularity* [11]. The communities found in this way are usually associated with groups of friends or acquaintances, or similarity in traits [9, 12, 13]. If these communities overlap with social or cultural groups, the use of language should vary between different communities in a social network [3]. Taking word usage as a proxy for variation in language [14, 15], we hypothesise that this variation should closely match the community structure of the network.

To test this hypothesis, we studied word usage in a weighted network created from communication between about 250,000 users of the social networking and microblogging site Twitter, and analysed if groups identified within the interaction network indeed had unique language features. Twitter communication is unstructured in the sense that every user can send a message to any other user. In constructing our network, we formed a link only when users had mutually directed messages at each other, analogously to what has been done in the study of mobile phone networks [16]. We used methods from statistical physics and network theory to identify groups in the network structure that emerge from user interaction, and linked this to word frequencies in the messages generated by each user.

Results and discussion

The network analysed had 189,000 nodes (each corresponding to a single user) with 75 million mutual tweets between them (mean degree of 28) and a global clustering coefficient of 0.084.

Characterising communities through word usage

Partitioning the sampled network of twitter users into groups so that the proportion of messages between users of the same group was maximised [17] yielded pronounced community structure (Figure 1). The modularity found with this *maximum modularity* algorithm is $Q = 0.78$, in the order of previously studied social networks [17] and far greater than the expected maximum modularity for a random network of the same degree distribution ($Q_{random} = 0.15$) [18]. For the larger communities identified, the algorithm we used identified sub-communities forming a hierarchy of communities (modularity at the lowest level was $Q = 0.66$). Testing the network for community structure using a second algorithm which uses the *map equation* to partition users into groups such that flow in the network stays within groups [19–21] yielded modularity $Q = 0.67$. We focus on the high-level partition generated by the modularity maximisation algorithm, but will return to the map equation algorithm to verify results.

We characterised each of the communities according to the words used in messages sent by the users of the community. To do this, we ranked words in each community by the Z-score of their usage to identify the words most representative of that community. Figure 1 gives illustrative examples of words that characterise each English-speaking community of more than 250 users (see Additional file 1 for the lists of top-ranked words). We surveyed the mean global frequencies for the 100 top-ranked words of each community, finding a broad range. Some communities used relatively common words (at 13% of global usage), while others used much rarer words (at 0.04% of global usage).

To determine the significance of word usage differences, we calculated the Euclidean distance of relative word usage frequencies for each pair of English-language communities using a bootstrap. For each such pair of communities, we sampled two new groups (with replacement) from their union until they had the same sizes as the communities being compared. Repeating this procedure 1,000 times for each pair of communities, we found that for 248 of the 253 pairs of communities the distance between the original pair

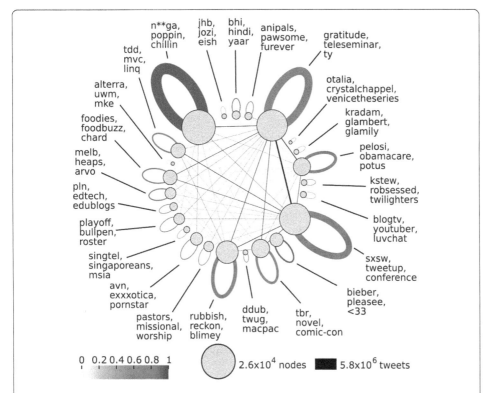

Figure 1 Partition of users sampled from Twitter into communities. The partition of users sampled from Twitter into communities, annotated with words selected to be typical of those used significantly commonly by each community (only English-speaking communities shown). The top word given for each community is the most significant one in that community. Users send a high proportion of their messages (0.91) to other users within the same community. Circles represent communities, with the area of the circle proportional to the number of users (>250 shown). The widths of the lines between circles represent the numbers of messages (>5000 shown) between or within community. The colours of the self-loops represent the proportion of messages that are within users from that group. A word has been starred to avoid offence.

was greater than all of the 1,000 resampled pairs. For the other five pairs of communities, the distance between them was greater than most ($\geq$95%) of the resamples. Comparable results were found for the communities generated with the hierarchical map equation algorithm. In other words, the community membership can explain part of the variance of word usage.

One could argue that the within-community similarities between word frequencies arise because users within a group communicate about one or a limited number of subjects. In contrast, there are revealing differences in word usage that go beyond subject area (see Table 1). To quantify differences beyond subjects of conversation, we tested other statistics using the same method we used for testing differences in word usage: frequency of letter usage, letter pair usage, word length and three-letter word ending. For all these statistics, the distances between almost all the community pairs (>98.8%) was greater than the distances between 95% of the 1,000 pairs of groups resampled from the unions of communities. The best-performing statistics were word ending and letter-pair frequency, and the worst was word-length frequency. Only a very small fraction of these matching word features (<10%) came from the same words. These results suggest that the communities used different language patterns, even when considering quite subtle differences that go beyond common subjects of conversation, such as word endings or word lengths.

Table 1 Language patterns of communities

Community	Language feature	Number of occurrences
n**ga, poppin, chillin	shortened endings ('er' → 'a' or 'ing' → 'in')	50
pln, edtech, edublogs	amalgamated words	31
anipals, pawsome, furever	animal based puns	31
bieber, pleasee, <33	lengthened endings (repeated last letter)	28
kstew, robsessed, twilighters	amalgamations/puns around Twilight movie genre	28
tdd, mvc, linq	acronyms	25
kradam, glambert, glamily	puns around pop star Adam Lambert	15

Language patterns found in communities from Figure 1. We looked at the top 100 words used significantly more than the rest of the population for each community, identified language patterns, and counted the number of occurrences. A word has been starred to avoid offence.

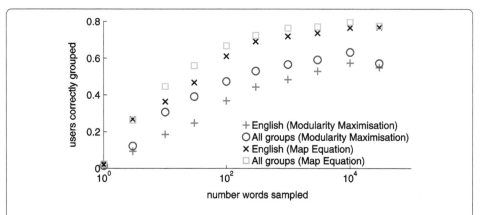

Figure 2 Proportion of users whose community is correctly predicted. The proportion of users whose topological community association is correctly predicted by analysing a random sample of words, as a function of the number of words sampled. Results are presented for both the modularity maximisation partition (users from only English-speaking communities are shown as red pluses, users from any community as blue circles), and the Map Equation partition (English-speaking communities are shown as black crosses, all communities are as blue squares). For each data point, 5,000 users were tested. Standard error of each point is <1%.

Predicting community membership from word usage

We also tested whether individual word usage can predict the community membership of users by comparing their own word frequencies with community word usage (see Materials and Methods). The more words we sampled from a test user, the more likely we were to associate the same community with the user as that which was found from topological community detection (Figure 2).

Comparing different partitions, the hierarchical map equation predicted the community of more users correctly than the high-level modularity maximisation partition. Analysing a random sample of 1,000 words of each user, we were able to predict the correct map equation community for approximately 72% of English-speaking users, compared to 48% with the modularity maximisation partition. Using the numbers of communities generated by each algorithm ($N = 322$ for the map equation versus $N = 413$ for modularity maximisation), we calculated the Z-score for these prediction scores. The Z-score for the map equation ($Z = 911$) was greater than that for the modularity maximisation ($Z = 687$). When, on the other hand, considering the lowest-level partition produced by the modularity maximisation algorithm, the fraction of users predicted correctly drops to 38%. When taking into account the number of communities ($N = 8,738$), though, the Z-score is greater than for both of the other partitions ($Z = 2,511$).

Given the community structure of the network, around half of messages will be directed to users in the high-level communities we predict. This means that, once a network is analysed, it is possible to assign the most likely community or communities for any user that was not part of the community detection. This can be done solely on the basis of the word frequencies in a relatively small sample of text written by that user. The proportion of topological groups predicted correctly from analysis of word usage increases roughly exponentially with the number of words sampled from each user (Figure 2).

Conclusions

We studied the relation between community structure in an online social network and language use in messages within that network, and found a striking overlap, whether we considered words, word fragments or word lengths. Moreover, we were able to predict the network community of a user, a purely structural feature, by studying his or her word usage, and we found that this was possible with rapidly growing accuracy for relatively few words sampled. This indicates how the language we use bears the signature of societal structure, and is suggestive of the enormous potential in using topological analysis to identify cultural groups.

A pair of users that engage in a online conversation would be expected to have some language in common. When groups of individuals share language, and also converse with each other, then it is possible to use our method to identify these groups and enrich them with the language they are using. A wide range of alternative algorithms may also be used [22]. A full exploration of these is beyond the scope of this paper, but may show improvements in identifying communities with more unique language patterns. Further improvements might be made by replacing Z-score metric we have used to identify words that stand out with a term frequency-inverse document frequency metric [23].

Our sample is only a small proportion of the much larger twitter network and one could ask whether the sampling process introduces a bias in the community structure we detect. Our sample network has small-world properties (average shortest path length $L = 4.4$), indicating that the sampling process should very quickly reach every community in the network. Resampling the network confirms this intuition. For very small resamples (<1%), the shortest path length L_r is greater than L, but on further sampling it converges towards L. Similarly, modularity decreases initially with the size of the resample before it converges, indicating that after enough sampling the process is no longer biased toward any particular community. This is consistent with previous analysis of this type of sampling process which showed that (given certain assumptions) it is a regular Markov process [24], and thus that the community being sampled is independent of the community at the origin of the sample [25]. Overall, this resampling analysis demonstrates that our sampling procedure quickly discovers the larger communities in the network if they are not completely isolated. With more sampling, smaller communities and sub-communities can also be discovered.

The finding that people can be placed in a community by analysing their language usage is consistent with evidence that humans make long-term decisions about relationships very quickly [26]. Our results give an indication that words could be markers of desirable underlying traits or social norms [27], allowing people to make quick decisions about the type of relationship they want from a new acquaintance. The community structure we observe in the network could be explained through homophily [13, 28], that is, through people biasing their interactions to others that are similar in some way, or through dyadic interactions [16]. More generally, any process that structures people into groups could play a strong role in cultural evolution [29–32], as well as in the spread of information or pathogens [33, 34]. If people with a negative attitude towards vaccination are preferentially in contact with those of the same opinion, this could lead to clusters of susceptibles and increased risk of outbreaks [35]. There is clearly scope for further study of the role such structuring plays in the evolution of cooperation in humans [36].

Online social networks offer us an unprecedented opportunity to systematically study the large-scale structure of human interactions [37]. Our approach suggests that groups with distinctive cultural characteristics or common interests can be discovered by identifying communities in interaction networks purely on the basis of topological structure. This approach has several benefits when compared to surveying groups identified on a smaller scale: it is systematic, and groups are identified and classified in an unbiased way; when applied to online social networks it is non-intrusive; and it easily makes use a large volume of rich data. In this study we characterise groups by their word frequencies, but this could be extended to quantify other cultural characteristics. Moreover, methods to detect overlapping communities could be used to test in how much these overlap [38], and whether individuals belong to multiple communities and use different word sets in each of them [39]. There are numerous applications of our method, including social group identification, customising online experience, targeted marketing, and crowd-sourced characterisation.

Methods
Network sampling
Our sample network was formed using a process called snowball-sampling [40]: For each user sampled, all their conversational tweets (*i.e.*, tweets that are directed at another user) were recorded and any new users referenced added to a list of users from which the next user to be sampled is picked. Starting from a random user, conversational tweets, time-stamped between January 2007 to November 2009 were sampled from the Twitter web site during December 2009, yielding over 200 million messages. We ignored messages that were copies of other messages (so called retweets, which are identified by the text 'RT'). The links in the network were bidirectional and weighted by the number of tweets sent between the two users linked.

Ranking words within a community
In order to establish which words characterise each community, we compared the fraction of users that use each word within a community with the fraction of users that used the word globally. We then assessed how unlikely it was that the difference between these two fractions could have happened by random chance. This is given by the standardised Z-score which, for each word used in community c, is

$$Z = \frac{\mu_c - \mu_g}{\sigma_g/\sqrt{N_c}},$$

where μ_c is the fraction of users in community c which have used the word, μ_g is the fraction of all users that have used it, N_c is the number of users in community c, and σ_g is the standard deviation of usage of the word amongst all users

$$\sigma_g^2 = \frac{1}{N}\left(\mu_g N(1 - \mu_g)^2 + (1 - \mu_g)N\mu_g^2\right)$$
$$= \mu_g(1 - \mu_g),$$

where N is the global number of users.

Comparing communities using a bootstrap

For each word i used by each community j we calculated its relative word usage frequency $f_j(i)$, *i.e.*, the proportion of the total word instances that were word i. Using this, we were able to measure the difference between two communities j and k by the Euclidean distance as follows,

$$d(j, k) = \sqrt{\sum_i \left[f_j(i) - f_k(i)\right]^2}.$$

To assess the likelihood that a distance calculated could have happened by chance we performed a bootstrap. For each pair of communities we took the union of users and resampled a new pair of communities (j' and k') of the same sizes as the original pair. For each resampled pair we calculated whether the Euclidean distance of the resampled pair was greater than that of the original pair, *i.e.*, if

$$d(j', k') > d(j, k).$$

We confirmed that the distribution of resampled distances was close to a normal distribution. Over many resampled pairs, the frequency of instances when this inequality was true gave us the probability that the difference in word usage between the two communities could have happened by chance if words were randomly distributed amongst communities.

Predicting communities of individual users

To predict the communities of individual users we compared individual word usage with community word usage to select the best matching community (see Figure 3). To do this we divided the users into two equal halves: a randomly selected set of test users and a base set of the remaining users. We then randomly sampled words from test users and compared the probability that the frequency with which that user uses the sampled word would have been obtained by randomly sampling words from all users (the p-value of its relative frequency) with the same p-values in the communities of base users (*i.e.*, considering the frequency with which that word is used in the community). We then associated the community with the smallest mean difference in p-values to the test user for the sampled words with that test user. For English-speaking users, we only tested users from communities larger than 250 users.

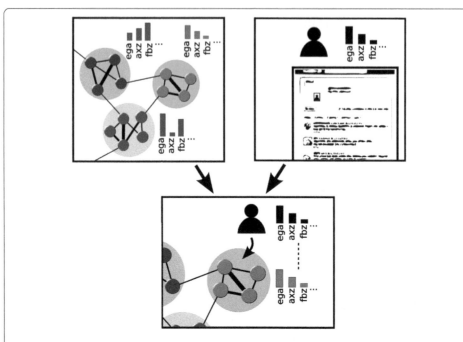

Figure 3 Method for predicting the community of a user. An illustration of the method for predicting which community a user is embedded in. Words are assigned scores (shown as bars above the words in the figure) based on how significantly different their usage is when compared with the global usage (see main text for more details). These scores are generated for the amalgamated text of the users of each community (top left panel), and for the text of the user being tested (top right panel). The scores are compared between a user and all communities and the best match is chosen as the predicted community (bottom panel).

Additional material

Additional file 1: Community word lists. The top-ranked words for English-speaking communities with more than 250 users. The communities at the highest level are numbered as in the figure, sub-communities are shown after each community. Listed are the words with Z-score, frequency in the whole network (*global freq*), frequency within the community (*group freq*) and the ratio of the frequency within the community to the frequency in the whole network (*ratio*).

Competing interests
Royal Holloway, University of London has filed a patent application, published as WO2012/080707, which seeks to protect many of the techniques described in this paper. Royal Holloway is currently pursuing commercial exploitation of this patent. JB and VAAJ are employees of Royal Holloway so may, in future, benefit directly or indirectly from any such exploitation.

Authors' contributions
JB conceived the study, collected the data, performed the analyses and contributed to the writing, SF led the writing, VAAJ contributed to the writing and supervised the project. All authors were involved in interpretation of the results.

Author details
[1]School of Biological Sciences, Royal Holloway, University of London, Egham, TW20 0EX, UK. [2]Department of Ecology and Evolutionary Biology, Princeton University, Princeton, NJ 08544, USA. [3]London School of Hygiene & Tropical Medicine, Keppel Street, London, WC1E 7HT, UK.

Acknowledgements
The authors would like to express their gratitude to Edwin van Leeuwen for helpful discussions. This work was supported by the Engineering and Physical Sciences Research Council through standard research grant number EP/D002249/1, by the Biotechnology and Biological Sciences Research Council grant BB/I000151/1 (to V.A.A.J.), by the Economic and Social Research Council grant (ES/L000113/1), by the EU FP7 funded integrated project EPIWORK (grant agreement number 231807), by the US Department of Homeland Security and by the Bill and Melinda Gates Foundation.

References

1. Gumperz J (1958) Dialect differences and social stratification in a North Indian village. Am Anthropol 60(4):148-170
2. Labov W (1966) The linguistic variable as structural unit. Wash Linguist Rev 3:4-22
3. Chambers JK (1997) Sociolinguistic theory. Blackwell, Oxford
4. Carroll KS (2008) Puerto Rican language use on myspace.com. Cent J 20:96-111
5. Mæhlum B (2010) Language and social spaces. In: Auer P, Schmidt JE (eds) Language and space: theories and methods, vol 1. de Gruyter, Berlin
6. Labov T (1982) Social structure and peer terminology in a black adolescent gang. Lang Soc 11:391-411
7. Mendoza-Denton N (2007) Homegirls: language and cultural practices among Latina youth gangs. Blackwell, Oxford
8. Milroy L (1980) Language and social networks. Blackwell, Oxford
9. Porter MA (2009) Communities in networks. Not Am Math Soc 56(9):1164-1166
10. Fortunato S (2010) Community detection in graphs. Phys Rep 486:75-174
11. Newman MEJ (2006) Modularity and community structure in networks. Proc Natl Acad Sci USA 103(23):8577-8582
12. Traud AL, Kelsic ED, Mucha PJ, Porter MA (2011) Comparing community structure to characteristics in online collegiate social networks. SIAM Rev 53(3):526-543
13. Bryden J, Funk S, Geard N, Bullock S, Jansen VAA (2011) Stability in flux: community structure in dynamic networks. J R Soc Interface 8(60):1031-1040
14. Kucera H, Francis WN (1982) Frequency analysis of English usage: lexicon and grammar. Houghton Mifflin, Boston
15. Michel J, Shen YK, Aiden AP, Veres A, Gray MK, The Google Books Team, Pickett JP, Hoiberg D, Clancy D, Norvig P, Orwant J, Pinker S, Nowak MA, Aiden AL (2010) Quantitative analysis of culture using millions of digitized books. Science 331:176-182
16. Kumpula JM, Onnela JP, Saramaki J, Kaski K, Kertesz J (2007) Emergence of communities in weighted networks. Phys Rev Lett 99:228701
17. Blondel VD, Guillaume J, Lambiotte R, Lefebvre E (2008) Fast unfolding of communities in large networks. J Stat Mech Theory Exp 2008(10):P10008
18. Reichardt J, Bornholdt S (2007) Partitioning and modularity of graphs with arbitrary degree distribution. Phys Rev E 76:015102
19. Rosvall M, Bergstrom CT (2008) Maps of random walks on complex networks reveal community structure. Proc Natl Acad Sci USA 105(4):1118-1123
20. Rosvall M, Axelsson D, Bergstrom CT (2009) The map equation. Eur Phys J Spec Top 178:13-23
21. Rosvall M, Bergstrom CT (2011) Multilevel compression of random walks on networks reveals hierarchical organization in large integrated systems. PLoS ONE 6(4):e18209. http://dx.doi.org/10.1371%2Fjournal.pone.0018209
22. Lancichinetti A, Fortunato S (2009) Community detection algorithms: a comparative analysis. Phys Rev E 80:056117
23. Salton G, Buckley C (1988) Term-weighting approaches in automatic text retrieval. Inf Process Manag 24(5):513-523. http://www.sciencedirect.com/science/article/pii/0306457388900210
24. Heckathorn DD (1997) Respondent-driven sampling: a new approach to the study of hidden populations. Soc Probl 44:174-199
25. Kemeny JG, Snell JL (1960) Finite Markov chains. Van Nostrand, Princeton
26. Sunnafrank M, Ramirez A Jr (2004) At first sight: persistent relational effects of get-acquainted conversations. J Soc Pers Relatsh 21(3):361-379
27. McElreath R, Boyd R, Richerson PJ (2003) Shared norms and the evolution of ethnic markers. Curr Anthropol 44:122-129
28. McPherson JM, Smith-Lovin L, Cook J (2001) Birds of a feather: homophily in social networks. Annu Rev Sociol 27:415-444
29. Fehr E, Fischbacher U (2004) Social norms and human cooperation. Trends Cogn Sci 8(4):185-190
30. Centola D, Gonzalez-Avella JC, Eguiluz VM, Miguel MS (2007) Homophily, cultural drift, and the co-evolution of cultural groups. J Confl Resolut 51(6):905-929
31. Boyd R, Richerson PJ (2009) Culture and the evolution of human cooperation. Philos Trans R Soc Lond B 364(1533):3281-3288
32. Hill KR, Walker RS, Božičević M, Eder J, Headland T, Hewlett B, Hurtado AM, Marlowe F, Wiessner P, Wood B (2011) Co-residence patterns in hunter-gatherer societies show unique human social structure. Science 331(6022):1286-1289
33. Funk S, Gilad E, Watkins C, Jansen VAA (2009) The spread of awareness and its impact on epidemic outbreaks. Proc Natl Acad Sci USA 106(16):6872-6877
34. Salathé M, Jones JH (2010) Dynamics and control of diseases in networks with community structure. PLoS Comput Biol 6(4):e1000736
35. Salathé M, Bonhoeffer S (2008) The effect of opinion clustering on disease outbreaks. J R Soc Interface 5(29):1505-1508
36. Efferson C, Lalive R, Fehr E (2008) The coevolution of cultural groups and ingroup favoritism. Science 321(5897):1844-1849
37. Lazer D, Pentland A, Adamic L, Aral S, Barabasi A, Brewer D, Christakis N, Contractor N, Fowler J, Gutmann M, Jebara T, King G, Macy M, Roy D, Alstyne MV (2009) Computational social science. Science 323(5915):721-723
38. Ahn YY, Bagrow JP, Lehmann S (2010) Link communities reveal multiscale complexity in networks. Nature 466:761-764
39. Clark HH, Brennan SE (1991) Grounding in communication. In: Resnick LB, Levine JM, Teasley SD (eds) Perspectives on socially shared cognition. Am Psychol Assoc, Washington
40. Goodman LA (1961) Snowball sampling. Ann Math Stat 32:148-170

3

The geography and carbon footprint of mobile phone use in Cote d'Ivoire

Vsevolod Salnikov[1], Daniel Schien[2], Hyejin Youn[3,4,5], Renaud Lambiotte[1] and Michael T Gastner[6,7*]

*Correspondence:
m.gastner@bristol.ac.uk
[6]Department of Engineering
Mathematics, University of Bristol,
Merchant Venturers Building,
Woodland Road, Bristol, BS8 1UB, UK
[7]Institute of Technical Physics and
Materials Science, Research Centre
for Natural Sciences, Hungarian
Academy of Sciences, P.O. Box 49,
Budapest, 1525, Hungary
Full list of author information is
available at the end of the article

Abstract

The newly released Orange D4D mobile phone data base provides new insights into the use of mobile technology in a developing country. Here we perform a series of spatial data analyses that reveal important geographic aspects of mobile phone use in Cote d'Ivoire. We first map the locations of base stations with respect to the population distribution and the number and duration of calls at each base station. On this basis, we estimate the energy consumed by the mobile phone network. Finally, we perform an analysis of inter-city mobility, and identify high-traffic roads in the country.

Keywords: mobile phone; Cote d'Ivoire; carbon footprint; human mobility

1 Introduction

The availability of mobile phone records has revolutionised our ability to perform large-scale studies of social networks and human mobility. Traditionally, researchers had to rely on a combination of surveys, census data and vehicle counting. These methods are costly and time consuming so that data were collected either infrequently or for small population samples only. In the last few years, while searching for innovative methods to circumvent these limitations, researchers have turned their attention to mobile phones as sensors to collect communication and mobility data [1]. The vast majority of studies were carried out in developed countries where mobile communication competes with established landline technologies. However, mobile phones are nowadays commonplace in developing countries too. Especially in Africa, mobile phones now provide affordable telecommunication where no alternative had previously existed [2, 3].

The data bases for Cote d'Ivoire, made accessible during the Orange D4D challenge [4], present the first opportunity to analyse a nationwide mobile phone network in Africa. The data are obtained from the so-called Call Detail Records (CDRs) which contain an approximate location of mobile phones every time they connect to a cell tower (e.g. due to a phone call). A growing body of research has shown that CDRs can accurately characterise many aspects of human mobility [5]. Practical examples include the tracking of population displacements after disasters [6, 7], the estimation of traffic volumes in cities [8], the calculation of carbon emissions due to commuting [9] and transport mode inference [10]. CDRs have become the basis for simulating epidemics [11], quantifying linguistic barriers [12] and optimising public transport [13]. Here we apply geospatial techniques to address several questions related to social and economic development. How is mobile phone infrastructure related to its use (Sections 2 and 3)? How much energy is needed to operate the network (Section 4)? Is the road infrastructure adapted to the population mobility patterns (Section 5)?

2 Mapping base station locations with respect to population density

Where to place the base stations that house the antennas is a central decision for any mobile communication provider. It determines how many people can access the network, the quality of calls and the ease with which the provider can operate the facilities. Optimising the base station locations is a difficult task, complicated by spatially heterogeneous demand and topological obstacles such as tall buildings or mountains. As a rule of thumb, however, population density is a crucial factor: where there are more people, we expect a higher density of base stations. Conversely, if rural areas with lower population are served by a disproportionately low number of base stations, these communities would be left with little or no access to the network. As mobile communication has enormous potential to improve the lives of the rural population (e.g. by access to banking and real-time information about agricultural commodity prices), one development objective must be to provide a roughly equal per-capita number of base stations for the entire population of Cote d'Ivoire.

We map the 1,238 base station coordinates given in the D4D file ANT_POS.TSV on a standard latitude-longitude projection (left map in Figure 1). Since Cote d'Ivoire is close to the equator, such a projection is nearly distance-preserving. The base stations (coloured dots on the map) are spatially very unevenly distributed: in some parts of Abidjan there are more than ten base stations per square kilometre, whereas some subprefectures in the north of the country have no base station at all. That there should be many base stations in Abidjan is quite obvious because ≈20% of all citizens live in the country's most populous city. However, whether the number of base stations is proportional to its population is not immediately apparent from the latitude-longitude projection.

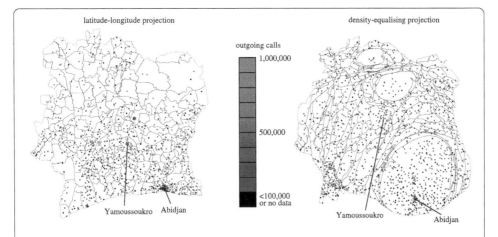

Figure 1 Base station locations. Base station locations on a conventional longitude-latitude projection (left) and a cartogram where areas are rescaled to be proportional to the number of inhabitants (right). The colours of the dots indicate the number of outgoing calls at each base station. The boundaries of subprefectures are shown for ease of orientation. The geographic distribution of the base stations are largely explained by the heterogeneous population distribution so that the point pattern appears less clustered on the right than on the left. Still, regions of significantly higher per-capita base station density remain (see Figure 2), especially in Abidjan, where even on the cartogram the dots are noticeably aggregated. The colours of the dots do not exhibit any clearly visible large-scale trends. However, a more careful statistical analysis shows that a significant correlation between traffic at nearby base stations exists (see Figure 3b).

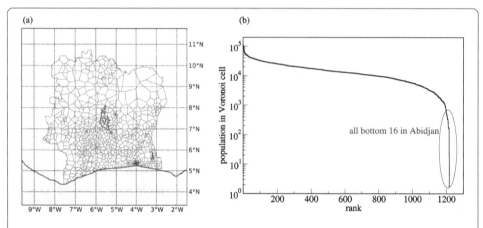

Figure 2 Rank plot of populations in Voronoi cells. (a) Voronoi cells of the 1,217 distinct base station locations in the Orange D4D challenge data base. **(b)** Rank plot of the population inside the Voronoi cells. Although a majority of 616 cells are within 50% of the median population (12,897 inhabitants), there are significant outliers at both top and bottom ranks. While the bottom ranked cells are predominantly in Abidjan, the top ranks are in rural areas as well as smaller cities.

We will thus have to combine the base station coordinates with information about the population distribution. Here we use census estimates from the AfriPop project (http://www.afripop.org) [14]. Based on these numbers, we project the map of Ivory coast so that all regions of the country are represented by an area proportional to its population [15]. Such a density-equalising map - also known as a cartogram - has become a popular tool to visualise inequality and development challenges [16]. Plotting the base station locations on the cartogram (right map in Figure 1) reveals a nuanced picture. On one hand, the point distribution is much less aggregated on the cartogram and thus is indeed largely proportional to population. On the other hand, the points are far from a homogeneous pattern. In Abidjan, in particular, a dense cluster of base stations remains clearly visible, indicating a disproportionately high per-capita connectivity there.

We confirm this observation by calculating the population in the base stations' Voronoi cells (Figure 2a). (The Voronoi cell of a given base station is the polygon that contains the area closer to this base station than to any other.) A population-proportional base station distribution would result in an equal population inside each Voronoi cell. A rank plot of population numbers (Figure 2b), however, has a clear S-shape: although most cells have a population of around 15,000 (mean 15,500, median 12,897), there are outliers in both directions. Interestingly, the 16 lowest ranked cells are all in Abidjan, making it by far the region with the highest per-capita base station density. By contrast, the Voronoi cells with the largest populations are in rural areas near inland borders (e.g. the second ranked base station at 7.267° N, 8.160° W is 20 km east of the Liberian border and the fifth ranked at 9.803° N, 3.303° W is 6 km south of the border with Burkina Faso) or near smaller cities (the top and third ranked base station are only a few kilometres outside Bouaké and the fourth and sixth ranked near Korhogo, the country's third and seventh largest cities respectively). Because many facility location models suggest that a fair distribution of resources should intentionally be skewed in favor of less populated areas [17, 18], our finding suggests these regions as targets for a future expansion of the network.

3 Spatial correlation between the population density and the number of calls

Recent studies of mobile phone records in developed countries [19] have argued that the number of human interactions in cities increases faster than linearly with the city population. This poses the question: does the number of calls in Cote d'Ivoire depend similarly on population density? We count the population and the number of calls on a square grid. We investigate squares of size 5 km × 5 km, 10 km × 10 km and 20 km × 20 km. We generally find that the number of calls is less correlated for smaller than for larger populations so that we divide the data into two distinct regions: one for sparsely and another for densely populated squares. We show the results for ordinary least-squares fits of the form log(number of calls) = a log(population) + b in Figure 3a for the 5 km × 5 km grid.[a] In the densely populated regime (population > 10,000), regression yields a slope $a = 0.87$ with a 95% confidence interval [0.70, 1.03].[b] (The formula for computing confidence intervals can be found for example in [20].) For larger sizes (10 km × 10 km, 20 km × 20 km) the least-squares exponent for dense populations increases, but all 95% confidence intervals include 1, the dividing line between sub- and superlinear scaling (see Table 1). This finding remains true even if the call intensity is measured by the total duration rather than the number of calls. Hence, the available data give neither sufficient evidence for nor against superlinear scaling for large populations.

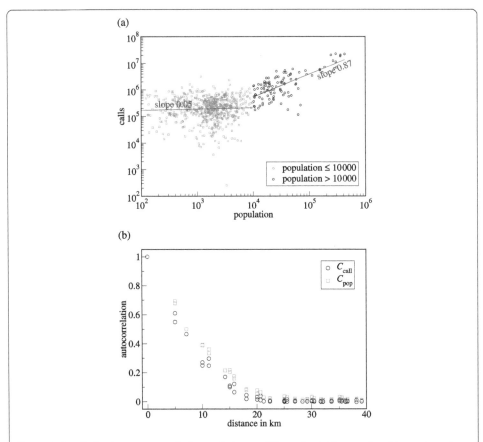

Figure 3 Correlation between population and phone call intensity. (a) Scatter plot of the total number of outgoing calls versus the population. Both variables are counted on a 5 km × 5 km square grid. An ordinary least-squares fit yields different slopes for small and large populations. **(b)** The spatial autocorrelation functions for the number of calls and the population size exhibit significant non-zero correlations up to ≈15 km.

Table 1 Regression of call intensity versus population

Grid	Intensity	Small population		Large population	
		a	95% CI	a	95% CI
5 km × 5 km	number of calls	0.05	[−0.04, 0.13]	0.87	[0.70, 1.03]
	duration of calls	0.06	[−0.02, 0.14]	0.86	[0.70, 1.02]
10 km × 10 km	number of calls	0.06	[−0.05, 0.17]	1.00	[0.77, 1.23]
	duration of calls	0.08	[−0.03, 0.18]	1.01	[0.78, 1.23]
20 km × 20 km	number of calls	0.27	[0.11, 0.43]	1.24	[0.91, 1.57]
	duration of calls	0.28	[0.12, 0.43]	1.27	[0.93, 1.60]

Results of regression to log(intensity) = a log(population) + b. The cutoff between small and large populations is 10,000 for the 5 km × 5 km grid, 20,000 for the 10 km × 10 km grid and 40,000 for the 20 km × 20 km grid. The cutoffs were chosen so that the number of data points in the large population regime are approximately equal (105, 74 and 80 respectively).

For small populations, however, superlinear scaling can be firmly ruled out. In this regime, the least-squares exponents for the 5 km × 5 km and the 10 km × 10 km grids are not even significantly different from zero, so that population hardly influences the call intensity at all. The explanation lies in infrastructure located away from population centres. Among the 5 km × 5 km squares with a population below 10,000, three of the ten squares with the largest number of calls are near the Buyo hydroelectric plant (6°14′ N, 7°3′ W). The other seven squares in the top ten are near major highways (San Pedro - Betia Road, San Pedro - Tabou Road, A4, A6, A7, A8 and A100). These locations are in zones with low population density, but the local infrastructure generates a relatively high call intensity.

Despite the weak correlation between calls and population size, the spatial distribution of calls is far from random. In Figure 3b we plot the spatial autocorrelation function C_{call} on the 5 km × 5 km grid. Although C_{call} decays quickly, the correlation is nevertheless >0.1 up to a distance of ≈15 km. For comparison, we also plot the autocorrelation C_{pop} of the population. C_{pop} is generally a little larger than C_{call}, but it decreases at a similar rate. It remains an intriguing question for future research whether both autocorrelations are generated by similar social mechanisms. In particular, an analysis based on a more careful socio-economic definition of 'city size' [21] may still unearth more details.

4 Energy and carbon footprint of wireless cellular networks in Cote d'Ivoire

In this section we estimate the energy and greenhouse gas (GHG) emissions, contributing to climate change, of the wireless cellular network in Cote d'Ivoire and compare its share of the national GHG emissions with that of wireless networks in other countries.

While mobile network operators are increasingly transparent about their environmental impact and GHG emissions, few data are available about the energy consumption and resulting GHG emissions of mobile networks in developing countries. Moreover, the Orange Cote d'Ivoire (OCI) data permits discussing energy consumption of parts of the entire network in relationship to population density. Thus, this work contributes to ongoing research that investigates the direct environmental impact of ICT (Information and Communication Technology) of systems in general, independent of development contexts, by estimating an entire network's footprint from the number of its base stations.

Much research has shown that mobile technologies are an important instrument of current information and communication technologies for development (ICT4D) strategies, for example [22]. On the other hand, the increasing deployment of these technologies can result in increasing GHG emissions, sometimes labelled 'footprint,' which recently has also received increasing interest by the community of ICT4D researchers [23, 24]. It is our aim to contribute to a more informed discussion through provision of quantitative estimates of energy consumption and GHG emissions. We want to precede this analysis with a qualification: in or outside of a development context the analysis of environmental impact of a technical system and its results can stand separately from the interpretation of these results towards decision making for policy formation. In this text we estimate the annual GHG emissions of the mobile network in Cote d'Ivoire and suggest directions for existing or future development of these networks from the perspective of their technical operation. However, this analysis would only provide an incomplete basis for policy making towards a development strategy as it does not include an analysis of the social or economic impacts and benefits of the wireless network.

The goal of our assessment is to estimate the national energy consumption and GHG emissions using the number of base stations as an input parameter. This requires an estimate of the power consumption per base station and the overhead from the remaining parts of the network. Depending on its type, the power consumption of a base station can vary between 800 and 2,800 W (estimations presented in [25]). Without additional information about the specific types of base stations, the OCI data can only be parameterised with average data. Additionally, an assessment of the energy consumption of a mobile network should include all relevant system parts in order to enable greater transferability of results. We assume the following composition of the wireless network: the base stations, which house the antennas and amplifiers, and auxiliary equipment for cooling and power transformation provide the radio signal to subscribers. They are controlled by several base station controllers and a few mobile service centres to which they are connected via a radio or fixed network. This network also provides connectivity with the Internet or networks of other operators. In our estimate of the GHG emissions we had to make some simplifying assumptions about the network infrastructure. We estimated the energy consumption for a single base station (including overhead for other system parts such as base station controllers) of around 2,100 W based on similar assumptions made in [25] and [26] that are based on publicly available data by Vodafone. This value is a top-down estimate based on the total energy consumption of the network and the total number of base stations. The corporate responsibility report of the Vodafone Group states that in 2011 the company globally operates 224,000 base stations and that the energy consumption was 4,117 GWh [27]. This value does not account for energy consumption in offices. Given that the average power consumption per base station is around 1.5 kW, the resulting value of 2,100 W per base station is plausible and further corroborated by other studies such as [28] who state that the energy consumption of the base stations constitutes 60-80% of the total energy consumption of the network.

An estimate of the contribution of the remaining parts of a mobile operator's organisation to energy and carbon footprint can, for example, be based on corporate social responsibility reports by Vodafone and O2, which state that the network accounts for around 80% to 90% of an operator's energy consumption [29, 30] and constitutes a similar portion of its GHG emissions [31]. The GSMA Mobile Green Manifesto report [32] makes similar assumptions. We assume that these ratios also apply to the OCI network and networks of other operators in Cote d'Ivoire.

Based on the data inventory we have a precise count of mobile base stations (1,238). In order to estimate the total annual national energy consumption by mobile networks we had to also estimate the number of base stations by competitors of OCI in addition to the power consumption by the other system parts. We assumed that all mobile operators deploy their network on average with similar density. Based on the market share of subscriptions (between 33% OCI [33] and 35% [34]) we estimate that the total number of base stations in Cote d'Ivoire is around 3,700.

Given these assumptions, we estimate that the GHG emissions of the wireless mobile networks by all operators in Cote d'Ivoire amount to about 29.1 kilo tonnes carbon dioxide equivalent per year (ktCO2e). This is about 0.4% of the total annual carbon emissions of 6,596.933 ktCO2e [35]. We further estimate the energy consumption to be 68 GWh which is about 1.9% of the total annual energy production of Cote d'Ivoire [36]. Compared to the pro-rata energy consumption and GHG emissions by mobile networks in Germany, this value is relatively high. Based on publicly available data by Vodafone Germany energy consumption by the network accumulated circa 600 GWh [30] in 2011. Assuming other wireless networks are equally efficient and Vodafone's market share of 32.97% [37], the energy consumption by mobile networks in Germany would be about 0.3% of the absolute energy consumption in the country in 2011 [38]. In [32] it is found that on global average, mobile networks result in 0.2% of all GHG emissions. Based on the Vodafone data, however, the portion of German mobile networks of the national GHG emissions is only around 0.1%.

Given the lack of data on the power consumption by each base station, there is a relatively high uncertainty to the estimate of the total annual energy consumption by all networks. The estimate of the carbon emissions is further affected by uncertainty in the parameter for the carbon intensity of electricity. In OECD countries, base stations are typically operated with energy from the electrical grid. In developing countries, however, electrical energy is possibly supplied by diesel generators to a significant degree. Diesel generators result in a greater carbon intensity per generated kWh of electricity (0.788 kgCO2-eq/kWh [39], as compared to 0.426 kgCO2-eq/kWh of the average intensity of grid electricity).

In Table 2 we evaluate the influence of these parameters on the estimates of GHG emissions and energy consumption. In scenario I, we consider how the energy consumption and GHG emissions would change if the average power consumption per base station was reduced by 25% relative to our base line. The resulting average power consumption per base station, including a portion for remaining network parts, is 1.58 kW. In this case the carbon footprint of the network is 0.33% and slightly closer to the global average value estimated by GSMA in [32] of 0.2%.

Table 2 Energy consumption of Cote d'Ivoire's mobile phone network

	BASE	I	II
Carbon intensity of electricity (kgCO2e/kWh)	0.43	0.43	0.60
Average aggregate power consumption per BS (kW)	2.10	1.58	2.10
Total national energy consumption by mobile networks (GWh)	68.32	51.24	68.32
National energy consumption by mobile networks (percent of total)	1.90	1.43	0.95
Total national GHG emissions by mobile networks (ktCO2e)	29.11	21.83	41.13
National GHG emissions by mobile networks (percent of total)	0.44	0.33	0.62
Annual energy consumption per subscriber (kWh/sub)	3.83	2.88	3.83

Scenarios of alternative input parameters. Scenario 'base' assumes average values for all parameters, scenario 'I' assumes a value for the power consumption per base station compared to 25% from base. Scenario 'II' assumes that 50% of the electricity consumed by base stations is supplied by diesel generators.

Secondly, we evaluate the scenario that half of the electricity consumed by the base station was provided by diesel generators and the other half by the electrical grid which would increase the carbon intensity from 0.426 kgCO2e/kWh to 0.602 kgCO2e/kWh. We include the assumption that this would free capacity in the electrical grid. In our scenario, the mobile network would consume 0.95% of Cote d'Ivoire's electrical energy and constitute 0.62% of the national GHG emissions. We also considered evaluating more complex assumptions about the types of base stations. Such a scenario would assume that network planners generate relatively precise predictions of demand in a cell. However, the number of outgoing calls that we plot in Figure 1 together with incoming calls are only a possible proxy to overall demand of voice traffic. Data services and number of calls at peak time must both be considered to estimate the minimum capacity of a base station. We believe that the results of such a scenario would have too much uncertainty to bring significant value for our discussion.

Given this sensitivity analysis it remains clear, that mobile networks in Cote d'Ivoire contribute to a greater degree to the total GHG emissions of the country than those in Germany. One of the main reasons for this difference is likely to be the contrasting structure of the German and Ivorian economy to which the energy intensive manufacturing industry in Germany is likely to contribute. This assumption is also supported by a comparison of street lighting as another energy consuming infrastructure. A report by the World Bank mentions in passing that 400,000 public street lights are operated in Cote d'Ivoire [40]. Assuming that street lights have a power consumption between 35 and 400 W [41] each, they constitute a share of the total energy consumption in Cote d'Ivoire between 1.4 and 16 percent. In contrast, the street lighting in Germany constitutes only 0.56% of the total energy consumption [42].

Interestingly, if apportioned to each subscriber, the annual energy consumption of the OCI mobile network is 3.83 kWh/sub which is much lower than the same metric for customers of Vodafone Germany (16.5 kWh/sub). The value is also a lot lower than the values reported in [43] (values between 7 and 34 kWh/sub with an average of 16.7 kWh/sub). In the case of Cote d'Ivoire, this is likely to be partly the result of a sparser deployment of base stations, in particular outside of Abidjan as we illustrate in Section 2. One contributing factor to this sparser deployment is likely to be the lower degree of urbanisation (52% compared to 74% Germany [35]). Another factor is the delayed introduction of data services to Cote d'Ivoire. Third generation services are only just being introduced to this market. Energy consumption on the user side of the mobile network by mobile phones and chargers is significantly lower than this. Phone models such as the Nokia 108 Dual-Sim [44] draw a power between as little as 5.86 mW and about 0.254 W while talking. Estimating the total energy consumption over the year depends on the user behaviour but even if customers spent 1 h talking on the phone per day, which is about 4 times higher than the average time spent in Europe, the total energy consumption by the phone would be about 0.18 kWh which is about 5% of the per-user energy consumption by the equipment on the operator side. Similarly, the energy consumption by chargers will vary if they remain plugged in while not connected to the phone. Yet, even if they are never disconnected, their power draw would result in a total energy consumption of 0.876 kWh which is about 23% of the operator side equipment.

These figures have relevance to the ICT4D community because development in Cote d'Ivoire can be seen as indicative for many other African countries. Cote d'Ivoire currently is among the countries with the highest mobile phone penetration [45]. As our estimates illustrate, the uptake of mobile phone technologies is accompanied by an increase in energy consumption. For Cote d'Ivoire specifically, it is likely that the energy consumption by the network will increase in the near future with an increasing adoption of data services.

Meanwhile, network coverage in Cote d'Ivoire is not homogenous as was described in Section 2. The Voronoi plot of the country in Figure 2a shows that the Voronoi cells around base stations are significantly larger in the region north of the 8th degree latitude. Indeed, the average population per cell in this northern region is 26,405 while it is 14,414 in the south. A further 94 base stations were needed in the north in order to achieve the same population density per base station which would increase the energy consumption in Orange's network by 7.6%.

5 Detecting important routes for inter-city mobility

CDRs provide a cheap and efficient source of data to study human mobility patterns at a large scale [1]. Yet they suffer from limitations that need to be carefully considered, and in some case dealt with, to ensure the validity of the observations. A key limitation is the sparse and heterogeneous sampling of the trajectories, as the location is not continuously provided but only when the phone engages in a phone call or a text message exchange. Moreover, the spatial accuracy of the data is determined by the local density of base stations. When estimating mobility from CDRs, different approaches have been developed in the literature (see Figure 4 for illustration).

First, researchers interested in statistical models of human mobility have adopted a Brownian motion approach [46], where each individual is considered as a particle randomly moving in its environment. Mobility is considered as a path between positions at successive position measurements. Authors have observed statistical properties reminis-

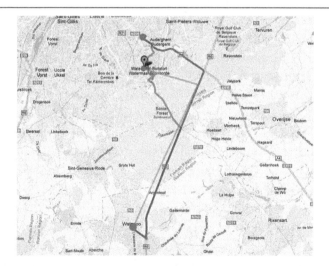

Figure 4 Detecting mobility patterns. To illustrate the different ways to uncover mobility patterns from CDRs, let us focus on the motion of an individual in Brussels, as measured by his GPS. In this small experiment, the user took his car in Watermael and went to two shops, one in Auderghem and one in Waterloo. The three locations are plotted in red. Three phone calls were made. One at home, one on the highway, and one in Waterloo. An approach where a path is composed of successive position measurements is shown in pink. In contrast, an approach where paths are based on important locations would detect the stop in Waterloo, rightly discard the one on the highway, but would still be blind to the location in Auderghem, because that stop was too short.

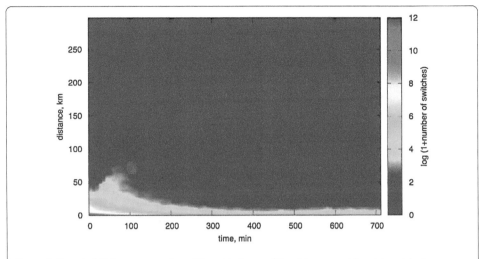

Figure 5 Traveled distance versus travel time. Heat map of the distances and time intervals between consecutive CDRs in the D4D dataset. The burstiness of phone activity leads to a broad distribution over time. Keeping transitions from different regions in the two-dimensional space allows for the identification of different aspects of human mobility.

cent of Levy flights, together with a high degree of regularity. Yet, the usefulness of these observations is limited by the bursty nature of phone activity, as burstiness is expected to alter basic statistical properties of the jumps, such as their distance distribution (see Figure 5). Even in studies where the positions are evaluated at regular intervals, the nature of the jumps remains unclear, as the method tends to detect short trips due to localisation errors, and is blind to the type of the places sampled from the real trajectory. As a side note, let us mention recent work using geo-localised web services, such as Foursquare, where users voluntarily check-in at places [47, 48]. Foursquare check-ins are also characterised by a bursty behaviour, but they provide a GPS accuracy, and semantic information (at the office, travelling, etc.) that might solve the aforementioned problems.

The second approach relies on the idea that mobility consists of moving from one place to another. The observation of mobility patterns thus requires one to define and identify important locations. A trajectory is seen as a set of consecutive locations visited by the user. Important locations can either be defined as a place where a user spends a significant amount of time, which he visits frequently, or where he has stopped for a sufficiently long time [1, 49–51]. This approach provides a more intuitive picture of mobility, where the sampling is determined by the periods of rest of the user. However, it is blind to the multi-scale nature of human mobility, as it requires the parametrisation of thresholds in time and in space to identify important locations. The value of the threshold and the corresponding granularity of the places depends on the system under scrutiny, say cities for international mobility or rooms for human mobility inside hospitals [52].

When measuring human mobility from CDRs, it is important to remember that mobility is about space and time. Both aspects must be carefully considered to provide a faithful description of human trajectories, especially in situations where the sampling of the data is heterogeneous. For this reason, each transition should be remembered as a jump in space over an interval in time and, if possible, be put in relation to the previous and following transitions. Contrary to the universality viewpoint of [46], not all transitions are alike. On the contrary, it is possible to extract different information and different types of mobility patterns by focusing on different regions in space-time. This filtering has been adopted in various studies, but usually either in space or in time. Let us mention [51], where transitions between identified places are considered only if they are registered within two hours of each other; in [50] the daily range of mobility is calculated, and in [8] a trip is defined as a displacement between two distinct base stations occurring within one hour in each time period. More complex filters can be defined on so-called *handoff patterns*, that is a sequences of cell towers that a moving phone uses while engaged in one voice call, e.g. in [49] where only sequences of more than 5 cell towers are included. Let us note that a filtering in space and in time allows for the selection of a characteristic velocity and, if needed, of the removal of noisy transitions occurring at a small spatial scale, e.g. transitions between neighbouring cells of a static user, or long temporal scale, e.g. transitions over several days where several intermediate steps are expected to be missing.

This overview of recent research suggests direct applications that would be of particular interest in a developing country, where empirical data on human mobility tend to be lacking. Using the aforementioned methodologies, it would be possible, for instance, to identify and map nationwide commuting patterns. Traffic tracking and route classification would also be possible after additional data is collected from test drives or signal strength data collected by high-resolution scanners [49]. In this work, we illustrate the potential benefits of a CDR analysis by focusing on the detection of high-traffic roads between cities. Such a detection might help deploy new infrastructure where the population actually needs it, e.g. in regions where mobility is high but the infrastructure is poor. Finding high-traffic roads requires one to filter transitions in the two-dimensional space of Figure 5. To do so, we apply the following procedure. We consider only transitions in a certain velocity range and occurring in less than a predefined time interval. Our choice of velocity range for car mobility is [15, 150] km/h, in order to discard pedestrian motion and noisy points, i.e. due to antenna switching instability. For our analysis, we have used the data from POS_SAMPLE_X.TSV source files, containing separate users' traces, in the form of a list of user - antenna - timestamp for each call or SMS, together with the antenna positions from the ANT_POS.TSV file. The lower bound for the time interval between two points has been set as the minimal value between two actions. For the upper bound, a one hour limit has been chosen in order to balance between sufficient data points and accuracy. Moreover, to remove noisy connections and to identify persistent motion, we have removed weak transitions between antennas, i.e. occurring less than 10 times. This operation leads to a fragmentation of the network into connected components which we further exploit by keeping only components composed of at least ten vertices. This operation has the advantage of removing undesired connections due to antenna switching and not associated to motion. Our results are robust under variations of the above parameters.

The described technique gives a good approximation of the most important human migration pathways (see Figure 6) and thus can be used for alternative road construction or improvement. Interestingly, it also allowed us to identify unknown roads, which we could validate *a posteriori*. Examples are shown in Figure 7 and Figure 8 where roads that were absent in Microsoft maps but found by our algorithm are found in maps provided by OpenStreetMap and Yahoo respectively. This can be of particular interest for a semi-automated map improvement technique: if a strong connection is found from the CDR information, but there is no road on the map, it should be analysed carefully whether an existing road has so far been overlooked.

Figure 6 High-traffic roads from mobile phone records. High-traffic road detection, as obtained from CDR data.

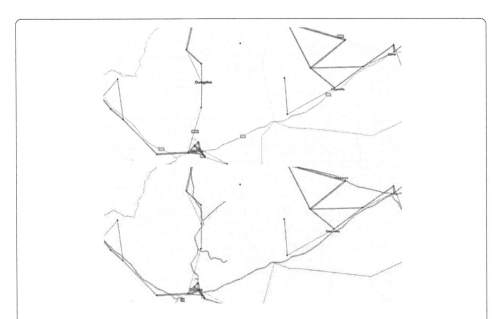

Figure 7 Road identification on Microsoft and OpenStreetMap maps. Roads that are identified from CDR data and are absent on a Microsoft map (upper panel) can be identified on an OpenStreetMap (lower panel).

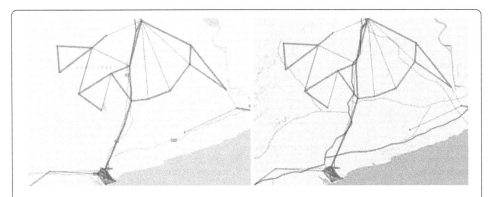

Figure 8 Road identification on Microsoft and Yahoo maps. Roads that are identified from CDR data and are absent on a Microsoft map (left panel) can be identified on a Yahoo map (right panel).

6 Conclusion

In this article we have presented how an analysis of the Orange D4D mobile phone data base reveals important patterns of communication infrastructure and mobile phone use in Cote d'Ivoire. The placement of base stations is biased towards Abidjan so that one development goal is an enhancement of the network in smaller cities and rural regions. We estimate that the network currently consumes between 2.88 and 3.83 kWh of energy annually per subscriber. Although this figure is less than in an industrial country such as Germany, the fraction of the national energy consumption spent on mobile telephony (estimated between 0.95% and 1.90%) is actually higher. Finally, we argued that mobility data from CDRs need further filtering to extract truly meaningful commuting patterns. We used the mobility traces that were part of the Orange D4D database to demonstrate how the main roads in Cote d'Ivoire can be identified.

Competing interests
The authors declare that they have no competing interests.

Authors' contributions
MTG performed the analysis of base station locations. HY and MTG calculated the correlation between phone calls and population density and drafted the text of Sections 2 and 3. DS calculated the energy consumption and drafted Section 4. VS performed the analysis of mobility traces. VS and RL drafted Section 5. All authors reviewed and approved the complete manuscript.

Author details
[1]naXys, University of Namur, Rempart de la Vierge 8, Namur, 5000, Belgium. [2]Department of Computer Science, University of Bristol, Merchant Venturers Building, Woodland Road, Bristol, BS8 1UB, UK. [3]Santa Fe Institute, 1399 Hyde Park Road, Santa Fe, NM 87501, USA. [4]Institute for New Economic Thinking, Oxford Martin School, Walton Well Rd, Oxford, OX2 6ED, UK. [5]Mathematical Institute, University of Oxford, Oxford, UK. [6]Department of Engineering Mathematics, University of Bristol, Merchant Venturers Building, Woodland Road, Bristol, BS8 1UB, UK. [7]Institute of Technical Physics and Materials Science, Research Centre for Natural Sciences, Hungarian Academy of Sciences, P.O. Box 49, Budapest, 1525, Hungary.

Acknowledgements
We thank Orange for making the D4D data set available. VS and RL acknowledge financial support from FNRS. MTG is grateful for financial support from the University of Bristol and the EPSRC Building Global Engagements in Research (BGER) grant. He also acknowledges support from the European Commission (project number FP7-PEOPLE-2012-IEF 6-456412013). This paper presents research results of the Belgian Network DYSCO (Dynamical Systems, Control, and Optimization), funded by the Interuniversity Attraction Poles Programme, initiated by the Belgian State, Science Policy Office. HY acknowledges the support by grants from the Rockefeller Foundation and the James McDonnell Foundation (no. 220020195).

Endnotes
[a] Five kilometres is approximately the reception radius of a base station, which is the relevant length scale in this problem. However, we also state the results for the other grids in Table 1.
[b] Because the logarithm of zero is undefined, the regression is calculated by ignoring cells where there were no calls.

References
1. Becker R, Cáceres R, Hanson K, Isaacman S, Loh JM, Martonosi M, Rowland J, Urbanek S, Varshavsky A, Volinsky C (2013) Human mobility characterization from cellular network data. Commun ACM 56:74-82
2. Heeks R, Jagun A (2007) Mobile phones and development. id21 insights 69:1-2. Available at http://www.dfid.gov.uk/r4d/PDF/Articles/insights69.pdf
3. Singh R (2009) Mobile phones for development and profit: a win-win scenario. Overseas development institute opinion 128. Available at http://www.odi.org.uk/sites/odi.org.uk/files/odi-assets/publications-opinion-files/3739.pdf
4. Blondel VD, Esch M, Chan C, Clerot F, Deville P, Huens E, Morlot F, Smoreda Z, Ziemlicki C (2012) Data for development: the D4D challenge on mobile phone data. arXiv:1210.0137
5. Hoteit S, Secci S, Sobolevsky S, Pujolle G, Ratti C (2013) Do mobile phone data allow estimating real human trajectory? In: Proc. of 3rd int. conference on the analysis of mobile phone datasets
6. Bengtsson L, Lu X, Thorson A, Garfield R, von Schreeb J (2011) Improved response to disasters and outbreaks by tracking population movements with mobile phone network data: a post-earthquake geospatial study in Haiti. PLoS Med 8:e1001083
7. Lu X, Bengtsson L, Holme P (2012) Predictability of population displacement after the 2010 Haiti earthquake. Proc Natl Acad Sci USA 109:11576-11581
8. Wang P, Hunter T, Bayen AM, Schechtner K, González MC (2012) Understanding road usage patterns in urban areas. Sci Rep 2:1001

9. Isaacman S, Becker R, Cáceres R, Kobourov S, Martonosi M, Rowland J, Varshavsky A (2011) Identifying important places in people's lives from cellular network data. In: Proc. of the 9th international conference on pervasive computing, pp 133-151

10. Wang H, Calabrese F, Di Lorenzo G, Ratti C (2010) Transportation mode inference from anonymized and aggregated mobile phone call detail records. In: Proc. of the 13th international IEEE conference on intelligent transport systems, pp 318-323

11. Lima A, De Domenico M, Pejovic V, Musolesi M (2013) Exploiting cellular data for disease containment and information campaigns strategies in country-wide epidemics. Technical report CSR-13-01, School of Computer Science, University of Birmingham

12. Amini A, Kung K, Kang C, Sobolevsky S, Ratti C (2013) The differing tribal and infrastructural influences on mobility in developing and industrialized regions. In: Proc. of 3rd int. conference on the analysis of mobile phone datasets

13. Berlingerio M, Calabrese F, Di Lorenzo G, Nair R, Pinelli F, Sbodio M (2013) AllAboard: a system for exploring urban mobility and optimizing public transport using cellphone data. In: Blockeel H, Kersting K, Nijssen S, Železný F (eds) Machine learning and knowledge discovery in databases, lecture notes in computer science. Springer, Heidelberg

14. Tatem AJ, Noor AM, von Hagen C, Di Gregorio A, Haym SI (2007) High resolution population maps for low income nations: combining land cover and census in East Africa. PLoS ONE 2:e1298

15. Gastner MT, Newman MEJ (2004) Diffusion-based method for producing density-equalizing maps. Proc Natl Acad Sci USA 101:7499-7504

16. Dorling D, Newman MEJ, Barford A (2010) The atlas of the real world: mapping the way we live, 2nd edn. Thames & Hudson, London

17. Gastner MT, Newman MEJ (2006) Optimal design of spatial distribution networks. Phys Rev E 74:016117

18. Gastner MT (2011) Scaling and entropy in p-median facility location along a line. Phys Rev E 84:036112

19. Schläpfer M, Bettencourt LMA, Raschke M, Claxton R, Smoreda Z, West GB, Ratti C (2012) The scaling of human interactions with city size. arXiv:1210.5215

20. Warton DI, Wright IJ, Falster DS, Westoby M (2006) Bivariate line-fitting methods for allometry. Biol Rev 81:259-291

21. Arcaute E, Hatna E, Ferguson P, Youn H, Johansson A, Batty M (2013) City boundaries and the universality of scaling laws. arXiv:1301.1674

22. Aker JC, Mbiti IM (2010) Mobile phones and economic development in Africa. J Econ Perspect 24:207-232

23. Roeth H, Wokeck L (2011) ICTs and climate change mitigation in emerging economies. Technical report. Available at http://www.niccd.org/sites/default/files/RoethWokeckClimateChangeMitigationICTs.pdf

24. Paul DI, Uhomoibhi J (2012) Solar power generation for ICT and sustainable development in emerging economies. Campus-Wide Inf Syst 29:213-225

25. Schien D, Shabajee P, Yearworth M, Preist C (2013) Modeling and assessing variability in energy consumption during the use stage of online multimedia services. J Ind Ecol 17:800-813

26. Schien D, Shabajee P, Wood SG, Preist C (2013) A model for green design of online news media services. In: Proc. of the 22nd international world wide web conference

27. Vodafone Group (2011) Sustainability report

28. Oh E, Krishnamachari B, Liu X, Niu Z (2011) Toward dynamic energy-efficient operation of cellular network infrastructure. IEEE Commun Mag 49:56-61

29. O2 (2011) O2 Sustainability report

30. Vodafone Deutschland (2011) Corporate responsibility report 2010/2011

31. Vodafone Group (2012) Sustainability report. Available at http://www.vodafone.com/content/dam/vodafone/about/sustainability/reports/2011-12/vodafone_sustainability_report_2011-12.pdf

32. GSMA (2012) Mobile's green manifesto. Technical report

33. Abidjan.net (2012) Téléphonie mobile : Les parts de marché de chaque entreprise. Available at http://news.abidjan.net/h/435550.html

34. Liberation (2012) La Côte-d'Ivoire, un terrain trop mobiles. Available at http://www.liberation.fr/economie/2012/05/28/la-cote-d-ivoire-un-terrain-trop-mobiles_822054

35. World Bank (2009) World development indicators. Available at http://data.worldbank.org/data-catalog/world-development-indicators

36. data base Electric power consumption (kWh) in Cote d'Ivoire. Available at http://www.tradingeconomics.com/cote-d-ivoire/electric-power-consumption-kwh-wb-data.html

37. Wikipedia (2011) Vodafone

38. Statistisches Bundesamt (2011) Erzeugung

39. Sovacool BK (2008) Valuing the greenhouse gas emissions from nuclear power: a critical survey. Energy Policy 36:2950-2963

40. World Bank (2007) Cameroun : Plan d'Action National Energie pour la Réduction de la Pauvreté. Technical report

41. BBC News (2008) How much does it cost to operate a street light? Available at http://news.bbc.co.uk/1/hi/magazine/7764911.stm

42. Bundesministerium für Wirtschaft und Technologie (2011) Energieverbrauch des Sektors Gewerbe, Handel, Dienstleistungen (GHD) in Deutschland für die Jahre 2007 bis 2010

43. Malmodin J, Moberg Å, Lundén D, Finnveden G, Lövehagen N (2010) Greenhouse gas emissions and operational electricity use in the ICT and entertainment & media sectors. J Ind Ecol 14:770-790

44. Nokia Nokia 108 dual sim specifications. Available at http://www.nokia.com/mea-en/phones/phone/108-dual-sim/specifications/

45. GSMA (2012) Sub-Saharan Africa mobile observatory 2012. Technical report

46. González MC, Hidalgo CA, Barabási A-L (2008) Understanding individual human mobility patterns. Nature 453:779-782

47. Noulas A, Scellato S, Mascolo C, Pontil M (2011) Exploiting semantic annotations for clustering geographic areas and users in location-based social networks. AAAI Workshop - Technical report, pp 32-35

48. Noulas A, Scellato S, Lambiotte R, Pontil M, Mascolom C (2012) A tale of many cities: universal patterns in human urban mobility. PLoS ONE 7:e37027

49. Becker RA, Cáceres R, Hanson K, Meng Loh J, Urbanek S, Varshavsky A, Volinsky C (2011) Route classification using cellular handoff patterns. In: Proc. of the 13th international conference on ubiquitous computing, pp 123-132
50. Isaacman S, Becker R, Cáceres R, Kobourov S, Rowland J, Varshavsky A (2010) A tale of two cities. In: Proc. of the 11th workshop on mobile computing systems, pp 19-24
51. Quercia D, Di Lorenzo G, Calabrese F, Ratti C (2011) Mobile phones and outdoor advertising: measurable advertising. IEEE Pervasive Comput 10:28-36
52. Lucet J-C, Laouenan C, Chelius G, Veziris N, Lepelletier D, Friggeri A, Abiteboul D, Bouvet E, Mentré F, Fleury E (2012) Electronic sensors for assessing interactions between healthcare workers and patients under airborne precautions. PLoS ONE 7:e37893

4

Link creation and information spreading over social and communication ties in an interest-based online social network

Luca Maria Aiello[1*], Alain Barrat[2,3], Ciro Cattuto[3], Rossano Schifanella[1] and Giancarlo Ruffo[1]

*Correspondence: aiello@di.unito.it
[1]Department of Computer Science, University of Torino, Torino, Italy
Full list of author information is available at the end of the article

Abstract

Complex dynamics of social media emerge from the interaction between the patterns of social connectivity of users and the information exchanged along such social ties. Unveiling the underlying mechanisms that drive the evolution of online social systems requires a deep understanding of the interplay between these two aspects. Based on the case of the aNobii social network, an online service for book readers, we investigate the dynamics of link creation and the social influence phenomenon that may trigger information diffusion in the social graph. By confirming that social partner selection is strongly driven by structural, geographical, and topical proximity, we develop a machine-learning social link recommender for individual users trained on a set of features selected as best predictive out of several and we test it on the still widely unexplored domain of a network of interest. We also analyze the influence process from the two distinct perspectives of users and items. We show that link creation plays an immediate effect on the alignment of user profiles and that the established social ties are a good substrate for social influence. We quantitatively measure influence by tracking the patterns of diffusion of specific pieces of information and comparing them with appropriate null models. We discover an appreciable signal of social influence even though item consumption is a very slow process in this context. All the detected patterns of social attachment and influence are observed to be stronger when considering the social subgraph on which communication effectively occurs. Based on our study of the dynamics of the aNobii social network, we investigate the possibility to predict the evolution of such a complex social system.

1 Introduction

Global dynamics of online social media emerge from the aggregation of the behavioral footprints generated by the activity of the users and their interactions. Such complex information ecosystems are characterized by two fundamental components, namely the creation of *social connections* between individuals and the *information exchange* between them. Mining the static and evolutionary patterns of such phenomena is the key to understand and predict micro and macroscopic dynamics of the whole system.

So far, many efforts have been focused on investigating the causes that determine the creation of social links and the process of information diffusion along these links. If, on the one hand, some results obtained by previous work are supported by well-known sociological theories, on the other hand many dynamics characterizing online social systems are not intuitive, difficult to model accurately, and still widely unknown.

Among others, the microscopic dimension of the process of *link creation*, and the *influence* phenomenon that triggers the diffusion of a piece of information or the spreading of a behavioral norm across the social network have still many unexplored sides. In the first case, even though many studies have addressed the problem of predicting the global evolution of social graphs, only few investigations have been performed from the individual perspective, namely trying to predict future social connections of a single social agent. Similarly, even if several models of information spreading on social networks have been proposed in the past, it is still not clear to what extent information can spread quickly and effectively in the network, and whether the factors that determine influence between peers are generalizable across different social systems.

We contribute to shed light on these questions through the analysis of aNobii, an online social network for book lovers. Unlike the mainstream, general-purpose social networks (*e.g.*, Facebook, Twitter, Google+), aNobii is a *network of interest*, where social aggregation is determined by the topical interests of the readers. Moreover, the contact network can be retrieved *via* crawling without restrictions, thus allowing the analysis of all the nodes reachable *via* crawling. The specificity of the domain considered and the richness of the features publicly exposed by the users allow the exploration of the social dimensions from an unusual angle. Our analysis is driven by two main goals:

1. Designing an effective strategy for the *recommendation* of new links to single users and verifying its effectiveness in an interest-based network. As opposed to the task of link prediction, link recommendation is a widely unexplored task and it has been addressed only for general-purpose networks. We survey a large amount of structural and topical features and we determine the best ones for recommendation purposes. We verify that recommendation in the considered domain is a harder task if compared to general purpose networks and we provide insights on the origin of this difference.

2. Providing quantitative measure of influence in an interest-driven domain by investigating the perspectives of both users (pairs of individuals interacting and exerting influence on one another) and items (books spreading in the network by word-of-mouth process). In the analysis of book spreading, we provide a novel comparison of diffusion traces with null models, we detect a clear signal of influence in a domain in which the consumption of items is a slow process, and we highlight some factors that foster the adoption of books by individuals.

A number of results emerge from the present study, including:

- The analysis of static properties of the aNobii online social system, including geographical and topical bias in link connectivity;
- The discovery of a relation between an item popularity and its viral diffusion potential;
- The detection of the importance of communication patterns over mere social links in the process of social link creation and influence;
- The introduction of a metric of structural node similarity inspired by graph-centrality metrics.

Overall, we present here a comprehensive study of the structure and dynamics of a social system that can be a valuable reference in online social network analysis, as it proceeds all the way from the data collection to the study of the complex dynamics of the system.

In the following we give an overview of the related work in the field (Section 2), we introduce the details of the aNobii social network and we discuss its static and dynamic structural properties (Sections 3, 4). The dynamics of link connectivity and social influence are discussed in Section 5, and the link recommendation algorithm is presented in Section 6.

2 Related work

Several studies have described online social systems from the point of view of their static network properties [1] and in the dynamics of their overall evolution [2, 3]. Temporal fluctuations of network topological features such as diameter, clustering coefficient and mixing patterns [4] and dynamics of link creation in social networks [5] have been explored in depth through the analysis of large-scale real world datasets. Previous works on link characterization, focusing on the patterns that describe the creation of links and how social ties features evolve in time, reveal that link creation is driven by *proximity*, *triangle closure*, *reciprocation* and *homophily* [5–9].

Among the topics related to the analysis of multi-agent systems, in this paper we focus on three broad areas that have attracted a strong interest; namely, the study of the *communication* patterns between users, the *influence* phenomenon, and the *link prediction* problem.

2.1 Communication networks

Recently, findings from social network analysis have been corroborated and expanded by the study of communication networks - also denoted as *activity* networks [10] or *interaction* networks [11] - that often coexist with social networks. The comparison of the graph of user-to-user interactions with the social network reveals similar connectivity patterns driven by reciprocity and triangle closure [12].

Activity networks are more dynamic than social networks and reflect changing trends in user interaction and information flow. Communication graphs have shown to be strongly clustered and to change over many time scales, even if the structural features of the activity network remain stable over time [13]. It has been observed that the average interaction level with neighbors in the social network is very low [14] and often decreasing with time [13]; in agreement with this, studies on the Facebook interaction graph [11] reveal that the social links that are effectively exploited for user-to-user communication are a minority. Moreover, recent studies on Twitter revealed that users can entertain no more than 100-200 stable relationships among all their social contacts [15]. Such results confirm the intuition that online social ties are not always good proxies to extract information exchange patterns.

Although the importance of communication links has been assessed in the past, many social phenomena such as homophily and influence have been studied using the graph of conventional social ties as reference. The effectiveness of modeling and predicting some social phenomena using communication networks instead of social networks has not been explored thoroughly, and has not been considered in the case of networks of interest like aNobii. We compare social and interaction ties in the context of link creation and information diffusion, finding that the information they carry have a different potential in predicting the formation of new links or the diffusion of information. For the link recommendation task, we introduce a metric that combines the information from both social and interaction networks to enhance the prediction accuracy.

2.2 Influence and diffusion

The task of capturing the dynamics of information spreading and influence that occur in networked environments has received much attention recently. Diffusion models of word-of-mouth processes have been developed in the past to enhance viral marketing strategies [16]; more recently, due to the large diffusion of social media, detection of influence patterns and of influential individuals has become important to capture the interaction dynamics in social networks and in real-time information networks.

Analysis of information propagation in Flickr [17] showed that diffusion is limited to individuals who reside in the close neighborhood of the seed user and the spreading process is very slow. Analysis of message cascading on Twitter has been used to estimate the degree of influence of users [18]; the most influential among a pair of users is determined using the difference between some activity metric, like the number of followers or number of tweet replies. In partial disagreement with this study, it has been shown that the number of followers (or of social contacts in general) does not imply a high influence degree [19].

A crucial task in the analysis of influence patterns is to discern real influence from unobserved factors, like homophily or confounding variables, that can induce statistical correlation between the behaviors or the profiles of connected users even without one being influenced by the other. Shuffling or randomization tests on user features are commonly used to detect a signal of influence inside noisy patterns of correlation between pairs of users [20]. Investigations on the interplay between homophily-driven creation of social connections and the influence that neighbors exert on each other's behavior have been made by Crandall *et al.* [21] on the Wikipedia collaboration network. Bakshy *et al.* [22] have reported a large scale experiment performed on the Facebook social network by randomizing the exposition of users to the items published by their friends, in order to expose the role of the social links in the propagation of an information, and to show the existence of a genuine influence phenomenon between Facebook friends.

Instead of representing the influence as an infection phenomenon between connected individuals, Yang and Leskovec [23] recently proposed a linear influence model which is agnostic on the network structure and relies only on the time of the contagion. These observations imply the presence of a hidden contagion web that is different from the observed social network [24]. Based on similar observations, other probabilistic models that represent influence effects between peers disregarding social links structure have been proposed [25].

To complement previous studies, we focus here on the influence phenomenon in a social context where item consumption (reading books) is a much slower process than in general-purpose online social and news media. We explore the influence process both from the point of view of users and items, exposing strong signals of influence at the moment of social link creation and the generation of information fluxes over the existing links. We characterize the spreading traces (*i.e.*, graphs of item adopters expanding in time), compare then to null models and provide some insights into the still open question of whether the fraction or the number of influencing neighbors has a stronger impact on the diffusion probability.

2.3 Link prediction

Predicting the presence of a link between two entities in a network is one of the major challenges in the area of *link mining* [26]. Such edge-related mining task is usually defined as *link detection* [27] when it aims to disclose the presence of unobserved or unknown links on a static network or as *link prediction* when it aims to foresee whether a connection will arise in the future between nodes that are unlinked at the current time. *Link recommendation* finally is a task whose goal is to provide to a target user a list of contacts that he will likely be keen to form a social link with [28].

Seminal work on link prediction was presented by Liben-Nowell and Kleinberg [29, 30]. They identify structural properties of the graph which can be used to build a ranking of the node pairs based on their structural similarity, which is in turn exploited to predict future interactions. Several slight variants of this approach have been adopted [31]. Another early work by Popescul *et al.* [32] focused instead on link detection using a classifier trained on the *feature vectors* that describe the nodes of the graph.

Combining structural graph similarity measures and simple node-based features in a supervised learning approach to link prediction has been also tried in the past [9, 33], showing the improvement of the prediction performance compared to predictors based solely on topological features. Geographical proximity between nodes [34] and groups affiliation [35] have been effectively used as node-based feature as well. Recently, some tests have been done also on the predictive power of some network clustering algorithms in link prediction tasks [36].

The best-known topological measures of structural similarity between pairs of nodes are reviewed and refined by Zhou *et al.* [37] and Lü *et al.* [38]. The authors compare several structural similarity metrics for link prediction in terms of accuracy and computational efficiency. Novel local proximity measures are also proposed and shown to be efficient and accurate in link detection. Efficiency of structural proximity metrics on graphs is addressed also by Song *et al.* [39].

Detection of links based only on the information extracted from folksonomies is performed by Schifanella *et al.* [40]. Similarity measures explicitly designed for the folksonomic space are used to compute a lexical proximity between users. A similar context is considered by Leroy *et al.* [41], who leverage the group membership information from Flickr to build a probabilistic graph and detect the hidden social graph with a good accuracy.

The problem of detecting both unknown links and missing node attributes in a network is addressed by Bilgic *et al.* [42]. They propose an iterative method that refines at each step the prediction of one of the two features considered leveraging the information gained on the other feature at the previous step.

The role of temporal aspects in prediction is explored by Tylenda *et al.* [43], who exploit the information of recent interaction between individuals to improve the prediction accuracy. Dunlavy *et al.* [44] use a matrix-tensor method to predict links that will be created in the future in networks with an underlying periodic structure.

Even if the majority of papers is focused on link prediction on simple graphs, a few techniques have been developed also for different kinds of networks. Work has been made in link detection on weighted networks [45–47], bipartite networks [44, 48, 49] and signed social graphs [50]. Very recently, an approach that combines supervised learning and random walks has been shown to have a promising accuracy for both prediction and recommendation of new links [28].

Finally, some approaches based on probabilistic models such as relational Markov networks [51] and probabilistic relational models [52] deserve to be cited. These approaches have however not been proven to be scalable and they have not been extensively tested on real-world datasets.

Despite the large amount of work in the prediction area, few efforts have been devoted to the task of link recommendation, which is inherently different (and more relevant for real social media services) since it aims to the satisfaction of single users and not just to maximize the ability of predicting the global evolution of the social graph. Moreover, to the best of our knowledge, link recommendation has not been studied in networks of interest but only in general-purpose online social graphs like Facebook. In our recommendation method we collect all the most relevant state-of-the-art features used for link prediction, define an additional feature, and we rank them according to their effectiveness in the recommendation task.

3 aNobii dataset

We analyze a temporal dataset taken from aNobii.com, a website for book lovers. The main feature of aNobii is the personal digital *library* that every user can build by picking titles from a vast database of more than 30 millions publications along with their metadata (such as author, publication year, *etc.*). Every book in the library can be marked with a reading status (*e.g.*, 'finished reading') and can be annotated with keywords (tags), a rating (from 1 to 5 stars) and a review. There is also a *wishlist* containing titles that users have planned to read. Users can enrich their profile with other personal information like their gender, age, marital status and a geo-location composed by a country and, optionally, a town. Country is specified in 97% and city in roughly 40% of the profiles.

Channels of social interaction form another crucial component of aNobii. The social network is composed by two different kinds of mutually-exclusive ties, namely the *friendship* and the *neighborhood* relations. Even if it is up to the users to choose one or another, the aNobii website suggests to establish a friendship tie with people that you already know in real life, while neighborhood should be used for people that you do not know, but whose library you consider interesting. Except for this usage recommendation, the two types of link have the same characteristics. They are directed, they can be established even without the approval of the linked user, and they enable the notification of the linked library updates. Social aggregation can be achieved also through the affiliation to *groups*. Thematic groups can be created by any user and the membership is open to anyone. The last channel of interaction is the *message wall* (also called 'shoutbox'). Users can write messages on the walls of any other individual, independently of the existence of a relationship in the social network. Self-posting is also allowed. Message exchange defines a different social network that we call *communication graph*, and whose properties are discussed in detail in Section 4.3. Self-posting is also allowed, yielding self-loops in the communication graph.

We explored the aNobii social networks through *web crawling* and collected all the public user data through page scraping. We took several snapshots, 15 days apart, using a BFS strategy initialized with a random seed and expanding the user list following the links of the contacts lists and in the shoutboxes. Since social and communications connections are directed we were only able to collect the information of the largest strongly connected component and the out component.[a] However, we collected the full information of both components, thus avoiding the possible biases related to incomplete sampling of a connected component.

4 Structure and dynamics of social network

4.1 Overview on network structure

Friendship and neighborhood networks have similar global properties, with however some structural differences. As shown in Table 1, both networks have a high percentage of reciprocated links and a strongly connected kernel that includes the majority of nodes. However, the neighborhood network is slightly smaller, denser, and has higher degree centralization [54]. Its size is smaller because neighborhood ties tend not to be used by less active members and it is more centralized because of very popular libraries with many 'followers': the range of variation of the in- and out-degree are broader for neighborhood than for friendship (for the in-degree, the maximal values are 1,708 for neighborhood and 453 for friendship; for the out-degree, the maximal values are respectively 6,537 and 705). These differences reveal that the two social ties are used slightly differently by users, and are in agreement with the intuition that friendship links correspond to individuals the user really knows, while neighborhood links can be established towards any other user whose library seems of interest. In the context of properties that apply in a comparable quantitative and qualitative way to both networks, it is however more convenient to consider the *union* between them. In the following, for simplicity, we will refer to the union network as the aNobii social network.

As a direct result of their structural differences, the diameters of the two networks (computed as the maximum shortest path length) are appreciably different. Still, they are both very high if considered that similar diameter values have been found for many other online social networks with much greater size [1]. The strong geographical clustering of the social network is the main reason behind this feature. The country-level graph of the social network depicted in Figure 1 reveals that the network has two main geographic communities, namely Italy (with roughly 60% of users) and Far East (composed by Taiwan, Hong Kong and China, that include less than 30% of users altogether). Since these two clusters are loosely connected to each other, the network has a dual core structure where connection between the two cores is mostly mediated by smaller communities (*e.g.*, the USA cluster). Paths between individuals residing in different cores are thus longer if compared to a more ordinary single core configuration and, consequently, the diameter is higher.

Table 1 Statistics concerning the friendship and neighborhood networks, their union (*i.e.*, the full social network) and the communication network in April 2011

	Friendship	Neighborhood	Union	Communication
Nodes	126,858	77,356	140,686	80,303
Links	557,258	633,635	1,187,650	574,285
Loops	0	0	0	22,579
Reciprocation	0.60	0.43	0.54	0.61
$\langle k_{out} \rangle$	4.4	8.2	8.4	7.2
$\langle w \rangle$	-	-	-	1.8
$\langle m \rangle$	-	-	-	12.9
WCC size	121,143	76,760	140,686	75,965
SCC size	81,292	41,063	100,492	38,336
Density	$3.4 \cdot 10^{-5}$	$1.1 \cdot 10^{-4}$	$6.0 \cdot 10^{-5}$	$8.9 \cdot 10^{-5}$
Average SPL	7.3	4.7	5.3	4.8
Diameter	25	15	20	17
Degree centr. [53]	0.0072	0.0875	0.0486	0.0650

SPL = shortest path length; WCC = weakly connected component; SCC = strongly connected component; $\langle k_{out} \rangle$ average out degree, $\langle w \rangle$ average edge weight (only for the communication network, see Section 4.3), $\langle m \rangle$ average number of messages in the shoutbox. Degree centralization is given by Freeman's formula $C_D = \frac{\sum_{i \in G}(k_{max} - k_i)}{(|G-1| \cdot |G-2|)}$.

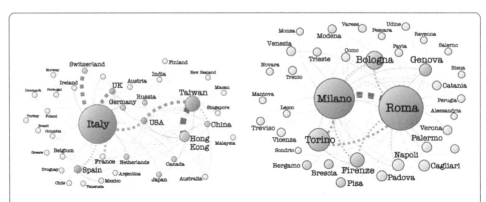

Figure 1 Graphs of home countries and towns of aNobii users. Nodes are scaled according to the size of the communities and the width and colors of edges depend on the number of links that connect nodes between the communities. In the graph of countries, communities with less than 20 members and edges with weight less than 20 are not shown. In the Italian towns graph, communities with less than 100 members and edges with weight less than 100 are not displayed.

The separation between the geographical regions in the graph can be quantified by measuring the *conductance* φ of the graph cut separating the users who reside in a given region R from the rest of the network, and comparing the value with the conductance of a random cut φ^{rand} between a region R' and the rest of the graph, where R' has the same size and degree distribution than R. The conductance is defined as the ratio between the number of edges crossing the cut and the minimum number of edges inside one of the two regions separated by the cut: small values denote well-separated regions while values close to 1 denote strong connectivity between regions [55]. Italy and Far East regions have a much smaller conductance than their random counterparts ($\varphi_{\text{IT}} = 0.08$, $\varphi_{\text{IT}}^{\text{rand}} = 0.69$, $\varphi_{\text{FE}} = 0.05$, $\varphi_{\text{FE}}^{\text{rand}} = 0.24$), while 'bridge' regions have a conductance comparable to the random case ($\varphi_{\text{USA}} = 0.66$, $\varphi_{\text{USA}}^{\text{rand}} = 0.60$).

Narrowing down the view on town-level graphs inside clusters, the intra-cluster connections appear denser and structured around a single core of nodes (Figure 1). Of course, since aNobii is focused on books, language is the main reason that leads to this sharp separation.

In addition to the geographical location, aNobii profiles contain a rich information about users. User activity, along with social ties, can be measured by several indicators. The corresponding probability distributions are shown in Figure 2. Not surprisingly, the most popular activity is filling the library with books (94% of users have at least one book). Approximatively 50% of users added at least one book in the wishlist and roughly the same portion of users is member of at least one group. Books are annotated with reviews by around 40% of users and rated by 75%. Tagging activity is quite unfrequent. Around 75% of users declare at least one friend or neighbor. Moreover, and as expected from studies in other online social systems [56], the activity distributions are all very broad, displaying heavy tails that highlight a strong heterogeneity in the behavior of users: no typical value of any user activity can thus be defined.

Different activities exhibit strong correlations between each other, as also investigated for other social networks like Last.fm and Flickr [40, 56]. Graphically, correlations can be depicted by showing the average activity of users who exhibit a given engagement level for another activity; in Figure 3 we display some correlation graphs of the out-degree and the number of books with other activities. Even if the observed patterns are noisy for users

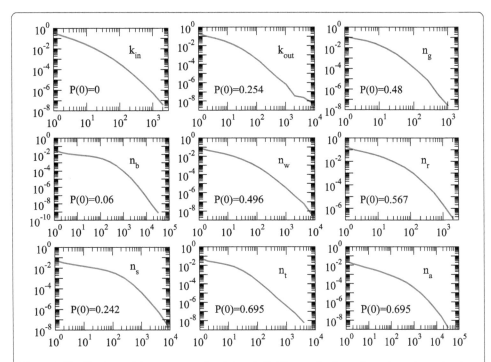

Figure 2 Distributions of the measures of activity of aNobii users. In-degree k_{in} and out-degree k_{out} in the social network, number of group memberships n_g, number of books in library and wishlist (n_b and n_w), number of reviews n_r and books rated with stars n_s, number of distinct tags n_t and total number of tag annotations n_a.

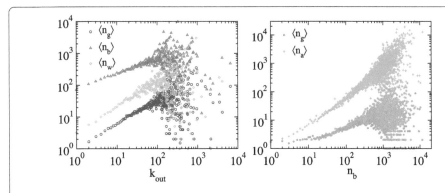

Figure 3 Correlations between different activities in aNobii. Left: Average number of group memberships $\langle n_g \rangle$, of books in library $\langle n_b \rangle$ and wishlist size $\langle n_w \rangle$ against the number of social out-links k_{out}. Right: Average number of group memberships and tag annotations $\langle n_a \rangle$ against the number of books in the library.

with a large number of connections and books (due to the low number of users over which the averages are performed), all the activities considered show a clear increasing trend for increasing values of k_{out} and n_b, corresponding to a positive correlation between activities.

The correlations between the activity of social network neighbors, commonly known as *mixing patterns* [57], can be measured by plotting the average amount of activity of the neighbours of all the users with the same value for that activity (*e.g.*, with the same number of books). The positive slopes of the scatterplots in Figure 4 (modulo the noise for the less frequent activity values) reveal an assortative mixing for all the activities, meaning that

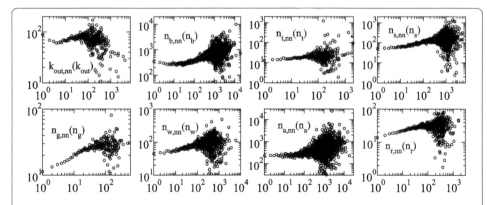

Figure 4 Mixing patterns for different activities in aNobii. The notation $n_{x,nn}(n_x)$ indicates the average amount of an activity x performed by the nearest neighbors of those users that expose the same amount n_x of that activity. As defined before, k_{out}, n_b, n_w, n_g, n_t, n_a, n_r, n_s denote respectively the out-degree and the number of books, wishlist items, group memberships, tags, tag annotations, reviews and ratings.

Table 2 Evolution of some quantities from one snapshot to the next

	1 → 2	2 → 3	3 → 4	4 → 5	5 → 6
New nodes	2,241	2,121	1,911	3,214	3,567
Removed nodes	239	222	230	220	684
New edges	19,472	18,324	17,618	24,805	26,883
Removed edges	642	763	713	782	700
New edges existing nodes	10,044	9,296	9,758	11,925	12,520
$u \rightarrow v$	54%	53%	54%	55%	51%
Reciprocated	10%	13%	13%	13%	14%
$u \leftrightarrow v$	36%	34%	33%	32%	35%
Simple closure	21%	21%	22%	21%	19%
Double closure	9%	10%	9%	9%	9%

The last two sections report the fractions of different edge types among the new edges created between nodes already existing at the beginning of the time window considered.

users are likely to be linked to other individuals with comparable amount of activity, a typical pattern of social networks.

4.2 Evolution of the network

Our temporal dataset allows to study the evolution of the social network. In Table 2 we report the evolution of some network parameters in a time span of 2 and a half months, with a granularity of 15 days. The largest component grows steadily due to the arrival of new nodes, and new ties are also created between existent users. Node and edge deletion are much rarer events.

We classify newly created edges among existing nodes in three categories. $u \rightarrow v$ denotes the category of unidirectional links while $u \leftrightarrow v$ represents the new reciprocal links. 'Reciprocated' denotes instead the new links from a node u to a node v, such that a link from v to u already existed. Links of the type $u \rightarrow v$ and $u \leftrightarrow v$ can be further described as 'Simple closure' and 'Double closure' ties respectively if they close at least a directed triangle (*i.e.*, there existed a node w such that the arcs $u \rightarrow w$ and $w \leftrightarrow v$ already existed). This fits the expectation that in a social network links are often established toward 'friends of friends'. This *triangle closure* phenomenon is evident also by looking at the distribution at time t of the distances of nodes that become linked at time $t + 1$. The comparison be-

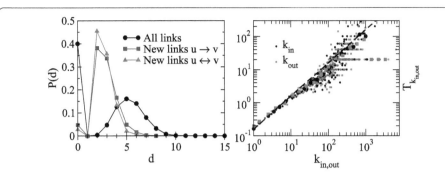

Figure 5 Link creation in aNobii. Left: Distribution at snapshot 4 of the distances of nodes which become linked between snapshots 4 and 5, compared with the distribution at snapshot 4 of distances between all pairs of users. The points in $d = 0$ give the portion of pairs of nodes between which no directed path exists in snapshot 4. Right: Measure of the preferential attachment. T_k is the probability for a new node to create a link toward a node of degree k. Black circles and red squares account for in and out degree, respectively. Thick dots represent the log-binning of the values, and the dashed line represents a linear relationship $T_k \propto k$.

tween such distribution and the distribution of distances between all the node pairs in the network (Figure 5, left) reveals that the process of social partner selection is biased towards the topological vicinity of the user. In particular, more than 40% of the new arcs close triangles and more than 80% are established between nodes residing at distance at most 3.

Besides *triangle closure*, another phenomenon that underlies link creation in growing graphs is *preferential attachment, i.e.* users with large number of connection are preferentially chosen to establish a social link [58]. We test this hypothesis using the following method [59]. Let us denote by T_k the *a priori* probability for a newcomer to create a link toward a node of degree k, between time $t-1$ and t. Given that at time $t-1$ the degree distribution of the $N(t-1)$ nodes is $P(k, t-1)$ (*i.e.*, there are $N(t-1)P(k, t-1)$ nodes of degree k), the probability to observe a new link from a new node to a node of degree k between $t-1$ and t is $T_k P(k, t-1)$. Therefore, we can measure T_k by counting for each k the fraction of links created by new nodes that reach nodes of degree k, and dividing by $P(k, t-1)$. As shown in Figure 5 (right), we obtain a linear behavior $T_k \propto k$, both when considering for k the in and the out-degree (which are strongly correlated). This is a clear signal of a linear preferential attachment. T_k values for $k > 1,000$ falling far from the diagonal are just statistical noise due to the low number of high-degree nodes.

Clearly, users do not have any knowledge of the overall network topology at any time, so they cannot be more motivated to connect to the most connected users. It is more likely that this preferential attachment arises from the fact that a new user creates links not only towards another user but also towards some of this user's neighbors. It has been shown that this locally-driven connection pattern results in effective preferential attachment [60, 61]. Indeed, we verified in our dataset that many newcomers join the network by creating links to pairs of already connected users.

4.3 Communication and interaction networks

Ties in social media are most often not categorized based on the intensity or on the type of the connections. However, in a social context, ties might have different strength and meaning, depending on the information that flows on them and from the features that describe the individuals they connect. To reach a deeper understanding of social dynamics, the information on the social connections must be complemented with other relational data. In this respect, the communication network carries a useful information to augment the description of the social substrate as given by the user-declared 'friendship' or 'neighborhood' ties: some user-declared ties might not be the support of any communication, and communication may occur between users that are neither 'friends' nor 'neighbors'.

The most extensive way in which the communication history between individuals can be defined is through a temporal graph, where each edge corresponds to a single message and carries a timestamp. In this temporal graph, the frequency of messages exchanged by two users might change, with periods of inactivity followed by bursts of messages. The detailed study of this dynamics goes beyond the scope of the present study, so that we consider an aggregation over the whole data set time window, and define the *communication graph* as a directed graph where each edge between two nodes is weighted by the number of messages sent between these nodes.

Similarly to previous work [11], we observe that macroscopic structural features of communication graph are analogous to those of the social networks. Degree distributions are very close to those found for the social networks (not shown) and the strength distributions (*i.e.*, number of received or sent messages) reveal an expected broad behavior (not shown). The statistics shown in Table 1 indicate that this graph has high reciprocation and centralization. Note that the communication network has self-links since it is possible for a user to write messages on his/her own shoutbox. Users keeping alive conversation threads on a single shoutbox or announcements published by the shoutbox owner are the main causes of this phenomenon. This behavior concerns however only 28% of the users, and the self-links represent only 4% of the total number of links. In Figure 6 we observe that the social connectivity and the amount of books in the library are correlated with the activity on the communication network. A strong correlation is also found between in-degree and out-degree in the communication network.

As shown in Table 3, the difference between social and communication graphs is substantial. More than 75% of the socially connected pairs lack any form of public communication and, conversely, around 25% of the communication channels are established between non connected users. We call *interaction graph* the portion of the social graph that overlaps with the communication network (*i.e.* Social ∩ Comm in the notation of Table 3).

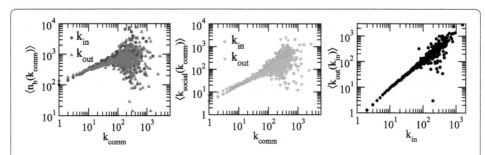

Figure 6 Correlation plots for the communication activity. The numbers of incoming and outgoing messages are strongly correlated with the number of social acquaintances (k_{social}) and with the size of the library (n_b). The high reciprocation in communication implies also a strong correlation between in- and out-degree in the communication network.

Table 3 Overlap between social networks and communication network

		Social\Comm	Comm\Social	Social ∩ Comm
#Nodes	Friendship	57,456	10,901	69,402
	Neighborhood	20,792	23,739	56,564
	Union	63,719	3,336	76,967
#Edges	Friendship	461,774	478,801	95,484
	Neighborhood	435,396	376,046	198,239
	Union	894,946	281,581	292,704

4.4 Topical alignment

Assortative mixing patterns suggest a propensity to the local alignment of behavioral patterns between connected nodes. While we explored only the mixing patterns relative to the amount of activity of neighboring users in Section 4.1, this tendency can be explored more in depth by taking into account the user profiles. More precisely we consider the similarity of users' profiles with respect to specific features, and measuring how it depends on the distance between nodes on the social network. We call *topical local alignment* a static property of the social network for which pairs of individuals that are close in the social graph are more similar than pairs separated by larger distances on the network. For instance, when considering books as a feature, the topical alignment can be measured by computing the similarity between the book sets of pairs of users as a function of their distance on the network. Similarity between two users u and v can be measured by counting the number of common books $n_{cb}(u, v)$ or by considering a normalized similarity measure such as the *cosine similarity*

$$\sigma_b(u, v) = \frac{\sum_b \delta_u(b)\delta_v(b)}{\sqrt{n_b(u)n_b(v)}}, \tag{1}$$

where the indicator function $\delta_x(b)$ is equal to 1 if user x has the book b in his/her library and to 0 otherwise. The cosine similarity is thus a scalar product of the 'book vectors' of users u and v, normalized by the library sizes $n_b(x) = \sum_b \delta_x(b)$.

To check if profiles of neighbors in the social network are topically aligned with respect to some features, we measure the average books and groups similarity of pairs separated by d hops in the social graph; results are shown in the first two columns of Figure 7. A quick decay of the similarity with the distance (for both the cosine similarity and the number of common items) gives a strong clue of the presence of a local topical alignment. However, the detected signal could *a priori* be ascribed to purely statistical alignment effects due to assortativity. For instance, since very active users tend to connect with other highly active users, their similarity could be high just because their feature sets are big, and thus they have a higher chance to share many elements. To tell apart real alignment from statistical effects, we need to compare the results obtained on the real data with a suitable *null model* [40]. Our null model is based on a random reshuffling of the items (*e.g.*, books) between user profiles, keeping unchanged both the size of the item sets and the social connections of each profile. This procedure preserves the assortativity patterns relative to activity intensity but wipes out the alignment due to the interaction between individuals. We note that the randomized curves exhibit a similar decay, that is due to the assortativity effect mentioned above. However, the difference between the curves for the reshuffled and the real data shows that the assortativity alone can not wholly account for the similarity detected in the real data, and that a genuine topical alignment effect is present: the presence

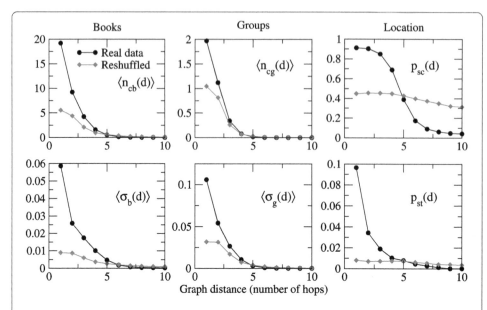

Figure 7 Topical and geographical alignment. Left and middle plots: Average similarity of the libraries (resp., groups) of aNobii users as a function of their distance in the social network. The similarity is measured by the average number of common books or groups (top, $\langle n_{cb} \rangle$, $\langle n_{cg} \rangle$), and by the average cosine similarity (bottom, $\langle \sigma_b \rangle$, $\langle \sigma_g \rangle$) between the books lists (resp., groups). In both cases, the same similarity after random reshuffling of items is shown. Right plots: Fraction of pairs of users at distance d in the union network residing in the same country (P_{sc}) or town (P_{st}). In both cases data from the network with reshuffled links are shown.

of a social link is correlated with the fact that the connected users are more likely to share interests and experiences or to be exposed to the same context or to each other's activity.

The same analysis can be performed on all the features of the users' profiles. For instance, the relationship between the geographic attributes and the distance on the social graph are explored in the right plots of Figure 7 that show the probability that two users at distance d on the social graph are from the same country or town. Again, to disentangle this signal from statistical effects (given for example by the imbalance of the number of users in each nation) we use as null model a random network with the same degree sequence as the original network but reshuffled geographic attributes. The alignment on the nationality feature is strong up to a distance of 4 hops and a strong effect is observed as well for towns, most of all for directly connected users.

This result suggests that people preferentially establish social ties with others who speak the same language, but also that the social selection process is driven by the geographic proximity (e.g., people that reside in the same town). In particular, 90% of the social edges connect users from the same country and there is a 10% probability that two connected users are from the same city. This result indicates a decreasing trend of the probability of connection with geographic distance, as also found in other online social networks that are not based on a particular interest (here, the books) but have broader scopes [62, 63].

As seen in the previous subsection, the fact that two users are connected does not automatically mean that they exchange information through messages. It is therefore of interest to compare the topical alignment on the social links that effectively are the support of communication ('Social ∩ Comm', in the notation of Table 3) with the alignment along the subset of social links on which no communication is observed ('Social \ Comm', in the notation of Table 3). Figure 8 shows that the former is larger than the latter, but only slightly:

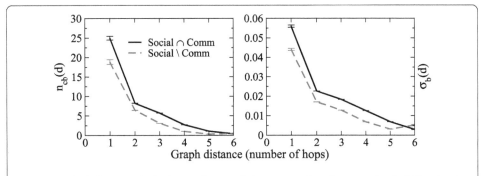

Figure 8 Topical alignment in the interaction graph. Average number of common books (left) and cosine similarity (right) against distance on the interaction graph and on the graph made by social contacts on which no communication occurs (Social\Comm). Standard error bars are shown for each curve.

interestingly, strong alignment effects exist even on a network along which no explicit communication flows, and are almost as strong as in the network of communication.

5 Homophily, selection and influence

5.1 Causal connection between similarity and link creation

In Section 4.4 we observed topical alignment as a static property of the network. Here we investigate the evolution of this phenomenon. Since we verified that the topical alignment, which denotes a homophily phenomenon between users [64], is not purely due to assortative patterns, we can ascribe this phenomenon to selection or to social influence. *Selection* corresponds to a process in which the choice of a social partner (here as 'friend' or 'neighbor') that is driven by the similarity between connecting individuals, while *social influence* [20] denotes the tendency of individuals to be influenced in their behavior by others, and in particular by their neighborhood in the social network. As we now show, both phenomena can be exposed in aNobii.

To check whether the occurrence of selection-driven attachment, one needs to compare the topical similarity, computed at time t, between pairs of users who create a social connection between t and $t + 1$, with the similarity of another set of users. Choosing for comparison a random set of pairs of users would trivially yield a strong difference, as we have shown previously that (i) most pairs of users creating a link between t and $t + 1$ reside at distance 2 or 3 on the network at t, and (ii) the similarity of users at distance 2 or 3 is much stronger than the one of users lying farther apart. We therefore compare the average similarity of connecting users with the average similarity of all the pairs of nodes residing two hops away in the social graph at t. Table 4 shows that pairs of users that are about to get connected are on average more similar than the average over all the nodes that are two hops away (except for the case of the number of common groups averaged over all pairs of users who establish a non-reciprocal link between t and $t + 1$). For new bidirectional links, and pairs of users who were at distance 2 and create a link (thus closing a triangle), the average similarity before the creation of the link is particularly strong. This result applies for all the similarity measures considered. The probability that two users at distance 2 have 0 similarity is also much smaller for the users who become linked between t and $t + 1$.

The picture emerging from this analysis and from the results presented in Sections 4.2 and 4.4 is the following: users connect to others residing close in the social graph, very

Table 4 Average similarity for snapshot $t = 4$ of pairs forming new links between t and $t + 1$ (either non-reciprocal, $u \rightarrow v$ or reciprocal, $u \leftrightarrow v$), compared with the average similarity of all pairs at distance 2 at t

	$\langle n_{cb} \rangle$	σ_b	$\langle n_{cg} \rangle$	σ_g
$d_{uv} = 2$	9.5 (0.2)	0.02	1.12 (0.61)	0.05
$u \rightarrow v$	12.9 (0.16)	0.04	1.1 (0.6)	0.08
$u \leftrightarrow v$	18.5 (0.06)	0.04	1.67 (0.44)	0.11
Simple closure	18.2 (0.09)	0.04	1.81 (0.45)	0.1
Double closure	23.4 (0.03)	0.05	2.2 (0.36)	0.12

Single and double closure refers respectively to new links $u \rightarrow v$ and $u \leftrightarrow v$ that close triangles. The similarity is measured by the number of common books n_{cb} or groups n_{cg}, and by the corresponding cosine similarities σ_b and σ_g. The numbers in parenthesis give the probability to have similarity equal to 0.

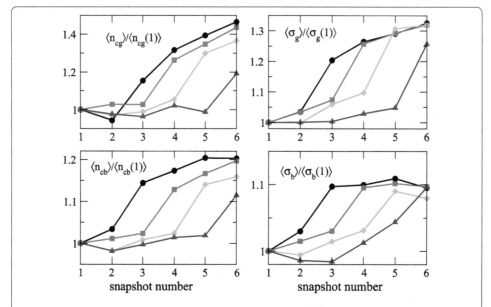

Figure 9 Evolution of the average similarity of user profiles. Similarity, as measured by the numbers of common books or groups, and by the cosine similarity, is shown for links created between t and $t + 1$, for $t = 2$ (black circles), 3 (red squares), 4 (green diamonds), 5 (blue triangles), normalized by the average similarity in the first snapshot. Values are quite stationary before t_0, and clear jumps are observed between t and $t + 1$.

often neighbors of neighbors; moreover, these individuals have on average more similar profiles than other pairs of users at distance 2. In this respect, one can infer that a selection process is at work and is one of the reasons of the observed local topical alignment: among the users who are already close in the graph (distance 2 and 3), the ones who become even closer are the ones who were more similar to each other.

In order to investigate social influence, we instead study the time evolution of the similarity between connected user profiles. In Figure 9 we plot the average similarity for library and group membership features for pairs of users that become connected between t and $t + 1$. Before the link is created the similarity score is rather stationary and a sudden increase is observed when the connection is created; the similarity then continues to grow, albeit at a slower rate. The following scenario emerges from this result: after a link creation, newly connected individuals take inspiration from each other for new books to read and new groups to join. The direct consequence of this reciprocal influence is a further alignment of the profiles, *i.e.*, a reinforcement of the homophily.

Note that the similarity metric used is symmetrical, therefore it does not account for the directionality of the newly created link. We decided not to consider the link directionality in the computation of the similarity, as close to 50% of the newly created links are bidirectional (see Table 2), and because a user receiving a new incoming connection is notified about it on his/her personal homepage: the influence at the time of the connection can potentially flow in both directions.

To summarize, our analysis on the dynamics of social aggregations show the presence of a *bidirectional* causal relationship between social connections and similarity. A higher similarity leads to a higher connection probability and, on the other hand, users who get connected become more similar due to the influence that new acquaintances exert on one another. These results apply not only for collaboration networks [21], but also for the present case of interest-based networks such as aNobii, where the similarity between users is evaluated on the basis of profile items, shared metadata, and topics of interest.

5.2 Structure of book graphs

Influence can also be investigated from a different angle, focusing on items rather than on users. The influence observed at the time of a link creation might indeed remain effective for the whole life span of the social link, and, at any time, may lead a user to adopt a new item (in particular a book) from his/her neighbors and, in turn, to influence others to adopt the same item. This phenomenon gives origin to adoption *cascades* that can be studied within the more general scope of information spreading [65]. Better understanding the spreading of items on the network can shed a clearer light on the overall role of influence in the online social network.

In this perspective, we study the static and dynamic properties of the book graphs: a book graph $G(b)$ is defined as the social subgraph composed by the users having the book b in their library or wishlist and by the links between them. We differentiate the analysis by classes of book popularity as measured by the size of the set $A(b)$ of the users who adopted the book b (*i.e.*, the nodes in $G(b)$). In particular, we introduce three popularity classes, namely the *rare* ($|A(b)| \in [10, 500)$), the *middle* ($|A(b)| \in [500, 1,000)$), and the *popular* ($|A(b)| \geq 1,000$) books. The boundaries of the popularity classes are chosen based on the empirical observation of the popularity distribution of books. Even neglecting very rare books with less than 10 readers we have more than 200K book graphs.

The size of the book graphs are broadly distributed between 1 and 20,000. Book graphs can be formed by several disconnected components, and around 12% of them are composed just by isolated nodes (this is only observed for graphs with at most 100 nodes). The connectivity patterns of books graphs can be detected by measuring how their topological features depend on their size. In Figure 10 we report the relative size of the greatest connected component ($S_{gcc}/|A(b)|$), the relative number of connected components ($N_{cc}/|A(b)|$), and the clustering coefficient (C) against the size of the book graph ($|A(b)|$). For the sake of comparison, for every point in the scatterplot we also depict two twin points representing the same topological measure calculated for two different random graphs taken as null models.

The first is an Erdős-Rényi graph with the same number of nodes and edges. The latter is a random subgraph of the social network with the same number of nodes and the same degree sequence. The purpose of the random subgraph is to model a process in which the book is adopted by the different users at random and independently. If such a

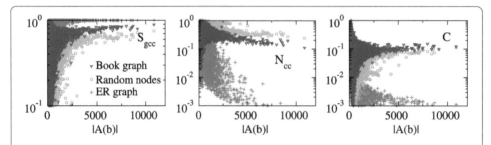

Figure 10 Properties of the book graphs. Scatterplots of relative size of the greatest connected component ($S_{gcc}/|A(b)|$), relative number of connected components ($N_{cc}/|A(b)|$), and clustering coefficient (C) vs. number of nodes in the $G(b)$ graph. For each graph, values for an Erdős-Rényi graph with the same number of nodes and edges are reported, as well as for a subgraph of $|A(b)|$ randomly chosen nodes in the aNobii social graph.

process is considered by simply selecting nodes at random in the network, the resulting subgraphs will be almost always composed of isolated nodes or small disconnected components, therefore we impose that the resulting subgraph has the same degree sequence as the original subgraph.

Book graphs exhibit a weaker connectivity but a much more clustered shape than the corresponding ER graphs, at fixed size. The relative number of connected components slowly decreases with size but remains considerably higher than the ER corresponding values; as a consequence, the relative size of the greatest component asymptotically stabilizes around a value smaller than in the ER graphs; conversely, real book graphs are much more clustered. Structural properties of the random-node-graphs are closer to those of the real book graphs, meaning that the measured levels of clustering and connectivity of the book graphs can partly be ascribed to the degree distribution of their nodes. Nevertheless, the random-node model still exhibits lower clustering and higher sparsity than the empirical book graphs.

To investigate more in depth the differences between the random-node model and the real data, we measure the same structural properties at given average node connectivity, and we study the three book popularity classes separately. Figure 11 shows the values of S_{gcc} and C against the average out-degree $\langle k \rangle$ in the book graphs.

The case of ER graphs is the simplest to interpret and is used as a reference for the other two cases. For ER graphs we observe a relatively rapid transition from 0 to 1 for S_{gcc} as $\langle k \rangle$ crosses 1, which is expected given the known transition between a set of small disconnected components and a giant connected component as the probability of connection crosses $1/N$. Instead, the clustering values remain very small (as also expected in ER graphs). In the case of the real book graphs, the size of the greatest component grows smoothly with the average degree, showing no sign of any abrupt transition, suggesting that the connectivity in book graphs is not driven by any threshold mechanism driven by the average node connectivity. Furthermore, for any average connectivity, a non-negligible portion of nodes remains in small isolated components. This can be due to the fact that several users adopt a book independently, without being directly influenced by their online social contacts. However, the clustering coefficient is very large, suggesting that the groups of adopters are tightly knit communities. The random-node model follows the same trend as the real data, but both the size of the largest component and the clustering are lower, showing that the connectivity patterns are not completely due to the degree distribution.

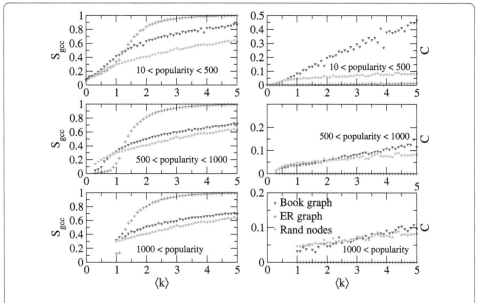

Figure 11 Properties of the book graphs. Relative size of greatest connected components ($S_{gcc}/|A(b)|$) and clustering coefficient (C) vs. average out degree ($\langle k \rangle$), averaged at fixed values of $\langle k \rangle$. Comparison values from corresponding ER graphs is resported.

For books with large popularity, the empirical data and the random-node case become closer.

The overall picture tends to indicate that book graphs may be originated by a process of expansion and densification of clustered cores of readers, and that a process of 'contagion' between users might have taken place in the shaping of the subgraphs of adopters $G(b)$. Nevertheless, as the book popularity grows such effect fades, presumably because the adoption of a very popular book is not mainly driven by inputs received within the social network, but can be in large part driven by stimuli and mechanisms external to the online social network. As the correlations shown here correspond to static snapshots, they cannot however be used to infer causality relations between connectivity and book adoption. It is therefore also possible that the structure of the book graphs is due to the fact that people sharing the same rare book are more likely to establish social contacts than people sharing a very common book.

5.3 Spreading of books

To better understand if a user might be led to adopt a book through the influence of his/her social neighborhood, it is necessary to analyze the temporal evolution of the $G(b)$ graphs. We call $G(b, t)$ the social subgraph of users having book b at time t. $G(b, t)$ can evolve because of new users arriving in the social network who have b in their library, users leaving, or users adding/removing b to/from their library. For the purpose of detecting influence patterns, we disregard the newcomers (who might or not fill their own library with the books they have read) and users leaving the network, and focus on the graph $G^*(b, t)$ restricted to the users who are present in all the considered snapshots. Moreover, for simplicity, we neglect the (very rare) events of book deletion: once a book is adopted by a user, we assume that it is present in his/her library at any future time. In this context, we formally define the set of *adopters* of a book b between time $t-1$ and t as $A^*(b, t) = G^*(b, t) \backslash G^*(b, t-1)$.

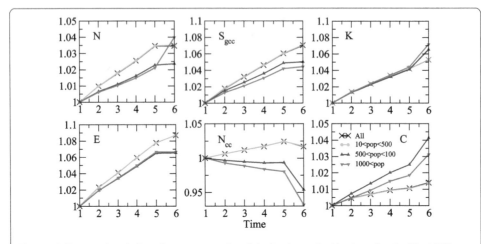

Figure 12 Temporal evolution of some properties of the book graphs. Number of nodes ($N = |A(b)|$), number of edges (E), size of the greatest connected component (S_{gcc}), number of connected components (N_{cc}), average out-degree (K) and clustering coefficient (C) are shown. All values are normalized by the initial value (at $t = 1$).

In Figure 12 the evolution of some properties of the graphs $G^*(b,t)$ is shown. Most of the values (N, E, K, C, S_{gcc}) grow in time, revealing the expansion and the increase of density and cohesion of the greatest component. The only exception is observed for the decreasing trend in the number of connected components for the graphs of the books with medium or high popularity. This can be explained by the fact that if a book is widespread over the social network it is more likely that a new adopter can create a bridge between two components of $G^*(b,t-1)$, thus reducing their number.

For every adopter, we measure the fraction of users that could potentially have played an influence in the book adoption process. If a book is adopted in the time span $[t,t+1]$, the users that may have influenced the adopter are her out-neighbors who already have that book in their library at time t.[b] We specifically focus only on the out-neighbors because users are explicitly notified of their new book adoptions, while a user may not be aware of the activity of his/her in-neighbors. Consequently, we denote the number of user u's out-neighbors at time t having book b as $K_b(u)$ and the fraction of such users over all u's out-neighbors as $F_b(u) = K_b(u)/K_{out}(u)$.

The distributions of K_b and F_b for the users u who adopt b in $[t,t+1]$ are shown in Figure 13, together with the same distributions restricted to the users u who still do not have adopted b at $t+1$. The curves for the two user categories are very different for both measures, thus revealing that users who adopt a particular book have been exposed, on average, to a higher number of users who had previously put that book in their libraries. In particular, the probability of having no out-neighbors at t with the target book in their library is much lower for the adopters (0.66) than for the non-adopters (0.98). Furthermore, as shown in Figure 14, the average K_b at fixed values of K_{out} is much higher for adopters than for non-adopters, even if a positive correlation is found in both cases, meaning that adopters have been considerably more exposed, on average, to other users exposing the adopted book. Such clear differences between the two cases of adopters and non-adopters represents a very strong evidence of the presence of an influence effect in the process of book adoption.

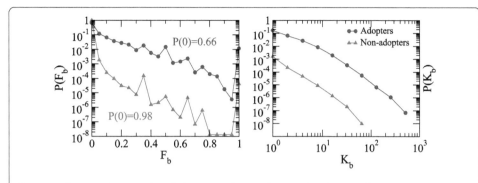

Figure 13 Compared properties of adopters and non-adopters. Distributions of portion (F_b) and number (K_b) of neighbors on the social network having book b at time t for adopters of book b between t and $t+1$ and for non-adopters. For the adopters, the same distributions computed on the interaction network only are shown.

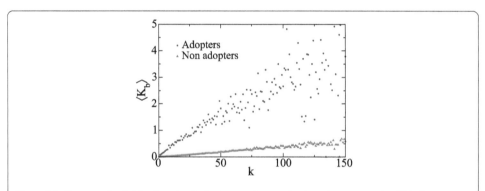

Figure 14 Compared neighborhoods of adopters and non-adopters. Average number (K_b) of out-neighbors on the social network having book b at time t, for the users having k out-neighbors. The cases of adopters and non-adopters are shown.

Interestingly, the vast majority (74%) of adopters with $F_b > 0$ exhibit values smaller than 0.2, and the average value of F_b for these adopters is rather small (0.189); on the other hand, the numbers K_b of neighbors of an adopter who already have the book b are broadly distributed. This could support two distinct hypothesis: the first one is that only a rather small number of neighbors are really influential among the neighborhood of a user; the second is that the important criterion in the adoption of a book (an 'influence threshold') is not the bare number of neighbors who have adopted a book, but the corresponding fraction among all out-neighbors, and that the influence threshold in such context is rather low.

5.4 Influence factors

As previously mentioned, users are notified of the adoption of a book by their out-neighbors: information flows in an automated way along the friendship and neighborhood links. It is thus interesting to compare the potential existence of influence effects in the book adoption process along the social links that do not support additional (non automated) communication between the users (Social\Comm) with respect to the case of social links that do (Social ∩ Comm). To this aim, we compute the probability of adoption at time t of a book b given a fixed number of neighbors who already have b at time $t-1$, formally: $P_a(b, t|K_b)$ with $K_b = |\Gamma_{out} \cap G^*(b, t - 1)|$, where Γ_{out} is the set of out-neighbors of u.

The computation of P_a for the pure social network must use out-neighbors because the information (*i.e.*, automatic notifications) flows against the direction of the edges. In the interaction network instead, both directions should be taken into account because a message sent from u to v may imply a particular interest of u in v's library or, conversely, that u is proactively suggesting a book to v. For this reason in the interaction network we consider two separate cases where K_b is computed considering the set of in-neighbors Γ_{in} or out-neighbors Γ_{out}.

Figure 15 shows the values of $P_a(b, t|K_b)$ averaged over all books and time steps, for the pure social network (Social\Comm) and the interaction network (Social $\cap$ Comm).

Interesting features emerge: (i) the probability of adoption is very small if $K_b = 0$ (less than $2 \cdot 10^{-4}$), and increases very rapidly as the number of out-neighbors having the considered book at $t - 1$ increase; (ii) this probability tends to saturate as K_b increases above 20, showing that an additional increase in the number of out-neighbors reading the book do not increase the user's adoption probability; (iii) the probability of adoption at fixed number of out-neighbors reading the book is much larger for out-neighbors with whom an explicit communication is established; (iv) when focusing on interaction ties, receiving messages from a certain number of early adopters of a book b implies a higher probability of adoption of b than sending messages to the same number of owners of b.

The first result is a strong indication in favor of the hypothesis of effective influence between neighbors on the social graph. The second indicates that the number of influential neighbors is limited, in support of the first hypothesis outlined above. The third result supports a scenario in which direct suggestions from neighbors with whom an explicit communication exists have a stronger influencing power than the automated notification system and, in particular, the fourth result suggests that adoption is at least partially triggered by direct recommendations received by earlier adopters.

The saturation of the influence probability over a certain threshold of K_b still does not answer the long lasting question whether the adoption probability rises more with the increase of the fraction (F_b) or the number (K_b) of neighbors who are potential influencers (in this case, earlier book adopters). To give some insight into this issue, we adopt a prediction approach in which, given a book graph $G^*(b, t)$, we try to predict the shape of the

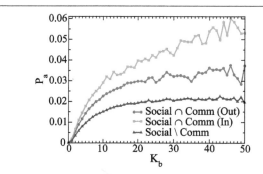

Figure 15 Book adoption probability. Probability of adoption of a book averaged on all the books and snapshots, at fixed values of the number of neighbors who have already adopted the book. Curves are depicted for the pure social network (**Social\Comm**), considering only the out-neighbors, and for the interaction network (**Social $\cap$ Comm**) considering the two cases of in- and out-neighbors.

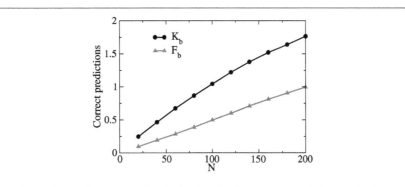

Figure 16 Prediction performance for book adoption. Prediction of new nodes being added to a book graph $G(b)$ between time t and $t + 1$, based on the lists of non-adopters at time t ranked by K_b and F_b values. The number of correct prediction against the length of the prediction list is shown.

graph $G^*(b, t + 1)$ based on the F_b and K_b values at time t of the users who will adopt book b at time $t + 1$. In short, we rank all the users who do not have book b at time t by their F_b and K_b values, and we count how many of them in the top N entries of the rank are adopters at time $t + 1$. Figure 16 shows the comparison between the metrics. For the purpose of this experiment we focus only on books with at least 20 new adopters in the time frame considered. Diffusion prediction falls out from the scope of this work, therefore we are not interested in evaluating the absolute but rather the relative performance of the two predictions. In fact, as expected, the absolute number of correctly predicted new adopters is always very low, due to the extremely high sparsity of the problem (the books spread slowly compared to the overall number of users that may potentially be influenced by their neighbors) and the simplicity of the features. However, the difference between the two curves shows clearly that K_b outperforms F_b for every value of N. This finding tends to support further the theory that influence is triggered more likely by few contacts that are able to communicate to the user and persuade him directly rather than by the portion of the social neighborhood that adopted the new item.

6 Recommending social contacts

The analysis reported in the previous sections sheds light on the dynamics of link creation in social media. Understanding the processes behind the creation of social connections allows to infer some model of network growth that can be exploited to predict the evolution of the system. In this section we will use the acquired knowledge of network dynamics to predict the creation of new links. More specifically, we propose a methodology for personalized contact recommendation that could be directly implemented on any social media like aNobii.

6.1 Prediction features

The task of predicting user pairs that will be connected in the future by a social tie can rely on two main sources of information: the structural features of the graph and the features from the user profiles. We use both types of features, considering the three main evolutionary patterns of the social graph that we previously detected.

1. *Proximity-driven link creation.* In the vast majority of cases, new neighbors are chosen among the nodes at distance 2 (*i.e.*, closing triangles) or 3 in the social graph. Restricting the analysis to pairs that reside near in the graph may miss some potential

new connections but dramatically lowers the time needed by practical algorithms for
partner recommendation.

2. *Strong interaction links.* Users are influenced and inspired more by the social contacts
   with whom they carry out a regular communication. Taking into account the
   strength of the interaction links rather than (or in addition to) pure social ties could
   improve the prediction.

3. *Homophily-driven attachment.* Users create new connections preferentially with their
   most similar acquaintances. Similarity is a notion that involves all the different facets
   of the user profile (from geographic location to favorite books). Pairs of more similar
   users should therefore be considered as more likely candidates for a link creation.

A list of features that synthesizes these three principles is shown in Table 5. Most of the
topological features presented have been used independently in literature for link prediction in undirected networks but can be easily adapted to the directed case. To also take
into account the information concerning the weighted interaction network, we introduce
a new index, the *weighted flow*, inspired by previous work on generalized degree centrality
in social networks [66]. It is defined as:

$$wf(u, v) = CN(u, v) + \frac{\sum_{x \in CN(u,v)} \min(w(u, x), w(x, v))}{CN(u, v)}. \tag{2}$$

Assuming that weights on arcs denote some information flow passing between nodes,
weighted flow combines the definition of common neighbors with the normalized sum of
the minimum flow of information passing from the arcs connecting the two target nodes
through their common neighbors. Applied to the interaction network, this metric measures both the number of potential communication channels between the two nodes and
the amount of information that could have been possibly exchanged between them using
their directed common neighbors as proxies.

**Table 5 List of features used in the prediction of a directed link between generic users u
and v, along with their description**

Feature	Description	Rank
Location	Binary attribute, whether u and v belong to the same city	14
Gender	Binary attribute, whether u and v belong to the same gender	15
Age	Absolute difference of ages	12
Library	Cosine similarity between library vectors	**5**
Groups	Cosine similarity between group membership vectors	**7**
Group size	Size of the smallest group the two users have in common	**6**
Vocabulary	Cosine similarity between sets of tags used	16
Contact list	Cosine similarity of the vectors of social contacts	**2**
Outdegree	Sum of the out degrees ($k_{out}(u) + k_{out}(v)$)	11
Preferential attachment	Product of the out degrees ($k_{out}(u) \cdot k_{out}(v)$)	13
Common neighbors	Number of common neighbors, directed case ($CN(u, v) = \|\Gamma_{out}(u) \cap \Gamma_{in}(v)\|$)	**4**
Triangle overlap	$\frac{CN(u,v)}{\Gamma_{out}(u)}$	**1**
Reciprocation	Binary attribute, whether the inverse link (v, u) is already present	9
Resource allocation	$\sum_{z \in (\Gamma_{out}(u) \cap \Gamma_{in}(u))} (\frac{1}{k_{out}(z)})$ [37]	**3**
Local path	Linear combination of common neighbors and common distance-2 neighbors ($CN + \epsilon \cdot CN_2$) [37]	10
Weighted flow	$wf(u, v) = CN(u, v) + \frac{\sum_{x \in CN(u,v)} \min(w(u,x), w(x,v))}{CN(u,v)}$	**8**

$\Gamma_{in/out}(u)$ denotes the set of u's in/out neighbors, $k_{out}(u) = \|\Gamma_{out}(u)\|$, and $w(x, y)$ is the weight of the tie between x and y. The
rank reported is the result of the Chi Squared attribute selection method applied to our test set; the bold font of the rank
indicates that the corresponding feature has been selected for the restricted feature set.

6.2 Classifier training and feature selection

Features can be combined through a supervised machine learning approach. A classifier properly trained on the mentioned features can determine, given any pair of nodes, if they are likely to create a social link between each other in the future. By knowing in advance the user pairs with higher connection probability, social contact recommendations can be sent to the endpoints, with the aim of notifying the two endpoints of the possibility of establishing a potentially interesting social connection that they may not have noticed otherwise or at least to speed up the linking process between them. We follow this approach and we discuss its effectiveness in a link recommendation scenario.

We choose to use a Rotation Tree classifier [67] that turned out, a posteriori, to be the best performing among all WEKA's [68] classifiers, and we train it with all the available features. The positive sample of the training set is built by about $10k$ pairs of users who reside at distance 2 on the social graph at the time of snapshot 1 and get connected before snapshot 6. The negative sample is given by as many pairs residing 2 hops away at snapshot 1 and that do not become connected. We consider only distance-2 neighbors because in the link recommendation task we will restrict our prediction to the closest non-connected pairs for computational efficiency reasons. Note that taking into account only distance-2 pairs makes the prediction task harder than selecting the non-connected pairs at random; this is due to the fact that the distribution of similarity values of pairs of users lying at distance 2 on the graph are more similar between positive and negative samples than for pairs of users taken at random (and hence farther away on the network with high probability).

As a preliminary check of the accuracy of the classifier, and in order to measure the relative predictive power of different features, we perform a 10-fold cross validation on the training set. Results for four different combinations of features are listed in Table 6; the predictive effectiveness of the features is measured through standard metrics such as the number of false positives and false negatives, accuracy, F-value, and area under the ROC. From the comparison it emerges clearly that the combination of structural and profile features leads to an appreciable improvement of the prediction quality, for all the performance indexes considered. Furthermore, aside from assessing that the combination of feature sets of different natures is good for the prediction, a more fine-grained exploration of the predictive potential of the features considered can help to exclude more redundant features, thus simplifying the decision process of the classifier and avoid overfitting. To this end, we executed the Chi Squared analysis for feature selection [69] to get a ranking of the predictive potential for all the features (see Table 5). We observe that features like vocabulary, gender, and preferential attachment have much less relevance than other features like the contact list or the library. In particular, we notice that features based on the triangle closure phenomenon are the most predictive.

Table 6 Prediction performance on the training set using the Rotation Forest classifier, 10-fold cross validation, with balanced positive and negative samples (10,000 examples)

Features	FP rate	FN rate	Accuracy	F-value	AUC
Profile	0.279	0.364	0.679	0.678	0.741
Structural	0.241	0.298	0.730	0.730	0.805
All	0.223	0.264	0.757	0.757	0.835
Restricted	0.219	0.279	0.751	0.751	0.826

Four different combinations of features are considered, the "Restricted" category includes a smaller sets of features designated as more predictive by the feature selection process.

By only using the top 9 features we verify that the prediction accuracy remains very stable and the False Positive rate is even slightly lower than with the full feature set (Table 6). We therefore retrain the classifier using the restricted feature set and use such classifier as the fundamental building block of our social contact recommender, described in the next subsection.

6.3 Contact recommendation

A contact recommendation service should be able to provide suggestions in real-time and on demand. Screening all the users that are not connected with the client requires a too high computational effort to meet this requirement. Therefore, we adopt a local search limited to the distance-2 neighborhood of the target user; among those potential contacts, the system outputs a fixed number N of suggestions.

To evaluate the effectiveness of this approach we build a test set of active users who established at least 20 new social ties between snapshots 1 and 6 with people who reside at distance 2 from them at snapshot 1. For each user u among such set, we apply our classifier to every pair $(u, v)|d(u, v) = 2$ and, from the set of pairs labeled positively by the classifier, we select N contacts to compose the recommendation list. The list is sorted according to the confidence score given by the classifier for each prediction. The number of actual ties created by the sampled users between time 1 and 6 is around $3k$, while the number of potential ties that could have been established by these users towards distance-2 neighbors is higher than $650k$. The goal of the classifier is to identify the $3k$ correct pairs among the $650k$ possible, with the lowest number of misclassifications. Such huge disproportion of positives and negatives instances determines a very high sparsity of the problem (density is less than 0.005), thus making the recommendation task particularly hard to solve with high accuracy.

Recommendation results are depicted in Figure 17, to measure the recommendation effectiveness we count the number of correctly predicted link creations, which account for the number of successful recommendations in this setting. We compare our recommender with two unsupervised techniques taking into account two single features separately, namely the number of common neighbors and the cosine similarity between libraries. In such unsupervised strategies, the recommendation lists are created by simply picking the N pairs with the highest scores for the considered metric. Results show that

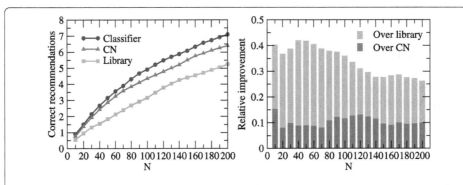

Figure 17 Recommendation results. Left: Precision at N for the recommendation made with the classifier combining all the relevant features and for two unsupervised baselines (common neighbors and library similarity). Right: Relative improvement on the classifier-based approach over the baselines.

the classifier outperforms appreciably the baselines and the number of the correctly predicted contacts grows steadily with the size of the recommendation list. However, it is surprising to observe that the relative precision (*i.e.*, the number of correct recommendations divided by the recommendation list size) is rather low, being less than 0.10 up to $N = 20$ and around 0.04 for $N = 200$.

To investigate the causes of such modest performance, we compare the obtained results with another attempt of tackling the link prediction problem from a recommendation perspective made in the Facebook social network [28]. The evaluation of the recommendation is very similar to ours with respect to the size of the network sample, the time span of the prediction and the activity of the target users. Among all the experiments that authors report, recommendation through logistic regression combining several structural graph features compares well to our approach. Nevertheless the number of correct recommendations is higher than in the aNobii case (correct recommendations at 20 is around 7.50 against ours 1.50). The main reason is due to the different sparsity of the problem. Specifically:

- In the same time span, the average number of new contacts per user in Facebook is more than six times larger than in aNobii (26 new links in Facebook *vs.* 4 in aNobii);
- The portion of new contacts residing at distance larger than 2 in aNobii is around 0.4, while in the Facebook dataset it is negligible;
- Contrary to Facebook, the aNobii network is directed and the predictions must take into account the directionality of the edge.

In Facebook, users are much more active and faster in establishing new contacts and they focus much more on their distance-2 neighbors, thus increasing the number of potential true positives over the total number of potential new contacts. Nevertheless, we underline that even in aNobii's more challenging setting the relative improvement of machine learning combination of different profile and structural features over the performance of common neighbors is comparable to the improvement obtained in the case of Facebook by previous work.

In short, the difference between the two cases can be summarized as follows. In Facebook, the decision of link creation among two people depends largely on the fact that the two endpoints have a social connection in the offline world, so that the decisional process to determine whether to add a new contact or not can be fast and simple. Conversely, in social networks with a stronger emphasis on topical interests, the items shared are more important than the personal user features (especially for neighborhood links that relate individuals who do not know each other *a priori*) and they are the main driver for the establishment of new social connections. The creation of links in such an interest network is therefore determined by the complex cognitive processes needed to relate multifaceted objects like books. This implies also a slower pace in such decisional process. Reaching definitive conclusions on this matter would require an extensive comparison between social media with different scopes (*e.g.*, music, news, photos), we believe our study can represent a contribution in this direction.

7 Discussion and conclusions

Link creation and influence are the processes on which most of the dynamics of online social media are based. In this work, we have characterized such phenomena in the case of aNobii, a network of interest for book lovers.

We have found that link formation has a strong propensity to topical and structural selection effects, reciprocity, and proximity-driven attachment. Based on these observations, we have collected a large number of both novel and state-of-the-art metrics that have a potential in predicting the formation of new links. Among such features, ranging from topical (*e.g.*, similarity between items owned by two users) to structural ones (*e.g.*, estimation of the amount of information potentially flowing from one person to the other *via* social links), we have detected the most predictive, thus shedding some light on the relative effectiveness of the main features that have been used in past work on link prediction. We have combined the best features into a classifier able to output a prediction about the future creation of a connection between any pair of nodes in the social network. We have used such classifier to produce recommendations of new social contacts for users. Differently from link prediction, that aims at predicting the global evolution of the network, link recommendation provides a contact list for every single individual and succeeds when many of the recommended contacts are actually linked by the target user. Such task is still widely unexplored and has been attempted only on general-purpose social networks with a strong accent on the user profile (*e.g.*, Facebook) rather than in interest networks like aNobii. The classifier considerably improves accuracy over simple yet very strong baselines, but the obtained performance is lower than the one reported for general-purpose online social media in previous work. The reasons for this gap likely reside in the different nature of the two cases. While in profile-focused services social aggregation is often based on the existence of a relation in the real world, that can be detected easily with simple metrics (*e.g.*, number of common friends), in interest-based networks the creation of new links is driven by cognitive processes needed to evaluate the topical interest in one profile rather than on another, that are more difficult to capture and anticipate. This finding opens the way to the exploration of the potential of prediction and recommendation in social platform with different topical focuses.

Investigation of influence complements the study on link creation. Unlike previous work, we investigate influence from both user and item perspectives. From the user side, we support with strong evidences the thesis that similarity patterns that are detected in the static network are also determined by the influence that connected users exert on each other. In particular, we observe that link creation triggers a noticeable sudden increase in the similarity between the endpoints, particularly in terms of books adopted. We inspect patterns of book adoption by modeling graphs of book spreading in time and comparing them with null models to point out their clustered and expanding nature. Based on this model, we find that the fraction of neighboring users that may have influenced an adopter is on average rather small, that the probability of adopting a book saturates as the number of neighbors already having that book increases and that the probability to adopt a book in function of the number of earlier adopters in the social neighborhood is higher if explicit communication channels exist with these neighbors. By adopting a prediction perspective, we also shed some light on the question about the fraction or the absolute amount of earlier adopter neighbors being the best indicator of higher probability of adoption, and we find that the absolute number is by far more predictive of a future adoption (even if accurate spreading prediction remains a difficult task due to the extreme sparsity of the problem and to external unobservable factors determining adoption). All these results support the idea that the 'information contagion' is a slow but relevant phenomenon in the social network and that it is usually triggered by a small number of influential users.

Another finding involves the analysis of the interaction network. For both link creation and information spreading, the interaction network has an important role in determining new connections and preferential channels of item diffusion. Many previous work showed that communication graph conveys a much stronger social signal than the pure social graph, but the implication of such stronger connections on sociological phenomena like homophily and influence had not been investigated directly before.

This work opens several natural research directions. Among possible research lines we mention the development of a model of spreading that relies on some user metadata other than the topology of the network and that could fit the phenomenon of book spreading we observed. A more thorough exploration of the possibility of predicting item spreading in contexts with slow content consumption like aNobii is also an interesting possible future extension and may open up the way to new item recommendation techniques.

Competing interests
The authors declare that they have no competing interests.

Authors' contributions
All authors designed the research. AB, LMA, and RS performed the data analysis. LMA performed the recommendation experiments. All authors analyzed the results, wrote, reviewed and approved the manuscript.

Author details
[1]Department of Computer Science, University of Torino, Torino, Italy. [2]Centre de Physique Théorique, Aix-Marseille Université et Université du Sud Toulon Var, CNRS UMR 6207, Marseille, France. [3]Data Science Laboratory, ISI Foundation, Torino, Italy.

Acknowledgements
This work has been partially supported by the Italian Ministry for University and Research (MIUR), within the framework of the project 'Information Dynamics in Complex Data Structures' (PRIN). We acknowledge support from the Lagrange Project of the ISI Foundation supported by the CRT Foundation.

Endnotes
[a] Strictly speaking, it is impossible to prove that our crawls reached effectively the largest component. Given its characteristics and size, which are in agreement with known properties of the aNobii social system, it is however a reasonable assumption.

[b] We disregard here the possibility of interactions between users taking place outside the social network. It is clear that what can be inferred from the analysis of the online social network are only tendencies and indications, and that no absolute proof of influence effects can be obtained, as one cannot rule out effects external to the network.

References
1. Mislove A, Marcon M, Gummadi KP, Druschel P, Bhattacharjee B (2007) Measurement and analysis of online social networks. In: IMC '07: proceedings of the 7th ACM SIGCOMM conference on Internet measurement. ACM, New York, pp 29-42
2. Kumar R, Novak J, Tomkins A (2006) Structure and evolution of online social networks. In: Proceedings of the 12th ACM SIGKDD international conference on knowledge discovery and data mining, KDD '06. ACM, New York, pp 611-617. http://doi.acm.org/10.1145/1150402.1150476
3. Leskovec J, Backstrom L, Kumar R, Tomkins A (2008) Microscopic evolution of social networks. In: Proceedings of the 14th ACM SIGKDD international conference on knowledge discovery and data mining, KDD '08. ACM, New York, pp 462-470. http://doi.acm.org/10.1145/1401890.1401948
4. Ahn YY, Han S, Kwak H, Moon S, Jeong H (2007) Analysis of topological characteristics of huge online social networking services. In: WWW '07: proceedings of the 16th international conference on World Wide Web. ACM, New York, pp 835-844
5. Aiello LM, Barrat A, Cattuto C, Ruffo G, Schifanella R (2010) Link creation and profile alignment in the aNobii social network. In: SocialCom '10: proceedings of the second IEEE international conference on social computing. IEEE Press, Minneapolis, pp 249-256
6. Mislove A, Koppula HS, Gummadi KP, Druschel P, Bhattacharjee B (2008) Growth of the Flickr social network. In: WOSN '08: proceedings of the first workshop on online social networks. ACM, New York, pp 25-30
7. Lauterbach D, Truong H, Shah T, Adamic L (2009) Surfing a web of trust: reputation and reciprocity on CouchSurfing.com. In: Computational science and engineering, IEEE international conference on, vol 4, pp 346-353
8. Weng J, Lim EP, Jiang J, He Q (2010) TwitterRank: finding topic-sensitive influential twitterers. In: Proceedings of the third ACM international conference on web search and data mining, WSDM '10. ACM, New York, pp 261-270. http://doi.acm.org/10.1145/1718487.1718520

9. Aiello LM, Barrat A, Schifanella R, Cattuto C, Markines B, Menczer F (2012) Friendship prediction and homophily in social media. ACM Trans Web 6:9

10. Chun H, Kwak H, Eom YH, Ahn YY, Moon S, Jeong H (2008) Comparison of online social relations in volume vs. interaction: a case study of cyworld. In: Proceedings of the 8th ACM SIGCOMM conference on Internet measurement, IMC '08. ACM, New York, pp 57-70. http://doi.acm.org/10.1145/1452520.1452528

11. Wilson C, Boe B, Sala A, Puttaswamy KP, Zhao BY (2009) User interactions in social networks and their implications. In: Proceedings of the 4th ACM European conference on computer systems, EuroSys '09. ACM, New York, pp 205-218. http://doi.acm.org/10.1145/1519065.1519089

12. Leskovec J, Horvitz E (2008) Planetary-scale views on a large instant-messaging network. In: Proceedings of the 17th international conference on World Wide Web, WWW '08. ACM, New York, pp 915-924. http://doi.acm.org/10.1145/1367497.1367620

13. Viswanath B, Mislove A, Cha M, Gummadi KP (2009) On the evolution of user interaction in Facebook. In: WOSN '09: proceedings of the 2nd ACM workshop on online social networks. ACM, New York, pp 37-42

14. Benevenuto F, Rodrigues T, Cha M, Almeida V (2009) Characterizing user behavior in online social networks. In: Proceedings of the 9th ACM SIGCOMM conference on Internet measurement conference, IMC '09. ACM, New York, pp 49-62. http://doi.acm.org/10.1145/1644893.1644900

15. Gonçalves B, Perra N, Vespignani A (2011) Modeling users' activity on Twitter networks: validation of Dunbar's number. PLoS ONE 6(8):e22656. http://dx.doi.org/10.1371%2Fjournal.pone.0022656

16. Kempe D, Kleinberg J, Tardos E (2003) Maximizing the spread of influence through a social network. In: Proceedings of the ninth ACM SIGKDD international conference on knowledge discovery and data mining, KDD '03. ACM, New York, pp 137-146. http://doi.acm.org/10.1145/956750.956769

17. Cha M, Mislove A, Gummadi KP (2009) A measurement-driven analysis of information propagation in the Flickr social network. In: Proceedings of the 18th international conference on World Wide Web, WWW '09. ACM, New York, pp 721-730. http://doi.acm.org/10.1145/1526709.1526806

18. Ye S, Wu SF (2010) Measuring message propagation and social influence on Twitter.com. In: Proceedings of the second international conference on social informatics, SocInfo '10. Springer, Berlin, pp 216-231. http://portal.acm.org/citation.cfm?id=1929326.1929342

19. Cha M, Haddadi H, Benevenuto F, Gummadi KP (2010) Measuring user influence in Twitter: the million follower fallacy. In: ICSWM '10: proceedings of the 4th international AAAI conference on weblogs and social media

20. Anagnostopoulos A, Kumar R, Mahdian M (2008) Influence and correlation in social networks. In: Proceedings of the 14th ACM SIGKDD international conference on knowledge discovery and data mining, KDD '08. ACM, New York, pp 7-15. http://doi.acm.org/10.1145/1401890.1401897

21. Crandall D, Cosley D, Huttenlocher D, Kleinberg J, Suri S (2008) Feedback effects between similarity and social influence in online communities. In: KDD '08: proceeding of the 14th ACM SIGKDD international conference on knowledge discovery and data mining. ACM, New York, pp 160-168

22. Bakshy E, Rosenn I, Marlow C, Adamic L (2012) The role of social networks in information diffusion. In: Proceedings of the 21st international conference on World Wide Web, WWW '12. ACM, New York, pp 519-528. http://doi.acm.org/10.1145/2187836.2187907

23. Yang J, Leskovec J (2010) Modeling information diffusion in implicit networks. In: Proceedings of the 2010 IEEE international conference on data mining, ICDM '10. IEEE Computer Society, Washington, pp 599-608. http://dx.doi.org/10.1109/ICDM.2010.22

24. Gomez Rodriguez M, Leskovec J, Krause A (2010) Inferring networks of diffusion and influence. In: Proceedings of the 16th ACM SIGKDD international conference on knowledge discovery and data mining, KDD '10. ACM, New York, pp 1019-1028. http://doi.acm.org/10.1145/1835804.1835933

25. Au Yeung CM, Iwata T (2010) Capturing implicit user influence in online social sharing. In: Proceedings of the 21st ACM conference on hypertext and hypermedia, HT '10. ACM, New York, pp 245-254. http://doi.acm.org/10.1145/1810617.1810662

26. Getoor L, Diehl CP (2005) Link mining: a survey. ACM SIGKDD Explor Newsl 7(2):3-12

27. Cooke RJE (2006) Link prediction and link detection in sequences of large social networks using temporal and local metrics. Master thesis, Department of Computer Science, University of Cape Town

28. Backstrom L, Leskovec J (2011) Supervised random walks: predicting and recommending links in social networks. In: Proceedings of the fourth ACM international conference on web search and data mining, WSDM '11. ACM, New York, pp 635-644. http://doi.acm.org/10.1145/1935826.1935914

29. Liben-Nowell D, Kleinberg J (2003) The link prediction problem for social networks. In: CIKM '03: proceedings of the twelfth international conference on information and knowledge management. ACM, New York, pp 556-559

30. Liben-Nowell D, Kleinberg J (2007) The link-prediction problem for social networks. J Am Soc Inf Sci Technol 58(7):1019-1031

31. Pavlov M, Ichise R (2007) Finding experts by link prediction in co-authorship networks. In: FEWS2007: proceedings of the workshop on finding experts on the web with semantics at ISWC/ASWC2007, Busan, South Korea

32. Popescul A, Popescul R, Ungar LH (2003) Structural logistic regression for link analysis. In: Proceedings of the second international workshop on multirelational data mining

33. Hasan MA, Chaoji V, Salem S, Zaki M (2006) Link prediction using supervised learning. In: Proceedings of SDM '06 workshop on link analysis, counterterrorism and security

34. O'Madadhain J, Hutchins J, Smyth P (2005) Prediction and ranking algorithms for event-based network data. ACM SIGKDD Explor Newsl 7(2):23-30

35. Zheleva E, Getoor L, Golbeck J, Kuter U (2008) Using friendship ties and family circles for link prediction (poster paper). In: 2nd SNA-KDD workshop on social network mining and analysis. ACM, Las Vegas

36. Sachan M, Ichise R (2010) Using semantic information to improve link prediction results in networked datasets. Int J Eng Technol 2(4):334-339

37. Zhou T, Lü L, Zhang YC (2009) Predicting missing links via local information. Eur Phys J B 71(4):623-630. Special issue: The physics approach to risk: agent-based models and networks

38. Lü L, Ci-Hang J, Zhou T (2009) Effective and efficient similarity index for link prediction of complex networks. arXiv:0905.3558

39. Song HH, Cho TW, Dave V, Zhang Y, Qiu L (2009) Scalable proximity estimation and link prediction in online social networks. In: IMC '09: proceedings of the 9th ACM SIGCOMM conference on Internet measurement conference. ACM, New York, pp 322-335
40. Schifanella R, Barrat A, Cattuto C, Markines B, Menczer F (2010) Folks in folksonomies: social link prediction from shared metadata. In: WSDM '10: proceedings of the third ACM international conference on web search and data mining. ACM, New York, pp 271-280
41. Leroy V, Cambazoglu BB, Bonchi F (2010) Cold start link prediction. In: SIGKDD '10: proceedings of the 16th ACM conference on knowledge discovery and data mining. ACM, Washington
42. Bilgic M, Namata GM, Getoor L (2007) Combining collective classification and link prediction. In: ICDMW '07: proceedings of the seventh IEEE international conference on data mining workshops. IEEE Computer Society, Washington, pp 381-386
43. Tylenda T, Angelova R, Bedathur S (2009) Towards time-aware link prediction in evolving social networks. In: SNA-KDD '09: proceedings of the 3rd workshop on social network mining and analysis. ACM, New York, pp 1-10
44. Dunlavy DM, Kolda GK, Acar E (2010) Temporal link prediction using matrix and tensor factorizations. arXiv:1005.4006
45. Onnela JP, Saramäki J, Hyvönen J, Szabó G, Lazer D, Kaski K, Kertész J, Barabási AL (2007) Structure and tie strengths in mobile communication networks. Proc Natl Acad Sci USA 104(18):7332-7336. http://dx.doi.org/10.1073/pnas.0610245104
46. Lü L, Zhou T (2009) Role of weak ties in link prediction of complex networks. In: CNIKM '09: proceedings of the 1st ACM international workshop on complex networks meet information and knowledge management. ACM, New York, pp 55-58
47. Gilbert E, Karahalios K (2009) Predicting tie strength with social media. In: Proceedings of the 27th international conference on human factors in computing systems, CHI '09. ACM, New York, pp 211-220. http://doi.acm.org/10.1145/1518701.1518736
48. Benchettara N, Kanawati R, Rouveirol C (2010) Supervised machine learning applied to link prediction in bipartite social networks. In: Social network analysis and mining, international conference on advances in. IEEE Computer Society, Los Alamitos, pp 326-330
49. Kunegis J, De Luca E, Albayrak S (2010) The link prediction problem in bipartite networks. In: Hullermeier E, Kruse R, Hoffmann F (eds) Computational intelligence for knowledge-based systems design. Lecture notes in computer science, vol 6178. Springer, Berlin, pp 380-389
50. Leskovec J, Huttenlocher D, Kleinberg J (2010) Predicting positive and negative links in online social networks. In: WWW '10: proceedings of the 19th international conference on World Wide Web. ACM, New York, pp 641-650
51. Taskar B, Wong MF, Abbeel P, Koller D (2003) Link prediction in relational data. In: NIPS '03: neural information processing systems conference, Vancouver, Canada
52. Getoor L, Friedman N, Koller D, Taskar B (2003) Learning probabilistic models of link structure. J Mach Learn Res 3:679-707
53. Freeman LC (1979) Centrality in social networks: conceptual clarification. Soc Netw 1(3):215-239. http://dx.doi.org/10.1016/0378-8733(78)90021-7
54. Wasserman S, Faust K (1994) Social network analysis: methods and applications. Cambridge University Press, Cambridge
55. Bollobas B (1998) Modern graph theory. Springer, Berlin
56. Marlow C, Naaman M, Boyd D, Davis M (2006) HT06, tagging paper, taxonomy, Flickr, academic article, to read. In: HYPERTEXT '06: proceedings of the seventeenth conference on hypertext and hypermedia. ACM, New York, pp 31-40
57. Newman MEJ (2002) Assortative mixing in networks. Phys Rev Lett 89:208701
58. Albert R, Barabási AL (2002) Statistical mechanics of complex networks. Rev Mod Phys 74:47-97
59. Newman MEJ (2001) Clustering and preferential attachment in growing networks. Phys Rev E 64(2):025102
60. Kleinberg JM, Kumar R, Raghavan P, Rajagopalan S, Tomkins AS (1999) The web as a graph: measurements, models and methods. In: Computing and combinatorics. Lecture notes in computer science, vol 1627, pp 1-18
61. Kumar R, Raghavan P, Rajagopalan S, Sivakumar D, Tomkins A, Upfal E (2000) Stochastic models for the web graph. In: Proceedings of the 41th IEEE symposium on foundations of computer science (FOCS), pp 57-65
62. Liben-Nowell D, Novak J, Kumar R, Raghavan P, Tomkins A (2005) Geographic routing in social networks. Proc Natl Acad Sci USA 102(33):11623-11628
63. Lee C, Scherngell T, Barber MJ (2009) Real-world separation effects in an online social network. Technical report. http://arxiv.org/abs/0911.1229
64. McPherson M, Lovin LS, Cook JM (2001) Birds of a feather: homophily in social networks. Annu Rev Sociol 27:415-444. http://dx.doi.org/10.1146/annurev.soc.27.1.415
65. Barrat A, Barthlemy M, Vespignani A (2008) Dynamical processes on complex networks, 1st edn. Cambridge University Press, New York
66. Opsahl T, Agneessens F, Skvoretz J (2010) Node centrality in weighted networks: generalizing degree and shortest paths. Soc Netw 32(3):245-251
67. Rodriguez JJ, Kuncheva LI, Alonso CJ (2006) Rotation forest: a new classifier ensemble method. IEEE Trans Pattern Anal Mach Intell 28(10):1619-1630
68. Hall M, Frank E, Holmes G, Pfahringer B, Reutemann P, Witten IH (2009) The WEKA data mining software: an update. ACM SIGKDD Explor Newsl 11:10-18
69. Liu H, Setiono R (1995) Chi2: feature selection and discretization of numeric attributes. In: Proceedings of the seventh international conference on tools with artificial intelligence, TAI '95. IEEE Computer Society, Washington, pp 388-391

5

Uncovering nodes that spread information between communities in social networks

Alexander V Mantzaris[*]

[*]Correspondence:
alexander.mantzaris@strath.ac.uk
Department of Mathematics and
Statistics, University of Strathclyde,
26 Richmond Street, Glasgow, G1
1XH, UK

Abstract

From many datasets gathered in online social networks, well defined community structures have been observed. A large number of users participate in these networks and the size of the resulting graphs poses computational challenges. There is a particular demand in identifying the nodes responsible for information flow between communities; for example, in temporal Twitter networks edges between communities play a key role in propagating spikes of activity when the connectivity between communities is sparse and few edges exist between different clusters of nodes. The new algorithm proposed here is aimed at revealing these key connections by measuring a node's vicinity to nodes of another community. We look at the nodes which have edges in more than one community and the locality of nodes around them which influence the information received and broadcasted to them. The method relies on independent random walks of a chosen fixed number of steps, originating from nodes with edges in more than one community. For the large networks that we have in mind, existing measures such as betweenness centrality are difficult to compute, even with recent methods that approximate the large number of operations required. We therefore design an algorithm that scales up to the demand of current big data requirements and has the ability to harness parallel processing capabilities. The new algorithm is illustrated on synthetic data, where results can be judged carefully, and also on a real, large scale Twitter activity data, where new insights can be gained.

Keywords: social network analysis; community analysis; Twitter; viral content; community connectivity; betweenness; information diffusion

1 Introduction

Online social networks (OSNs) such as Facebook, LinkedIn and Twitter have inspired a great amount of research. Whether it is regarding their uses [1] in different aspects of our daily lives or on how a important scientific breakthrough can spread around the world [2]. These networks can be very large, for example Facebook currently holds around 1 billion user accounts. Despite the obvious computational challenges, analysis of these large datasets provides the opportunity to test hypothesis about human social behavior on an unprecedented scale, and hence to reveal deeper understandings of human social behavior [3]. Furthermore, commercial, government and charitable enterprises can utilize the networks to inform campaigning, advertising and promotion. Hence, there is great potential impact for improvements in the analytical tools designed for analysing social networks.

Within the OSNs generated by users, community structures form naturally, and research into their detection is very active [4, 5]. These developments in community detection have produced a diverse set of methods which are at our disposal. Run times of the algorithms are a major concern, and current datasets can be too large for many of the algorithms available. One approach to deal with the size is by using network samples; for example, [6] analyzes community structure in a subset of millions of nodes taken from Facebook. However, for the types of effects that span over the entirety of the networks, we wish to avoid sampling and deal with complete networks.

Communities in OSNs can emerge for many reasons. A key driver can be homophily [7], where some underlying similarity between users in a community leads to a higher number of edges between these users than with users in a different community. [8] investigates homophily formation and evolution in a online social buyers setting. Here, a community builds trust and supports the activity of online purchases, which is the motivation for more in depth research into the nature of the inter-community connections. Companies have an interest in their brand identity within OSN communities, as users now have the ability to broadcast brand information to many other users within their social reach. Although not based on data from OSNs, [3] discusses the attributes that users exhibit to utilize their business associations, and how companies should work to cultivate their brand presence with customers. The authors also raise many interesting questions concerning the dynamic elements of brand presence which are relevant to this work.

It is also interesting to elaborate on how distinct communities are brought together to create large connected graphs. Without the connectivity between dense communities, isolated components would not support many of the fascinating phenomena that have been observed, notably the hugely influential small world effect [9], where there exist surprisingly short paths between members of the network located in different communities. By definition, the density of those edges connecting communities is less than the density of edges within communities. The sparsity of the between-community connectivity is the basis for community separation quality measures such as the modularity index, [10]. The relatively low number of these edges connecting communities together gives them special importance as they are critical for the graph's connectivity. A recent study explores this network feature using examples from brain connectivity, [11], concluding that connection costs can explain these modular networks. For the applications in OSNs, where companies seek to harness the power of Internet advertising, nodes which offer community traversal connections are critical targets [12]. The aim of this work is therefore to give a simple and scalable methodology for defining and discovering this type of key structural component. For the remainder of this paper an edge connecting two different communities will be referred to as a *boundary edge* and the nodes on either side of these edges as *boundary nodes*.

It is important to have in mind that the edges created facilitate an information exchange but when a node receives content, independently it decides on whether to repeat this received information to its follower node set. In future time steps this can include nodes that were previously not included in the sharing of this content for whatever reasons or constraints might exist. For content to spread throughout the network this decision to repeat the content must be consistently agreed on independently. The number of times this must occur is increased when there is a large number of distinct communities and only a few boundary nodes acting as regulators for the content to cross communities and become *viral*. The term viral usually assumes that a large portion of the nodes in network are aware of a piece of information or content regardless of the specific niche community they may belong to. Viral activity can be identified through conversation volume spikes, or cascades, as users share a common piece of content in a short amount of time.

In general the content users would classify as *news* has many examples of viral spreading of content. Twitter is sometimes considered to be a news source, with [13] counting at least 85% of Tweets being related to headline news. Much of which includes news of commercial interest and opens possibilities for real time engagement. Real time monitoring of these events being discussed is therefore essential for automated engagement. With spikes in topics lasting in the order of minutes, the run time of an algorithm should be reduced as much as possible and the ability of the algorithm to utilize the hardware of multiple processors is highly desirable. The works [14, 15] discuss this real time monitoring of events and gives a number of case studies, comparing techniques for spike detection. Our work has a slightly different emphasis, since we aim to detect nodes and edges that facilitate propagation of information, and hence would be natural candidates for monitoring and intervention.

To introduce notation and background, we consider a graph $G = (V, E)$, with $N = |V|$ number of nodes and $M = |E|$ as the number of edges. The standard centrality measure most relevant to our work is betweenness (shortest path betweenness), [16]. For a node v, this measure is defined as

$$b_v = \sum_{i \neq j \neq v} \frac{\sigma_{i,j}(v)}{\sigma_{i,j}}, \qquad (1)$$

where $\sigma_{i,j}$ counts the total number of shortest paths between i and j, and $\sigma_{i,j}(v)$ counts how many of these pass through node v. Hence, b_v gives an indication for the amount of potential control or influence node v has on the information flow between all other nodes in the network. Computing this measure straightforwardly for each node requires a large number of operations, $\Theta(N^3)$, leading to a run time that is impractical for large networks. Using Brandes algorithm [17] a complexity of $\Omega(M \times N)$ is possible, which is still time consuming for the networks with millions of nodes.

The strict assumption that information flows along shortest paths (geodesics) is not always appropriate, as discussed, by Newman [18], who proposes a *random walk betweenness* measure computed using matrix methods. An important criticism of the geodesic viewpoint, which also motivates the random walk alternative, is that when passing messages to target nodes, typical users do not have the global network information and hence may not be aware of the shortest paths between pairs of nodes to be able to place them along the correct route. The runtime for this *random walk betweenness* measure is $\Omega((M + N)N^2)$ and the algorithm requires matrix inversions. We also note that these two betweenness measures above are designed for static networks, and changes in the size of communities over time can affect the distribution of the betweenness values amongst the nodes.

2 Methodology

Given networks arising from online social media, there are many cases where rich community structure is observed. The edges connecting these separately clustered groups

Table 1 Outline of the boundary node vicinity algorithm

1	Extract the set of connected graphs from the original graph
2	For each connected component obtain the community labels for the graph
3	Obtain the set of boundary nodes
4	Measure the local vicinity of each boundary node using the fixed length random walk method and aggregate all of the values in the graph into a normalized score

of nodes are referred to as boundary nodes here, and those edges connecting them are boundary edges. In this section our algorithm for measuring the boundary node proximity is described. The goal is to be able to rank nodes in a network according to their ability to influence nodes across different communities by the information (content) they exchange. This will reveal the boundary nodes, which play a key role in exchanging information between different communities, and those nodes surrounding them in their local vicinity. The algorithm is based on the premise that information travels via a random walk rather than through a shortest path route.

An adjacency matrix A of dimension N will be used to represent the original network, where $A_{i,j} = 1$ when there is an edge between nodes i and j. Once the network has been decomposed into its connected subcomponents and the community labelling has been assigned, the set of boundary edges, connecting two nodes (i,j) belonging to different communities, can then be defined as:

$$\mathbf{W}_{i,j} = \big\{(i,j) : i \in C_1, j \notin C_1, i \notin C_2, j \in C_2\big\}. \tag{2}$$

Here (C_1, C_2) are two communities belonging to the list of community labels, $\mathbf{C}$, in the graph. We assume that the number of community labels will be much less than the number of nodes, $|\mathbf{C}| \ll N$. From the boundary edge set $\mathbf{W}$, the boundary nodes $\mathbf{B}$, can be found. Due to the typical sparsity of the community connectivity, the number of boundary nodes will be much less than the total number of nodes, $|\mathbf{B}| \ll N$.

The algorithm proposed here iterates through the boundary node set and performs a set of independent truncated random walkers originating at each boundary node, until convergence is reached in the distribution of visits to the nodes in the vicinity of each boundary node. It is the counts of the visits from the random walkers to the boundary nodes and nodes of the same community in their vicinity which allows a ranking in terms of being able to influence another community by spread of content. The description of the algorithm is summarized in steps 1 to 4 of the outline given in Table 1. In the first step of the algorithm the set of connected graphs is extracted from the original graph of the network, $\mathbf{G}$, using breadth first search (BFS). BFS can be performed with run time linear in terms of the number of edges and vertices, $O(N + M)$, and space complexity linear in terms of N. Given that most social networks will be small-world and scale-free, the number of edges will not grow too fast with the number of vertices. A relatively small subset of high degree nodes are responsible for the connectivity. The degree distribution following a power law [19] means that the majority of nodes will have a small number of edges. The second step is to label each node according to the community it belongs to and can be computed in $O(N)$. There is a wide selection of algorithms for obtaining the community structure, [5, 20]. In our work, we use the Louvain method of [21]. The run time of the Louvain algorithm is $\Omega(N \log N)$, and there is an efficient implementation available. Tests run with this method report working with millions of nodes under 2 minutes on a standard PC. It is a greedy algorithm using the modularity index, [22], as an optimization criteria, which has the benefit that the number of iterations taken by the algorithm can be controlled to some extent by examining the value of change in the index per iteration. Other algorithms for community detection were experimented with and produced similar results in datasets where the community separation was clear. In situations where different approaches produce different community labellings the algorithm proceeds to focus on a different set of nodes which is likely to have a large amount of overlap. The third step extracts the set of boundary nodes which controls the information exchange between different communities as they are the only nodes that connect directly to nodes in a different community.

The final step in Table 1 runs a number of i.i.d. random walkers from each boundary node until a convergence criterion is satisfied based on the number of visits to the nodes in the network. The number of visits to each node is counted and is a measure of ability to disseminate information across boundary edges and influence different communities. Steps 3 and 4 are described in more detail in the next subsection. This algorithm can be referred to as the boundary vicinity algorithm (BVA).

2.1 Boundary node analysis

To obtain the boundary nodes/edges of a connected graph as defined in (2), we use the vector of community labellings for the set of nodes in the network $\mathbf{C}$ and look for adjacent nodes with different community labellings. With an edge list of the adjacency matrix of the graph, L, each edge is represented as a row number and a column number in this two column matrix. Where the two labels differ on a row in this edge list, a boundary edge has been detected;

$$\mathbf{W} = \big\{ \mathbf{C}\big(L(s,1)\big) \neq \mathbf{C}\big(L(s,2)\big) \big\}. \tag{3}$$

The adjacency matrix of the community specific graph is the matrix $A_C(i,j)$, where

$$A_{C_l:i,j} = \begin{cases} 1, & A_{i,j} \times \delta(C_l(i), C_l(j)) = 1, \\ 0 & \text{otherwise.} \end{cases} \tag{4}$$

Here the $\delta(\cdot, \cdot)$ is the Kronecker delta where the value of one is given when both inputs are equal. To obtain these matrices it is not a requirement to iterate through each element. This will be clarified below. With the community adjacency matrices for each community label A_C and the boundary nodes belonging to the network $\mathbf{B}$ we can iterate through the nodes of $\mathbf{B}$ and run the series of random walkers localized on each boundary node and confined to each A_C.

The random walks used to measure the ability for nodes to influence and affect the boundary nodes have a fixed number of steps. For the walks to represent the localized region of these nodes, $\mathbf{B}$, the walks cannot be given an excessively large length as this would dilute the importance of nodes closer to the boundary nodes. The Barabási-Albert model [19, 23] uses the mechanism of preferential attachment to reproduce the growth characteristics of many networks. The average path length for these networks is $\log(N)/\log(\log(N))$, where we assume that the ceiling of the value is taken. We use this value as a baseline in deciding the number of random walk steps that must be taken before a piece of information loses the consistency and relevance of the original content. Various other values can

```
procedure BNV(G,walknum,stepnum)
    visitCounts = ← zeros(1,N)
    ids ← connected_components(G)
    for all  id ∈ ids do
        G_i ← G(id,id)                                          ▷ G_i is a connected graph
    end for
    for all  g ∈ G do
        (C,Q) ← community(g)                                    ▷ infer community structure
        if Q < threshold then
            continue
        end if
        W = g(i,j) × (1 − δ(C_i ≠ C_j))                         ▷ boundary edge list
        A_C =community_mask(g,C)
        for all node ∈ W do
            A = A_{node∈C}
            present_node = node
            w = 0
            walks = null
            while w < walknum do                                ▷ i.i.d walkers
                pWeightsVec(node) = 1
                s = 0
                while s < stepnum do                            ▷ random walker
                    node = randomStateTransition(A,node)
                    pWeightsVec(node) = 1 + pWeightsVec(node)
                    s = s + 1
                end whilewalks = append(walks, pWeightsVec];
                w = w + 1
                if w =walknum then
                    psrf = GelmanRubinDiagnostic(walks);
                    if psrf < 0.95 — psrf> 1.05 then
                        w = 0                                    ▷ more walks for convergence
                    else
                        pWeights = scaleCommunityWeights(pWeightsVec)
                        visitCounts = append(visitCounts,pWeightsVec)
                    end if
                end if
            end while
        end for
    end for
    return visitCounts
end procedure
```

Figure 1 Boundary vicinity algorithm (BVA).

be used for the number of steps taken in the random walks. The method is not sensitive towards this value as long as the chains do not reach the stationary distribution where the initial state of the chain has not affected the final results, since we are interested in the locality of nodes surrounding the initial state which is one of the boundary nodes. Alternatives which worked well are the average path length, and the longest path length from the boundary node to another node in the same community.

Based on this idea, Figure 1 displays the pseudocode of the algorithm for measuring the boundary node proximities. The first input is the data structure for the connectivity of the nodes in the network. The second input is *walknum*, which is the number of random walkers that are started from each boundary node before convergence is tested. The third input, *stepnum*, is the number of steps/node traversals taken by each random walker. The vector *visitCounts* holds the number of visits by random walkers which are made to each node in the network throughout the algorithm. As a variation this vector could be made into a sparse matrix where each row is the contribution of an i.i.d. walker, so that more information from the walks can be found. The function call here, connected_components(G), is to the breadth-first-search algorithm which produces a list of the elements in G which are connected to each other. Using the identifiers of connected graph membership, a list of the connected components is produced, **G**. In the loop of the elements of **G**, g is a connected network. Here the function call community(g), is to the community detection algorithm of choice (in this work the Louvain algorithm is used). This returns the community membership labels **C** for the networks and modularity index Q. If the modularity index is not larger than a certain threshold of choice, then it is considered that g has no evident community structure and therefore no boundary nodes and the loop continues to the next connected graph component g. The boundary edges, **W**, can be extracted by including only edges which connect different community labels. We obtain the adjacency matrices for each community label by including only the nodes in each community label in a separate adjacency matrix. For each unique *node* in the list of **W** the algorithm then proceeds through the standard method of a set of random walks on the adjacency matrix. After the completion of *walknum* number of walks, the trajectories are tested for convergence using the potential scale reduction factor (PSRF) of [24]. If the set of trajectories have not converged, more walkers are computed until the required amount of convergence is achieved. Upon convergence, the values counts of visits to each node by the walkers is normalized to remove the effects of more walks due to lack of convergence. The results are scaled according to the relative size of the community in relation to the whole graph because of the impact it may have on the large scale of the information flow, so that the nodes in larger communities deliver a larger impact than small ones.

The run time of this algorithm is dominated by the community detection phase. Due to the boundary node set being much smaller in size than the number of nodes, the loops required to iterate through them and perform the random walks will typically cost less than N.

Each component of the BVA algorithm, Table 1, can be made more efficient using parallelization methods. The first step requiring breadth first search can be parallelized using shared or distributed memory, following the works [25, 26], where the number of edges visited is significantly reduced. Another approach to BFS is [27] that utilizes the Nvidia GPUs, but the authors note the memory restrictions for large graphs that take up more than the graphics card memory of around 1 GB. When the number of nodes goes beyond a few million nodes and tens of millions of edges, memory becomes a concern and the method of [28] shows that the step of acquiring the set of connected components can be performed in log space. The community detection component can also be parallelized by using the method of [29] resulting in a completely parallelizable algorithm. The last steps of the algorithm can naturally be parallelized by running the i.i.d. random walkers on separate processors at the same time. After they have completed their walks the trajectories can then be monitored for convergence.

3 Results

Here the results of using the algorithm on synthetic datasets and a real dataset are shown. One synthetic network used for testing is a set of random Erdös-Rényi (ER) graphs produced and connected together to from a connected network by choosing randomly members to act as boundary nodes, shown in Figure 2. The other synthetic network is produced from connecting independent communities graphs produced using preferential attachment, shown in Figure 3. These synthetic datasets are used because the results of using them are easy interpret and compare when using BVA and betweenness. The well known Zachary Karate club dataset [30] is analyzed and presented in Figure 4. The Enron email

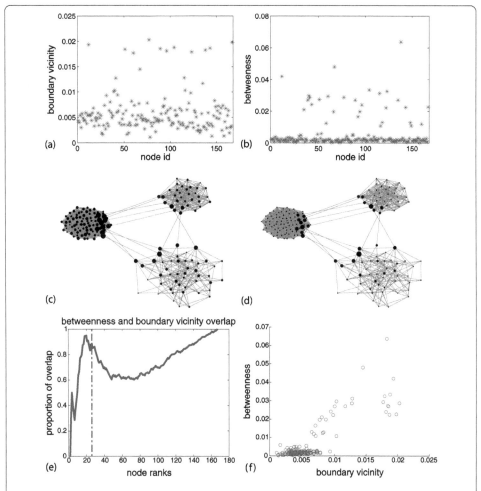

Figure 2 3 ER communities connected and analysed with BVA and betweenness. The first row of plots show the scores given to the node IDs with the boundary vicinity algorithm and betweenness respectively. The second row of plots is the network visualizations with the nodes scaled in size according the normalized scores from the boundary vicinity algorithm and betweenness respectively. Subplot **(e)** shows the proportion of overlap between the top ranking nodes from BVA and betweenness for different sizes of the ranking size. Subplot **(f)** is a scatter plot of the BVA and betweennes values for each node.

dataset [31] is also analysed utilizing the valuable semantic data associated with the nodes to show the qualitative validity of the algorithm. Lastly two new datasets collected from monitoring Twitter hashtags are presented where the volume of Tweets and the volume of boundary nodes are presented against a random set.

Figure 2 shows the results of using the boundary vicinity algorithm (BVA) and calculating betweenness on a synthetically produced network. Three communities were generated independently with the ER model and then a set of random nodes (26 here) were selected from these communities to be connected to a different community. These selected nodes become the *boundary nodes* in the network. There are 167 nodes, and the three communities have 87, 47 and 33 nodes with a total of 13 bridges between them. The chains of random walkers used were run until the convergence diagnostic of PSRF was below 1.2. There are six subfigures labelled (a)-(f), where (a) and (b) show the normalized values from the algorithms (y-axis) given to each node in the network (x-axis). Subfigure (a) for the boundary vicinity algorithm has a more evenly spread distribution across the nodes

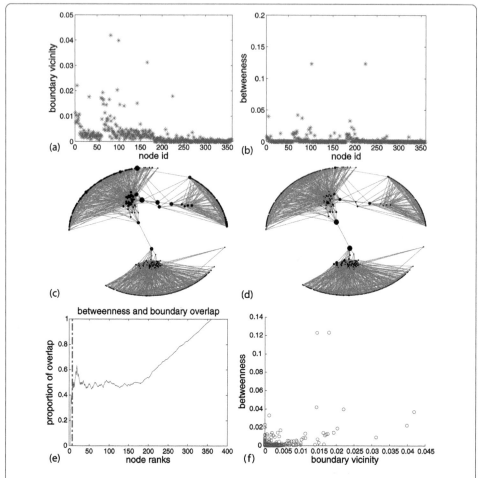

Figure 3 3 communities produced with preferential attachment connected and analysed with BVA and betweenness. The first row of plots show the scores given to the node IDs with the boundary vicinity algorithm and betweenness respectively. The second row of plots is the network visualizations with the nodes scaled in size according the normalized scores from the boundary vicinity algorithm and betweenness respectively. Subplot **(e)** shows the proportion of overlap between the top ranking nodes from BVA and betweenness for different sizes of the ranking size. Subplot **(f)** is a scatter plot of the BVA and betweennes values for each node.

than what betweenness produces in subfigure (b). We can see that betweenness gives almost absolute importance to the nodes on the boundary with little emphasis for the nodes in the vicinity of those boundary nodes. Subfigures (c) and (d) display the networks with the vertices scaled according to the boundary vicinity measure and betweenness respectively. In (c) we can see the neighboring nodes of the boundary scaled as well. Subfigure (e) counts the proportion of overlap in the ranking between BVA and betweenness for an increasing number of nodes. We can see that both algorithms have almost complete overlap in choosing the top 26 nodes but differ in the order for the subsequent nodes. Subfigure (f) shows a scatter plot of the values for all the nodes with both algorithms. We can see how the top ranking nodes are clearly distinct from the bulk of the network and how BVA produces a greater variance for nodes not in the boundary set. These results are consistent with multiple runs, and alternative networks which varied the number of bridges connecting communities and the density of edges between nodes in a community.

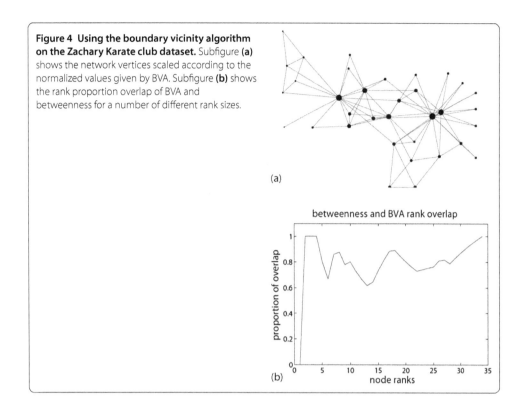

Figure 4 Using the boundary vicinity algorithm on the Zachary Karate club dataset. Subfigure **(a)** shows the network vertices scaled according to the normalized values given by BVA. Subfigure **(b)** shows the rank proportion overlap of BVA and betweenness for a number of different rank sizes.

Subfigure (a) in Figure 5 shows the results of simulating an S-I epidemic on the network of three connected ER communities. Each simulation begins where a single node is put into the infected state and each infected node can infect the nodes in its locality of a single edge according to the adjacency matrix. Three hundred independent simulations are run for each different configuration of the transmission probability and the average percentage of the network that is infected at each iteration is shown. In the first plot the black line shows the results where the transmission probability is uniform across all nodes, and is 0.2 in this case. The blue and red lines show where the top ten BVA and betweenness scoring nodes are removed/immunized from the spread of the infection. The rate of network infection is reduced in both cases showing that both scores provide useful targets for limiting spread. The second plot shows a slightly different strategy where for the blue and red lines, instead of removing the top ten nodes based on BVA and betweenness, their probability to move from susceptible to the infected state is 0.01 compared to the rest of the nodes with probability 0.2. The black line here is still the case of the uniform 0.2 probability used across the network.

In Figure 3 3 communities are produced using the Barabási-Albert model [19, 23] algorithm of preferential attachment and then these communities are connected by choosing nodes uniformly from each group. There are 360 nodes, 3 communities of 60, 120, and 180 nodes with a total of 13 bridges. When BVA is run the chains of random walkers that begin from the boundary nodes were run until the convergence diagnostic of PSRF was below 1.2. The same format as with the previous figure is used. In the first row of subplots, (a) and (b), we can see again that there is a wider distribution in the scores for the nodes with the BVA algorithm on non-boundary nodes. In subfigures (c) and (d) we visualize the networks with the nodes scaled according to the BVA and betweenness respectively. We can see that the highest degree nodes which are central to the community they belong to

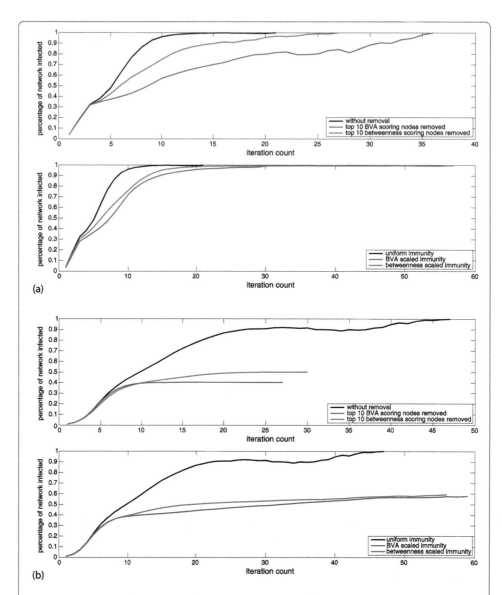

Figure 5 An S-I epidemic simulated on the networks of 3 connected communities and the Zachary Karate club. We test the ability of BVA and betweenness to prevent spread in an S-I epidemic. A single node at random is chosen as the initial infected node and the simulation is run until all nodes in the network are infected or there is no further spread after 100 iterations. The simulations are run 300 times and the average percentage of the network infected at each iteration is plotted. The results for each situation are shown up to the iteration number there was on average a increase in the network infected where the maximum permitted was 60. In subfigure **(a)** the graph of Figure 2 is used for the S-I simulation. The first subplot shows the results of the simulations using a uniform transmission probability of 0.2 in a black line, in blue the results of removing the top 10 nodes which BVA gave the highest score to, and in red the results of removing the top 10 nodes which betweenness produced. In the second subplot in black is the results of using a uniform transmission probability of 0.2, the blue line the results of giving only the top 10 BVA nodes a probability of 0.01 of becoming infected, and the red line where the top 10 betweenness nodes become infected with 0.01. We can see in both plots that BVA and betweenness target nodes which assist slowing down the spread. In subfigure **(b)** we see the results of the same simulations using the network of communities shown in Figure 3 produced using preferential attachment. With the case of removal both BVA and betweenness significantly reduce the spread and restrict the ability of the spread through the whole network. In the last subplot the rate of infecting the whole network is also significantly reduced although the simulation do not terminate as with the situation of removal. Subfigure **(c)** shows the epidemic simulation using the Zachary Karate club network presented in Figure 4 with nodes scaled according to the BVA score. The plot shows the results of giving the top 3 BVA and betweenness scored nodes the same reduced probability of infection. The reduced rate of infection is visible for this network as well.

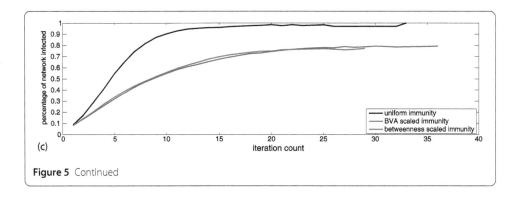

Figure 5 Continued

are scaled and highlighted in both cases. A critical difference is that the boundary nodes at the top which receive a large score with BVA but are given minimal importance with betweenness. With betweenness the role of these nodes is redundant given alternative routes through nodes with higher degree and direct connections to many nodes in the community. In the effort to inspire cross pollination of communities with promoted content, the ability to saturate a user with fewer connections may be advantageous, and worth considering because they may be influenced more easily. In (e) we look at the overlap proportion of the ranking between nodes for a number of nodes in both algorithms. We can see the local peak of the number of overlaps for more nodes than the number of boundary nodes. This is because the structure of the network includes nodes in the vicinity of the boundary which lay on the shortest paths to other nodes in the community. In the last subfigure we can see the scatter plot of the BVA values and betweenness. The ranking of the algorithms may be more similar to each other than with the ER communities connected but the distribution is much more narrow for betweenness in this case, highlighting the few boundary nodes that are also core to the communities.

Subfigure (b) in Figure 5 shows the results of simulating an S-I epidemic on the network of three connected ER communities. Each simulation begins where a single node is put into the infected state and each infected node can infect the nodes in its locality of a single edge according to the adjacency matrix. Three hundred independent simulations are run for each different configuration of the transmission probability and the average percentage of the network that is infected at each iteration is shown. The percentage of the infected network is stops where simulations no longer continued infecting new nodes on average. The maximum permitted iteration number for each simulation was set at 60. In the first plot the black line shows the results where the transmission probability is uniform across all nodes, and is 0.2 in this case. The blue and red lines show where the top ten BVA and betweenness scoring nodes are removed/immunized from the spread of the infection. The rate of network infection is reduced in both cases showing that both scores provide useful targets for limiting the spread. Since the communities had a very sparse interconnectivity the removal restricted the between community spread limiting the number of infected nodes. The second plot shows a slightly different strategy where for the blue and red lines, instead of removing the top ten nodes based on BVA and betweenness, their probability to move from susceptible to the infected state is 0.01 compared to the rest of the nodes with probability 0.2. The black line here is still the case of the uniform 0.2 probability used across the network. The rate of transmission is significantly reduced from the uniform case and even more than the results on the ER graph in the first subfigure since the community connectivity relies on few edges.

Figure 4 shows the results of using BVA on the Zachary Karate club dataset. In subplot (a) the network is visualized and the vertices are scaled according to normalized scores given by the BVA algorithm. The central members of the communities are given large values as are the boundary nodes since they are within the vicinity of the boundary. In subfigure (b) the overlap of the rankings with BVA and betweenness is shown for the number of nodes included, and as with the previous two figures the overlap for both methods peaks when including the top number of nodes which corresponds to the number of boundary nodes. In Figure 5, subfigure (c) shows the results of simulating an S-I epidemic on this network. The case of removal of top scoring BVA and betweenness nodes is not presented due to the size of the network. Here only the top 3 scoring nodes for BVA and betweenness are given the reduced probability of infection 0.01. As with the simulations on the other networks, BVA and betweenness target nodes which reduce the rate of infection.

When analyzing the Enron email dataset, a subset of the nodes are included where the position in the company is known. BVA and betweenness scores are calculated for each of the nodes in the network and the top ten nodes for which their roles are known are compared. BVA selects 3 vice presidents, 1 CEO, 2 managers, 2 traders, and 2 employees to be in the top ten. Betweenness selects 1 vice president, 1 managing director, 2 managers, 1 director of trading, 2 traders, 1 secretary and 2 employees. The list provided by BVA contains more company members with higher positions than by betweenness. This may not be always the case, but it does show that the features of the network extracted by BVA captures importance in the node placements.

Figure 6 shows the Twitter activity of a TV show *FearneHolly* which is monitored in real time using the paid Twitter API service that does not deliver such a limited subset of the Tweets being sent regarding the hashtag, as does the free service. We look at the Tweet volumes over time for this topic and plot them in the bottom subplot of the figure. We can see a single dominating conversation intensity spike. We wish to see the activity of the boundary node set, $\mathbf{W}$, according to the large conversation volumes. BVA focuses on the boundary nodes since it supposes that they are key in facilitating the productions of these large spikes of conversation activity in Twitter. Since these dominant spikes observed in Twitter stand out so much from smaller oscillations it can be assumed that it is due to the conversation taking place across the entire network of different communities and not confined to the locality of clustered nodes in a single community. The boundary nodes of the network are found, and over time the number is counted at each time point, shown in the blue line in the first subplot. We see a single dominant spike for the number of boundary nodes in the same region as that for the total conversation intensity in the bottom subplot. There is a need to test whether the boundary node increase at the same time as the total volume indicates that they provided vital routes for content to spread or is their number only a consequence of the overall activity of the nodes uniformly over the network and not in any way dependent on the presence of the boundary nodes. To investigate this, we select a random set of nodes in the network of equal size to that of the boundary node set and look for spikes in the volume of communication in this random set. A threshold is set at a standard deviation above the mean Tweet count per minute for each subplot and is shown as a dashed black line. Using a confusion matrix gives us a table of values for the false positives (FP), false negatives (FN), true positives (TP), and true negatives (TN) for a predictor. A confusion matrix for the boundary node set activity as an indicator of the

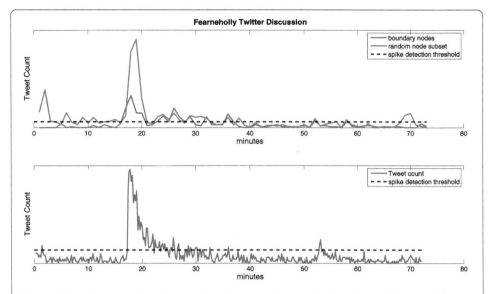

Figure 6 Boundary node detection over time from real time monitoring of events in FearneHolly Twitter discussion. The Twitter activity of a TV show, FearneHolly, is monitored and the Tweets are gathered. The top plot shows the number of boundary nodes that produce a Tweet between time points in blue, and in red is shown the number of Tweets from a random set of nodes of equal size to the boundary node set of the Twitter network. In the bottom plot is the total volume of Tweets over time and we see a single dominant spike in the conversation activity with a decay trailing afterwards. The black dashed line in each subplot is a threshold for spike detection which is one standard deviation from the average Tweet count over time. We can see that the boundary nodes produce a single dominant spike mirroring that of the total conversation activity. The random set of nodes is selected to see whether the boundary node activity simply reflects the total number of Tweets, but we can see a spike in the activity occurs at the start of the monitoring which is not present in either of the other trajectories.

total Tweet volume is calculated:

$$
\begin{array}{c}
\quad\quad\quad\text{Boundary Spike}\quad\text{No Boundary Spike}\\
\begin{array}{l}
\text{Volume Spike}\\
\text{No Volume Spike}
\end{array}
\left(
\begin{array}{cc}
7 & 3\\
5 & 58
\end{array}
\right).
\end{array}
\tag{5}
$$

For the randomly selected group of nodes of equal size to the boundary nodes set the confusion matrix is:

$$
\begin{array}{c}
\quad\quad\quad\text{Random Group Spike}\quad\text{No Random Group Spike}\\
\begin{array}{l}
\text{Volume Spike}\\
\text{No Volume Spike}
\end{array}
\left(
\begin{array}{cc}
8 & 2\\
16 & 47
\end{array}
\right).
\end{array}
\tag{6}
$$

Given the scope of the application BVA the precision of the indicator is the most relevant measure to compare from the confusion matrices. For the boundary node set the precision ($TP/(TP + FP)$) for this dataset is 0.58 and for the randomly selected group of nodes 0.33 (two significant figures given). The boundary node vicinity algorithm focusing on the boundary node activity is working with a subset of the network which is appears to have value during the intense information exchange events (the dataset can be provided by contacting the author).

We look at the Tweets gathered from another TV show *Got to Dance*, shown in Figure 7, in a similar way to the previous *FearneHolly* example. A confusion matrix for the boundary

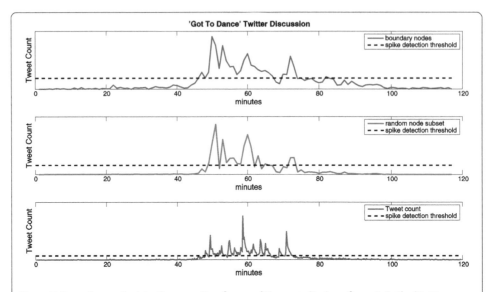

Figure 7 Boundary node detection over time from real time monitoring of events in the 'Got to Dance' Twitter discussion. The Twitter activity of a TV show is monitored and the Tweets are gathered. The first subplot shows the number of boundary nodes that produce a Tweet, and in the second subplot is shown the number of Tweets from a random set of nodes of equal size to the boundary node set taken from this Twitter network. In the bottom plot is the total volume of Tweets over time, and we see a time frame of intense conversation activity. The dashed lines in black are a threshold for the number of Tweets in a minute that are considered to be a spike and is a standard deviation above the mean Tweet count. The boundary nodes as well as the rest of the network are taking part in the conversation with the ability for information exchange between communities.

node set activity as an indicator for the total Tweet volume is calculated:

$$\begin{array}{c} & \text{Boundary Spike} \quad \text{No Boundary Spike} \\ \begin{array}{l} \text{Volume Spike} \\ \text{No Volume Spike} \end{array} \left(\begin{array}{cc} 18 & 1 \\ 8 & 90 \end{array} \right). \end{array} \tag{7}$$

For the randomly selected group of nodes of equal size to the boundary nodes set the confusion matrix is:

$$\begin{array}{c} & \text{Random Group Spike} \quad \text{No Random Group Spike} \\ \begin{array}{l} \text{Volume Spike} \\ \text{No Volume Spike} \end{array} \left(\begin{array}{cc} 12 & 7 \\ 6 & 92 \end{array} \right). \end{array} \tag{8}$$

The precision values are 0.69 and 0.67 for the boundary nodes and random node subset respectively. Both network subsets show substantial alignment with the conversation spikes in the total volume count. The added value of looking at the boundary nodes in this type of situation is to exploit the unique positioning for efficient spreading between communities.

4 Discussion

The work presented here gives an efficient algorithm for ranking the ability of nodes in a network, with community structure, to spread information between clusters. Previously proposed methods impose large computational difficulties or are not based on principles which realistically model how information across the communities can spread. Focusing attention on these boundary nodes in a network can be critical for monitoring whether content may reach the point of becoming *viral*. In practice not all of the nodes in the network may be directly influenceable. An alternative approach can be to indirectly influence a chosen node by targeting the local vicinity of the node in the network. The boundary vicinity algorithm (BVA) acknowledges nodes that may be placed in such a position to have more or less influence on content leaving or entering a community of nodes in network.

A strength of this boundary vicinity algorithm is that it combines the power of community detection algorithms with the use of random walkers to assist in the process of investigating the range of influence of the boundary nodes. The results show that this algorithm is comparable with betweenness centrality without the requirement for full the maturity of a network to be visible. In situations where the observed connectivity is changing, analysing the network in sections based on a community structure is an approach to provide more consistent results over time. The algorithm has a single tuning parameter which determines the number of steps a random walker takes from the boundary nodes. Using a fraction of the average path length for networks constructed with the Barabási-Albert model has given stable results in our experiments.

Measures such as betweenness can provide a set of optimal targets for spreading content along shortest path routes throughout the complete connected network. This task ignores the challenges that might be faced which attempting to promote activity in the critical set of nodes which lay on the boundary of the communities making up the complete network. A list of the nodes which are best positioned to quickly spread a piece of content does not address many of the practical challenges in inspiring activity as a non-invasive influencer. Assessing the vicinity of the influencers for the boundary nodes gives a reasonable subset for which attention must be given to ensure that cross pollination between clustered sets of nodes can occur.

Overall, the proposed algorithm has the potential to quickly handle the task of analysis with an online stream of large datasets. In particular real time event monitoring in environments such as Twitter where topic discussions can grow and decay rapidly, this is especially important. With the goal of spreading the content as far as possible the boundary nodes, and those nodes in its close vicinity, in a community must be targeted, which is at the core of this method proposed here.

Competing interests
The author declares that they have no competing interests.

Acknowledgements
Thanks is given to Peter Laflin for providing feedback over the course of this work, and to Bloom Agency, Leeds, for supplying anonymised Twitter data. This work was performed as part of the Mathematics of Large Technological Evolving Networks (MOLTEN) project, which is supported by the Engineering and Physical Sciences Research Council and the Research Councils UK Digital Economy programme, with grant EP/I016058/1, and the support of the University of Strathclyde with Bloom Agency for the follow-on support from the Impact Acceleration Account.

References
1. Skeels MM, Grudin J (2009) When social networks cross boundaries: a case study of workplace use of Facebook and LinkedIn. In: Proceedings of the ACM 2009 international conference on supporting group work. ACM, New York, pp 95-104
2. De Domenico M, Lima A, Mougel P, Musolesi M (2013) The anatomy of a scientific gossip. arXiv:1301.2952
3. McAlexander JH, Schouten JW, Koenig HF (2002) Building brand community. J Mark 66:38-54
4. Leskovec J, Lang KJ, Dasgupta A, Mahoney MW (2009) Community structure in large networks: natural cluster sizes and the absence of large well-defined clusters. Internet Math 6(1):29-123

5. Fortunato S (2010) Community detection in graphs. Phys Rep 486(3):75-174
6. Ferrara E (2012) A large-scale community structure analysis in Facebook. EPJ Data Sci 1(1):1-30
7. McPherson M, Smith-Lovin L, Cook JM (2001) Birds of a feather: homophily in social networks. Annu Rev Sociol 27:415-444
8. Matsuo Y, Yamamoto H (2009) Community gravity: measuring bidirectional effects by trust and rating on online social networks. In: Proceedings of the 18th international conference on World Wide Web. ACM, New York, pp 751-760
9. Travers J, Milgram S (1969) An experimental study of the small world problem. Sociometry 32:425-443
10. Newman ME, Girvan M (2004) Finding and evaluating community structure in networks. Phys Rev E 69(2):026113
11. Clune J, Mouret J-B, Lipson H (2013) The evolutionary origins of modularity. Proc R Soc Lond B, Biol Sci 280(1755):20122863
12. Subramani MR, Rajagopalan B (2003) Knowledge-sharing and influence in online social networks via viral marketing. Commun ACM 46(12):300-307
13. Kwak H, Lee C, Park H, Moon S (2010) What is Twitter, a social network or a news media? In: Proceedings of the 19th international conference on World Wide Web. ACM, New York, pp 591-600
14. Weng J, Lee B-S (2011) Event detection in Twitter. In: ICWSM
15. Nichols J, Mahmud J, Drews C (2012) Summarizing sporting events using Twitter. In: Proceedings of the 2012 ACM international conference on intelligent user interfaces. ACM, New York, pp 189-198
16. Freeman LC (1977) A set of measures of centrality based on betweenness. Sociometry 40:35-41
17. Brandes U (2001) A faster algorithm for betweenness centrality. J Math Sociol 25(2):163-177
18. Newman ME (2005) A measure of betweenness centrality based on random walks. Soc Netw 27(1):39-54
19. Barabási A-L, Albert R (1999) Emergence of scaling in random networks. Science 286(5439):509-512
20. Lancichinetti A, Fortunato S (2009) Community detection algorithms: a comparative analysis. Phys Rev E 80(5):056117
21. Blondel VD, Guillaume J-L, Lambiotte R, Lefebvre E (2008) Fast unfolding of communities in large networks. J Stat Mech Theory Exp 2008(10):P10008
22. Clauset A, Newman ME, Moore C (2004) Finding community structure in very large networks. Phys Rev E 70(6):066111
23. Albert R, Barabási A-L (2002) Statistical mechanics of complex networks. Rev Mod Phys 74(1):47
24. Gelman A, Rubin DB (1992) Inference from iterative simulation using multiple sequences. Stat Sci 7:457-472
25. Beamer S, Asanović K, Patterson D (2013) Direction-optimizing breadth-first search. Sci Program 21(3):137-148
26. Beamer S, Buluc A, Asanovi K, Patterson DA (2013) Distributed memory breadth-first search revisited: enabling bottom-up search. Technical report, DTIC document
27. Harish P, Narayanan PJ (2007) Accelerating large graph algorithms on the GPU using CUDA. In: High performance computing—HiPC 2007. Springer, Berlin, pp 197-208
28. Reingold O (2008) Undirected connectivity in log-space. J ACM 55(4):17
29. Martelot El, Hankin C (2013) Fast multi-scale community detection based on local criteria within a multi-threaded algorithm. arXiv:1301.0955
30. Zachary WW (1977) An information flow model for conflict and fission in small groups. J Anthropol Res 33:452-473
31. Chapanond A, Krishnamoorthy MS, Yener B (2005) Graph theoretic and spectral analysis of Enron email data. Comput Math Organ Theory 11(3):265-281

6

The impact of social segregation on human mobility in developing and industrialized regions

Alexander Amini, Kevin Kung, Chaogui Kang, Stanislav Sobolevsky[*] and Carlo Ratti

[*]Correspondence: stanly@mit.edu
SENSEable City Laboratory,
Massachusetts Institute of
Technology, 77 Massachusetts
Avenue, Cambridge, 02139, USA

Abstract

This study leverages mobile phone data to analyze human mobility patterns in a developing nation, especially in comparison to those of a more industrialized nation. Developing regions, such as the Ivory Coast, are marked by a number of factors that may influence mobility, such as less infrastructural coverage and maturity, less economic resources and stability, and in some cases, more cultural and language-based diversity. By comparing mobile phone data collected from the Ivory Coast to similar data collected in Portugal, we are able to highlight both qualitative and quantitative differences in mobility patterns - such as differences in likelihood to travel, as well as in the time required to travel - that are relevant to consideration on policy, infrastructure, and economic development. Our study illustrates how cultural and linguistic diversity in developing regions (such as Ivory Coast) can present challenges to mobility models that perform well and were conceptualized in less culturally diverse regions. Finally, we address these challenges by proposing novel techniques to assess the strength of borders in a regional partitioning scheme and to quantify the impact of border strength on mobility model accuracy.

Keywords: predictive human mobility; social networks; cultural diversity

Introduction

Transportation and communication networks form the fabric of industrialized nations. The roll-out of such infrastructure in such regions can play a major role in supporting, or deterring, a regions' ability to thrive economically and socially. Likewise, citizens' use of these networks can tell us much about the region, including insight on how ideas and diseases may be spreading, or how to most effectively augment services, such as health care and education [1].

Existing studies of mobile phone data have given us insight on numerous aspects of human mobility [2–6]. However, these studies tend to focus on regions with the highest mobile phone coverage, which also happens to be in more stable, mature, and developed regions. Thus, the models produced based on this data might not be as appropriate for developing regions with a substantially different patterns of social interactions and human mobility. However, these highly industrialized and wealthy regions represent less than one-third of the world's population, with the remaining two-thirds living in developing and less economically mature regions. Accurate models for developing regions are critical as these regions are facing the most rapid demographic and economic shifts worldwide, and are in even greater need of such models to help inform policy makers, urban planners, and service providers. Yet, little work has been done to assess the appropriateness of models conceptualized for industrialized regions for use in developing regions.

Obtaining a comprehensive and accurate dataset of the telecommunications activity in developing regions can be extremely difficult due to security and privacy considerations, limited coverage by any single provider, and the need for a rigorous data capture methodology and infrastructure. The Data4Development (D4D) dataset [7] provided a unique opportunity by collecting data throughout the Ivory Coast and releasing it specifically for research purposes, so that developing regions could also be analyzed in greater detail. The contrast of long-standing cultural and linguistic diversity with relatively recent and rapid urbanization offered researchers a unique opportunity to understand the communication and mobility patterns and needs of a developing nation during key phases of its transformation.

Our study brought the D4D data from Ivory Coast together with mobility data from an industrialized nation (Portugal) in order to assess the ability of human mobility models developed for industrialized regions to accurately model developing regions. We focus on the comparison of these two countries at very different stages in their industrialization and in their levels of cultural and linguistic diversity, and sheds new light on the applicability of metrics and models conceptualized for industrialized regions to developing regions. Our results demonstrate the importance of considering cultural and linguistic diversity in the construction of new models to address the challenges of developing regions. The insights gained from our study have important applications to policymaking, urban planning, and the services deployments that are transforming Ivory Coast and many other developing countries.

In the following sections, we provide additional details on the data used in this study, the results derived, and the conclusions drawn.

Related works

Leveraging mobile phone data to elucidate and quantify many aspects of human life is growing in popularity. For example, mobile phone data has been used to gain insights from a diversity of cultures, ranging from university students to professionals in the US, Finland, and Africa [8]. Targeted cultural patterns included pace of life, reaction to outlier events, and social support, as opposed to the mobility focus of our study. Eagle et al used mobile phone communication logs and top up records to conduct a comprehensive comparison of urban and rural life within a small country, as opposed to across countries as targeted by our research [9]. Mobile phone data has also been used to study the seasonal consumption patterns of tourists in Estonia [10].

As part of the D4D competition, researchers studied a wide range of topics ranging from social behaviors, economics, health, transportation, and mobility. Several studies [11–13] considered mobility patterns for the purpose of improving the planning or efficiency of the transportation systems. While some articles [14, 15] targeted mobility within the largest city, Abidjan, and others considered mobility across the country, none tackled the challenge of assessing mobility models created for mature and industrialized nations on the developing nation of Ivory Coast. Additionally, ours is the first study to have considered the linguistic and cultural barriers and affinities that we have shown to be significantly stronger in the developing nation of Ivory Coast, in comparison the more industrialized nation of Portugal. Thus our study represents a novel and important contribution to understanding the challenges of creating globally applicable mobility models.

Data description

We used four datasets to assess and compare the human mobility patterns in the Ivory Coast and Portugal. The first dataset, *D1* was provided by Orange Telecom as *SET2*, via the Data for Development (D4D) Challenge [7]. This dataset was based on anonymized Call Detail Records (CDRs) of 2.5 billion calls and SMS exchanges between 5 million users December 1, 2011 until April 28, 2012 (150 days).

SET2 contains consecutive call activities of each subscriber over the study period. Each record in this dataset represents a single connection to an antenna and contains the following fields: timestamp, anonymized ID of the user, and the antenna ID they connected to. To further anonymize this data, the original dataset was subsampled to the calls of 50K randomly sampled individuals for each of 2-week periods in the dataset. The geographical positions of the antenna for *D1* was also provided and visualized in Figure 1B according to the density of antennae in every region. Black lines overlaid on the country represent the corresponding first-level administrative boundaries (19 Ivorian régions and 20 Portuguese

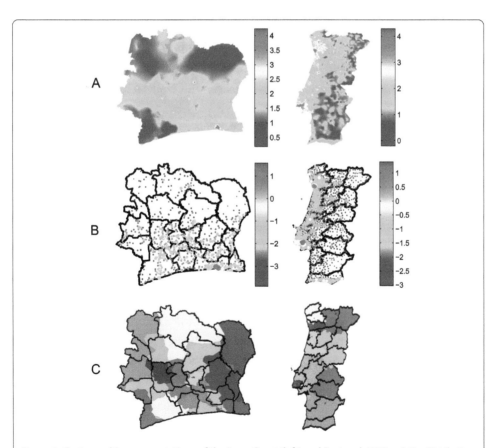

Figure 1 Cartographic representations of the Ivory Coast (left) and Portugal. (A) *Population Distribution*, where colors are logarithmically based on the population density. **(B)** *Geographic cell tower position*, where the size and color of the antennae are logarithmically mapped based on the density of antennae in the area. **(C)** *Community Partitioning*, where communities are built from human migrations over a 24 hour time window and visually displayed along with the countries official administrative boundaries.

districts). Records without antenna IDs were removed; 107 antennae had no calls and 128 antennae had no population movements.

The second dataset, $D2$, provided 400 million anonymized CDRs across Portugal for the time period of January 1, 2006 to December 31, 2007. $D2$ was also provided by Orange Telecom with 2000 antennae distributed across Portugal, and the same data fields as in $D1$.

Datasets $D3$ and $D4$ provided a high-resolution population density data for Ivory Coast [16] and Portugal [17], respectively. To map the population data to the antennae, we created a Voronoi tessellation [18] of each country based on the antennae location. For the 12 locations that had 2-3 antennas in a single location, those 2-3 antennas were collapsed into a single Voronoi cell. Each antenna was assigned the total population within the corresponding Voronoi cell. Figure 1A provides a logarithmic scale population density distribution map using the data from $D3$ and $D4$. The population maps were created as an interpolation of the population density at each antenna.

Although used widely for human mobility studies, mobile phone data provides only a proxy for human mobility, for example, callers are tracked only to the spatial resolution of the antenna (which may be up to 70 km, depending on tower height and terrain), and usually only when the phone is in use while not everyone uses a mobile phone while traveling. However, even in developing regions, mobile phone penetration is high. Ivory Coast has 85% mobile phone coverage, with Orange Telecom (the provider of the data for Ivory Coast and Portugal used in this study) being the top mobile phone provider having a market share of 42.5%. In general mobile phone penetration in Portugal is almost absolute, while the total number of phone accounts is even higher than the total number of people - 142% of the country population owns a mobile device, with Orange Telecom at 19% of market share.

Collective mobility patterns

We first performed a bulk mobility pattern analysis based on $D1$ and $D2$ by plotting the probability density function $P(\Delta r)$ of the individual travel distances (or jump sizes) Δr in a trace of agglomerated de-identified callers over a period of two weeks, for Ivory Coast (left plot, solid black line) and Portugal (right plot, solid black line), as shown in Figure 2A. The distributions were qualitatively similar to each other except that at the administrative level, the distributions in Ivory Coast are much more scattered than those observed in Portugal, suggesting greater regional variance. We fit the density function to a truncated power law of the form $P(\Delta r) = (\Delta r + \Delta r_0)^{-\beta} \exp(-\Delta r/\kappa)$, as described in [2], where Δr_0, β, and κ are the fit constants. While the two distributions had similar cutoff distance ($\kappa_{Portugal} = 106 \pm 10$ km; $\kappa_{Ivory} = 122 \pm 5$ km), the two countries have slightly different power law coefficients ($\beta_{Portugal} = 1.37 \pm 0.06$; $\beta_{Ivory} = 1.62 \pm 0.03$). This higher coefficient in Ivory Coast indicates that the likelihood of displacement generally decays faster with distance in comparison to Portugal.

We also investigated regional differences in the mobility patterns. In both cases of Ivory Coast and Portugal, we identified the first level administrative boundaries as the highest country-defined level of partitioning. For Ivory Coast these are called 'régions,' while in Portugal they are referred to as 'districts.' We partitioned the mobility data by the different level-one administrative regions and overlaid the same density functions specific for each administrative region on the same plots above. Different administrative regions are

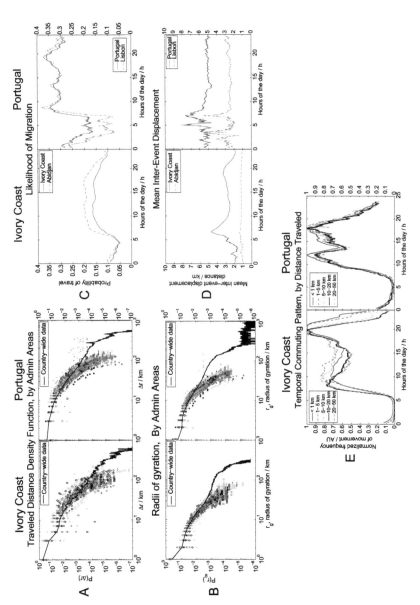

Figure 2 Comparative mobility functions for Ivory Coast (left) and Portugal (right). Probability density functions for *distance traveled* **(A)** and *radius of gyration* **(B)** for each administrative area (differentiated by different color/shape markers). Comparison of country-wide data to capital city daily commuting profiles through respective *probabilities of displacement* **(C)** and *mean inter-event migration distance* **(D)**. Country wide temporal commuting profiles *separated by the distance traveled* **(E)**.

identified by different scatter marker types and colors. We observed the same truncated power law behavior across the different regions, but the Ivory Coast regions exhibited significantly greater diversity than similarly defined regions in Portugal. This would indicate that in Ivory Coast the likelihood that people migrate and commute with respect to distance is much more dependent on what part of the country they are in, as opposed to in Portugal where the different administrative regions show very little diversity from each other.

Another important metric for assessing mobility patterns is the radius of gyration. As defined in [2], the radius of gyration for each caller is the characteristic distance traveled by each caller when observed up to time t, and is computed as the probability distribution function of the mean squared variance of the center of mass of each user's set of catchment locations. The results are plotted in Figure 2B, with t = the period of data collection for each of the datasets.

The distributions plotted in Figure 2B and show that the bulk mobility data from Ivory Coast adheres well to the scale-free framework proposed in [2]. The similarity in the bulk mobility characteristics between Ivory Coast and Portugal serves to strengthen the argument that we can make valid comparisons between the two datasets, as described in the sections below.

Commuting patterns

Daily commuting patterns are a critical component of any region's mobility requirements. Displacement is defined as movement from one cell tower to another cell tower between two consecutive calls, and is a key marker for assessing mobility. To focus on daily commuting patterns, we excluded data collected during weekends, and computed the fraction of inter-call events that were accompanied by displacements in a moving 40-minute window of time for Ivory Coast and Portugal. We averaged the fraction of displacement for each 40-minute window across 45 weekdays to get a 24-hour temporal profile of the probability of displacement during a workday.

The first and probably the most significant difference is the absolute difference in the probability of displacement, which can be seen in Figure 2C. We observe that in Portugal, in a given period, people are much more mobile compared to their counterparts in Ivory Coast.

Both countries exhibit a commuting pattern; there is a sharp rise in the probability of displacement around 7-9 a.m. The evening decline is not as sharp, suggesting that people leave work at different times in the evening.

Significant quantitative differences between the countries can also be seen throughout the day. In Portugal, people in Lisbon and across the nation exhibited similar likelihood to commute during the busiest hours. However, a significantly higher percentage of people in Abidjan were mobile than across the nation. Additionally, while displacement levels in Abidjan and across Ivory Coast were similar during the lowest period (4-7 a.m.). Displacement for the same period is significantly higher for Portugal than for Lisbon, and is likely an indicator of more significant numbers of suburban commuters in Portugal than in Ivory Coast.

Figure 2D provides a comparison of the mean migration distances between the 2 countries for the same period. Here again, the average distance traveled is significantly less in Ivory Coast and its capital city, than in Portugal. In the country-wide data, we observe a sharp increase in the mean inter-event displacement distance near the morning peak commute (around 5-9 a.m.) in both Ivory Coast and Portugal. However, the spike in distance encountered in Lisbon during morning commute does not occur in Abidjan. This difference may be indicative of people both living and working in close proximity in Abidjan, as opposed to commuting in from outside or across the city as is often the case in developed regions with more comprehensive public transport facilities.

We examined the country-specific commuting pattern more closely by looking at how the distance commuted may affect the daily behaviors. The observed distances traveled were binned (0-1 km, 1-5 km, 5-10 km, 10-20 km, and 20-50 km), and the daily temporal profile of the probability of displacement was computed for each bin for the two countries, as shown in Figure 2E.

The temporal profiles for both Ivory Coast and Portugal show a bimodal pattern in Figure 2E. For Ivory Coast the morning peak is around 7 a.m. and the evening peak is around 8 p.m., as opposed to roughly 10 a.m. and 6 p.m. for Portugal. Note that the peaks for Portugal are much sharper than those of Ivory Coast. Overall these differences indicate a shorter prime commuting period for Portugal, which is likely indicative of the ability for commuters to travel more efficiently to their destinations.

Community structure

Large networks, such as the telecommunications or transportation networks of a nation, often exhibit community structure, i.e., the organization of vertices into clusters with many edges joining vertices of the same cluster and comparatively few edges joining vertices of different clusters. Identifying the community structure in such networks has many applications, such as better placement and provisioning of services. Recently, this type of community structure analysis has been performed on land-line communications in Great Britain [19], mobile connections in Belgium [20], United States [21], and various other countries across Europe, Asia, and Africa [22, 23]. While there is research investigating the impact of physical human mobility on the space-independent community structure [21] there has been a lack of similar research for developing nations.

Network modularity [24] is a measure of the strength of the division of a network into clusters. Networks with high modularity have dense connections between nodes within clusters, and sparse connections between nodes in different clusters. Modularity is computed as the fraction of edges that fall within a cluster, minus the expected such fraction if the edges were distributed at random with respect to the node strength distribution. The value of modularity lies in the range $[-1, 1]$, and is positive if the edges within groups exceeds the number expected on the basis of chance.

The definition of network modularity is:

$$Q = \frac{1}{2m} \sum_{ij} \left[A_{ij} - \frac{k_i k_j}{2m} \right] \delta(c_i, c_j), \tag{1}$$

where A_{ij} is the weight of the link from i to j, k_i is the sum of the weights from node i, c_i is the community that node i was assigned to, $m = \frac{1}{2} \sum_{ij} A_{ij}$, and $\delta(c_i, c_j)$ is 1 if $c_i = c_j$ and 0 otherwise.

High modularity in mobility networks may point to an efficient organization of residences, employment, and services all in close proximity, or it may point to restrictive policies or infrastructures that limit free movement across communities. We were interested

Table 1 Comparison of different similarity indices to compare similarity between community partitioning (generated from network of human mobility) and the respective administrative boundaries

Similarity Index	Portugal	Ivory Coast	Difference
Wallace [30]	0.482813	0.199134	0.283679
Adjusted Rand [31]	0.495536	0.258351	0.237184
Jaccard [32]	0.377999	0.184733	0.193266
Fowlkes-Mallows [33]	0.553788	0.378296	0.175491
Melia-Heckerman [34]	0.659385	0.515347	0.144037
Hubert [35]	0.806411	0.707795	0.098615
Larsen [36]	0.58273	0.525396	0.057334
Rand [31]	0.903205	0.853898	0.049308

in the community structure of developing nations, such as Ivory Coast, especially in comparison to more developed nations, such as Portugal.

We used datasets *D1* and *D2* to build the human mobility networks and identify the community structure of antennae within the Ivory Coast and Portugal. We set nodes to the locations of each cell tower, and edges to the total number of migrations of all people that placed two consecutive calls between the two nodes within a time window of 24 hours. We tested the following Community Detection algorithms: Louvain [25], Le Martelot [26], Newman [27], Infomap [28], and a new method of community detection suggested in [29]. We computed the modularity of community structures identified by each of these methods. The method described in [29] provided the highest modularity, and was subsequently chosen to be used for this part of the study. Figure 1C graphically compares the communities identified (in color) with their first level administrative boundaries (outlined in black).

An especially interesting difference in the communities identified for Ivory Coast and those identified for Portugal was the similarity between identified communities and the official administrative boundaries of the nations. We calculated 7 different clustering coefficients, each representing the qualitative similarity between the two different partitions of each region. While the communities identified for Portugal exhibited high similarity with the 20 official administrative boundaries (districts), this was not the case for the Ivory Coast's 19 official administrative boundaries (régions). As shown in Table 1, communities identified for Portugal show significantly higher similarity (as much as 28% higher clustering coefficients) to administrative boundaries, in comparison to that of the Ivory Coast.

While this significant difference in community and official boundary alignments may be attributable to the layout of infrastructure along official boundaries, we began to question whether there might be more fundamental differences. Previous studies have shown that other factors, such as geographical features, can play an important role in how communities are formed and services are sought [19, 37]. However, little has been done to investigate the direct impact of culture and language on human mobility.

Ivory Coast represents an especially interesting context to investigate cultural and linguistic influences on mobility within a single nation. The Ivory Coast is a nation made up of more than 60 distinct tribes, classified into 5 principle regions [38]. The official language is French, although many of the local languages are widely used, including Baoulré, Dioula, Dan, Anyin and Cebaara Senufo, and an estimated 65 languages are spoken in the country.

Intuitively, these cultural and linguistic differences are likely to influence mobility patterns in the region. However, it is also known that as regions become more industrialized, cultural ways are often blended or lost altogether. Portugal represents an interesting context for the latter, as Portuguese is the single national language of Portugal, and any tribal boundaries pre-date Roman times.

Due to the vast differences seen in the network community structure to administrative-defined boundaries, our goal in the next section was to understand if tribal structure of the Ivory Coast could be the influential factor of the mobility patterns in the region.

Tribal community analysis

Since the communities detected in Section IV exhibited low similarity to administrative boundaries, we began to investigate the impact of certain factors present in the Ivory Coast that may be attributable to such a substantial difference. Since people and their behaviors throughout a large portion of Africa are still impacted by their tribal affiliations while any tribal boundaries in Portugal predate Roman times, studying the tribal boundary impact in Ivory Coast represented a perfect example of this. We generated digital shape files for each of the eight distinct tribal regions in Ivory Coast [39]. Such tribal maps do have a level of uncertainty associated with them due to migrations over time; however, we used the most recent versions of tribal boundaries available.

We then modified the community detection approach to use the tribal boundaries as the Level 1 boundaries and subsequently ran a hierarchical community detection using the Louvain method [25] in each of these Level 1 tribal partitions in order to produce the sub-communities inside different tribal regions which we will refer to as sub-tribal communities. The Louvain method provided the closest final number of partitions to the administratively defined subprefectures of the algorithms that we tested, and was thus chosen as the most appropriate for current purposes. By doing so, we were able to generate sub-tribal communities while also conserving the physical shape of each tribal region. Figure 3A demonstrates this by showing the official prefecture and subprefecture boundaries (left) and the tribal and sub-tribal communities (right) that were created using this approach. The larger first level partitions (prefecture and tribal) are indicated as a single color, while the smaller secondary partitions (subprefecture and sub-tribal) are indicated as black lines within their respective first level partition. The number of subprefectures and sub-tribal regions are very similar (approximately 250 and 220 respectively) and thus can be used as a valid comparison against each other.

As a first measure of impact of tribes on mobility, we aggregated the mobility network between communities. Figure 3B provides a plot of the mobility network with each node representing a sub-tribal community, and each edge is colored on a logarithmic scale to reflect the number of migrations between the connected nodes in the mobility network. Nodes are colored with the same logarithmic scheme and represent the sum of all migrations into this location. The intra-tribal community mobility network is plotted separately from the inter-tribal community mobility network, in order to facilitate comparison. The intra-tribal network plots only those edges between communities in the same tribe. The inter-tribal network plots only edges between communities of differing tribes.

This diagram provides a first insight into tribal influences on mobility. Note that the number of intra-tribal migrations (as indicated by the color coding of edges) dwarfs the number of inter-tribal migrations. Additionally, the inter-tribal migrations are largely dominated by connections to the largest city, Abidjan.

The impact of the tribal borders versus administrative borders in Ivory Coast on human mobility could be also directly demonstrated by measuring the strength of normalized mobility fluxes at different geographical distances in case they cross or do not cross those

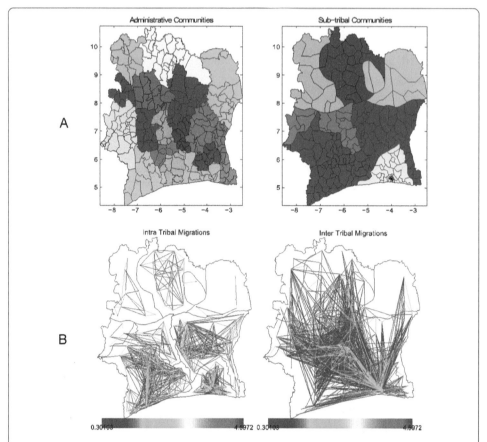

Figure 3 Hierarchical boundary and human migration visualization in Ivory Coast. (A) *Partitionings of Ivory Coast* by administrative prefectures/sub-prefectures (left) and tribal/sub-tribal communities (right). **(B)** *Intra-Inter tribal migrations*, where each node represents an individual sub-tribal community, and each link is logarithmically colored to represent the number of migrations (extracted from call records) between the two nodes.

borders. Figure 4B provides a zoomed in version of the statistically significant data points of Figure 4A and shows that for any given distance, the flux between intra-Administrative and intra-Tribal regions is consistently higher than the flux between inter-Administrative and inter-Tribal regions. One can then conclude that the fluxes crossing the tribal border are much weaker on average compared to fluxes at the same geographical distance but crossing an administrative border instead.

We also quantified the strength of these partitioning ties by computing the network modularity of the sub-tribal communities versus that of the administrative boundaries. The network modularity of the sub-tribal communities was 0.6548, in comparison to a network modularity of 0.6158 for the administrative boundaries. Given that the number of regions for both partitions (sub-tribal and sub-prefecture) is very similar, this increase of network modularity corresponding to sub-tribal communities by the definition of network modularity shows again that mobility patterns have a stronger connection in a sub-tribal country partitioning compared to that of an administrative partitioning.

Modeling human mobility

Accurately modeling human interactions between regions can present many challenges; however, effectively doing so can provide a crucial piece of information to efficiently dis-

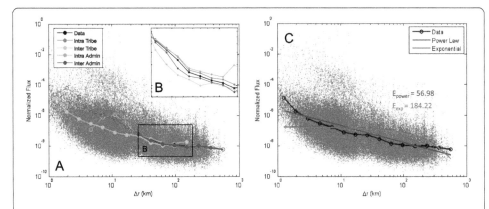

Figure 4 Normalized migration fluxes between two locations. Gray data-points represent the individual fluxes, while the black line indicates the data averaged into smaller bins. Fluxes are separated into 4 additional categories **(A)**, depending whether the flux was intra/inter and tribal/admin regions of the Ivory Coast. The marker of a given bin is filled if that bin contains more than 1% of all data points, (i.e., the bin is considered statistically significant if it is filled). A zoomed in version of **(B)** over the part of the graph where all signal bins are statistically significant is shown in (A). The data is also fitted to a power-law and exponential distribution **(C)** and visualized. The MAPE for each fit is also given.

tribute resources, health services, etc. throughout a given area. The Gravity Model, whose origins trace back to Ravenstein's laws of migration [40], was formulated on Newton's Law of gravity, and predicts flux between a source and destination based on the populations of the source and destination, and the distance between the source and destination. More specifically, according to the gravity model, the average flux migrations from regions i to j is:

$$T_{ij} = A\frac{p_i p_j}{r_{ij}^{\gamma}}, \tag{2}$$

where i and j are origin and destination locations with populations p_i and p_j respectively at a distance of r_{ij} from each other. A is a normalization factor and γ is an adjustable parameter chosen to fit the data.

An alternative version of the gravity model using an exponential fit can be also described as:

$$T_{ij} = Ap_i p_j e^{-\gamma r_{i,j}}. \tag{3}$$

To determine which model would be more appropriate we plotted the normalized flux between two locations separated by a given distance in Figure 4C. We fit these normalized migrational fluxes to both a power-law and exponential fit (blue and red lines) and observe that the power-law distribution is much more consistent for modeling our data (which is also confirmed by comparing mean absolute percent error values reported on the plot). Therefore, for the remainder of this study we used the gravity model in Equation (2).

In order to apply the model one must inherently define the appropriate spatial resolution (i.e., the areas to model migrations between/within). By monitoring the resulting accuracy of the model, it is possible to gain insight on what type of partitioning of an area will most effectively allow for human mobility to be modeled. We started by investigating if the use of these sub-tribal communities would provide an advantage in modeling the mobility network of the Ivory Coast compared to an administrative (subprefecture) partitioning.

We computed the Gravity model using dataset *D1*, and specifically modeled the migrations for both administrative and sub-tribal partitioning of the country, and subsequently tested the accuracy of the model from the mean average percent error (MAPE) with respect to the true network of human mobility. MAPE has been shown to be a very effective measure of error in model predictions, especially when considering population forecasting [39, 41].

We compute MAPE according to:

$$M = \frac{100}{n} \sum_{t=1}^{n} \left| \frac{A_t - F_t}{A_t} \right|, \tag{4}$$

where A_t is the actual value, F_t is the forecasted value, and n is the number of data points. Therefore, an inaccurate model will subsequently yield a high MAPE value; whereas an accurate model will yield a much smaller MAPE value.

To further explore the relationship between tribal and administrative boundaries we applied an alternative approach for modeling human mobility and interaction, the Radiation Model. The Radiation Model [5] was recently proposed as a parameter free mobility model in which individuals move and interact based on the population density of the source and destination regions, and that of the surrounding regions. Using the Radiation Model, the average flux between two regions i and j is:

$$T_{ij} = T_i \frac{m_i n_j}{(m_i + s_{i,j})(m_i + n_j + s_{i,j})}, \tag{5}$$

where i and j are origin and destination locations with populations m_i and n_j respectively, at distance $r_{i,j}$ from each other, with $s_{i,j}$ representing the total population in the circle of radius $r_{i,j}$ centered at i (excluding the source and destination population). T_i signifies the total outgoing flux that originates from region i. Since, our system represents a finite space (the regions and boundaries within a country), we subsequently normalize T_i by a factor of $(1 - \frac{m_i}{M})$ where M is the total sample population in the system [42].

Figure 5A shows the normalized MAPE comparison for the sub-tribal and administrative boundaries, and demonstrates that the MAPE for Gravity Model predictions made via administrative boundaries ranged from 150% to 230% higher than that of sub-tribal communities, while the Radiation Model also yielded 20% to 50% higher MAPE values for administrative boundaries. This indicates a higher accuracy (lower MAPE) produced when sub-tribal communities were used, as opposed to administrative boundaries. This subsequently suggests that, in terms of mobility patterns of Ivory Coast, it is more effective to model mobility on a partition that accounts for tribal, cultural, and lingual differences in groups of people, as opposed to the current administratively defined country partition.

We also partitioned the mobility model predictions according to intra-tribal and inter-tribal flux in order to quantify the *strength of the connectivity of the tribes*. Quantitatively, the MAPE for the inter-tribal mobility was 11.3% higher than the MAPE of the intra-tribal mobility predictions, and supports the dominant pattern of intra-tribal migrations over inter-tribal migration which may require special consideration in terms of mobility modeling. Again, the fact that the Radiation model produces more accurate results for migrations within a single tribe compared to those between tribes suggests that the tribes themselves are playing a key role in the overall improved accuracy of the model.

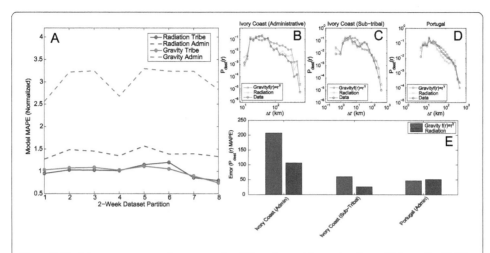

Figure 5 Model accuracy comparison across the different countries and regions. (A) *Normalized MAPE values* for Administrative and Tribal partitionings for Radiation and Gravity Model. The migration models for *Ivory Coast's administrative* **(B)** and *sub-tribal boundaries* **(C)**, as well as in *Portugal's administrative partitioning* **(D)** are also compared where each signal represents the probability of migration to a location 'r' kilometers away from the originating location. MAPE values for each model and partitioning to the respective data are shown in **(E)**.

Figures 5B-D compare the probability of migration predicted by both the Gravity and Radiation Models, to the actual migration percentages as computed from CDR data. While the CDR data is not the ground truth for migration, for example because it is a sample of the total population and is tracked only to the antenna level, it is also the basis for both models and thus represents a valid comparison for this study. As a more direct comparison of accuracy, Figure 5E provides the error (MAPE) for the models plotted in Figures 5B-D. For the Ivory Coast, these figures show the higher accuracy (i.e., lower error) of Radiation Model for both administrative and sub-tribal communities, and it shows that using the Radiation Model with sub-tribal communities provides the highest accuracy (i.e., lowest MAPE).

Figure 5D illustrates the Portuguese administrative municipality boundaries perform well for both the Radiation and Gravity Models. This may be indicative of municipal boundaries that were designed to align with cultural and social communities or that cultural and social communities have adapted to fit administrative boundaries.

However, we believe a more likely explanation is the growing homogeneity of language and culture that comes with maturing industrialization and urbanization. This is reflected in the predominance of Portuguese as the national language in Portugal, compared to the more than 60 local languages spoken in Ivory Coast.

There are several important implications from these findings.

1 Models of mobility, migration, and interaction that are conceptualized in mature and industrialized regions may not directly map to developing regions with more pronounced cultural and linguistic differences. Such models need to better account for these differences.

2 If administrative boundaries are drawn and services are placed based on models that do not accurately reflect these influences, results could include inefficiencies, leading to inequality of services (e.g., longer or less accessible commutes), and potentially discrimination and alienation of segments of the population.

3 Techniques for assessing the strength of borders in a given regional partitioning
   scheme are critical to ensuring the accuracy of mobility and migration modeling, and,
   perhaps more importantly, to enabling sound decision-making by authorities tasked
   with setting effective administrative boundaries.

In the following section, we propose novel techniques for quantifying the impact of a
regional partition scheme on model accuracy, and for assessing the strength of borders in
a given partitioning scheme.

Assessing regional affinities and border strength

In previous sections, we demonstrated the issues arising from using mobility models, such
as the Gravity and Radiation models, on regions where the partitioning scheme, such as
Ivory Coast administrative boundaries, does not reflect the regional affinities and border
strengths these models assume. We illustrated techniques to create more appropriate partitioning schemes, such as the tribal communities, and demonstrated the ability to achieve
higher accuracy mobility modeling using this improved partitioning.

However, it may not always be possible to simply re-draw borders. Instead, tools are
needed to assess the efficacy of an existing partitioning scheme, in terms of the affinities
within the identified borders and the strength of the borders.

In this section, we propose two novel techniques to address the above challenge. Firstly,
we present a metric to determine whether affinities exist within borders that may impact
the accuracy of mobility modeling. We test our metric on the tribal and administrative
boundaries used in the previous sections. Secondly, we propose a technique to assess the
strength of existing borders, and we demonstrate our technique on the existing administrative borders of Portugal and Ivory Coast. Our techniques use the same mobility data
used in previous sections and can be performed on any regional partitioning scheme, and
thus provide valuable tools to mobility researchers and to urban planners.

Regional affinity

The accuracy of both the Gravity Model and the Radiation Model depends on the ability to
accurately model, for a given time epoch, movement from any region to any other region,
and lack of movement to another region. Inter-region movements are driven by opportunities and resources, which are reflected in the population of region, and constrained
by distance. Intra-region affinities, such as physical proximity to home, work, family, and
friends, tend to limit movement from a given region. Improperly partitioning a region to
account these affinities results in over or under predicting flux, and therefore, poor model
performance.

We propose a metric to assess whether such affinities exist, and test that metric on the
tribal and administrative boundaries used in previous sections. To compute this metric, we
segregated all migrations into two categories: intra- and inter-regional migrations. Referring to Figure 3A, an inter-region migration is a migration that crosses a color boundary.
Likewise, an intra-region migration is a migration that does not cross a color boundary.
When a model over-predicts the number of inter-region migrations, it is under-estimating
the strength of the affinities within that region.

We use S to denote the bias of a regional partitioning to over or under estimate flux
across regional boundaries. We compute S as:

$$S = \frac{\sum_1^n \frac{R}{T}}{n},$$

(6)

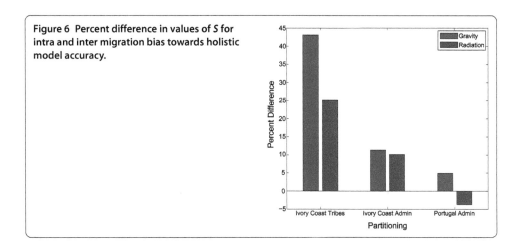

Figure 6 Percent difference in values of *S* for intra and inter migration bias towards holistic model accuracy.

where R is the modeled flux, T is the true flux, and n is the total number of predictions made. In other words, S represents the average ratio of modeled to predicted fluxes in the system. Therefore, relatively high values of S indicate the model is generally *over* predicting, while lower values indicate a general *under* prediction by the model. We compute separate S_{inter} and S_{intra} values, where the S_{inter} value includes only inter-region flux and S_{intra} includes only intra-region flux.

The percent difference (D) between S_{intra} and S_{inter} for all partitions provides a measure of bias. That is, the larger the value of D, the stronger the bias for over estimating inter-region flux. Figure 6 illustrates that both the Gravity and Radiation Models exhibited the most significant over estimation of inter region flux for Ivory Coast Tribes. Recall that significant over estimation of inter region flux is a result of significant under estimation of intra region affinities. Consistent with the results of previous sections, the administrative boundaries of both Portugal and Ivory Coast demonstrate substantially less bias. Thus our metric performs well in highlighting the strong affinities (in this case tribal), which must be accounted for in the model.

Border strength
Background

Just as human mobility may be constrained by affinities, it is similarly impacted by the strength of surrounding borders. Mobility models must accurately and succinctly reflect borders that may be physical, such as gates or other guards, or abstract, such as lack of opportunities. However, neither the Gravity Model nor the Radiation Model provide a means to assess border strength.

In this section, we propose a novel metric for assessing the strength of borders within a region. We demonstrate our metric by computing the strengths of the administrative borders of Portugal and Ivory Coast used in previous sections. As predicted by the Gravity and Radiation Models, we show that borders surrounding the heavily populated region of Abidjan are more penetrable than borders elsewhere in the Ivory Coast. Similarly, our results show that the borders throughout the country of Portugal are much more uniform, even showing consistency with the more heavily populated Lisbon. Our metric allows us to show that while these two cities, located in two very different regions, share a higher penetrability of borders than surrounding regions, they also exhibit significant differences in the distribution of border strength.

Methodology

To compute border strength, we start by defining the connectedness of each node (in our study, cell-tower) to each partition. The connectedness of node i to partition P is denoted by $C_{i,P}$, and computed as:

$$C_{i,P} = \frac{\sum_{\substack{j \in P \\ j \neq i}} (e_{i,j} + e_{j,i})}{S_i + T_i - 2m_{i,i}}, \tag{7}$$

where i and j are nodes, $w_{i,j}$ is the weighted directed matrix of human mobility, $m_{i,j} = \frac{w_{i,j}}{\sum w_{i,j}}$, $S_i = \sum_j m_{i,j}$, and $T_j = \sum_i m_{i,j}$. Finally, $e_{i,j} = m_{i,j} - S_i T_j$ is the difference between the actual number of migrations and the expected number of migrations from i to j.

For any given node i (located within partition P_i), if there exists a partition P_q ($i \neq q$) for which $C_{i,P_q} > C_{i,P_i}$ (i.e., node i is more strongly connected to partition P_q than to the partition in which it is located), then we say node i is not stable within partition P_i. We compute the stability of node i as s_i, where:

$$s_i = C_{i,P_i} - \max_{D \neq P_i} \{C_{i,D}\}. \tag{8}$$

Therefore, for any given node i, $-1 \leq s_i \leq 1$. Further, $s_i = 0$ indicates node i is as strongly connected to at least one partition other than the partition P_i to which it is assigned, and thus we say node i is not stable within the partition P_i it is located. Negative values of s_i indicate node i is more strongly connected to partitions other than the partition P_i to which it is assigned (i.e., the considered partitioning is not optimal in terms of the modularity score), and positive values of s_i indicate node i is more strongly connected to its assigned partition P_i.

Figure 7A illustrates the stability values (s_i) for each node (i.e., cell tower) in Ivory Coast, relative to the partitioning imposed by administrative borders, and colored on a logarithmic scale. By performing a linear interpolation of the s_i values across the entire map of Ivory Coast (Figure 7B), we obtain an estimate of the stability across the entire region. This linear interpolation assigns a stability measure to each pixel in the XY plane ($s_{x,y}$),

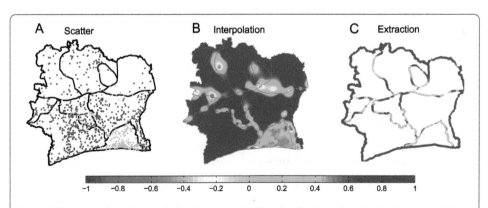

Figure 7 The procedure for calculating the strength of borders for Ivory Coast's tribal regions. Cell tower antennas are plotted on a map of the country and colored by their respective s_i value **(A)**. A two dimensional interpolation across the entire map is then performed **(B)** to estimate the s_i value at any point throughout the country. The pixels that subsequently lie along the tribal borders are then extracted and visualized **(C)**.

and thus enables us to compute a border strength metric for a given border as the mean of the stability values of the pixels that directly lie on that border (Figure 7C). We denote the border strength metric of any given border b as s_b. Thus $s_b = \text{mean}(s_{x_b,y_b})$ where (x_b, y_b) are all coordinates of pixels that lay on a border.

Note also that by computing s_b from the linearly interpolated values across the entire region, our approach enables a border strength metric that reflects the aggregate impact of cells that are not well connected, even if those cells are not physically close to borders.

Analysis

In addition to providing a single border strength metric by which any border may be assessed, our method enables analysis of the distribution of stability values ($s_{x,y}$) for each border. Figures 8A-D illustrate how significantly more penetrable borders surrounding the densely populated Abidjan are in comparison to other portions of the country. This higher penetrability of borders surrounding Abidjan holds for both tribal (Figure 8A) in comparison to the remainder of tribal borders (Figure 8B). This effect is again prominent with the administrative border surrounding Abidjan (Figure 8C) relative to the rest of the country (Figure 8D). Furthermore, Figure 8A illustrates the mean positive penetrability ($\overline{s_b}$) of 0.2847 for the borders surrounding Abidjan, versus 0.4767 for borders throughout the rest of Ivory Coast (Figure 8B). Also note that penetrability in Abidjan is markedly higher than in the remainder of Ivory Coast, whereas the Lisbon borders (Figures 8E-F) are only marginally less penetrable than in the remainder of Portugal. This supports our ear-

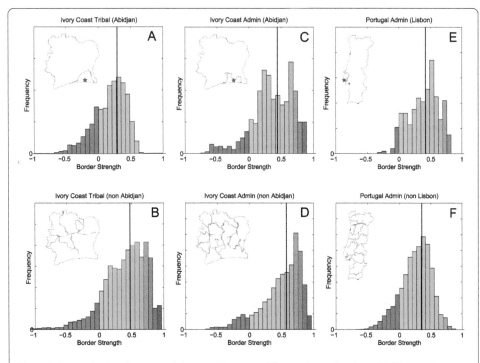

Figure 8 Strength of node connectivity visually mapped from values of s_i along (A)-(B) *Ivory Coast Tribal*; (C)-(D) *Ivory Coast Administrative*; and (E)-(F) *Portuguese Administrative* boundaries. Border categories are separated according to whether they contain the main city of the respective country (i.e., (A) & (C) *Abidjan, Ivory Coast* and (E) *Lisbon, Portugal*). Histograms display the distribution of the border strength values along the border(s). Black vertical lines are indicative of the mean positive border strength value.

lier finding that mobility in Portugal is much more uniform throughout the entire country compared to the Ivorian Coast context.

The distributions illustrated in Figure 8 also provide interesting insights into mobility in Ivory Coast and Portugal. More specifically, notice the tight clustering of border strengths for Abidjan under the Tribal partitioning (Figure 8A) versus more widely distributed border strength values for the rest of Ivory Coast. This supports our early findings that Tribal boundaries play a key role in mobility throughout the country, except in highly industrialized regions such as Abidjan.

Conclusion

Africa is a continent that has been shaped by human migration over tens of thousands of years. Indeed, migrations within and beyond the African borders have recently been shown as influencing all civilizations as we know them. However, until recently, there has been a dearth of data on the forms and patterns of migration within the nations of Africa. Moreover, much of the mobility research is based on theories that have emerged from highly industrialized nations and lack validation in the context of developing environments.

Our study has demonstrated that many of these conceptions are not necessarily applicable in the African context. We have made these differences clear by comparing our findings in Ivory Coast to one such industrialized nation, Portugal. For example, we have shown that the probability of displacement during normal commuting hours in Portugal is often nearly double that of Ivory Coast for the same time of day. Similarly, average distances traveled by commuters in Portugal is nearly double that of commuters in Ivory Coast.

While differences in the likelihood of travel and average distance travel can be attributed to quantitative differences in infrastructural support for mobility this already strongly affects the whole mobility picture leading to a number of quantitative dissimilarities. Our study shows evidence of more fundamental differences in infrastructural support for mobility, such as tribal, cultural, and lingual differences. In addition, we demonstrate that the similarity between administrative boundaries and communities detected in mobile phone data is markedly lower in Ivory Coast than in Portugal.

By identifying the tribal influence on mobility in the Ivory Coast, we were able to illuminate further differences in mobility patterns. For example, we were able to show intra-tribal migrations were much more frequent than that of inter-tribal migrations over the same distance and therefore are under or overestimated by the models. Taking this into account by exploiting our tribally aligned communities for the mobility models drastically improves modeling of human mobility in Ivory Coast. We validated this higher accuracy by computing the MAPE across all data points for both models, and found a 20% to 50% higher error for the models using administrative boundaries. We also validated our results by computing the distribution of migrations by distance migrated and found that by using this sub-tribal method of spatial units definition in modeling human mobility we were able to improve the accuracy of the models so drastically, that the Ivory Coast performed even better than its developed country-counterpart, Portugal.

We propose novel techniques for assessing the strength of borders within a regional partitioning scheme, and for assessing the impact of inappropriate partitioning on model accuracy. Our results offer improved insights on why models developed for mature and stable regions may not translate well to developing regions, and provide tools for urban planners and data scientists to address these deficiencies.

We believe that the findings of this study demonstrate important differences that exist between developing and industrialized regions. Using these two countries as an example, we are motivated to further explore these differences by considering more countries and areas with diverse cultural, economical and social backgrounds.

Competing interests
The authors declare that they have no competing interests.

Authors' contributions
The main idea of the paper was proposed by SS and CR. SS and AA designed the research steps. AA prepared the manuscript initially and performed the key steps of the research. KK and CK participated in performing research steps. All authors read and approved the final manuscript.

Acknowledgements
The authors wish to thank Orange and D4D Challenge for providing the datasets used throughout this study. We further thank Ericsson, the MIT SMART Program, the Center for Complex Engineering Systems (CCES) at KACST and MIT CCES program, the National Science Foundation, the MIT Portugal Program, the AT&T Foundation, Audi Volkswagen, BBVA, The Coca Cola Company, Expo 2015, Ferrovial, The Regional Municipality of Wood Buffalo and all the members of the MIT SENSEable City Lab Consortium for supporting the research.

References

1. Robertson C, Sawford K, Daniel SL, Nelson TA, Stephen C (2010) Mobile phone-based infectious disease surveillance system, Sri Lanka. Emerg Infect Dis 16(10):1524
2. Gonzalez MC, Hidalgo CA, Barabasi A-L (2008) Understanding individual human mobility patterns. Nature 453(7196):779-782
3. Ratti C, Williams S, Frenchman D, Pulselli R (2006) Mobile landscapes: using location data from cell phones for urban analysis. Environ Plan B, Plan Des 33(5):727
4. Reades J, Calabrese F, Ratti C (2009) Eigenplaces: analysing cities using the space-time structure of the mobile phone network. Environ Plan B, Plan Des 36(5):824-836
5. Simini F, González MC, Maritan A, Barabási A-L (2012) A universal model for mobility and migration patterns. Nature 484(7392):96-100
6. Kang C, Sobolevsky S, Liu Y, Ratti C (2013) Exploring human movements in singapore: a comparative analysis based on mobile phone and taxicab usages. In: Proceedings of the 2nd ACM SIGKDD international workshop on urban computing. ACM, New York, p 1
7. Blondel VD, Esch M, Chan C, Clerot F, Deville P, Huens E, Morlot F, Smoreda Z, Ziemlicki C (2012) Data for development: the d4d challenge on mobile phone data. Preprint arXiv:1210.0137
8. Eagle N (2008) Behavioral inference across cultures: using telephones as a cultural lens. IEEE Intell Syst 23(4):62-64
9. Eagle N, de Montjoye Y, Bettencourt LM (2009) Community computing: comparisons between rural and urban societies using mobile phone data. In: International conference on computational science and engineering, vol 4, 2009. CSE'09, pp 144-150, IEEE
10. Ahas R, Aasa A, Mark Ü, Pae T, Kull A (2007) Seasonal tourism spaces in Estonia: case study with mobile positioning data. Tour Manag 28(3):898-910
11. Berlingerio M, Calabrese F, Di Lorenzo G, Nair R, Pinelli F, Sbodio ML (2013) Allaboard: a system for exploring urban mobility and optimizing public transport using cellphone data. In: Proceedings of the third international conference on the analysis of mobile phone datasets (NetMob)
12. Liu F, Janssens D, Wets G, Cools M (2013) Profiling workers' activity-travel behavior based on mobile phone data. In: Proceedings of the third international conference on the analysis of mobile phone datasets (NetMob)
13. Zilske M, Nagel K (2013) Building a minimal traffic model from mobile phone data. In: Proceedings of the third international conference on the analysis of mobile phone datasets (NetMob)
14. Naboulsi D, Fiore M, Stanica R et al(2013) Human mobility flows in the city of Abidjan. In: 3rd international conference on the analysis of mobile phone datasets
15. Yan X-Y, Zhao C, Wang W (2013) Predicting human mobility patterns in cities. In: 3rd international conference on the analysis of mobile phone datasets
16. AfriPop: Cote D'Ivoire. http://www.clas.ufl.edu/users/atatem/index_files/CIV.htm
17. Portal do Instituto Nacional de Estatística. http://www.ine.pt
18. Voronoï G (1908) Nouvelles applications des paramètres continus à la théorie des formes quadratiques. Deuxième mémoire. Recherches sur les parallélloèdres primitifs. J Reine Angew Math 134:198-287
19. Ratti C, Sobolevsky S, Calabrese F, Andris C, Reades J, Martino M, Claxton R, Strogatz SH (2010) Redrawing the map of Great Britain from a network of human interactions. PLoS ONE 5(12):14248
20. Expert P, Evans TS, Blondel VD, Lambiotte R (2011) Uncovering space-independent communities in spatial networks. Proc Natl Acad Sci USA 108(19):7663-7668
21. Calabrese F, Dahlem D, Gerber A, Paul D, Chen X, Rowland J, Rath C, Ratti C (2011) The connected states of America: quantifying social radii of influence. In: 2011 IEEE third international conference on privacy, security, risk and trust (passat) and 2011 IEEE third international conference on social computing (socialcom), pp 223-230. IEEE
22. Sobolevsky S, Szell M, Campari R, Couronné T, Smoreda Z, Ratti C (2013) Delineating geographical regions with networks of human interactions in an extensive set of countries. PLoS ONE 8(12):81707

23. Sobolevsky S (2013) Digitale ansätze für eine regionale abgrenzung. In: Offenhuber D, Ratti C (eds) Die stadt entschlüsseln: wie echtzeitdaten den urbanismus verändern, Bauwelt fundamente, vol 150. Birkhäuser, Basel
24. Newman ME (2006) Modularity and community structure in networks. Proc Natl Acad Sci USA 103(23):8577-8582
25. Blondel VD, Guillaume J-L, Lambiotte R, Lefebvre E (2008) Fast unfolding of communities in large networks. J Stat Mech Theory Exp 2008(10):10008
26. Le Martelot E, Hankin C (2011) Multi-scale community detection using stability as optimisation criterion in a greedy algorithm. In: KDIR, pp 216-225
27. Newman ME (2006) Finding community structure in networks using the eigenvectors of matrices. Phys Rev E 74(3):036104
28. Lancichinetti A, Fortunato S (2009) Community detection algorithms: a comparative analysis. Phys Rev E 80(5):056117
29. Sobolevsky S, Campari R, Belyi A, Ratti C (2013) A general optimization technique for high quality community detection in complex networks. Preprint arXiv:1308.3508
30. Wallace DL (1983) Comment. J Am Stat Assoc 78(383):569-576
31. Rand WM (1971) Objective criteria for the evaluation of clustering methods. J Am Stat Assoc 66(336):846-850
32. Jaccard P (1901) Étude comparative de la distribution florale dans une portion des alpes et des jura. Bull Soc Vaud Sci Nat 37:547-579
33. Fowlkes EB, Mallows CL (1983) A method for comparing two hierarchical clusterings. J Am Stat Assoc 78(383):553-569
34. Heckerman D, Meila M (1998) An experimental comparison of several clustering and initialization methods. Technical report, Citeseer
35. Hubert L, Arabie P (1985) Comparing partitions. J Classif 2(1):193-218
36. Larsen B, Aone C (1999) Fast and effective text mining using linear-time document clustering. In: Proceedings of the fifth ACM SIGKDD international conference on knowledge discovery and data mining. ACM, New York, pp 16-22
37. Onnela J-P, Arbesman S, González MC, Barabási A-L, Christakis NA (2011) Geographic constraints on social network groups. PLoS ONE 6(4):16939
38. Cote d'Ivoire - Encyclopedia Britannica Academic Edition Inc. http://www.britannica.com/EBchecked/topic/139651/Cote-dIvoire
39. Swanson DA, Tayman J, Bryan T (2011) Mape-r: a rescaled measure of accuracy for cross-sectional subnational population forecasts. J Popul Res 28(2-3):225-243
40. Ravenstein EG (1885) The laws of migration. J Stat Soc 48(2):167-235
41. Tayman J, Swanson DA (1999) On the validity of mape as a measure of population forecast accuracy. Popul Res Policy Rev 18(4):299-322
42. Masucci AP, Serras J, Johansson A, Batty M (2013) Gravity versus radiation models: on the importance of scale and heterogeneity in commuting flows. Phys Rev E 88(2):022812

7

Modeling dynamics of attention in social media with user efficiency

Carmen Vaca Ruiz[1,3]*, Luca Maria Aiello[2] and Alejandro Jaimes[2]

*Correspondence:
cvaca@fiec.espol.edu.ec
[1] Politecnico di Milano, Piazza Leonardo Da Vinci, 32, Milan, Italy
[3] FIEC, Escuela Superior Politecnica del Litoral, Campus Gustavo Galindo, Km 30.5 via Perimetral, Guayaquil, Ecuador
Full list of author information is available at the end of the article

Abstract

Evolution of online social networks is driven by the need of their members to share and consume content, resulting in a complex interplay between individual activity and attention received from others. In a context of increasing information overload and limited resources, discovering which are the most successful behavioral patterns to attract attention is very important. To shed light on the matter, we look into the patterns of activity and popularity of users in the Yahoo Meme microblogging service. We observe that a combination of different type of social and content-producing activity is necessary to attract attention and the efficiency of users, namely the average attention received per piece of content published, for many users has a defined trend in its temporal footprint. The analysis of the user time series of efficiency shows different classes of users whose different activity patterns give insights on the type of behavior that pays off best in terms of attention gathering. In particular, sharing content with high spreading potential and then supporting the attention raised by it with social activity emerges as a frequent pattern for users gaining efficiency over time.

Keywords: online attention; microblogging; social networks; time series

1 Introduction

Understanding users' activities in social media platforms, in terms of the actions they take and how those actions affect the attention they receive (e.g., comments, replies, re-posts of messages they post, etc.), is crucial for understanding the dynamics of social media systems as well as for designing incentives that lead to growth in terms of user activity and number of users. As expected, given the nature of such platforms, users who receive attention from their peers tend to be more engaged with the service and are less likely to churn out [1]. Insights on the kinds of actions that users take to gain more attention and become "popular" are therefore important because they can help explain how social media platforms evolve. In spite of the importance of analyzing such behavior at a large scale, the dynamics of attention are not well understood. This is largely due to two main reasons: on one hand that there are few datasets that show the evolution of a network from its very beginnings, and on the other hand, because most work has focused on the popularity of content rather than on analyzing the effects of user's behaviors on how other users react to them. For example, there have been many studies to establish the reasons behind user or item popularity in social networks (e.g., [2, 3]), but the effects that the patterns of attention received have on the activity and the engagement of the "average" users have not been thoroughly explored so far.

In this paper, we address questions that focus on social media users' behavior at different stages of their participation in social media platforms. In particular, we introduce a new way to examine attention dynamics, and from this perspective perform a deep analysis of the evolution of user activity and attention in a social network from its beginning until the service ceased to exist. Analyzing the weekly efficiency, i.e. the amount of attention received in the platform normalized by the amount of content produced, we observe that 56% of the users in the dataset exhibit a footprint of their efficiency with a clearly defined trend (i.e., sharply increasing/decreasing or peaking). We are able to extract patterns of user behavior from these temporal footprints that reveal differences in the activity behavior of users of different classes. We focus our analysis on Yahoo Meme, a microblogging service that was launched by Yahoo in 2009 and discontinued in 2012. While the mechanisms of interaction in Yahoo Meme were similar to those found in other social media platforms, to the best of our knowledge, this is the first study that examines in detail the questions we are addressing from the perspective of user efficiency, using data from a service from its initial launch.

The main contributions of this work include:

- Study of the attention dynamics in social networks from the angle of *efficiency*, namely the ratio between attention received and activity performed. The notion of efficiency in time allows to detect patterns that could not emerge using other raw popularity or activity indicators.
- Definition of a method to classify noisy time series of user-generated events. The method is successfully used to find classes of users based on the time series of their efficiency scores, with an accuracy ranging from 0.85 to 0.93, depending on the different classes.
- Extraction of insights useful to detect and prevent user churn. For instance, exploration of the efficiency time series reveals that increase in efficiency is determined by creation of high-quality content, but the acquired attention has to be sustained with additional social activity to keep the efficiency high. If such social exchange is missing, attention received drops very quickly.

2 Related work

Much effort has been spent lately in measuring the effect that the activity of content production and sharing has in influencing the actions of social media participants. Depending on whether the investigation adopts the perspective of the *user* who is sharing or of the *content* being shared, emphasis has been given to the characterization of either the influential users or the process of information spreading along social connections.

Different methods to identify influentials, namely individuals who seed viral information cascades, have been proposed recently [4], and it has been observed that simple measures such as the raw number of social connections are not good predictors of influence potential [5–7]. Instead, the ease of propagation of a piece of content is correlated with many other features, including the position of the content creator in the social network [8], demographic factors [9, 10], and the sentiment conveyed in the message [11].

For what concerns content-centered analysis, much attention has been devoted to the study of the structure and diffusion speed of information cascades in social and news media [12–14], including Yahoo Meme [14, 15]. Weng *et al.* [14] for instance have shown that triadic closure helps to explain the link formation in early stages of the user's lifetime but later in time it is the information flow the driver for new connections. Despite the difficulty of determining whether observed cascades are generated by a real influence effect [16] (unless performing controlled experiments [17]), the role of influence in social network dynamics is widely recognized, albeit not fully understood. Factors related to influence include geolocation, visibility of the content, or exogenous factors like major geopolitical or news events for news media [18–20].

Patterns of temporal variation of popularity have been investigated previously, mostly focusing on the attention given to pieces of user-generated content. Previous work includes characterization of the peakness and saturation of video popularity on YouTube in relation to content visibility [18], crowd productivity dependence on the attention gathered by videos [1], the classification of bursty Twitter hashtags in relation to topic detection tasks [21], and the clustering of hashtag popularity histograms based on their shape [22]. Time series has been used to predict popularity in blogs, where the early reactions of the crowd to a piece of content is strongly correlated to the expected overall popularity [3, 23].

In this work we focus on users as opposed to content and we analyze time series of a metric combining the user activity and the attention received. We do not focus on the popularity gained at a global scale, but instead we characterize temporal patterns of activity and attention of each individual. We show that time series of individual user activity cannot be clustered accurately based on their shapes by state-of-the art methods, so we propose an algorithm to fix that. Finally, except in rare cases (e.g., [24]), previous work on network analysis has relied mostly on limited temporal snapshots. In contrast, we use the temporal data of the entire life-span of Meme, from its release date until its shutdown.

3 Dataset description

Meme was a microblogging service launched by Yahoo in April 2009 and discontinued in May 2012. Users could *post* messages, receive notifications of posts published by people they *follow* (follower ties are *directed* social connections), and *repost* messages of other users or *comment* on those messages. The overall number of registered users grew at a constant pace, up to almost $700K$. When neglecting uninvolved users (i.e., users who were registered, but stopped explicit activity), we observe a growing trend up to a maximum of $60K$ users around the end of the first year, and then a slow but steady decline. In Table 1 we report general statistics on the follower network in the last week of the service. The final network contains a well-connected core of users resulting in a greatest connected component covering almost the full network, with a high clustering coefficient. As already observed for other online social networks, the average path length is proportional to $\log\log(N)$, and similarly to other news media the level of social link reciprocity is very low [25].

Table 1 Followers network statistics

Nodes	Edges	Density	$\langle k \rangle$	$\langle k_{in} \rangle$	GWCC$_\%$	Reciprocity	$\langle d \rangle$	d_{max}	C
568K	20M	$6.2 \cdot 10^{-5}$	71	35	0.996	0.096	2.59	11	0.433

Δ = density, GWCC$_\%$ = relative size of the greatest weakly connected component, d = geodesic distance, C = clustering coefficient.

4 Activity vs. attention

Activity and attention are the two dimensions we aim to examine with our study. After defining the features, we look at their relationship in terms of correlations of their raw indicators and then we study them from a novel perspective by defining a metric of user efficiency. We find that very efficient users tend to write fewer posts per week but are heavily involved in social activities such as commenting.

4.1 Activity and attention metrics

We define *activity* and *attention* indicators that are computed for every user. Activity indicators are measured by the number of posts (pd), reposts (rd), and comments done (cd), or by the number of new followees added ($fwee$), while attention is determined by the number of reposts (rr) ot comments received (cr) from others, and by the number of new incoming follower links (fw). Reposts received can be *direct* or *indirect* (i.e., reposting a repost). To measure attention we consider direct reposts.

The possibility of indirect reposting originates repost *cascades* that can be modeled as trees rooted in the original post and whose descendants are the direct (depth 1) and indirect (depth 2 to the leaves) reposts. Besides being another attention indicator, the cascade size (cs) is a good proxy for the *perceived interestingness* of the content because, intuitively, sharing a piece of content originated by someone who is not directly linked through a social tie, and therefore is likely to be unknown to the reposter, implies a higher likelihood that the reposter was interested in that piece content. Therefore, we consider the cascade size as a measure of content interestingness.

Even though several measure of influence, authoritativeness, or more in general importance of a user in a networked system have been developed in the past (see for instance the work by Romero *et al.* [7]), here we adopt the perspective of a single user, rather than of the whole community. Therefore, we are going to interpret the system as a black box that receives input from a user (activity) and returns some output (attention), without considering the actual effect that the input causes inside the system. Although this is a simplification, it allows us to better focus on the user dimension and to cluster users with respect to the perception they get from the interaction with the system (i.e., attention in exchange for activity).

4.2 Correlations

When dealing with multidimensional behavioral data, detecting causation between events can be difficult [16], but potential mechanisms driving the interactions between the different dimensions at play can be spotted through the investigation of correlations [26]. In this case, the correlations between activity and attention metrics give a first hint about the potential payoff of some user actions in terms of attention received.

In Figure 1, visual clues of the relationship between different metrics of activity and attention are shown in the form of heatmaps. The four plots on the left display the average values of attention indicators for users whose number of posts and comments resides in given ranges. To make sure that the trends emerging from the heatmaps are significant, we count the number of users falling in each of the range buckets. In Table 2 we report the average and the median number of users in each bucket of the heatmaps. As expected from the broad distributions of the activity and attention indicators, few actors have very high values for some pairs of indicators. For instance, in the heatmap in Figure 1(E), just

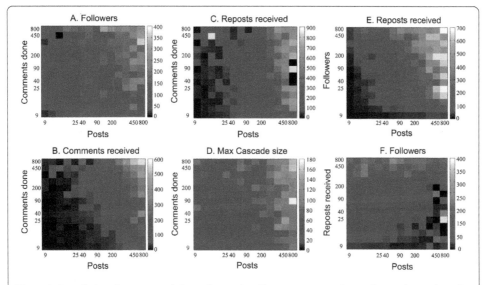

Figure 1 Correlations between activity and attention. Users were grouped according to the number of x and y values (plotted on a log scale) and, for each group, the average number of the z-value was calculated and mapped to a color intensity.

Table 2 Statistics for the number of users considered in each bucket of the heatmaps depicting the correlations between activity and popularity metrics (Figure 1)

x-axis	y-axis	Average	Median
Posts	Reposts received	73.1	39
Posts	Comments done	77.9	32
Posts	Followers	74.3	45

The average and median number of users per bucket in each combination of metrics is shown.

10 users are in the upper-right bucket (users with > 625 posts *and* and > 625 followers). However, in general the number of users per bucket is sufficiently high to consider the trend statistically significant, as shown by Table 2.

First, we observe that attention in terms of followers and comments (Figures 1(A)-(B)) is correlated with both number of posts and comments done, resulting in a color gradient becoming brighter when transitioning from the lower-left corner to the upper-right one. Users who gained more followers were heavier content producers and an even more evident correlation is found when considering comments received (Figure 1(B)), likely due to a comment reciprocity tendency (we calculated the comment reciprocity being around 24%, much higher than reciprocity in the follower network). We observe a partially similar effect when looking at content-centered indicators, namely the reposts received and the cascade size (Figures 1(C)-(D)). In these cases we find a positive correlation with the number of posts, but not with the amount of comments, suggesting that social interaction, such as commenting on other people posts, does not strongly characterize content propagation.

The two plots on the right of Figure 1 show the relation between pairs of attention metrics with the number of posts. From Figure 1(E) we learn that social exposure (i.e., being followed) and productivity (i.e., number of posts) are both heavily correlated with the number of reposts. However, people with moderate or heavy posting activity can reach a high level of attention even having a relatively small audience (as shown by the bright colors extending down along the right side of the map). This intuition is confirmed by the fact that swapping the axes of the two attention measures, the correlation is disrupted (Figure 1(F)), meaning that people with high number of posts and reposts do not necessarily have a large number of followers.

4.3 User efficiency

The above findings support on one hand the intuitive principle about: "the more you give, the more you get" and, on the other hand, they reinforce the hypothesis that visibility is not enough to grant a wide diffusion of content (similarly to the "million follower fallacy" in the context of Twitter [6]). However, the user perception of the interaction with peers through an online system is not dependent just by the raw number of feedback actions received, but also by the amount of attention in relation with the effort spent to gain it. Given this perspective, we define the *efficiency* η of a user u in a given time frame $[t_i, t_j]$ as the amount of attention received over the amount of activity performed between t_i and t_j, for any pair of activity (*Act*) and attention (*Att*) metrics:

$$\eta_u^{Act,Att}(t_i, t_j) = \frac{\sum_{t_i}^{t_j} Att_u}{\sum_{t_i}^{t_j} Act_u}. \tag{1}$$

Analogous definitions have been used in different disciplines such as physics and economics [27], and in most of the cases the efficiency is upper bounded to 1, i.e., the outcome from the system cannot exceed the energy given in input. On the contrary, in a social media setting the efficiency is unbounded and it constitutes an objective function to maximize in order to increase the engagement of the user base. Even if comments can be strong indicators of involved user participation, the main focus of the online service under study is posting and reposting, similarly to Twitter. Therefore we always consider the number of posts as the metric of activity in the efficiency formula. In the above definition (Formula (1)) we assume that the attention that we take into account should be the one that is directly triggered by the activity considered, we use either the number of reposts ($\eta_u^{Post,Repost}$) or the number of comments ($\eta_u^{Post,Comm}$) as proxies for attention received, since other metrics such as number of followers are not necessarily responses to the posting activity.

The distribution of $\eta_u^{Post,Repost}$ and $\eta_u^{Post,Comm}$ for all the users during the complete lifetime of the network is drawn in Figure 2. Even if the maximum efficiency scores span up to several hundreds, the majority of users have an efficiency lower than 1, and most of them

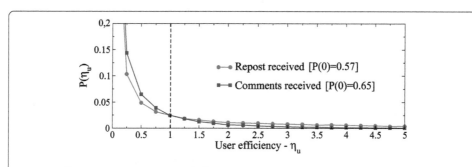

Figure 2 Efficiency scores. Distribution of efficiency scores, bucketed in 0.25-wide bins. Average scores are 0.38 for comments and 1.55 for reposts.

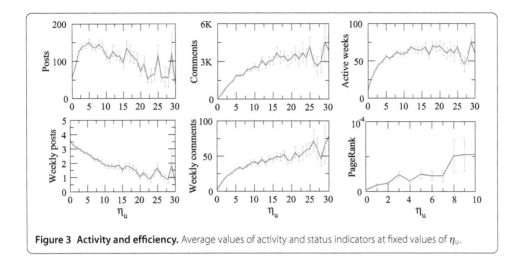

Figure 3 Activity and efficiency. Average values of activity and status indicators at fixed values of η_u.

have values close to zero. The average over the η_u values of all users is higher than 1 for reposts and much lower for comments. This is justified by the fact that Meme emphasized especially the repost feature. For this reason, next we consider only the efficiency of posts in relation to reposts, and we refer to it as η_u, for simplicity.

High activity is usually indicative of poor efficiency or, in other words, activity alone is not indicative of high potential of attention gain. To study more in depth the traits of efficient and inefficient users, we describe users with different η_u values according to several activity and status features, as shown in Figure 3.

Insightful patterns emerge. First, the higher the η_u, the lower the activity in terms of number of posts, but not in the range $0 \leq \eta_u \leq 5$ (containing most of the users), in which the number of posts grows with η_u. However, when looking at the average number of posts submitted per week instead, the trend becomes monotonic, confirming the theory about the limited attention of the audience being a barrier for attention gathering [20]. Second, the higher the η_u, the higher the amount of comments: the more efficient users are the ones who comment the most. Finally, the longevity of the profile and the prestige on the follower network (computed with standard PageRank) are also distinctive features of efficient users.

5 Evolution of efficiency in time

Attention attracted by users, and by consequence their efficiency, is not constant in time. It depends on the amount of activity, the position in the network and other factors. However next we show that, even if many users exhibit a oscillating but globally stable values of efficiency in time, more than half the users show sharp variations in their efficiency time series, that tell more about the activity behavior in different periods of the user lifetime. First, we give the definition of efficiency time series. Then, we explain the algorithm used to classify users efficiency traces according to the shape of their trend and discuss the properties of the four classes we found. We (i) find that state-of-the-art algorithms for clustering of timeseries do not perform well on the noisy traces such the ones generated by human activity, therefore, based on the observed shapes, (ii) we propose a new classification method and evaluate it against a human-curated ground truth, and (iii) we analyze the differences between user behaviors in the four main user efficiency classes around the main changepoint of the efficiency curve.

5.1 Efficiency time series definition

By adapting the efficiency formula for a discrete-time scenario, we model the temporal efficiency evolution using weekly time series for each user u measuring the efficiency η_u after each week. The elements of the series are generated as follows:

$$\eta_u(t_i) = \frac{rr(p_{t_i})}{|p_{t_i}|}, \quad t_i \in T_u = \{t_1, \ldots, t_n\},$$

where p_{t_i} represents the set of posts published by user u on week t_i, $rr(p_{t_i})$ is the total number of direct reposts received in the user's lifetime for the set of posts p_{t_i}, and T_u is the sorted list of weeks in which the user u published at least one post.

5.2 Time series type detection

Characterizing users based on the exhibited temporal behavior of their efficiency requires to extract automatically patterns out of the generated time series. There are two main families of state-of-the art methods for this task. The first one includes *feature-based* approaches that cluster series based on their kurtosis, skewness, trend, and chaos [28]. The latter one includes *area-under-the-curve* methods [29–31] that consist into dividing the time series into equally sized fragments, measure the area under the curve in each fragment, represent the time series as a vector of such quantities, and then apply a clustering algorithm over them (specifically, we used k-means). We first tried those state-of-the art methods to cluster the efficiency time series. We do not report extensively the results obtained for the sake of brevity, but both feature-based approaches area-under-the-curve methods produce clusters containing extremely heterogeneous curves, as we assessed by manual inspection. In addition to that, we tried also a separate approach, proposed few years ago, that transforms the curves through Piecewise Aggregate Approximation and Symbolic Aggregate Approximation and then clusters the resulting representations with k-means [32]. Also this method lead to very imbalanced clusters, being the 99% of curves put in one single cluster. The main issue with those approaches is that they have been tested in the past mainly on synthetic time series. When time series represent the activity of single actors they may have an extremely broad variety of length, shapes, and oscillation of the curve that the mentioned methods are not able to handle properly.

Even though the produced clusters were very noisy, the area-under-the-curve method tended to group together curves in four main clusters, with a predominance of well-recognizable shapes: *increasing, decreasing, peaky* and *steady*. Some examples of time series for each class are depicted in Figure 4 (top). Driven by the qualitative insights that the clustering produced, we developed a tailored classification algorithm to obtain cleaner groups, based on a qualitative, discrete representation of the temporal data, inspired by the representation of financial time series presented by Lee *et al.* [33]. Our algorithm executes the following steps:

1. *Smoothing.* Apply the kernel regression estimator of Nadaraya and Watson [34] to the user temporal data to obtain a smoothed time series t. The smoothing process gets rid of very sharp and punctual fluctuations, which are very frequent in human activity time series. Examples of raw curves compared to their smoothed versions are shown in Figure 4 (bottom).

2. *Linguistic transform.* Generate a qualitative representation of the time series t for a user u using three states: High, Medium, Low (H, M, L). We empirically set the

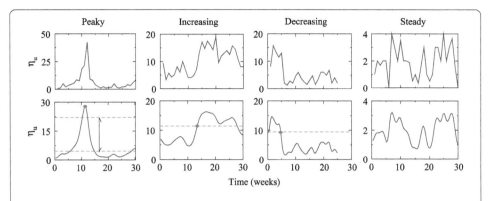

Figure 4 Time series examples for each class. Examples of efficiency time series for users of each class indicated by the clustering of time series. Top: raw time series, bottom: smoothed Time series. Threshold used to detect changepoints for the first three types are reported with dashed lines.

threshold for high values to 0.6 and for medium values to 0.3 (i.e., values greater than the 60% of the maximum efficiency reached by the user are considered High). The idea of using threshold values is supported by previous work in time-series segmentation [35].

3. *Fluctuation reduction.* Search for contiguous subsequences of a given state and drop the subsequences whose length is less than the 10% of the total length. Similarly to the smoothing procedure, this step helps to eliminate noisy fluctuations in the time series. For example, in the series *HHHMHHHMMMLLL*, the fourth element, *M* is dropped.

4. *String collapsing.* Collapse the string representation of *t* by replacing subsequences of the same state with a single symbol of the same type. For instance, the resulting series from the previous example, *HHHHHMMMMLLL*, is transformed to *HML*.

5. *Detection of Increasing/Decreasing classes.* Look for collapsed sequences with just two groups of symbols and classify as "Increasing" a sequence transitioning from *L* or *M* to the state *H* and as "Decreasing" those transitioning from *H* to *L* or *M*. The second and third columns in Figure 4 show the threshold for High values as a dotted red line.

6. *Detection of Peaky class.* For the unclassified series, find those exhibiting a peaky shape by looking at outliers in the series whose value is higher than *x* times the average value. This method has been successfully used before in the context of Twitter, with *x* = 5 [21]. Other methods for peak detection we tested [36] find just local peaks, which are very frequent in noisy time series.

7. *Detection of changepoint.* Accurately locating the point in which a curve transitions between different levels is important to study the behavior of users in their single activity and popularity metrics around the point in time when these changes occur [37]. For the peak type curves, the changepoint is intuitively defined by the highest peak, whereas for the increasing and decreasing types the point is identified by the time in which the linguistic representation of the series transitions from *H* to *M* or *L* status (decreasing) or from *L* or *M* to *H* status (increasing). For the sake of comparison, we match our simple technique with the statistical change point analysis recently proposed by Chen *et al.* [38]. We find that, although for most time series the values from the two methods were very close (at most 1 or 2 weeks difference in

around 80% of the cases), the statistical changepoint detection often identifies points right before or right after a change of efficiency.

8. *Detection of Steady class.* The remaining time series are classified as steady.

As in most previous work [39], in absence of an automatic way to compute the quality of the classes, two of the authors annotated a random sample of 1,000 time series per class to assess the goodness of our algorithm. Since the expected shapes of the curves for each class are very clear (see examples in Figure 4) a human evaluator can decide with certainty whether the instances from the sample match the expected template. The outcome of the labeling is very encouraging, with 93% correct instances in the Decreasing class, 86% in the Increasing, and 85% in Peak, and almost perfect agreement between evaluators (Fleiss $\kappa = 0.80$). For the Steady class, where shapes can vary much, we labeled as *misclassified* any curve belonging to the other classes. We found a low portion of *misclassifed* instances (12%). We observe that the users in the steady class are around 44%, meaning that 56% of the users exhibit a temporal footprint of the efficiency curve that has a clearly defined trend. This is a finding with important implications on the applicative side, meaning that the majority of users could be accurately profiled as having consistently increasing or decreasing efficiency patterns.

5.3 Changepoint detection

Accurately locating the point in which a curve transitions between different levels is important to characterize the user behavior when his efficiency significantly increases or drops, thus allowing to study how single activity and popularity metrics vary when these changes occur [37]. Changepoint detection refers to the problem of finding time instants where abrupt changes occur [37]. Except for the steady time series, which denote a user behavior that is quite constant in time (or for which transition to higher or lower efficiency levels are much slower), all the other three types have a changepoint in which the efficiency trend changes radically in a relatively short period of time compared to the total length of the user lifetime. For the peak type curves, the changepoint is intuitively defined by the highest peak, whereas for the increasing and decreasing types the point is identified by the time in which the linguistic representation of the series transitions from H or M to L status (decreasing) or from L or M to H status (increasing). More general methods to identify changepoints relying on the changes in mean and variance have been proposed in the past. For the sake of comparison, we match our simple technique with the statistical change point analysis recently proposed by Chen *et al.* [38]. We find that, although for most time series the values from the two methods were very close (at most 1 or 2 weeks difference in around 80% of the cases), the statistical changepoint detection sometimes identifies points right before or right after a change of efficiency. In fact, the generality of statistical methods is not a plus in cases in which the set of curves in input is quite homogeneous and for which ad-hoc methods result more reliable. For this reason, we use our definition of changepoint.

Once users with similar profiles in their temporal efficiency evolution have been grouped, time series are analyzed to identify meaningful changepoints.

6 User efficiency classes

For each detected class, we perform an analysis in aggregate over all the users first and then we characterize the evolution of the same metrics in time. We find that (i) publishing

Table 3 Activity, popularity and longevity indicators for the four user classes

Type	%users	Activity			Attention				Time	
		pd	*cd*	*fwee*	*cr*	*fw*	*rr*	*cs*	*days*	*weeks*
Decreasing	15%	6.11	2.78	10.7	4.90	3.57	25.3	34	491	53
Increasing	16%	10.3	4.74	9.69	6.14	4.82	43.4	51	690	92
Peak	25%	8.10	2.74	6.82	4.07	3.18	9.11	32	703	85
Steady	44%	8.22	3.75	10.3	5.50	4.35	29.1	40	610	72

Values are the median of the average weekly values. Abbreviations used are *pd* = posts, *cd* = commentsDone, *fwee* = followees, *fw* = followers, *rr* = repostsReceived, *cs* = cascadeSize, *days* = userLifetime, *week* = activeWeeks

interesting content helps to boost the efficiency of the subsequent posts through attention gathering and that (ii) the efficiency gained in that way should be sustained by intense social activity to avoid it to drop.

6.1 Static analysis of user classes

We aggregate different activity and attention indicator scores over users and weeks, for each of the four user classes. For all the indicators, we compute their average value per-week for every user and then we compute the median of all the results obtained for users of the same class. Median is used instead of average to account for the broad distribution of values. In addition, to get a measure of the adhesion of users to the service, we measure the median number of weeks of activity and the median number of days of duration of the user account. Values for all the metrics are shown in Table 3 and they show a first picture of the levels of activity performed and attention attracted by users of different classes. Users in the Increasing class have the highest values for almost all the metrics compared to other groups. They are able to attract high levels of attention (*fw*, *rr*), combined with the ability of conciliating the production of content of high interestingness for the community (high *cs*) with social activity (high *cd* and *fwee* values). As we will show later, the production of comments and addition of followees is a characteristic of this class through time. On the contrary, users belonging to the Peak class are the least active in terms of social activity (low *cd* and *fwee* values) but, surprisingly, they are relatively active content publishers and have the tendency to be active for long time, exhibiting a high number of active weeks and the highest account duration. They are quite involved in posting but are not much engaged in the social interactions that complements the content production and consumption process. As we will observe next, these users do some commenting activity at the beginning of their lifetime but they reduce significantly the number of followees or comments rapidly. Users in the Decreasing and Steady classes receive both a good amount of attention and establish a high number of social links, backed up by a high content-production activity in the Steady case. Given the shorter time of involvement and knowing about their sharp efficiency drop, the users in the Decreasing class are likely people with a good level of participation who, differently from the users in Steady, reduced significantly the involvement in the service at some point.

6.2 Variation around the changepoint

Here we investigate deeper how users in each class distribute the amount of activity in time. We perform an analysis around the changepoint of the efficiency curve, and see if the different temporal patterns can explain *why* their efficiency level changed over time. We decompose the timeseries into different *phases* and study the relations between them in terms of the activity and attention indicators. Specifically, for all the users belonging to the classes where the changepoint is given (i.e., all but the Steady class).

Let us define three user-dependent time steps: the week in which the user activity started w_{start}, the week of the changepoint of the efficiency curve w_{cp}, and the week of the end of the activity w_{end}, after which no other action is performed by the user. Accordingly, we define three *phases* of the user lifespan referred as *Before*, *CP*, *After*, which represent, respectively: the weeks in the $[w_{start}, w_{cp})$ interval, the changepoint week w_{cp}, and the weeks in the $(w_{cp}, w_{end}]$ interval. We calculate the average weekly amount of activity and attention metrics during these three macro-aggregates of weeks. The three values obtained for each indicator capture the variation of activity and attention when approaching the critical point in which a consistent change of efficiency is detected.

To detect the variation of the values in the three phases we compute two ratios for each user: (a) RatioCP = activity-or-attention metric measured in w_{cp} divided by the same metric computed in $[w_{start}, w_{cp})$, and (b) RatioAfter = activity-or-attention metric measured in $(w_{cp}, w_{end}]$ divided by the same metric during $[w_{start}, w_{cp})$. Ratios are then averaged over all the users of each class. Comparison of ratios between different user classes reveals the key differences between them: values above 1 mean that the value of the indicator grew in *CP* of in *After* phases compared to the *Before* phase. Final results for different values of activity and attention are reported in Figure 5. For instance, in Figure 5(a), we observe that RatioAfter is above 1 just for users in the Peaky class. It means that the users in that class have published more posts after the changepoint than they did before it. We can summarize our findings as follows:

- *Activity and attention at CP*. Users of all classes maintain a similar trend in the number of posts done in *CP* with a slight increase in the case of the Increasing class (Figure 5(a)). For Peak and Increasing classes, the number of reposts received, cascade size and followers increases significantly in *CP* compared to *Before* (Figure 5(d), (e), (f) respectively). Since reposts received and cascade size are proxies for content interestingness, this indicates the production of content that attracts the attention of a much higher number of users. For both classes, this is the most likely cause of the rise

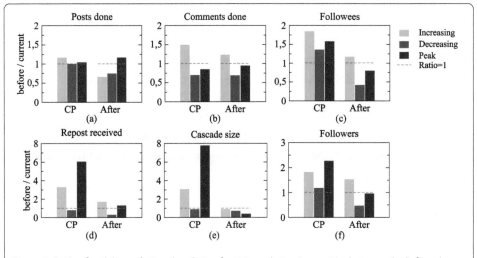

Figure 5 Ratio of activity and attention. Ratio of activity and attention metrics between the Before phase and later phases (Change Point and After), for the 3 user classes.

of their efficiency at *CP*. For the Decreasing class the attention values start dropping instead. Finally, differently from other classes, users in the Increasing class produce a higher number of comments in *CP* (Figure 5(b)).

- *Social activity after CP*. In the *After* phase, social interaction such as the number of comments and the addition of new followees considerably increase compared to *Before* for the Increasing class (Figures 5(b), (c)), while they remain stable or in slight decrease for the Peak class. Decreasing class values drop also in this case.
- *Content production activity after CP*. The reverse scenario is found when looking at the posting activity. In the *After* phase, Peak post messages at a higher rate than Before (Figure 5(a)), while *Increasing* posting activity drops in favor of a higher attention to social interaction.

The main lesson learned from the above findings is that the submission of pieces of "interesting" content, namely posts that attract the attention of a wider audience than usual, is the trigger to transition to higher efficiency levels. However, efficiency cannot be maintained without cost. Increasing engagement in social activity and expanding the potential audience turns out to be an effective strategy not to lose efficiency. Conversely, producing more content without reinforcing the social relationships with the potential consumers of the content results in a rapid drop of efficiency to the original levels. The difference between the Increasing and Peaky classes is particularly striking, having the Increasing-type users fully exploiting social activity with 17% more followees, 23% more comments and 61% reposts after their changepoint, while Peaky-type users keep their activity approximately stable (except for an increase of reposts done). Moreover, as expected, when a status of equilibrium between attention received and activity is disrupted by an arbitrary reduction of productivity and social interactions, the efficiency is destined to fade quickly.

7 Conclusions

We explored the interplay between activity and attention in Yahoo Meme by defining the notion of user *efficiency*, namely the amount of attention received in relation to the content produced. We find that, unlike the raw attention measures, efficiency has strong negative correlation with the amount of user activity and users who are involved in social activities such as commenting, have higher centrality in the social network than average, but are not necessarily heavy content producers.

However, if we consider commenting as a form of content creation, we observe that comment takes less effort than creating a post but, frequently, it can be more effective. It is so because the reciprocity plays a role and the comments network exhibits a higher reciprocity than that of the follower network. Users can, thus, benefit from the visibility of a post whenever they comments on it.

We classify into four main classes (sharp increasing/decreasing steps, peaks or stable trend) the time series of user efficiency with a novel algorithm that overcomes limitations of previous approaches and we find four main clusters. By analyzing the variation of activity and attention around the changepoints of the timeseries, we find evidences that user efficiency is boosted by a particular combination of production of interesting content and constant social interactions (e.g., comments). In these cases, users gather the attention from a wider audience by publishing content with higher spreading potential and then they manage to keep the attention high through regular and intensified social activity. These insights find direct application on the detection and prevention of user churn: being able to detect users who increase their efficiency but that are frustrated by not being able to keep it high can be helped either by recommending them social activities or pushing their contacts to interact with them. The task of churn prediction is a natural continuation of the present work that we plan to address in the future.

Competing interests
The authors declare that they have no competing interests.

Authors' contributions
CVR and LMA designed the methodology and conceived the experiments. CVR performed the data processing, the time series clustering and calculated the ratios. LMA calculated the overall network statistics. All authors wrote and revised the manuscript. This work was carried out while CVR was an intern at Yahoo Labs, Barcelona.

Author details
[1]Politecnico di Milano, Piazza Leonardo Da Vinci, 32, Milan, Italy. [2]Yahoo Labs, Av. Diagonal 177, 08018, Barcelona, Spain. [3]FIEC, Escuela Superior Politecnica del Litoral, Campus Gustavo Galindo, Km 30.5 via Perimetral, Guayaquil, Ecuador.

Acknowledgements
This work is supported by the SocialSensor FP7 project, partially funded by the EC under contract number 287975. Carmen Vaca research work has been funded by ESPOL and the Ecuadorian agency SENESCYT. We would like to thank Amin Mantrach, Neil O'Hare, Daniele Quercia, and Rossano Schifanella for the useful discussions.

References
1. Huberman BA, Romero DM, Wu F (2009) Crowdsourcing, attention and productivity. J Inf Sci 35(6):758-765
2. Ratkiewicz J, Fortunato S, Flammini A, Menczer F, Vespignani A (2010) Characterizing and modeling the dynamics of online popularity. Phys Rev Lett 105(15):158701
3. Szabo G, Huberman BA (2010) Predicting the popularity of online content. Commun ACM 53(8):80-88
4. Pal A, Counts S (2011) Identifying topical authorities in microblogs. In: Proceedings of the fourth ACM international conference on web search and data mining (WSDM), pp 45-54. ACM, New York
5. Asur S, Huberman BA, Szabo G, Wang C (2011) Trends in social media: persistence and decay. In: Proceedings of the 5th AAAI conference on weblogs and social media (ICWSM)
6. Cha M, Haddadi H, Benevenuto F, Gummadi PK (2010) Measuring user influence in Twitter: the million follower fallacy. In: AAAI conference on weblogs and social media (ICWSM), vol 10, pp 10-17
7. Romero DM, Galuba W, Asur S, Huberman BA (2011) Influence and passivity in social media. In: WWW'11: proceedings of the 20th international conference companion on world wide web. ACM, New York, pp 113-114
8. Hong L, Dan O, Davison BD (2011) Predicting popular messages in Twitter. In: WWW. ACM, New York
9. Strufe T (2010) Profile popularity in a business-oriented online social network. In: Proceedings of the 3rd workshop on social network systems (SNS). ACM, New York, p 2
10. Suh B, Hong L, Pirolli P, Chi EH (2010) Want to be retweeted? Large scale analytics on factors impacting retweet in Twitter network. In: 2010 IEEE second international conference on social computing (SocialCom). IEEE Press, New York, pp 177-184
11. Quercia D, Ellis J, Capra L, Crowcroft J (2011) In the mood for being influential on Twitter. In: 2011 IEEE third international conference on privacy, security, risk and trust (PASSAT) and 2011 IEEE third international conference on social computing (SocialCom). IEEE Press, New York, pp 307-314
12. Cha M, Mislove A, Gummadi KP (2009) A measurement-driven analysis of information propagation in the Flickr social network. In: Proceedings of the 18th international conference on world wide web (WWW). ACM, New York, pp 721-730
13. Bakshy E, Hofman JM, Mason WA, Watts DJ (2011) Everyone's an influencer: quantifying influence on Twitter. In: Proceedings of the fourth ACM international conference on web search and data mining (WSDM). ACM, New York, pp 65-74
14. Weng L, Ratkiewicz J, Perra N, Gonçalves B, Castillo C, Bonchi F, Schifanella R, Menczer F, Flammini A (2013) The role of information diffusion in the evolution of social networks. In: Proceedings of the 19th ACM SIGKDD international conference on knowledge discovery and data mining. KDD'13, pp 356-364
15. Ienco D, Bonchi F, Castillo C (2010) The meme ranking problem: maximizing microblogging virality. In: 2010 IEEE international conference on data mining workshops (ICDMW). IEEE Press, New York, pp 328-335
16. Shalizi CR, Thomas AC (2011) Homophily and contagion are generically confounded in observational social network studies. Sociol Methods Res 40(2):211-239
17. Bakshy E, Rosenn I, Marlow C, Adamic L (2012) The role of social networks in information diffusion. In: Proceedings of the 21st international conference on world wide web (WWW). ACM, New York, pp 519-528
18. Figueiredo F, Benevenuto F, Almeida JM (2011) The tube over time: characterizing popularity growth of YouTube videos. In: Proceedings of the fourth ACM international conference on web search and data mining (WSDM). ACM, New York, pp 745-754
19. Brodersen A, Scellato S, Wattenhofer M (2012) YouTube around the world: geographic popularity of videos. In: Proceedings of the 21st conference on world wide web (WWW). ACM, New York, pp 241-250
20. Weng L, Flammini A, Vespignani A, Menczer F (2012) Competition among memes in a world with limited attention. Sci Rep 2:335

21. Lehmann J, Gonçalves B, Ramasco JJ, Cattuto C (2012) Dynamical classes of collective attention in Twitter. In: Proceedings of the 21st international conference on world wide web (WWW). ACM, New York, pp 251-260
22. Yang J, Leskovec J (2011) Patterns of temporal variation in online media. In: Proceedings of the fourth ACM international conference on web search and data mining (WSDM). ACM, New York, pp 177-186
23. Mathioudakis M, Koudas N, Marbach P (2010) Early online identification of attention gathering items in social media. In: Proceedings of the third ACM international conference on web search and data mining (WSDM). ACM, New York, pp 301-310
24. Kooti F, Yang H, Cha M, Gummadi KP, Mason WA (2012) The emergence of conventions in online social networks. In: AAAI conference on weblogs and social media (ICWSM)
25. Kwak H, Lee C, Park H, Moon S (2010) What is Twitter, a social network or a news media? In: Proceedings of the 19th international conference on world wide web (WWW). ACM, New York, pp 591-600
26. Schifanella R, Barrat A, Cattuto C, Markines B, Menczer F (2010) Folks in folksonomies: social link prediction from shared metadata. In: Proceedings of the third ACM international conference on web search and data mining. ACM, New York, pp 271-280
27. Arthur S, Sheffrin SM (2003) Economics: principles in action. Prentice Hall, New York
28. Wang X, Smith K, Hyndman R (2006) Characteristic-based clustering for time series data. Data Min Knowl Discov 13(3):335-364
29. Fu T-C (2011) A review on time series data mining. Eng Appl Artif Intell 24(1):164-181
30. Geurts P (2001) Pattern extraction for time series classification. In: Principles of data mining and knowledge discovery. Springer, Berlin, pp 115-127
31. Warren Liao T (2005) Clustering of time series data - a survey. Pattern Recognit 38(11):1857-1874
32. Lin J, Keogh E, Wei L, Lonardi S (2007) Experiencing sax: a novel symbolic representation of time series. Data Min Knowl Discov 15(2):107-144
33. Lee CHL, Liu A, Chen WS (2006) Pattern discovery of fuzzy time series for financial prediction. IEEE Trans Knowl Data Eng 18(5):613-625
34. Härdle W, Vieu P (1992) Kernel regression smoothing of time series. J Time Ser Anal 13(3):209-232
35. Assfalg J, Kriegel HP, Kroger P, Kunath P, Pryakhin A, Renz M (2006) Similarity search on time series based on threshold queries. In: Advances in database technology - EDBT, pp 276-294
36. Palshikar G (2009) Simple algorithms for peak detection in time-series. In: Proceedings of the 1st international conference on advanced data analysis, business analytics and intelligence (ADABAI)
37. Basseville M, Nikiforov IV (1993) Detection of abrupt changes: theory and applications. Prentice Hall, New York
38. Chen J, Gupta AK (2011) Parametric statistical change point analysis: with applications to genetics, medicine, and finance. Birkhäuser, Basel
39. Lin J, Li Y (2009) Finding structural similarity in time series data using bag-of-patterns representation. In: Scientific and statistical database management. Springer, Berlin, pp 461-477

8

Scoring dynamics across professional team sports: tempo, balance and predictability

Sears Merritt[1] and Aaron Clauset[1,2,3]*

*Correspondence:
aaron.clauset@colorado.edu
[1] Department of Computer Science,
University of Colorado, Boulder, CO
80309, USA
[2] BioFrontiers Institute, University of
Colorado, Boulder, CO 80303, USA
Full list of author information is
available at the end of the article

Abstract

Despite growing interest in quantifying and modeling the scoring dynamics within professional sports games, relative little is known about what patterns or principles, if any, cut across different sports. Using a comprehensive data set of scoring events in nearly a dozen consecutive seasons of college and professional (American) football, professional hockey, and professional basketball, we identify several common patterns in scoring dynamics. Across these sports, scoring tempo - when scoring events occur - closely follows a common Poisson process, with a sport-specific rate. Similarly, scoring balance - how often a team wins an event - follows a common Bernoulli process, with a parameter that effectively varies with the size of the lead. Combining these processes within a generative model of gameplay, we find they both reproduce the observed dynamics in all four sports and accurately predict game outcomes. These results demonstrate common dynamical patterns underlying within-game scoring dynamics across professional team sports, and suggest specific mechanisms for driving them. We close with a brief discussion of the implications of our results for several popular hypotheses about sports dynamics.

Keywords: team sports; big data; dynamics; prediction

1 Introduction

Professional team sports like American football, soccer, hockey, basketball, etc. provide a rich and relatively well-controlled domain by which to study fundamental questions about the dynamics of competition. In these sports, most environmental irregularities are eliminated, players are highly trained, and rules are enforced consistently. These features produce a level playing field on which competition outcomes are determined largely by a combination of skill and luck (ideally more the former than the latter).

Modern sports in particular produce large quantities of detailed data describing not only competition outcomes and team characteristics, but also the individual events within a competition, e.g., scoring events, referee calls, timeouts, ball possessions, court positions, etc. The availability of such data has enabled many quantitative analyses of individual sports [1–12]. Relatively little work, however, has asked what patterns or principles, if any, cut across different sports, or whether there are fundamental processes governing some dynamical aspects of all such competitions. These questions are the focus of this study, and our results shed light on several other phenomena, including the roles of skill and luck in determining outcomes, and the extent to which events early in the game influence events later in the game.

Game theory provides an attractive quantitative framework for understanding the principles and dynamics of competition [13]. Given a set of payoffs for different actions, formal game theory can identify the optimal strategy or probability distribution over actions against an intelligent adversary. In simple decision spaces, like penalty shots in soccer [14] or serve-and-return play in tennis [15], professional athletes appear to behave as game theory predicts (although some do not [16]). However, most professional team sports exhibit large and complex decision spaces, with many possible actions of uncertain payoffs, and execution is carried out by an imperfectly coordinated team. Game theory provides less guidance within such complex games, and the resulting dynamics are often better described using tools from dynamical systems [17, 18].

Using such an approach, we investigate the within-game scoring dynamics of four team sports, college and professional (American) football, professional hockey, and professional basketball. Our primary goals are (i) to quantify and identify the common empirical patterns in scoring dynamics of these sports, and (ii) to understand the competitive processes that produce these patterns. We do not consider non-stationary effects across games, e.g., evolving team rosters or skill sets, playing field variables, etc. Instead, we focus explicitly on the sequence of scoring events within games. For each sport, we study three measurable quantities: scoring event tempo, balance, and predictability. We take an inferential approach to investigating their cross-sport patterns and present a generative model of competition dynamics that can be fitted directly to scoring event data within games. We apply this model to a comprehensive data set of 1,279,901 scoring events across 9 or 10 years of consecutive seasons in our four team sports.

There are many claims in both the academic literature and the popular press about scoring dynamics within sports, and sports are often used as exemplars of decision making and dynamics in complex competitive environments [16, 19–21]. Our results on common patterns in scoring dynamics and the processes that generate them serve to clarify, and in several cases directly contradict, many of these claims, and provide a systematic perspective on the general phenomenon.

1.1 Summary of results

Across all sports, scoring tempo - when scoring events occur - is remarkably well-described by a Poisson process, in which scoring events occur independently with a sport-specific rate at each second on the game clock. This rate is fairly stable across the course of gameplay, except in the first and last few seconds of a scoring period, where it is much lower or much higher, respectively, than normal. This common pattern implies that scoring events are largely memoryless, i.e., the timing of events earlier in the game have little or no impact on the timing of future events. Memorylessness contrasts with the dynamics of strategic games like chess or Go, in which events early in a game constrain and drive later events. Instead, professional sports appear to exhibit little strategic entailment, and events are driven instead by short-term optimization for scoring as quickly as possible.

The scoring balance between teams - how often a team wins a scoring event - is well-described by a common Bernoulli process, with a bias parameter that varies effectively over gameplay and across sports. Football and hockey exhibit a common pattern in which the probability of scoring again while in the lead effectively increases with lead size. In basketball, however, this probability decreases with lead size (a phenomenon first identified by [10]). The former pattern is consistent with the outcome of each scoring event being determined by a memoryless coin flip whose bias depends on the difference in the teams' inherent skill levels. The pattern in basketball is also consistent with such a process, but where on-court team skill varies inversely with lead size as a result of teams deploying their weaker players when they are in the lead and their stronger players when they are not. This player management strategy produces substantially more unpredictable games than in other sports, with winning teams losing their lead and losing teams regaining it much more often than we would normally expect.

Overall, these results reinforce the conclusions from scoring tempo, indicating that event outcomes early in a game have little or no impact on event outcomes later in the game, which reinforces statistical claims that teams do not become 'hot,' [10, 19, 22] with successes running in streaks. Instead, gameplay is largely a sequence of roughly independent, short-term optimizations aimed at maximizing near-term scoring rates, with little multi-play strategic efforts and few downstream consequences for mistakes or miscalculations. This memorylessness may be caused by a persistently level playing field, which lacks strategically exploitable environmental features [23] and forbids actions that might produce sustained competitive advantages [24] as a result of within-game choices, e.g., eliminating an opposing team's best players. Table 1 summarizes these results as they relate to a series of specific questions about scoring dynamics.

We combine these insights within a generative model of gameplay and demonstrate that it accurately reproduces the observed evolution of lead-sizes over the course of games in all four sports, and also makes highly accurate predictions of game outcomes, when only the first few scoring events have occurred. Cursory comparisons suggest that this

Table 1 A summary of our results, in question-and-answer format

Question	Answer
Does scoring in games of different team sports follow common patterns?	Yes. The pattern of when points are scored and who gets them are remarkably similar across sports.
What is the common pattern?	Events occur randomly (a Poisson process). Which team wins the points is coin flip (a Bernoulli process) that depends on the relative skill difference of the teams on the field.
What might cause this pattern?	A strong focus on short-term maximization of scoring opportunities, while blocking the other team from the same. There is no evidence of strategic planning across plays, as in games like chess or Go. Teams largely react to events as they occur.
What determines how often scoring occurs?	Each sport has a characteristic rate (see Table 3), which increases dramatically at the end of scoring periods.
What determines who wins an event?	Skill and luck, in that order.
Do events early in a game influence events later in a game?	No. Each scoring event or 'play' is effectively independent, once we control for relative team skill (and lead size in basketball). Gameplay is effectively 'memoryless.'
Can a team be 'hot,' where they score in streaks?	No. Just like players [19], teams do not get 'hot.' Scoring streaks are caused by getting lucky.
When is it easier or harder to score?	Every moment is equally easy or difficult. But, teams try harder at the end of a period.
Which sport is the most unpredictable?	Pro basketball, where lead sizes (spreads) tend to shrink back to zero. This tendency generates many 'ties' as a game unfolds.
Do other sports exhibit this pattern?	No. Pro basketball is the only sport where the spread tends to shrink. In football and hockey, the spread tends to grow over time.
Does being behind help you win, as argued by [21]?	No. Being behind helps you lose. Being ahead and being lucky helps you win.

model achieves accuracy comparable to or better than several commercial odds-makers, despite this model knowing nothing about teams, players, or strategies, and instead relying exclusively on the observed tempo and balance patterns in scoring events.

2 A null model for competition dynamics

We first introduce the limiting case of an *ideal competition*, which provides a useful tool by which to identify and quantify interesting deviations within real data, and to generate hypotheses as to what underlying processes might produce them. Although we describe this model in terms of two teams accumulating points, it can in principle be generalized to other forms of competition.

In an ideal competition, events unfold on a perfectly neutral or 'level' playing field, in which there are no environmental features that could give one side a competitive advantage over the other [23]. Furthermore, each side is perfectly skilled, i.e., they possess complete information both about the state of the game, e.g., the position of the ball, the location of the players, etc. and the set of possible strategies, their optimum responses, and their likelihood of being employed. This is an unrealistic assumption, as real competitors are imperfectly skilled, and possess both imperfect information and incomplete strategic knowledge of the game. However, increased skill generally implies improved performance on these characteristics, and the limiting case would be perfect skill. Finally, each side exhibits a slightly imperfect ability to execute any particular chosen strategy, which captures the fact that no side can control all variables on the field. In other words, two perfectly skilled teams competing on a level playing field will produce scoring events by chance alone, e.g., a slight miscalculation of velocity, a fumbled pass, shifting environmental variables like wind or heat, etc.

An ideal competition thus eliminates all of the environmental, player, and strategic heterogeneities that normally distinguish and limit a team. The result, particularly from the spectator's point of view, is a competition whose dynamics are fundamentally unpredictable. Such a competition would be equivalent to a simple stochastic process, in which scoring events arrive randomly, via a Poisson process with rate λ, points are awarded to each team with equal probability, as in a fair Bernoulli process with parameter $c = 1/2$, and the number of those points is an iid random variable from some sport-specific distribution.

Mathematically, let $S_r(t)$ and $S_b(t)$ denote the cumulative scores of teams r and s at time t, where $0 \leq t \leq T$ represents the game clock. (For simplicity, we do not treat overtime and instead let the game end at $t = T$.) The probability that S_r increases by k points at time t is equal to the joint probability of observing an event worth k points, scored by team r at time t. Assuming independence, this probability is

$$\Pr\big(\Delta S_r(t) = k\big) = \Pr(\text{event at } t)\Pr(r \text{ scores})\Pr(\text{points } = k). \tag{1}$$

The evolution of the difference in these scores thus follows an finite-length unbiased random walk on the integers, moving left or right with equal probability, starting at $\Delta S = 0$ at $t = 0$.

Real competitions will deviate from this ideal because they possess various non-ideal features. The type and size of such deviations are evidence for competitive mechanisms that drive the scoring dynamics away from the ideal.

Table 2 Summary of data for each sport, including total number of seasons, teams, competitions, and scoring events

Sport	Abbrv.	Seasons	Teams	Competitions	Scoring events
Football (college)	CFB	10, 2000-2009	486	14,588	120,827
Football (pro)	NFL	10, 2000-2009	31	2,654	19,476
Hockey (pro)	NHL	10, 2000-2009	29	11,813	44,989
Basketball (pro)	NBA	9, 2002-2010	31	11,744	1,080,285

3 Scoring event data

Throughout our analyses, we utilize a comprehensive data set of all points scored in league games of consecutive seasons of college-level American football (NCAA Divisions 1-3, 10 seasons; 2000-2009), professional American football (NFL, 10 seasons; 2000-2009), professional hockey (NHL, 10 seasons; 2000-2009), and professional basketball (NBA, 9 seasons, 2002-2010).[a] Each scoring event includes the time at which the event occurred, the player and corresponding team that won the event, and the number of points it was worth. From these, we extract all scoring events that occurred during regulation time (i.e., we exclude all overtime events), which account for 99% or more of scoring events in each sport, and we combine events that occur at the same second of game time. Table 2 summarizes these data, which encompass more than 1.25 million scoring events across more than 40,000 games.

A brief overview of each sport's primary game mechanics is provided in Additional file 1 as Appendix A. In general, games in these sports are competitions between two teams of fixed size, and points are accumulated each time one team places the ball or puck in the opposing team's goal. Playing fields are flat, featureless surfaces. Gameplay is divided into three or four scoring periods within a maximum of 48 or 60 minutes (not including potential overtime). The team with the greatest score at the end of this time is declared the winner.

4 Game tempo

A game's 'tempo' is the speed at which scoring events occur over the course of play. Past work on the timing of scoring events has largely focused on hockey, soccer and basketball [4, 6, 10], with little work examining football or in contrasting patterns across sports. However, these studies show strong evidence that game tempo is well approximated by a homogenous Poisson process, in which scoring events occur at each moment in time independently with some small and roughly constant probability.

Analyzing the timing of scoring events across all four of our sports, we find that the Poisson process is a remarkably good model of game tempo, yielding predictions that are in good or excellent agreement with a variety of statistical measures of gameplay. Furthermore, these results confirm and extend previous work [10, 19], while contrasting with others [12, 25], showing little or no evidence for the popular belief in 'momentum' or 'hot hands,' in which scoring once increases the probability of scoring again very soon. However, we do find some evidence for modest non-Poissonian patterns in tempo, some of which are common to all four sports.

4.1 The Poisson model of tempo

A Poisson process is fully characterized by a single parameter λ, representing the probability that an event occurs, or the expected number of events, per unit time. In each sport,

Table 3 Tempo summary statistics for each sport, along with simple derived values for the expected number of events per game and seconds between events

Sport	$\hat{\lambda}$ [events/s]	T [s]	$\hat{\lambda}T$ [events/game]	$1/\hat{\lambda}$ [s/event]
NFL	0.00204(1)	3600	7.34	490.2
CFB	0.00230(1)	3600	8.28	434.8
NHL	0.00106(1)	3600	3.81	943.4
NBA	0.03194(5)	2880	91.99	31.3

Parenthetical values indicate standard uncertainty in the final digit.

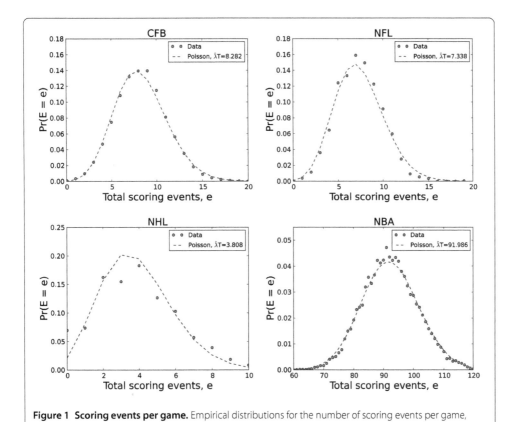

Figure 1 Scoring events per game. Empirical distributions for the number of scoring events per game, along with the estimated Poisson model with rate λT (dashed).

game time is divided into seconds and there are T seconds per a game (see Table 3). For each sport, we test this model in several ways: we compare the empirical and predicted distributions for the number of events per game and for the time between consecutive scoring events, and we examine the two-point correlation function for these inter-event times.

Under a Poisson model [26], the number of scoring events per game follows a Poisson distribution with parameter λT, and the maximum likelihood estimate of λ is the average number of events observed in a game divided by the number of intervals (which varies per sport). Furthermore, the time between consecutive events follows a simple geometric (discrete exponential) distribution, with mean $1/\lambda$, and the two-point correlation between these delays is zero at all time scales.

For the number of events per game, we find generally excellent agreement between the Poisson model and the data for every sport (Figure 1). However, there are some small de-

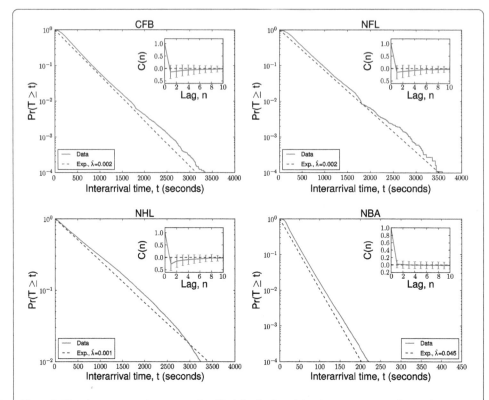

Figure 2 Time between scoring events. Empirical distribution of time between consecutive scoring events, shown as the complementary cdf, along with the estimated distribution from the Poisson model (dashed). Insets show the correlation function for inter-event times.

viations, which suggests some second-order, non-Poissonian processes, which we investigate below. Deviations are greatest in NHL games, whose distribution is slightly broader than predicted, underproducing games with 3 events, and overproducing games with 0 or with 8 or more events. Similarly, CFB games have a slight excess of games with 9 events, and NBA games exhibit slightly more variation in NBA games with scores close to the average (92.0 events) than expected. In contrast, NFL games exhibit slightly less variance than expected, with more games close to the average (7.3 events) than expected.

For the time between consecutive scoring events within a game, or the inter-arrival time distribution, we again find excellent agreement between the Poisson model and the data in all sports (Figure 2). That being said, in CFB, NFL and NBA games, there are slightly fewer gaps of the minimum size than predicted by the model. This indicates a slight dispersive effect in the timing of events, perhaps caused by the time required to transport the ball some distance before a new event may be generated. In contrast, NHL games produce as many short gaps, more intermediate gaps, and fewer very long gaps than expected were events purely Poissonian.

Finally, we calculate the two-point correlation function on the times between scoring events [27],

$$C(n) = \left(\sum_k \big(t_k - \langle t \rangle \big) \big(t_{k+n} - \langle t \rangle \big) \right) \Big/ \sum_k \big(t_k - \langle t \rangle \big)^2, \qquad (2)$$

where t_k is the kth inter-arrival time, n indicates the gap between it and a subsequent event, and $\langle t \rangle$ is the mean time between events. If $C(n)$ is positive, short intervals tend to be followed by other short intervals (or, large intervals by large intervals), while a negative value implies alternation, with short intervals followed by long, or vice versa. Across all four sports, the correlation function is close or very close to zero for all values of n (Figure 2 insets), in excellent agreement with the Poisson process, which predicts $C(n) = 0$ for all $n > 0$, representing no correlation in the timing of events (a result also found by [10] in basketball). However, in CFB, NFL and NHL games, we find a slight negative correlation for very small values of n, suggesting a slight tendency for short intervals to be closely followed by longer ones, and vice versa.

4.2 Common patterns in game tempo

Our results above provide strong support for a common Poisson-like process for modeling game tempo across all four sports. We also find some evidence for mild non-Poissonian processes, which we now investigate by directly examining the scoring rate as a function of clock time. Within each sport, we tabulate the fraction of games in which a scoring event (associated with any number of points) occurred in the tth second of gameplay.

Across all sports, we find that the tempo of events follows a common three-phase pattern within each distinct period of play (Figure 3). This pattern, which resembles an inverse sigmoid, is characterized by (i) an early phase of non-linearly increasing tempo, (ii) a middle phase of stable (Poissonian) or slightly increasing tempo, and (iii) an end phase of sharply

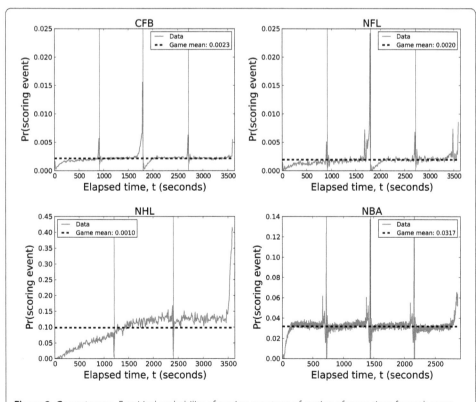

Figure 3 Game tempo. Empirical probability of scoring events as a function of game time, for each sport, along with the mean within-sport probability (dashed line). Each distinct game period, demarcated by vertical lines, shows a common three-phase pattern in tempo.

increasing tempo. This pattern is also observed in certain online games [23], which have substantially different rules and are played in highly heterogeneous environments, suggesting a possibly fundamental generating mechanism for team-competitive systems.

4.2.1 Early phase: non-linear increase in tempo

When a period begins, players are in specific and fixed locations on the field, and the ball or puck is far from any team's goal. Thus, without regard to other aspects of the game, it must take some time for players to move out of these initial positions and to establish scoring opportunities. This would reduce the probability of scoring relative to the game average by limiting access to certain player-ball configurations that require time to set up. Furthermore, and potentially most strongly in the first of these phases (beginning at $t = 0$), players and teams may still be 'warming up,' in the sense of learning [28] the capabilities and tendencies of the opposing team and players, and which tactics to deploy against the opposing team's choices. These behaviors would also reduce the probability of scoring by encouraging risk averse behavior in establishing and taking scoring opportunities.

We find evidence for both mechanisms in our data. Both CFB and NFL games exhibit short and modest-sized dips in scoring rates in periods 2 and 4, reflecting the fact that player and ball positions are not reset when the preceding quarters end, but rather gameplay in the new quarter resumes from its previous configuration. In contrast, CFB and NFL periods 1 and 3 show significant drops in scoring rates, and both of these quarters begin with a kickoff from fixed positions on the field. Similarly, NBA and NHL games exhibit strong but short-duration dips in scoring rate at the beginning of each of their periods, reflecting the fact that each quarter begins with a tossup or face-off, in which players are located in fixed positions on the court or rink. NBA and football games also exhibit some evidence of the 'warming up' process, with the overall scoring rate being slightly lower in period 1 than in other equivalent periods. In contrast, NHL games exhibit a prolonged warmup period, lasting well past the end of the first period. This pattern may indicate more gradual within-game learning in hockey, perhaps are a result of the large diversity of on-ice player combinations caused by teams rotating their four 'lines' of players every few minutes.

4.2.2 Middle phase: constant tempo

Once players have moved away from their initial locations and/or warmed up, gameplay proceeds fluidly, with scoring events occurring without any systematic dependence on the game clock. This produces a flat, stable or stationary pattern in the probability of scoring events. A slight but steady increase in tempo over the course of this phase is consistent with learning, perhaps as continued play sheds more light on the opposing team's capabilities and weaknesses, causing a progressive increase in scoring rate as that knowledge is accumulated and put into practice.

A stable scoring rate pattern appears in every period in NFL, CFB and NBA games, with slight increases observed in periods 1 and 2 in football, and in periods 2-4 in basketball. NHL games exhibit stable scoring rates in the second half of period 2 and throughout period 3. Within a given game, but across scoring periods, scoring rates are remarkably similar, suggesting little or no variation in overall strategies across the periods of gameplay.

4.2.3 End phase: sharply increased tempo

The end of a scoring period often requires players to reset their positions, and any effort spent establishing an advantageous player configuration is lost unless that play produces a scoring event. This impending loss-of-position will tend to encourage more risky actions, which serve to dramatically increase the scoring rate just before the period ends. The increase in scoring rate should be largest in the final period, when no additional scoring opportunities lay in the future. In some sports, teams may effectively slow the rate by which time progresses through game clock management (e.g., using timeouts) or through continuing play (at the end of quarters in football). This effectively compresses more actions than normal into a short period of time, which may also increase the rate, without necessarily adding more risk.

We find evidence mainly for the loss-of-position mechanism, but the rules of these games suggest that clock management likely also plays a role. Relative to the mean tempo, we find a sharply increased rate at the end of each sport's games, in agreement with a strong incentive to score before a period ends. (This increase indicates that a 'lolly-gag strategy,' in which a leading team in possession intentionally runs down the clock to prevent the trailing team from gaining possession, is a relatively rare occurrence.) Intermediate periods in NFL, CFB and NBA games also exhibit increased scoring rates in their final seconds. In football, this increase is greatest at the end of period 2, rather than period 4. The increased rate at the ends of periods 1 and 3 in football is also interesting, as here the period's end does not reset the player configuration on the field, but rather teams switch goals. This likely creates a mild incentive to initiate some play before the period ends (which is allowed to finish, even if the game clock runs out). NHL games exhibit no discernible end-phase pattern in their intermediate periods (1 and 2), but show an enormous end-game effect, with the scoring rate growing to more than three times its game mean. This strong pattern may be related to the strategy in hockey of the losing team 'pulling the goalie,' in which the goalie leaves their defensive position in order to increase the chances of scoring. Regardless of the particular mechanism, the end-phase pattern is ubiquitous.

In general, we find a common set of modest non-Poissonian deviations in game tempo across all four sports, although the vast majority of tempo dynamics continue to agree with a simple Poisson model.

5 Game balance

A game's 'balance' is the relative distribution of scoring events (not points) among the teams. Perfectly balanced games, however, do not always result in a tie. In our model of competition, each scoring event is awarded to one team or the other by a Bernoulli process, and in the case of perfect balance, the probability is equal, at $c = 1/2$. The expected fraction of scoring events won by a team is also $c = 1/2$, and its distribution depends on the number of scoring events in the game. We estimate this null distribution by simulating perfectly balanced games for each sport, given the empirical distribution of scoring events per game (see Figure 1). Comparing the simulated distribution against the empirical distribution of c provides a measure of the true imbalance among teams, while controlling for the stochastic effects of events within games.

Across all four sports, we find significant deviations in this fraction relative to perfect balance. NFL and CFB games exhibited more variance than expected, while NHL and NBA games exhibited the least. Within a game, scoring balance exhibits unexpected patterns. In particular NBA games exhibit an unusual 'restoring force' pattern, in which the probability of winning the next scoring event *decreases* with the size of a team's lead (a pattern first observed by [10]). In contrast, NFL, CFB and NHL games exhibit the opposite effect, in which the probability of winning the next scoring event appears to increase with the size of the lead - a pattern consistent with a heterogeneous distribution of team skill.

5.1 Quantifying balance

The fraction of all events in the game that were won by a randomly selected team provides a simple measure of the overall balance of a particular game in a sport. Let r and b index the two teams and let E_r (E_b) denote the total number of events won by team r in its game with b. The maximum likelihood estimator for a game's bias is simply the fraction $\hat{c} = E_r/(E_r + E_b)$ of all scoring events in the game won by r.

Tabulating the empirical distributions of $\hat{c}$ within each sport, we find that the most common outcome, in all sports, is $c = 1/2$, in agreement with the Bernoulli model. However, the distributions around this value deviate substantially from the form expected for perfect balance (Figure 4), but not always in the same direction.

In CFB and NFL, the distributions of scoring balances are similar, but the shape for CFB is broader than for NFL, suggesting that CFB competitions are less balanced than NFL competitions. This is likely a result of the broader range of skill differences among teams

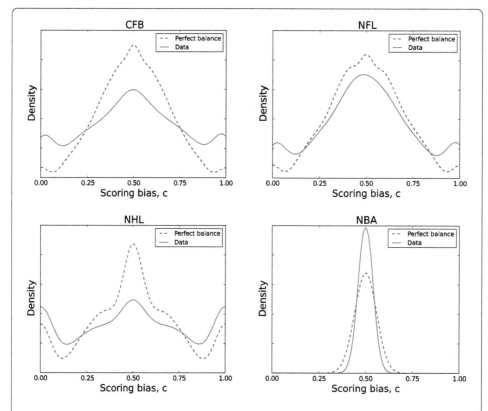

Figure 4 Game balance. Smoothed distributions for the empirical fraction $\hat{c}$ of events won by a team, for each sport, and the predicted fraction for a perfectly balanced scoring, when given the empirical distribution of events per game (Figure 1). Modes at 1 and 0 indicate a non-trivial probability of one team winning or losing every event, which is more common when only a few events occur.

at the college level, as compared to the professionals. Like CFB and NFL, NHL games also exhibit substantially more blowouts and fewer ties than expected, which is consistent with a heterogeneous distribution of team skills. Surprisingly, however, NBA games exhibit less variance in the final relative lead size than we expect for perfectly balanced games, a pattern we will revisit in the following section.

5.2 Scoring while in the lead

Although many non-Bernoulli processes may occur within professional team sports, here we examine only one: whether the size of a lead L, the difference in team scores or point totals, provides information about the probability of a team winning the next event. [10] previously considered this question for scoring events and lead sizes within NBA games, but not other sports. Across all four of our sports, we tabulated the fraction of times the leading team won the next scoring event, given it held a lead of size L. This function is symmetric about $L = 0$, where it passes through probability $p = 1/2$ where the identity of the leading team may change.

Examining the empirical scoring functions (Figure 5), we find that the probability of scoring next varies systematically with lead size L. In particular, for CFB, NFL and NHL games, the probability appears to increase with lead size, while it decreases in NBA games. The effect of the negative relationship in NBA games is a kind of 'restoring force', such that leads of any size tend to shrink back toward a tied score. This produces a narrower

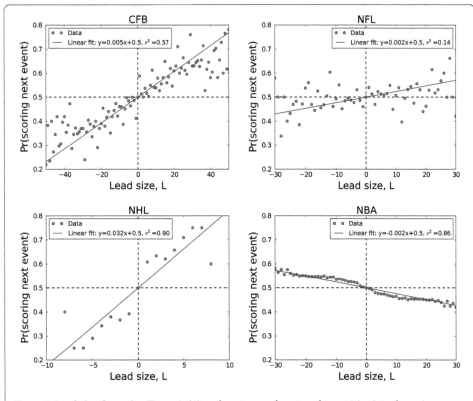

Figure 5 Lead-size dynamics. The probability of scoring as a function of a team's lead size for each sport, football, hockey, and basketball and a linear least-squares fit ($p \leq 0.1$), indicating positive or negative correlations between scoring and a competition's score difference.

distribution of final lead sizes than we would expect under Bernoulli-style competition, precisely as shown in Figure 4 for NBA games.

Although the positive function for CFB, NFL and NHL games may superficially support a kind of 'hot hands' or cumulative advantage-type mechanism, in which lead size tends to grow superlinearly over time, we do not believe this explains the observed pattern. A more plausible mechanism is a simple heterogeneous skill model, in which each team has a latent skill value π_r, and the probability that team r wins a scoring event against b is determined by a Bernoulli process with $c = \pi_r/(\pi_r + \pi_b)$. (This model is identical to the popular Bradley-Terry model of win-loss records of teams [29], except here we apply it to each scoring event within a game.)

For a broad class of team-skill distributions, this model produces a scoring function with the same sigmoidal shape seen here, and the linear pattern at $L = 0$ is the result of averaging over the distribution of biases c induced by the team skill distribution. The function flattens out at large $|L|$ assuming the value representing the largest skill difference possible among the league teams. This explanation is supported by the stronger correlation in CFB games (+0.005 probability per point in the lead) versus NFL games (+0.002 probability per point), as CFB teams are known to exhibit much broader skill differences than NFL teams, in agreement with our results above in Figure 4.

NBA games, however, present a puzzle, because no distribution of skill differences can produce a negative correlation under this latent-skill model. [10] suggested this negative pattern could be produced by possession of the ball changing after each scoring event, or by the leading team 'coasting' and thereby playing below their true skill level. However, the change-of-possession rule also exists in CFB and NFL games (play resumes with a faceoff in NHL games), but only NBA games exhibit the negative correlation. Coasting could occur for psychological reasons, in which losing teams play harder, and leading teams less hard, as suggested by [21]. Again, however, the absence of this pattern in other sports suggest that the mechanism is not psychological.

A plausible alternative explanation is that NBA teams employ various strategies that serve to change the ratio $c = \pi_r/(\pi_r + \pi_b)$ as a function of lead size. For instance, when a team is in the lead, they often substitute out their stronger and more offensive players, e.g., to allow them to rest or avoid injury, or to manage floor spacing or skill combinations. When a team is down by an amount that likely varies across teams, these players are put back on the court. If both teams pursue such strategies, the effective ratio c will vary inversely with lead size such that the leading team becomes effectively weaker compared to the non-leading team. In contrast to NBA teams, teams in CFB, NFL and NHL seem less able to pursue such a strategy. In football, substitutions are relatively uncommon, implying that π_r should not vary much over the course of a game. In hockey, each team rotates through most of its players every few minutes, which limits the ability for high- or low-skilled players to effectively change π_r over the course of a game.

6 Modeling lead-size dynamics

The previous insights identify several basic patterns in scoring tempo and balance across sports. However, we still lack a clear understanding of the degree to which any of these patterns is necessary to produce realistic scoring dynamics. Here, we investigate this question by combining the identified patterns within a generative model of scoring over time, and test which combinations produce realistic dynamics in lead sizes. In particular, we consider two models of tempo and two models of balance. For each of the four pairs of tempo and balance models for each sport, we generate via Monte Carlo a large number of games and measure the resulting variation in lead size as a function of the game clock, which we then compare to the empirical pattern.

Our two scoring tempo models are as follows. In the first (Bernoulli) model, each second of time produces an event with the empirical probability observed for that second across all games (shown in Figure 3). In the second (Markov), we draw an inter-arrival time from the empirical distribution of such gaps (shown in Figure 2), advance the game clock by that amount, and generate a scoring event at that clock time.

Our two balance models are as follows. In the first (Bernoulli) model, for each match we draw a uniformly random value c from the empirical distribution of scoring balances (shown in Figure 4) and for each scoring event, the points are won by team r with that probability and by team b otherwise. In the second (Markov), a scoring event is awarded to the leading team with the empirically estimated probability for the current lead size L (shown in Figure 5). Once a scoring event is generated and assigned, that team's score is incremented by a point value drawn iid from the empirical distribution of point values per scoring event for the sport (see Additional file 1, Appendix B).

The four combinations of tempo and balance models thus cover our empirical findings for patterns in the scoring dynamics of these sports. The simpler models (called Bernoulli) represent dynamics with no memory, in which each event is an iid random variable, albeit drawn from a data-driven distribution. The more complicated models (called Markov) represent dynamics with some memory, allowing past events to influence the ongoing gameplay dynamics. In particular, these are first-order Markov models, in which only the events of the most recent past state influence the outcome of the random variable at the current state.

Generating 100,000 competitions under each combination of models for each sport, we find a consistent pattern across sports (Figure 6): the Markov model of game tempo provides little improvement over the Bernoulli model in capturing the empirical pattern of lead-size variation, while the Markov model for balance provides a significant improvement over the Bernoulli model. In particular, the Markov model generates gameplay dynamics in very good agreement with the empirical patterns.

That being said, some small deviations remain. For instance, the Markov model slightly overestimates the lead-size variation in the first half, and slightly underestimates it in the second half of CFB games. In NFL games, it provides a slight overestimate in first half, but then converges on the empirical pattern in the second half. NHL games exhibit the largest and most systematic deviation, with the Markov model producing more variation than observed, particularly in the game's second half. However, it should be noted that the low-scoring nature of NHL means that what appears to be a visually large overestimate here (Figure 6) is small when compared to the deviations seen in the other sports. NBA games exhibit a similar pattern to CFB games, but the crossover point occurs at the end of period 3, rather than at period 2. These modest deviations suggest the presence of still other non-ideal processes governing the scoring dynamics, particularly in NHL games.

We emphasize that the Markov model's accuracy for CFB, NFL and NHL games does not imply that individual matches follow this pattern of favoring the leader. Instead, the pattern provides a compact and efficient summary of scoring dynamics conditioned on unobserved characteristics like team skill. Our model generates competition between two featureless teams, and the Markov model provides a data-driven mechanism by which

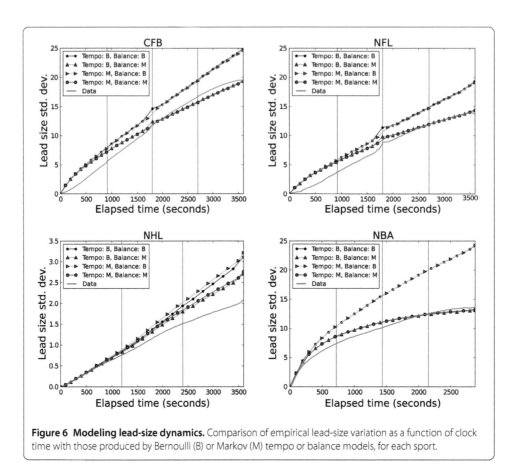

Figure 6 Modeling lead-size dynamics. Comparison of empirical lead-size variation as a function of clock time with those produced by Bernoulli (B) or Markov (M) tempo or balance models, for each sport.

some pairs of teams may behave as if they have small or large differences in latent skill. It remains an interesting direction for future work to investigate precisely how player and team characteristics determine team skill, and how team skill impacts scoring dynamics.

7 Predicting outcomes from gameplay

The accuracy of our generative model in the previous section suggest that it may also produce accurate predictions of the game's overall outcome, after observing only the events in the first t seconds of the game. In this section, we study the predictability of game outcome using the Markov model for scoring balance, and compare its accuracy to the simple heuristic of guessing the winner to be the team currently in the lead at time t. Thus, we convert our Markov model into an explicit Markov chain on the lead size L, which allows us to simulate the remaining $T - t$ seconds conditioned on the lead size at time t. For concreteness, we define the lead size L relative to team r, such that $L < 0$ implies that b is in the lead.

The Markov chain's state space is the set of all possible lead sizes (score differences between teams r and b), and its transition matrix P gives the probability that a scoring event changes a lead of size L to one of size L'. If r wins the event, then $L' = L + k$, where k is the event's point value, while if b wins the event, then $L' = L - k$. Assuming the value and winner of the event are independent, the transition probabilities are given by

$$P_{L,L+k} = \Pr(r \text{ scores } | L)\Pr(\text{point value } = k),$$

$$P_{L,L-k} = \big(1 - \Pr(r \text{ scores } | L)\big)\Pr(\text{point value } = k),$$

where, for the particular sport, we use the empirical probability function for scoring as a function of lead size (Figure 5), from r's perspective, and the empirical distribution (Additional file 1, Appendix B) for the point value.

The probability that team r is the predicted winner depends on the probability distribution over lead sizes at time T. Because scoring events are conditionally independent, this distribution is given by P^n, where n is the expected number of scoring events in the remaining clock time $T - t$, multiplied by a vector S_0 representing the initial state $L = 0$. Given a choice of time t, we estimate $n = \sum_{w=t}^{T} \Pr(\text{event} \mid w)$, which is the expected number of events given the empirical tempo function (Figure 3, also the Bernoulli tempo model in Section 6) and the remaining clock time. We then convert this distribution, which we calculate numerically, into a prediction by summing probabilities for each of three outcomes: r wins (states $L > 0$), r ties b (state $L = 0$), and b wins (states $L > 0$). In this way, we capture the information contained in the magnitude of the current lead, which is lost when we simply predict that the current leader will win, regardless of lead size.

We test the accuracy of the Markov chain using an out-of-sample prediction scheme, in which we repeatedly divide each sports' game data into a training set of a randomly selected 3/4 of all games and a test set of the remaining 1/4. From each training set, we estimate the empirical functions used in the model and compute the Markov chain's transition matrix. Then, across the games in each test set, we measure the mean fraction of times the Markov chain's prediction is correct. This fraction is equivalent to the popular AUC statistic [30], where AUC = 0.5 denotes an accuracy no better than guessing.

Instead of evaluating the model at some arbitrarily selected time, we investigate how outcome predictability evolves over time. Specifically, we compute the AUC as a function of the cumulative number of scoring events in the game, using the empirically observed times and lead sizes in each test-set game to parameterize the model's predictions. When the number of cumulative events is small, game outcomes should be relatively unpredictable, and as the clock runs down, predictability should increase. To provide a reference point for the quality of these results, we also measure the AUC over time for a simple heuristic of predicting the winner as the team in the lead after the event.

Across all sports, we find that game outcome is highly predictable, even after only a small number of scoring events (Figure 7). For instance, the winner of CFB and NFL games can be accurately chosen more than 60% of the time after only a single scoring event, and this rate increases to more than 80% by three events. NHL games are even more predictable, in part because they are very low-scoring games, and the winner may be accurately chosen roughly 80% of the time after the first event. The fast rise of the AUC curve as a function of continued scoring in these sports likely reflects the role played by differences in latent team skill in producing large leads, which make outcomes more predictable (Figure 5). In contrast, NBA games are the least predictable, requiring more than 40 events before the AUC exceeds 80%. This likely reflects the role of the 'restoring force' (Figure 5), which tends to make NBA games more unpredictable than we would expect from a simple model of scoring, and significantly more unpredictable than CFB, NFL or NHL games.

In all cases, the Markov chain substantially outperforms the 'leader wins' heuristic, even in the low-scoring NHL games. This occurs in part because small leads are less informative than large leads for guessing the winner, and the heuristic does not distinguish between these.

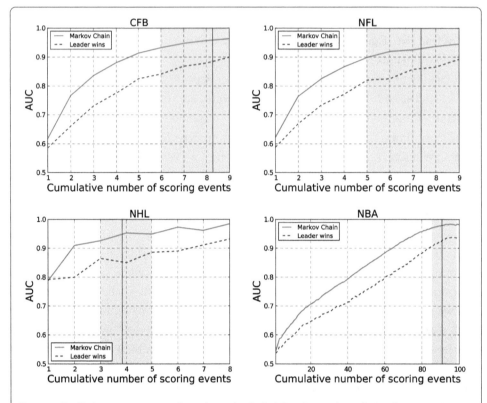

Figure 7 Predicting game outcome from dynamics. Probability of correctly predicting the game winner (AUC) using the Markov chain model and the 'leader wins' model for football, hockey, and basketball. The vertical line shows the average number of scoring events per game, and the highlighted region shows the middle 50% of games around this value.

8 Discussion

Although there is increasing interest in quantitative analysis and modeling in sports [31–35], many questions remain about what patterns or principles, if any, cut across different sports, what basic dynamical processes provide good models of within-game events, and the degree to which the outcomes of games may be predicted from within-game events alone. The comprehensive database of scoring events we use here to investigate such questions is unusual for both its scope (every league game over 9-10 seasons), its breadth (covering four sports), and its depth (timing and attribution information on every point in every game). As such, it offers a number of new opportunities to study competition in general, and sports in particular.

Across college (American) football (CFB), professional (American) football (NFL), professional hockey (NHL) and professional basketball (NBA) games, we find a number of common patterns in both the tempo and balance of scoring events. First, the timing of events in all four sports is remarkably well-approximated by a simple Poisson process (Figures 1 and 2), in which each second of gameplay produces a scoring event independently, with a probability that varies only modestly over the course of a game (Figure 3). These variations, however, follow a common three-phase pattern, in which a relatively constant rate is depressed at the beginning of a scoring period, and increases dramatically in the final few seconds of the period. The excellent agreement with a Poisson process implies that teams employ very few strategically-chosen chains of events or time-sensitive strategies in these games, except in a period's end-phase, when the incentive to score is elevated. These results provide further support to some past analyses [10, 19], while contrasting with others [12, 25], showing no evidence for the popular notion of 'hot hands', in which scoring once increases the chance of scoring again soon.

Second, we find a common pattern of imbalanced scoring between teams in CFB, NFL and NHL games, relative to an ideal model in which teams are equally likely to win each scoring event (Figure 4). CFB games are much less balanced than NFL games, suggesting that the transition from college to professional tends to reduce the team skill differences that generate lopsided scoring. This reduction in variance is likely related both to only the stronger college-level players successfully moving up into the professional teams, and in the way the NFL Draft tends to distribute the stronger of these new players to the weaker teams.

Furthermore, we find that all three of these sports exhibit a pattern in which lead sizes tend to increase over time. That is, the probability of scoring while in the lead tends to be larger the greater the lead size (Figure 5), in contrast to the ideal model in which lead sizes increase or decrease with equal probability. As with overall scoring balance, the size of this effect in CFB games is much larger (about 2.5 times larger) than in NFL games, which is consistent with a reduction in the variance of the distribution of skill across teams. That is, NFL teams are generally closer in team skill than CFB teams, and this produces gameplay that is much less predictable. Both of these patterns are consistent with a kind of Bradley-Terry-type model in which each scoring event is a contest between the teams.

NBA games, however, present the opposite pattern: team scores are much closer than we would expect from the ideal model, and the probability of scoring while in the lead effectively *decreases* as the lead size grows (Figure 5; a pattern originally identified by [10]). This pattern produces a kind of 'restoring force' such that leads tend to shrink until they turn into ties, producing games that are substantially more unpredictable. Unlike the pattern in CFB, NFL and NHL, no distribution of latent team skills, under a Bradley-Terry-type model, can produce this kind of negative correlation between the probability of scoring and lead size.

Recently, [21] analyzed similar NBA game data and argued that increased psychological motivation drives teams that are slightly behind (e.g., by one point at halftime) to win the game more often than not. That is, losing slightly is good for winning. Our analysis places this claim in a broader, more nuanced context. The effective restoring force is superficially consistent with the belief that losing in NBA games is 'good' for the team, as losing does indeed empirically increase the probability of scoring. However, we find no such effect in CFB, NFL or NHL games (Figure 5), suggesting either that NBA players are more poorly motivated than players in other team sports or that some other mechanism explains the pattern.

One such mechanism is for NBA teams to employ strategies associated with substituting weaker players for stronger ones when they hold various leads, e.g., to allow their best players to rest or avoid injury, manage floor spacing and offensive/defensive combinations, etc., and then reverse the process when the other team leads. In this way, a team will play more weakly when it leads, and more strongly when it is losing, because of personnel changes alone rather than changes in morale or effort. If teams have different thresholds for making such substitutions, and differently skilled best players, the averaging across these differences would produce the smooth pattern observed in the data. Such substitutions are indeed common in basketball games, while football and hockey teams are inherently less able to alter their effective team skill through such player management, which may explain the restoring force's presence in NBA games and its absence in CFB, NFL or NHL games. It would be interesting to determine whether college basketball games exhibit the same restoring force, and the personnel management hypothesis could be tested by estimating the on-court team's skill as a function of lead size.

The observed patterns we find in the probability of scoring while in the lead are surprisingly accurate at reproducing the observed variation in lead-size dynamics in these sports (Figure 6), and suggest that this one pattern provides a compact and mostly accurate summary of the within-game scoring dynamics of a sport. However, we do not believe these patterns indicate the presence of any feedbacks, e.g., 'momentum' or cumulative advantage [36]. Instead, for CFB, NFL and NHL games, this pattern represents the distribution of latent team skills, while for NBA games, it represents strategic decisions about which players are on the court as a function of lead size.

This pattern also makes remarkably good predictions about the overall outcome of games, even when given information about only the first ℓ scoring events. Under a controlled out-of-sample test, we found that CFB, NFL and NHL game outcomes are highly predictable, even after only a few events. In contrast, NBA games were significantly less predictable, although reasonable predictions here can still be made, despite the impact of the restoring force.

Given the popularity of betting on sports, it is an interesting question as to whether our model produces better or worse predictions than those of established odds-makers. To explore this question, we compared our model against two such systems, the online live-betting website Bovada[b] and the odds-maker website Sports Book Review (SBR).[c] Neither site provided comprehensive coverage or systematic access, and so our comparison was necessarily limited to a small sample of games. Among these, however, our predictions were very close to those of Bovada, and, after 20% of each game's events had occurred, were roughly 10% more accurate than SBR's money lines across all sports. Although the precise details are unknown for how these commercial odds were set, it seems likely that they rely on many details omitted by our model, such as player statistics, team histories, team strategies and strengths, etc. In contrast, our model uses only information relating to the basic scoring dynamics within a sport, and knows nothing about individual teams or game strategies. In that light, its accuracy is impressive.

These results suggest several interesting directions for future work. For instance, further elucidating the connection between team skill and the observed scoring patterns would provide an important connection between within-game dynamics and team-specific characteristics. These, in turn, could be estimated from player-level characteristics to provide a coherent understanding of how individuals cooperate to produce a team and how teams compete to produce dynamics. Another missing piece of the dynamics puzzle is the role played by the environment and the control of space for creating scoring opportunities. Recent work on online games with heterogeneous environments suggests that these spatial factors can have large impact on scoring tempo and balance [23], but time series data on player positions on the field would further improve our understanding. Finally, our data omit many aspects of gameplay, including referee calls, timeouts, fouls, etc., which may provide for interesting strategic choices by teams, e.g., near the end of the game, as with clock management in football games. Progress on these and other questions would shed more light on the fundamental question of how much of gameplay may be attributed to skill versus luck.

Finally, our results demonstrate that common patterns and processes do indeed cut across seemingly distinct sports, and these patterns provide remarkably accurate descriptions of the events within these games and predictions of their outcomes. However, many questions remain unanswered, particularly as to what specific mechanisms generate the modest deviations from the basic patterns that we observe in each sport, and how exactly teams exerting such great efforts against each other can conspire to produce gameplay so reminiscent of simple stochastic processes. We look forward to future work that further investigates these questions, which we hope will continue to leverage the powerful tools and models of dynamical systems, statistical physics, and machine learning with increasingly detailed data on competition.

Additional material

Additional file 1: Technical details on game mechanics (Appendix A) and points per scoring event, by sport (Appendix B).

Competing interests
The authors declare that they have no competing interests.

Authors' contributions
AC conceived the research and acquired the data. AC and SM designed the models and performed the data analysis. All authors wrote and approved the final version of the manuscript.

Author details
[1] Department of Computer Science, University of Colorado, Boulder, CO 80309, USA. [2] BioFrontiers Institute, University of Colorado, Boulder, CO 80303, USA. [3] Santa Fe Institute, 1399 Hyde Park Rd., Santa Fe, NM 87501, USA.

Acknowledgements
We thank Dan Larremore, Christopher Aicher, Joel Warner, Mason Porter, Peter Mucha, Pete McGraw, Dave Feldman, Sid Redner, Alan Gabel, Owen Newkirk, Oskar Burger, Rajiv Maheswaran and Chris Meyer for helpful conversations. This work was supported in part by the James S McDonnell Foundation.

Endnotes
  [a] Data provided by STATS LLC, copyright 2014.
  [b] See https://live.bovada.lv. Only data on NBA games were available.
  [c] See http://www.sbrforum.com/betting-odds.

References
1. Klaassen FJGM, Magnus JR (2001) Are points in tennis independent and identically distributed? Evidence from a dynamic binary panel data model. J Am Stat Assoc 96:500-509
2. Albert J, Bennett J, Cochran JJ (2005) Anthology of statistics in sports, vol. 16. SIAM, Philadelphia
3. Ben-Naim E, Vazquez F, Redner S (2007) What is the most competitive sport? J Korean Phys Soc 50:124-126
4. Thomas AC (2007) Inter-arrival times of goals in ice hockey. J Quant Anal Sports 3(3)
5. Duch J, Waitzman JS, Amaral LAN (2010) Quantifying the performance of individual players in a team activity. PLoS ONE 5:10937
6. Heuer A, Müller C, Rubner O (2010) Soccer: is scoring goals a predictable Poissonian process? Europhys Lett 89:38007
7. Buttrey SE, Washburn AR, Price WL (2011) Estimating NHL scoring rates. J Quant Anal Sports 7(3):24
8. Radicchi F (2011) Who is the best player ever? A complex network analysis of the history of professional tennis. PLoS ONE 6:17249
9. Radicchi F (2012) Universality, limits and predictability of gold-medal performances at the Olympics games. PLoS ONE 7:40335
10. Gabel A, Redner S (2012) Random walk picture of basketball scoring. J Quant Anal Sports 8
11. Goldman M, Rao JM (2012) Effort vs. concentration: the asymmetric impact of pressure on NBA performance. In: Proceedings MIT Sloan sports analytics conference, pp 1-10
12. Yaari G, David G (2012) 'Hot hand' on strike: bowling data indicates correlation to recent past results, not causality. PLoS ONE 7:30112
13. Myerson RB (1997) Game theory: analysis of conflict. Harvard University Press, Cambridge
14. Palacios-Huerta I (2003) Professionals play minimax. Rev Econ Stud 70(2):395-415

15. Walker M, Wooders J (2001) Minimax play at Wimbledon. Am Econ Rev 91(5):1521-1538
16. Romer D (2006) Do firms maximize? Evidence from professional football. J Polit Econ 114(2):340-365
17. Reed D, Hughes M (2006) An exploration of team sport as a dynamical system. Int J Perform Anal Sport 6(2):114-125
18. Galla T, Farmer JD (2013) Complex dynamics in learning complicated games. Proc Natl Acad Sci USA 110:1232-1236
19. Ayton P, Fischer I (2004) The hot hand fallacy and the gambler's fallacy: two faces of subjective randomness? Mem Cogn 32(8):1369-1378
20. Balkundi P, Harrison DA (2006) Ties, leaders, and time in teams: strong inference about network structure's effects on team viability and performance. Acad Manag J 49:49-68
21. Berger J, Pope D (2011) Can losing lead to winning? Manag Sci 57(5):817-827
22. Vergin RC (2000) Winning streaks in sports and the misperception of momentum. J Sport Behav 23:181
23. Merritt S, Clauset A (2013) Environmental structure and competitive scoring advantages in team competitions. Sci Rep 3:3067
24. Barney J (1991) Firm resources and sustained competitive advantage. J Manag 17:99-120
25. Yaari G, David G (2011) The hot (invisible?) hand: can time sequence patterns of success/failure in sports be modeled as repeated independent trials. PLoS ONE 6:24532
26. Boas ML (2006) Mathematical methods in the physical sciences, 3rd edn. Wiley, Hoboken
27. Box GEP, Jenkins GM, Reinsel GC (2013) Time series analysis: forecasting and control. Wiley, Hoboken
28. Thompson P (2010) Learning by doing. In: Hall B, Rosenberg N (eds.) Handbook of economics of technical change, pp 429-476. Elsevier, Philadelphia
29. Bradley RA, Terry ME (1952) Rank analysis of incomplete block designs: I. the method of paired comparisons. Biometrika 39(3/4):324-345
30. Bradley AP (1997) The use of the area under the ROC curve in the evaluation of machine learning algorithms. Pattern Recognit 30(7):1145-1159
31. Arkes J, Martinez J (2011) Finally, evidence for a momentum effect in the NBA. J Quant Anal Sports 7
32. Bourbousson J, Sève C, McGarry T (2012) Space-time coordination dynamics in basketball: Part 2. The interaction between the two teams. J Sports Sci 28(3):349-358
33. de Saá Guerra Y, Martín González JM, Sarmiento Montesdeoca S, Rodríguez Ruiz D, Arjonilla López N, García Manso JM (2013) Basketball scoring in NBA games: an example of complexity. J Syst Sci Complex 26(1):94-103
34. Everson P, Goldsmith-Pinkham PS (2008) Composite Poisson models for goal scoring. J Quant Anal Sports 4(2):13
35. Neiman T, Loewenstein Y (2011) Reinforcement learning in professional basketball players. Nat Commun 2:569
36. Price DDS (1976) A general theory of bibliometric and other cumulative advantage processes. J Am Soc Inf Sci 27(5):292-306

9

Sharing political news: the balancing act of intimacy and socialization in selective exposure

Jisun An[1]*, Daniele Quercia[2], Meeyoung Cha[3]*, Krishna Gummadi[4] and Jon Crowcroft[5]

*Correspondence: jan@qf.org.qa;
meeyoungcha@kaist.edu
[1]Qatar Computing Research
Institute, Majlis Al Taawon Street,
Doha, Qatar
[3]Graduate School of Culture
Technology, KAIST, 291 Daehak-ro,
Daejeon, Republic of Korea
Full list of author information is
available at the end of the article

Abstract

One might think that, compared to traditional media, social media sites allow people to choose more freely what to read and what to share, especially for politically oriented news. However, reading and sharing habits originate from deeply ingrained behaviors that might be hard to change. To test the extent to which this is true, we propose a *Political News Sharing (PoNS)* model that holistically captures four key aspects of social psychology: *gratification*, *selective exposure*, *socialization*, and *trust & intimacy*. Using real instances of political news sharing in Twitter, we study the predictive power of these features. As one might expect, news sharing heavily depends on what one likes and agrees with (*selective exposure*). Interestingly, it also depends on the credibility of a news source, i.e., whether the source is a social media friend or a news outlet (*trust & intimacy*) as well as on the informativeness or the enjoyment of the news article (*gratification*). Finally, a Twitter user tends to share articles matching his own political leaning but, at times, the user also shares politically opposing articles, if those match the leaning of his followers (*socialization*). Based on our PoNS model, we build a prototype of a news sharing application that promotes serendipitous political readings along our four dimensions.

Keywords: news sharing; political news; political diversity; social media; Twitter

1 Introduction

Media bias has been widely studied in cultivation theory. This holds that popular media such as newspapers, television, and now the Internet have the power to influence our view of the world and set our day-to-day norms. Media bias - appearing as either selecting what to report or choosing a slant on a particular report [1, 2] - matters because it affects the political beliefs of the audience, alters voting behavior [3, 4], and has negative societal effects like increasing intolerance of dissent and creating segregated and polarized communities [5].

Since social media sites have been recently used to share news stories at a global scale [6–8], they promise to connect millions of individuals who hold very diverse political views [9] and diversify their media consumption [10]. Unfortunately, in social media, people's news consumption patterns have not changed much compared to those in traditional media - people tend to avoid information that conflicts with their views, resulting in the old-fashioned problem of media bias, even reinforcing what is known as the filter bubble [11].

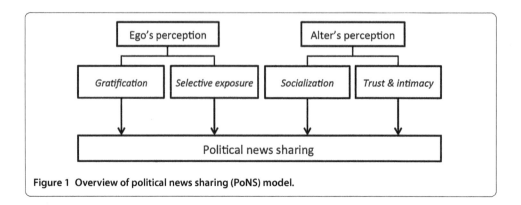

Figure 1 Overview of political news sharing (PoNS) model.

The choice of what to read and share is a process determined by a number of psychological factors such as cognition and motivation. Investigating them thoroughly will lead us to understand the media bias problem better and develop a tool mitigating this effect. One set of theories is related to the 'ego's perception' and includes two main factors: *gratification*, suggesting that people read and share news to satisfy their desires such as informativeness and entertainment [12] and *selective exposure*, suggesting that people like to read information in agreement with their views and avoid conflicting information [13]. Another set of theories is associated with 'alter's perception' and focuses on social aspects of information sharing: whether the person who passes the information is credible (trust & intimacy) and whether the person who will receive the news would like it (socialization). These two sets of theories have not been considered together, and we will do so here.

To this end, we propose a Political News Sharing (PoNS) model based on the two popular perspectives as theoretical foundation. The PoNS model is graphically summarized in Figure 1. There are four major factors that might impact news sharing: gratification, selective exposure, socialization, and trust & intimacy. We have evaluated the PoNS model with more than 150,000 cases of sharing political news in Twitter. Using data of twenty-four popular news media outlets and twenty-one million Twitter users, we study the predictive power of the four factors separately and collectively. More specifically, we make the following contributions:

1. We investigate the extent to which Twitter users are exposed to political diversity. We find that 90% of the users receive information from news media of only one political leaning - that is, most people do not subscribe to politically diverse media outlets. On the other hand, their friends' retweets lead them to diversify their news consumption, in that, 41% of the users are exposed to politically diverse news.

2. We test which factors motivate people to share news. The most important factor is the source's credibility: a user is 49% more likely to retweet news coming from media sources (original tweet) than news from other users (retweeted one). However, when sharing *political* news, people prefer those from friends (Trust & Intimacy). The second strongest factor is exposure: with an extra exposure to a news article, a user is 23% more likely to retweet the news (Gratification).

3. Political news is not generally considered to be a retweeting subject, but when people share, they mostly retweet articles they agree with (agreeable news), confirming the key role of selective exposure theory. We also find a weak evidence that when the articles is interesting to their followers, people share political news reflecting views different from their own (socialization).

4. These findings provide a holistic view of how people share political news. The first finding suggests that the formation of echo-chambers resulting from subscriptions to traditional media outlets is countered by the more serendipitous news sharing happening among users. Also, the fact that followers hold a certain influence over a user is not surprising, if one considers that people are influenced by peers who are up to three (social network) hops away from them [14]. Based on these four generic factors that motivate political news sharing, we demonstrate a new way of visualizing news articles that gives users a fine control over the PoNS' four dimensions.

2 Background

Researchers in media communication have long been studying the media effect, and we review some of those studies below.

2.1 Media bias and its consequences

Media bias has been shown to have negative societal consequences (e.g., intolerance of dissent, political segregation, group polarization) [5]. Republicans and Democrats read different newspapers and books [15] and geographically sort themselves by choosing in which neighborhoods to live [16]. Media slant changes people's beliefs, for example, in whom to vote [3, 17]. Group polarization is prevalent not only in the offline world (e.g., in the form of geographic sorting) but also in the online world. Blogs reflecting different political views rarely link to each other [18], and online news consumption is also biased, much like offline news [19].

A few recent studies examined how people exchange political content in online social networks. [20] has looked at Twitter use of U.S. political parties. [21] has shown a retweeting network of political hashtag that shows a clear segregation of two political parties; however they have found active interactions across those two parties in a mention network. Related to this work, [22] has reported that political discussions taking place in Twitter can go to extreme easily. We build upon this work and expand it by determining to which extent Twitter users segregate themselves into echo chambers, and what could be done about it.

2.2 News sharing in social media

Due to its popularity and the data's easy accessibility - Twitter data is publicly available - research on Twitter has been flourishing for the last few years. Kwak *et al.* [23] studied the topology of the Twitter graph, finding a non-power-law follower distribution, a short effective diameter, and low reciprocity. Other studies have provided insights into the patterns of user participation in Twitter by looking into the use of Twitter as a medium of information spreading, including sharing URLs and reporting news [24], posting local news [25], and promoting political views [26]. Despite a large body of research on information sharing being conducted, news articles published by media sources have less been examined.

A news article published in social media can reach many more audience members than media outlets' direct followers, passed through the social network. Consider the example of a news article exchanged by Twitter users in Figure 2. It shows how the same news could propagate with different sentiments (i.e., positive and negative comments). The article is originally tweeted by the Washington Times and is then received by followers of the media source, who might have different political views. Among the followers, two of them

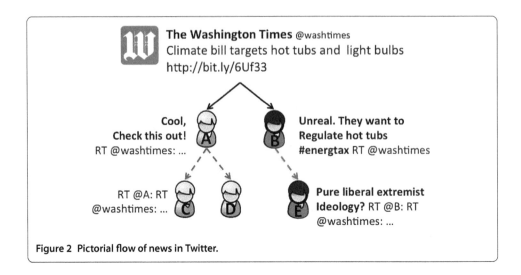

Figure 2 Pictorial flow of news in Twitter.

might decide to retweet the article to their followers. In the toy example, user A is in tune with the political view of the Washington Times and he adds a comment ('cool. check this out'). Then, user A's followers, user C and user D, get to receive the Washington Times' original tweet along with user A's positive recommendation. However, not all news articles are positively recommended. In the case of user B, he may decide to retweet the news, but with a negative comment ('Unreal. they want to regulate hot tubs #energtax' and his follower user E might further decide to add another negative comment 'pure liberal extremist ideology?') before he retweets.

2.3 Motivations of news sharing

A number of theories in media and communication research have been suggested to understand why people consume news. Gratification theory states that satisfying audiences' social and psychological needs is the key to attracting and keeping those audiences [12]. Specifically, desires such as entertainment, interpersonal communication, information learning, escapism, and surveillance are the general factors that are associated with news consumption on the Internet [27–30]. The few studies that have focused on content sharing activities in online communities found that gratification, social interaction, reciprocity, and self-identifications are strongly related to why people share knowledge online [31]. On the other hand, as an attempt to understand how people manage opinion conflicts, selective exposure theory hypothesizes that individuals tend to favor information that reinforces pre-existing views while avoiding contradictory information [13].

In the context of social media study, number of exposures has been widely considered as a proxy of social impact. Social impact theory states one's belief, motive, behavior changes as a result of presence or actions of other individuals' [32]. The first principle is that it is a multiplicative function of the strength, immediacy, and number of sources present in the environment. A number of studies have examined the impact of exposure in relation to whether it motivates people to share a piece of information. Previous work has found a strong evidence that the number of exposures is strongly related to a hashtag adoption [33] and a rapid growth of hashtags [34].

However, in this work, we use the number of exposures as a proxy to measure informativeness of a tweet. Social impact theory also states that the relative impact of each additional person decreases and when an individual is a part of a group, the impact of sources is divided among individuals exposed and is therefore reduced - as more people exposed, less likely to change their behavior. The theory also relates to a theory of 'diffusion of responsibility' in a socio-psychology phenomenon whereby a person is less likely to take responsibility for action or inaction when others are present [35, 36], hinting that one may feel less obligated to share a piece of information as more exposures happen. Thus, we do not use the number of exposures as directly connected to the motivation of sharing. We rather consider it as an additional context of the tweet.

3 Political news sharing model

When ideas spread, there are always three parties: the person(s) creating the news, the person passing on the news, and the person(s) receiving it. Considering how these three parties influence motivations of a person in sharing news, we identify four major factors: gratification, selective exposure, socialization, and trust & intimacy. Followed by relevant prior literature, we discuss corresponding Twitter specific measures of each factor.

3.1 Gratification

We assume that how a user perceives a given article contributes to whether or not he will share it. More precisely, informativeness describes the extent to which news shared can provide users with relevant and valuable information. A user would perceive a piece of information as valuable when he is exposed to it multiple times, resulting in motivating him to share it further. Related to this, entertainment is another key factor for understanding news consumption [29]. People are more likely to share news that they deeply care about and are interested in. To study why users retweet news articles, we derive two predictors from gratification theory:

1. *F1 numexposures* denotes how many times the retweeter repeatedly gets exposed to the article.

2. *F2 topic-interesting-me* reflects the extent to which the retweeter is interested in the article's topic. To compute it, we create, for each user, his *interest-vector* by considering each article the user posts, classifying the article's categories, and aggregating the classifications of all the user's articles into a unique *interest-vector*. The classification consists of 12 categories and is performed by the Alchemy Application Programming Interface (http://www.alchemyapi.com/), which is a popular text-mining web service that classifies news articles in a number of topic.

3.2 Selective exposure

Selective exposure theory states that individuals tend to favor information that reinforces pre-existing views and avoid contradictory information. In this theory, individuals are likely to choose political articles with opinions that fit with and support what they already know. Various studies have examined whether selective exposure exists in news consumption and consistent evidence has been found across a variety of media [37]. Below are the two predictors associated with the selective exposure theory:

3. *F3 political* reflects whether the article is about politics or not (binary).

4. *F4 leaning-matched-me* indicates that the retweeter's political views match those of the media outlet that published the article (binary). This factor is considered only if the news article is about politics.

3.3 Socialization

Socialization plays a critical role in determining whether a user will share a news article. This is particularly true in social networking sites. The experience that a user has in sharing news articles depends on the context created by the user's peers (e.g., only few reactions on what has been shared, being ignored). To encourage discussions or idea exchange and to ultimately enrich the social media experience, users might consider what their online friends like to read or agree with.

We thus expect that one retweets news articles that are relevant to one's followers. Hence the two predictors related to socialization are:

5. *F5 topic-interesting-followers* indicates the extent to which the retweeter's followers are interested in the article's topic. This is computing based on the average similarity between the categories of the article (as per Alchemy categories) and the interest-vectors of one's followers.

6. *F6 leaning-matched-followers* represents a fraction of retweeter's followers whose political views match that of the article. This factor is considered only if the news article is about politics.

3.4 Trust and intimacy

In social media, news articles are shared not just by news outlets but also by users. People easily turn their ears to a piece of information or an opinion coming from their 'friends.' The stronger the relationship, the more easily people accept what friends share. Through peer influence, users might receive news articles reflecting views different from their own. We would like to examine whether trust and intimacy affect a user's decision to share a given article. Trust in the sender might also impact one's willingness to retweet the article. To capture the impact of friendship on retweeting news articles, we consider a number of measures between a user who tweets an article and his follower who receive it. The predictors related to trust and intimacy are:

7. *F7 fromfriend* indicates whether a news article comes from one of the retweeter's friends or from a media source (binary).

8. *F8 mutualfriend* is a measure of whether the user and the propagator(s) are friends with each other (i.e., have a mutual relationship).

9. *F9 difference-in-followers* is the difference between the retweeter's number of followers and the propagator's. A friend having a greater number of followers may be a public figure or influential.

10. *F10 sharedfollowers* is the number of common followers between retweeter and propagator. Having more common followers may mean that the two have common interests.

11. *F11 sharedfollowees* is the number of common followees between retweeter and propagator.

12. *F12 sharedleaning* reflects whether the retweeter's political views match those held by the propagators.

4 Data

4.1 Collecting Twitter data

Twitter was created in 2006 and it has been rapidly growing, attracting 255M monthly active users [38]. In Twitter, the users share content composed from 140-character text messages called *tweets*. Users can choose whom to *follow* - a social relationship in Twitter is not necessarily mutual. Hence, topologically, a Twitter network is a directed graph: an individual has a number of 'followees' whom he follows and 'followers' who follow him. A user will receive all tweets posted by his followees. Unless a user sets his privacy setting as 'private' explicitly, all tweets he posts are visible to the public by default.

For our analysis, we gathered publicly available information from Twitter. We firstly identified a set of news media sources by consulting both the website http://newspapers. com (which listed the top 100 newspapers in the USA) and Twitter's 'Browse Interest' directory (its news directory) [39]. From these two lists, we generated a list of news providers, including mainstream news outlets such as the New York Times and CNN. We also included individual journalists and anchors as they are known to have a large audience and play a prominent role as news providers. We only considered US-based news media outlets, a total of 22.

Using the Twitter API, we obtained all follow links to media sources and their corresponding tweets for an 8-month period (from January to August 2009). To efficiently identify the consumption behavior of news on Twitter, we focus on the set of news media tweets that contain a URL. Through the Twitter API, we collected all tweets that contain any of the URLs posted by the 22 media sources. Not all of these users were directly following media sources. For each user who posted, retweeted, or replied to those URLs, we also gathered his follow links.

The resulting dataset includes 22 media sources with 55,777 tweets with a total of 8,793,507 subscribers. Among all tweets, there were 42,483 tweets containing URLs, 397,640 retweets, 21.4 million Twitter profiles, and 720 million directed follow links. For convenience, Table 1 shows a summary of the data collected from all media sources.

Table 1 Summary of the three media sources under study

Account	Subscribers	Tweets	URLs	RTs of URLs	Mondotimes
abcnews	16,397	3,800	3,729	10,412	left
ariannahuff	23,912	185	94	894	left
davidgregory	1,115,405	575	159	2,361	left
huffingtonpost	54,418	4,186	4,174	29,385	left
jdickerson	953,993	1,469	413	14,501	left
maddow	1,091,269	127	116	12,316	left
nbcnightlynews	12,602	2,118	2,105	3,234	left
nprnews	116,834	1,956	1,848	30,825	left
nprpolitics	1,272,479	2,803	2,342	20,238	left
nprscottsimon	887,009	893	68	763	left
nytimes	1,755,740	5,676	5,527	91,379	left
theearlyshow	6,873	1,524	1,413	4,191	left
todayshow	108,481	1,672	1,050	26,291	left
washingtonpost	27,196	1,903	1,617	9,619	left
andersoncooper	319,257	3,528	3,436	23,495	center
cnnbrk	2,596,796	524	240	32,131	center
jackgraycnn	587,758	3,109	368	26,598	center
richardpbacon	819,312	1,793	224	16,116	center
foxnews	100,272	6,401	6,361	15,699	right
chicagotribune	17,588	1,010	1,010	15,610	right
usnews	4,747	4,239	4,233	7,545	right
washtimes	6,954	2,025	1,956	4,037	right
all	8,793,507	55,777	42,483	397,640	

4.2 Extracting political discourse

To categorize the URLs in our tweets, we use, again, the Alchemy API. We use this API because it has been shown that it entails superior classification performance compared to other popular classifiers [40]. Given a URL, Alchemy extracts the associated text and returns featured words, the main topic, and a confidence value for the categorization which scales from 0 to 1 representing the API's degree of belief that the text pertains to that category. The main topic is chosen from the following 12 topics: Arts Entertainment, Business, Computer Internet, Culture Politics, Gaming, Health, Law Crime, Recreation, Religion, Science Technology, Sports, and Weather. We excluded URLs that are categorized as 'None' (e.g., video live streaming or personal photos) and URLs that have low confidence values (<0.5 on Alchemy's scale of $[0,1]$).

Out of 42,483 URLs from the 22 media sources, 23,017 URLs were successfully classified. For these categorized news articles, 41% of them have been retweeted at least once, where culture_politics is the mostly popular category, where 73% of articles in culture_politics has been retweeted at least once, followed by entertainment (68%), and science_technology (57%).

Next, to classify news outlets into liberal, conservative, or center, we consulted the website http://www.mondotimes.com and used the Americans for Democratic Action (ADA) scores of media sources [1] that is widely used for comparing media bias across different outlets [2]. The ADA score measures a media outlet's political bias based on the number of times the outlet cites various think-tanks and other politically-oriented groups. The score is on the scale from 0 to 100, where 0 indicates a strong conservative tendency. Four media outlets (Fox News, Chicago Tribune, U.S. News & World Report, and Washington Times) were classified as right-wing, five (including CNN) as center, and fourteen (including Huffington Post, NPR News, and New York Times) as left-wing. As we are interested in how different political opinions reach users having different political views, we chose to focus on left and right media outlets (18 in total), since they have a clear political stance.

4.3 Inferring political leaning of users

We inferred the political leaning of each user based on the set of media outlets that the user subscribed to. To reduce noise in the data, we only considered users who tweeted more than 5 times in the last three months of our data collection period (this leaves us with 2.9M users). Then we filtered out users who follow only one media source under the assumption that they are less interested in news reading through social media. After this pruning, 419,446 users were still left.

To infer the political leaning of individual users, we have used their subscriptions to media outlets, under the conservative assumption that one's political leaning can be determined only if all media outlets the user follows exhibit the same political leaning [41]. Recent study has shown this mapping method is valid [42]. To analyze the restrictions introduced by this assumption, we randomly picked 30 left-leaning users and 30 right-leaning users in our dataset, and asked them their political leanings. We received 22 and 16 responses from left and right-leaning, respectively, retaining a response rate of 63%. Among those 38 people who answered, we found 30 users (78.9%) were classified correctly (16 left-leaning users with 72.7% matching rate and 14 right-leaning users with higher matching rate of 87.5%). With such a high level of accuracy, we choose to use the conservative rule of thumb to assign political leanings of users. These users accounted for 380,568 or 90.7% of our users. Most were left-wing (88%) and only 44,943 users (12%) were right-wing.

Table 2 Summary of the two compared datasets

	Active followers	Classified URLs	Retweets (Retweeters)
Original dataset (14 left & 4 right)	419,446	22,179	154,078 (68,225)
Balanced dataset (4 left & 4 right)	146,480	11,289	60,524 (27,597)

The balanced dataset is a subset of the original dataset, where we balance the number of left and right media sources.

Because our original dataset includes many more left-wing media sources, it may over-represent left-leaning users. Even though they are over-represented compared to the general population, they are still representative of the Twitter population. We therefore generated a 'balanced dataset' that includes the same number of media sources from each political leaning (four of each are selected randomly). A summary of the two datasets is shown in Table 2. The numbers reported in the row 'balanced dataset' correspond to the mean values across 20 different reshuffled versions of the balanced dataset. All our analyses have been carried out on both datasets, and the corresponding results remain consistent between the two, suggesting that the ways in which we select outlets do not impact the results.

5 Status quo of media bias

Retweets from friends can expose individuals to diverse political views. To test the extent to which this is the case, we map retweets back to the original tweets by tracking URLs, which do not change from tweet to retweet. By consolidating all tweets containing the same URL, we build a propagation tree for each news article.

5.1 Top news covered by left and right media

From our eighteen media sources, 14,568 URLs were categorized as political news articles. These URLs spawned 31,473 retweets. 17.5% of users engaged in political news propagation, and users who follow both left and right media sources (following four media outlets at least) were three times more likely to propagate political news than others.

To give a sense of which political news stories are shared in Twitter, we listed the top stories in Table 3. One can see that the left and right media have a different tone of voice even on the same topic. For example, on an issue regarding North Korea, left-wing media reported 'North Korean Leader Pardons, Releases U.S. Journalists' while right-wing media said 'North Korea Threatens to Wipe Out U.S.'

5.2 Exposure to diverse opinions

To investigate whether Twitter users live in echo chambers or not, we examined what users receive and what they decide to promote by retweeting. More specifically, we initially consider two main sources of news articles (i.e., media sources a user follows and his Twitter friends) and compute the political diversity of news articles coming from the two sources based on the Shannon Index, which is defined as the (political) entropy of the news articles associated with the user. It is $-\sum_{i=1}^{S}(p_i \log p_i)$, where S is the total number of possible political preferences, and p_i is a proportion of news articles that reflects the ith political preference. If a user's articles reflect all political views to the same extent, then the Shannon Index (the user's political diversity) is maximum. While the Shannon Index

Table 3 The top 10 mentioned political news articles from the left-leaning and the right-leaning media sources in Twitter

Rank	Left-leaning media	Source	# of RT
1	The President's Opening Remarks on Iran	nytimes	203 (*l*100, *r*50, *b*53)
2	Cheney Is Linked to Concealment of C.I.A. Project	nytimes	113 (*l*97, *r*2, *b*14)
3	Sarah Palin Resigning as Alaska's Governor	nytimes	50 (*l*38, *b*12)
4	N. Korean Leader Pardons, Releases U.S. Journalists	nytimes	48 (*l*38, *b*10)
5	'Military Coup' Underway In Iran	nytimes	47 (*l*39, *r*3, *b*5)
6	Health Care Hecklers & the Rise of Right-Wing Rage	nytimes	43 (*l*41, *b*2)
7	Conservatives Don't Know He's Joking	nytimes	42 (*l*38, *b*4)
8	N.Y. Assembly Passes Gay Marriage Bill	nytimes	39 (*l*39)
9	10 Most Offensive Tea Party Signs From Tax Day Protests	nytimes	39 (*l*34, *b*5)
10	Rick Perry Calls For Fed Help With Swine Flu	nytimes	37 (*l*28, *b*9)

Rank	Right-leaning media	Source	# of RT
1	North Korea Threatens to 'Wipe Out' U.S.	foxnews	40 (*l*2, *r*20, *b*18)
2	Obama Claim of AARP Endorsement 'Inaccurate'	foxnews	30 (*r*16, *b*14)
3	House leaders drop their plans to buy fancy jets	foxnews	30 (*r*20, *b*10)
4	WH Says Girl Chosen at 'Random' to Speak at Town Hall	foxnews	28 (*l*2, *r*18, *bb*8)
5	Pelosi Calls Health Care Critics 'Un-American'	foxnews	28 (*r*14, *b*14)
6	Latino Leaders Call for Illegal Immigrants to Boycott Census	foxnews	24 (*l*2, *r*12, *b*10)
7	Outbursts, Hot Tempers Fill Town Hall Meetings	foxnews	24 (*r*16, *b*8)
8	Obama: Recovery Will Take Years Not Months	foxnews	24 (*r*20, *b*4)
9	AARP Faces Backlash From Seniors Over Health Care Reform	foxnews	22 (*r*16, *b*6)
10	Palin to stump for conservative Democrats	foxnews	20 (*r*6, *b*14)

The table also shows the news source of the article and the number of retweets of the article from different political groups, where *l* stands for liberals, *r* for conservatives, and *b* for others.

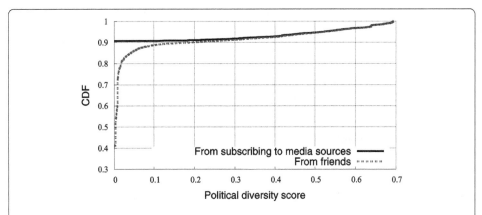

Figure 3 CDF of political diversity score. The plot shows the distribution of political diversity score from direct subscription (solid line) and that from social media friends (dotted line).

is popularly used as a measure of diversity, the resulted values may be biased as it does not take the sample size into consideration. To solve the bias problem, we apply Miller-Madow correction technique [43].

5.2.1 Diversity from subscribing to media sources

For each user, we consider the media sources the user follows, determine their political leanings, and compute their overall political diversity score using the Shannon index. Across all users, we find that the distribution of political diversity is skewed. Figure 3 shows that 90% of users have a political diversity score of 0, meaning that they only subscribe to media sources of their political leaning, and only 10% have diversity score greater than 0, meaning they subscribe to at least one media source whose political view is different from their own. Based on the classification of different 'user types' in previous studies [44], we could classify the users in the 90% group as either *challenge-averse* (i.e., users who seek out affirming opinions but reject the idea that they avoid challenging items) or *support-seeking* (i.e., users who are primarily interested in opinions that are similar to their own), while the remaining 10% would be classified as *diversity-seeking* (i.e., users who are interested in considering opinions that challenge their own).

To then distinguish who is support-seeking among the 90%, we consider which of these users have retweeted news articles containing political views different from their own. People in the support-seeking category do not like political diversity, yet they do not mind receiving a few articles they disagree with. We find that, among the low-diversity users in the 90% group, 86% are challenge-averse and 14% are support-seeking. Compared to the previous work suggesting that there was no evidence of the existence of support-seeking individuals [44], we observed three very distinct groups: users who do not subscribe media outlets nor share articles contrasting their political views, users who occasionally share articles even if they are in conflict with their views, and users who enjoy diverse opinions.

5.2.2 Diversity from friends

Having looked at the political diversity introduced by the media outlets users subscribe to, we now examine the diversity introduced by their Twitter 'friends'. Thus, for each user, we consider the news articles the user receives not only from media sources but also from friends. We then compute the diversity of political views contained in those articles using, again, the Shannon index.

We find that the distribution of political diversity score among users is still skewed as seen in Figure 3. However, there is a crucial difference: now the proportion of users with political diversity score of 0 drops from 90.7% to 40.7%, suggesting that social media friends are a primary source of political diversity in Twitter. At the population level, the geometric average of political diversity shows a 7.13-fold increase (the same goes for the politically balanced dataset in which the increase is even higher - it is 12.24-fold). We also find that the higher the diversity from direct media subscription, lower the changes in the diversity from friends with Pearson's correlation coefficients of $r = -0.29$ ($p < 0.0005$) and with a Spearman's correlation coefficients of $r = -0.14$ ($p < 0.0005$).

To see which set of media outlets gets more exposure through social media friends, we select users who follow: (1) only left-leaning media sources; and (2) only right-leaning media sources. We find that both left-leaning (55.6%) and right-leaning media outlets (56.7%) profit from the social network (Figure 4), reaching more than half of non-subscribers in our dataset. With a balanced set, 45.3% of left-leaning and 47.8% of right-leaning users are exposed to media outlets having views different than their friends'. The row percentages slightly change between the two cases yet they are comparatively the same and lead to the same conclusion: left-leaning media outlets reach non-subscribers slightly less than right-leaning media outlets do.

6 Evaluation of PoNS model

Having observed that users are exposed to politically diverse news articles far more by their friends than directly by the media sources, we now test the PoNS model and examine which of the four factors (gratification, selective exposure, socialization, and trust & intimacy) are better associated with the chance of sharing political news. We use a logistic

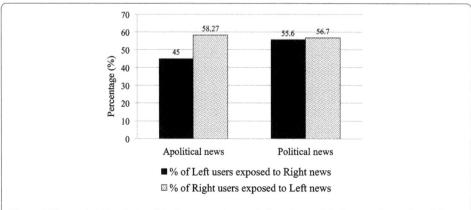

Figure 4 The probability that political news stories reach the other political group through social media friends. The bar plot shows an increase in political diversity after incorporating indirect media exposures through social media friends.

binomial regression, which models the probability that a user retweets a given news article based on twelve predictors extracted across the four factors. All predictors undergo a logarithmic transformation, when necessary (i.e., when they are skewed). The dependent variable is thus:

$$y_i = \begin{cases} 1 & \text{if user } i \text{ retweeted,} \\ 0 & \text{if user } i \text{ did not retweet.} \end{cases}$$

Since our data only includes positive cases - that is, the cases when people share the news articles - we need to augment our dataset with negative cases (by under-sampling them): we do so by adding an equal number of negative cases - that is, with a set of random news article-and-user pairs. By construction, the resulting sample is balanced (the response variable is split 50-50), and the accuracy of a random prediction model would thus be 50%. We model a retweeting probability as a linear combination of the predictive variables, plus terms for interactions. We use the first 7 and a half months of our data to calculate the independent variables and use the last two weeks of data for the test, which had 14,309 retweeting cases. Adding the same number of random negative cases, we use 28,618 cases to build the model.

The results of the logistic regressions are reported in Table 4. The coefficients reported tell us the extent to which the corresponding predictors explain the retweeting behavior. The p-values indicate the extent to which coeffiecients are statistically significant. To show how well the model fits the data, we use Hosmer-Lemeshow test of 'goodness-of-fit' and report χ^2 and its p-value. Please note that with Hosmer-Lemeshow test, the higher the p-value of the model, the better the model fits the data. The Hosmer and Lemeshow's (H-L) goodness of fit test divides subjects into deciles based on predicted probabilities, then computes a chi-square from observed and expected frequencies. Then a probability (p) value is computed from the chi-square distribution to test the fit of the logistic model. If the H-L goodness-of-fit test statistic is greater than 0.05, as we want for well-fitting models, we fail to reject the null hypothesis that there is no difference between observed and model-predicted values, implying that the model's estimates fit the data at an acceptable level. That is, well-fitting models show non-significance on the goodness-of-fit test, indicating model prediction that is not significantly different from observed values.

Table 4 Logistic regression results for retweeting news

Predictive variables	Original	Revised
Gratification		
F1 numexposures	0.93***	0.93***
F2 topic-interesting-me	−0.09	-
Selective exposure		
F3 political	−0.80***	−0.89***
F4 leaning-matched-me	0.72***	0.91***
Socialization		
F5 topic-interesting-followers	0.57***	0.49***
F6 leaning-matched-followers	−0.14	-
Trust and intimacy		
F7 fromfriend	−2.09***	−1.47***
F8 mutualfriend	0.13*	-
F9 difference-in-followers	0.05***	-
F10 sharedfollowers	−0.00	-
F11 sharedfollowees	−0.00***	-
F12 sharedleaning	−0.37***	−0.38***
F13 politicsfromfriend	0.31***	0.35***

Both models pass the goodness-of-fit tests: Original ($\chi^2 = 11.1629$, $p = 0.45$) and Revised ($\chi^2 = 13.2977$, $p = 0.39$). Signif. codes: 0 (***) 0.001 (**) 0.01 (*) 0.05 ().

Logistic regression coefficients cannot directly be interpreted on the scale of the data as models are nonlinear on the probability scale. To ease the interpretation of the logistic regression coefficients β, one could apply the 'divide by 4' rule which can be applied if the probabilities (i.e., values of the outcome variable) are close to 0.5, that is the case for our data [45]. To see how, take a predictor x (e.g., whether or not the article is about politics), its regression coefficient β_x, and the outcome variable y_i. From the idea that the slope of the logistic curve is maximized at the center point, one can take the logistic regression coefficient β_x and divide it by 4 to get an upper bound on how much a unit difference in x (e.g., whether article is about politics or not) would change the outcome variable (e.g., probability of retweeting the article). If β_x is, for example, 0.8, then articles about politics are likely to be retweeted with a probability 20% ($\frac{0.8}{4} = 0.2$) more than articles of any other subject.

6.1 General news sharing

We first investigate the generic news sharing pattern. We consider retweeting cases not only of political news but also of other kinds of news for comparison. Table 4 reports the results of the logistic regression: the 'original model' column fits the original dataset, while the 'revised model' column includes only the significant predictors whose sign remain unchanged compared to those of the original model. Both models fit the data better than the null model and the prediction error rate of our model is only 0.19, while that of the null model is 0.5. Below we discuss the findings.

Gratification: The F1 feature is statistically significant, while F2 is not. The number of repeated exposures to the same article (F1) is positively correlated with retweeting the news, emphasizing the importance of a news article being informative to be retweeted. The positive coefficient of 0.93 indicates that one extra exposure to the article increases one's retweeting probability by 23% (0.93/4 = 0.23). On the other hand, what a user generally likes is not correlated to what he shares (F2). This finding counters what had been found in more traditional settings: one major motivation for consuming and sharing news is entertainment [29].

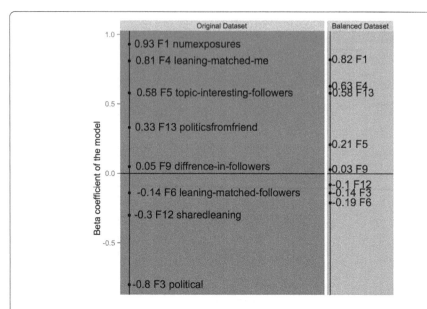

Figure 5 **Factors ranked based on their predictive power (i.e., beta coefficient value of the model) to retweeting behavior.** Each column reports the results from the original dataset and the balanced dataset. Even the scale of impacts may vary, the list of significant factors and their signs are matching in two models, which gives a confidence in the original dataset.

Selective exposure: Both F3 and F4 are statistically significant variables. People tend to retweet news articles in subject areas other than politics. The negative correlation for F3 indicates that a user is 20% less likely to retweet political articles as opposed to other types of news (−0.8). When articles about politics are concerned, one retweets them more with a high positive correlation, if they express political views one agrees with (F4, 0.72). This suggests that although Twitter allows the flow of politically diverse news articles, people have a strong tendency to retweet only what matches their views.

Socialization: We find that what one's followers are interested in (F5) is positively related to what one chooses to share (0.57). This finding is in line with findings from other work [31] in that social interaction is a key factor that encourages information sharing in the online world. Trying to please one's friends may be particularly important in Twitter.

Trust and intimacy: The results show that all the variables except for F10 are statistically significant, and few are mildly correlated. The significance of source credibility (F7) shows a negative correlation (−2.09). This indicates that a user is 52% more likely to retweet news articles that come from media sources than from friends. However, news from a friend who has a mutual relationship (F8) have a 3% higher probability of being retweeted (0.13). To a limited extent, one is also likely to preferentially retweet news coming from popular friends (F9). Finally, political news is unlikely to be shared, yet a user is 8% more likely to share a political article given that it was shared by a friend (F13, 0.31). This peer pressure effect was even true for friends who had opposing political views (F12, −0.37).

The regression analysis can determine the relative importance of the 13 predictors (in the following order): trust & intimacy, gratification, selective exposure, and socialization. Significant factors are ranked based on how much they increase the retweeting probability and are summarized in Figure 5. Each column reports the results for the original dataset

Table 5 Predictors for retweeting political news articles

Predictive variables	Agree with article	Disagree with article
F1 numexposures	0.74***	0.83***
F2 topic-interesting-me	0.16	1.23*
F5 topic-interesting-followers	0.22	−0.36
F6 leaning-matched-followers	−0.44*	1.55**
F8 mutualfriend	0.14*	0.52·
F9 difference-in-followers	0.06***	−0.13**
F10 sharedfollowers	0.00	0.00*
F11 sharedfollowees	0.00	−0.01*
F12 sharedleaning	−0.27***	−1.60**

Both models pass the Goodness-of-fit tests: Agree ($\chi^2 = 4.5227$, $p = 0.81$) and Disagree ($\chi^2 = 1.6879$, $p = 0.97$). Signif. codes: 0 (***) 0.001 (**) 0.01 (*) 0.05 (.).

and the politically balanced dataset, respectively. For the two datasets, the impact of each factor varies in scale, but their signs (positive or negative) do not, speaking for the validity of the results.

To sum up, the credibility of a news outlet (trust & intimacy) and the informativeness or the enjoyment of the articles themselves (gratification) are the two strongest factors that motivate people to share news. Socialization plays a role in choosing news topics to a certain extent - what a user shares depends on what his friends like. In sharing political news, we see that people share political news less frequently than other types of news; however, when they do so, the political stances of articles are likely to match those of the users (selective exposure) or of their friends. As one might expect, one's taste is a strong motivation to encourage to share a news article. However the above results also suggest that social relationships do affect media consumption in notable ways.

6.2 Political news sharing

Next, we focus on the specific question of whether users retweet articles differently depending on the article's political views. We consider two situations: one in which a news article matches the retweeter's political views - that incorporates 3,379 positive retweeting cases, and the other in which it does not match (701 negative retweeting cases). We run a logistic regression for these two cases separately, and report the results in Table 5. For the two regressions, the likelihood ratio test were significant at the 5% level. In both cases, the strongest predictor is *numexposures*, which is the number of times the retweeter has been exposed to the article. If the article agrees with the retweeter's political views, then the article does not necessarily agree with the followers' political views (−0.44) and is likely to come from reciprocal friends (0.14), who might happen to have diverse political views (−0.27).

In contrast, if the article disagrees with the retweeter's political views, then the article is likely to be of retweeter's interest (1.23) but not necessarily of followers' interest (−0.36), match followers' political preferences (1.546), come from friends who have different political views (−1.60), and come from friends with whom one has a mutual relationship (0.52). This means that, when people decide to retweet political articles, they do care about their online social relationships (e.g., who shared, who is the audience). When it is an article contrasting their views, then social context becomes more significant. As such, contextualizing the news reading experience could offer ways of nudging people to accept a variety of political views.

7 Limitations and implications

7.1 Limitations

This work has some main limitations. First, our dataset shows biases, which might inherently come from the biases of the Twitter population. For example, we have an over-representation of liberal users, but that is because the number of left-wing media outlets is higher than that of right-wing ones. To check whether this would impact our results, we have also considered a 'balanced' (sample) dataset that includes the same number of left and right media outlets, and we found the results to be consistent in both.

The second limitation of our work is the method we used for classifying the topic of news articles - Alchemy. We find that $F2$ *topic-interesting-me* factor is not strongly related to news sharing behavior, which is counter-intuitive. Had only Alchemy been used, we might have been unsure whether our results hold true in general, or whether they are the product of classification artifacts. To validate Alchemy's categorization of news articles, we compared the classifications for the New York Times articles returned by Alchemy and the official classifications offered on the New York Times site. For example, a url http://www.nytimes.com/2009/04/13/us/politics can be categorized as 'Culture Politics' based on the URL itself. Showing 82% mcathing probability with New York Times' categorization, we believe that is it acceptable to use Alchemy. However, there is still a room to examine whether the lack of correlation of $F2$ and retweeting probability is produced by the Alchemy or by its inherent absence of relationship.

Third, in building our PoNS model, we generate an artificial 50-50 positive-negative retweeting cases by taking random negative retweeting cases. Given a large number of tweets individuals receive, 50% of negative retweeting cases may not reflect the reality - in fact, only a few news articles are shared. However, such sample creation helps us to understand which of four factors in our PoNS model is the strongest one in relating to news sharing behavior. Yet, further investigation on the effect of samples can be conducted. For example one could test the model by changing the proportion of negative cases in generating samples.

Last but not least, we do not consider the sentiment of a user when he shares an article. If a user shares a news article of an hostile media outlet, it does not necessarily mean that he is vouching for it - he might simply make fun of it. Yet, what we observed from our analysis is that when an individual shares news articles that conflict with his own political view, it is about his friends' interests rather than his own, and this stays valid even thought we do not consider the sentiment of tweets. However, recent studies have emphasized the role of the sentiment of a tweet in its virality, especially when it is news content. Negative sentiment tends to be a strong promoter of news sharing [46, 47] and the stronger the emotion of a tweet is, the higher the chance it is retweeted [48, 49]. Thus investigating on how the sentiment of tweet come across with the factors we considered seems like an interesting follow up work. We leave this as future work.

7.2 Theoretical implications

This work has important implications for theories on information consumption, information sharing, and opinion diversity. Our results suggest that news sharing depends on four factors: (1) gratification; (2) selective exposure; (3) socialization; and (4) trust and intimacy. These factors have been studied before [28–31], but only separately, mainly because of lack of data. Here we have studied them together.

In terms of opinion spreading, it is tempting to think that Twitter allows us to connect to thousands of individuals who collectively hold diverse political views. The reality is that homophily limits who connects to whom (who one follows or is followed by, in Twitter parlance) - users are likely to connect to and exchange news articles with other like-minded users. As such, it is hard for ideas to pass between groups who are separated. Both online and offline, one important dimension separating groups of people is politics [50]. When people are separated by political views, they perceive each other as far apart and are unlikely to share opinions and offer any kind of support. This results into the creation of echo-chambers where like-minded individuals talk with each other and, as a result, reinforce each other's views. In our work, we found that Twitter users segregate themselves into echo chambers by sharing like-minded opinions even though they are exposed to different opinions.

In terms of opinion diversity, it is known that exposures to balanced information brings positive social consequences; it helps people set common grounds on important issues and improve group decision-making [51]. On the other hand, previous studies have also shown that exposure to balanced information does not change people's minds but, in contrast, increases commitment to original perceptions [52–54]. This effect is called *cognitive dissonance* [55], i.e., people tend to deny claims that contradict their beliefs. For example, exposing people to balanced political news generally leads them to hold more intense beliefs than they held beforehand. So the simple approach of exposing people to diverse political opinions might not work, and more sophisticated approaches should be used. Our study suggests that social context (e.g., one's followers) is associated with low levels of cognitive dissonance. Challenge-averse individuals were prepared to lose their reticence and retweet some articles with views different from their own - these articles generally came from friends.

In terms of information diffusion, there are a few studies on the relation of 'impact of number of exposures' to different outputs (e.g., hashtag adoption of Twitter [33] and Facebook fan page creation [56]). These studies all concluded that the more an individual is exposed to some piece of information, the more likely the individual will be persuaded by it. For example, [56] reports that '*after controlling for News Feed exposure variables, neither demographic characteristics nor number of Facebook friends seems to play an important role in the prediction of maximum diffusion chain length*'. Our study shows a similar trend and also finds that, after controlling for *numexposures*, other variables become important, and their importance changes across individuals: some users may like the popular stories (hence larger *numExposures*), while others value stories coming from close friends (hence *mutualfriend*).

7.3 Practical implications

We have found that users are more likely to retweet articles that are shared by their popular friends. This means that news aggregators might want to rank news depending on how popular or socially central the individual sources are. In general, offering personalized news articles on politics is more challenging than offering other types of articles. However, not all users find such exposure challenging. Support-seeking or diversity-seeking users are expected to be open minded and be willing to receive political news that do not necessarily reflect their own views. However, challenge-averse users may not appreciate such exposure. Our findings suggest that offering news through social-networking friends could be a reasonable way to 'scratch' challenge-averse users' echo chambers.

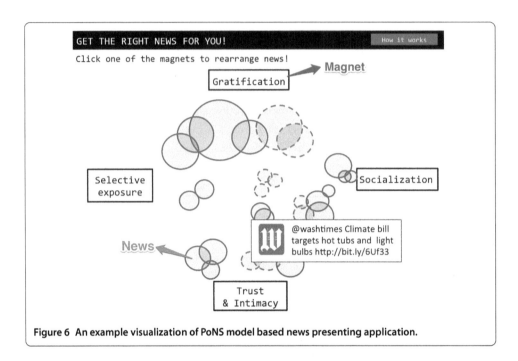

Figure 6 An example visualization of PoNS model based news presenting application.

Our findings have practical implications for the design of news aggregators. Twitter users strongly care about their followers' interests, including their political views. Traditional news aggregators return news a user might like based on the user's interest only. Our findings suggest that aggregators might also return news that not only are of interest to the user but also encourage interactions with friends.

Based on these findings, we introduce a new visualization for presenting news articles that gives users control over the PoNS' four dimensions (gratification, selective exposure, socialization, and trust & intimacy). This visualization is based on the Dust & Magnet visualization technique [57] that uses a magnet metaphor in which the individual data cases are represented as particles of iron dust, and magnets represent the different variables of the dataset. Users can interactively manipulate the magnets and then the dust moves appropriately.

One can develop an application that collects news articles a user receives in Twitter and present them with PoNS' four factors, providing more context to what they read. Figure 6 shows an example design of such application, which is run on a left-leaning user' news articles. The rectangles are magnets (i.e., PoNS' dimensions), and the circles are dust (i.e., news articles). The blue circles having solid line are news articles from left-wing media and the red ones having dotted line are from right-wing media. The size of each circle reflects the popularity of the news article based on the number of retweeted. By clicking any dust object, a user can see the detailed pop-up of the corresponding tweet.

A user can also click on any magnet to adjust the magnitude of attraction of magnet. When a magnet is clicked, dust particles are attracted to the magnet based on the value of the dimension corresponding to the magnet. For example, if the magnet represents socialization, a piece of dust with a higher value for socialization attracts more than a piece of dust with a lower value for it. As a result, users receives a sorted list of news articles. By allowing users to explore news articles along psychological dimensions, one could encourage them to expand their normal news reading patterns.

8 Conclusion

To counter information overload, people increasingly turn to their friends to receive filtered information as a proxy for relevance. If one hears about a story from a friend, then that story suddenly becomes relevant and salient even when its political orientation is different [58]. This established pattern of social behavior guides our actions not only offline but also online.

In Twitter, some of those who tend to be diversity-averse in their consumption of political news still promote stories they disagree with, and they do so because these stories are relevant to their online friends. This finding suggests that social ties are a proxy for relevance online. This striking resemblance with what happens offline happens likely because human behavior, which took thousands of years to evolve, changes much more slowly than the Web, which is only about 20 years old. As a result, it is easier for our online world to align itself with our offline world [59].

The media landscape continues to evolve over time and how people use certain medium also changes. This work has offered only one snapshot of the Twitter political landscape. To extend this, we will conduct a longitudinal study using the same 4-factor model, and see how the contributions of those factors changes over time and during large-scale events (e.g., elections).

Competing interests
The authors declare that they have no competing interests.

Authors' contributions
JA collected the data. JA, DQ, and MC performed the analysis. JA, DQ, MC, KG, and JC conceived the experiments and wrote the manuscript.

Author details
[1] Qatar Computing Research Institute, Majlis Al Taawon Street, Doha, Qatar. [2] Yahoo Labs, Avinguda Diagonal 177, Barcelona, Spain. [3] Graduate School of Culture Technology, KAIST, 291 Daehak-ro, Daejeon, Republic of Korea. [4] Max Plank Institute for Software Systems, Campus E1 5, Saarbrücken, Germany. [5] Computer Laboratory, University of Cambridge, 15 JJ Thomson Avenue, Cambridge, UK.

Acknowledgements
JA was supported in part by the Google European Doctoral Fellowship in Social Computing. MC was supported by the BK21 Plus Postgraduate Organization for Content Science in Korea.

References
1. Milyo J, Groseclose T (2005) A measure of media bias. Q J Econ 120(4):1191-1237
2. Gentzkow M, Shapiro JM (2010) What drives media slant? Evidence from U.S. daily newspapers. Econometrica 78(1):35-71
3. Della Vigna S, Kaplan E (2007) The Fox News effect: media bias and voting. Q J Econ 122:1187-1234
4. Zaller JR (1992) The nature and origins of mass opinion. Cambridge University Press, Cambridge
5. Glynn CJ, Herbs S, OKeefe GJ, Shapiro RY (1999) Public opinion. Westview Press, Boulder
6. Quirk PW (2009) Iran's Twitter revolution. http://www.fpif.org/articles/irans_twitter_revolution. Accessed 28 Jul 2014
7. Tumasjan A, Sprenger TO, Sandne PG, Welpe IM (2010) Predicting elections with Twitter: what 140 characters reveal about political sentiment. In: Proceedings of the 4th international AAAI conference on weblogs and social media (ICWSM'10)
8. Lotan G, Graeff E, Ananny M, Gaffney D, Pearce I, et al (2011) The Arab Spring - the revolutions were tweeted: information flows during the 2011 Tunisian and Egyptian revolutions. Int J Commun 5:1375-1405
9. Diakopoulos N, Naaman M (2011) Towards quality discourse in online news comments. In: Proceedings of ACM conference on computer supported cooperative work (CSCW'11)
10. An J, Cha M, Gummadi K, Crowcroft J (2011) Media landscape in Twitter: a world of new conventions and political diversity. In: Proceedings of the 5th international AAAI conference on weblogs and social media (ICWSM'11)
11. Pariser E (2012) The filter bubble: how the new personalized web is changing what we read and how we think. Penguin Books, London
12. Severin WJ, Tankard JW (2000) Communication theories: origins, methods and uses in the mass media. Addison-Wesley, Boston
13. Sears DO, Freedman JL (1967) Selective exposure to information: a critical review. Public Opin Q 31(2):194-213

14. Christakis NA, Fowler JH (2009) Connected: the surprising power of our social networks and how they shape our lives. Little Brown and Company, New York

15. Krebs V (2008) Political polarization in Amazon book purchases. http://www.orgnet.com/divided.html USA. Accessed 27 Jul 2014

16. Bishop B (2008) The big sort: why the clustering of likeminded America is tearing us apart. Houghton Mifflin Company, New York

17. Mutz DC (1996) Political persuasion and attitude change. University of Michigan Press, Ann Arbor

18. Adamic LA, Glance N (2005) The political blogosphere and the 2004 U.S. election: divided they blog. In: Proceedings of the 3rd international workshop on link discovery (LinkKDD'05)

19. Gentzkow M, Shapiro JM (2011) Ideological segregation online and offline. Q J Econ 126(4):1799-1839

20. Livne A, Simmons MP, Adar E, Adamic L (2011) The party is over here: structure and content in the 2010 election. In: Proceedings of the 5th international AAAI conference on weblogs and social media (ICWSM'11)

21. Conover MD, Ratkiewicz J, Francisco M, Gonçalves B, Menczer F, Flammini A (2011) Political polarization on Twitter. In: Proceedings of the 5th international AAAI conference on weblogs and social media (ICWSM'11)

22. Yardi S, Boyd D (2010) Dynamic debates: an analysis of group polarization over time on Twitter. Bull Sci Technol Soc 30(5):316-327

23. Kwak H, Lee C, Park H, Moon S (2010) What is Twitter, a social network or a news media? In: Proceedings of the 19th international world wide web conference (WWW'10)

24. Java A, Song X, Finin T, Tseng B (2007) Why we Twitter: understanding microblogging usage and communities. In: Proceedings of the 9th WebKDD and 1st SNA-KDD 2007 workshop on web mining and social network analysis (WebKDD/SNA-KDD'07)

25. Yardi S, Boyd D (2010) Tweeting from the town square: measuring geographic local networks. In: Proceedings of the 4th international AAAI conference on weblogs and social media (ICWSM'10)

26. Boyd D, Golder S, Lotan G (2010) Tweet, tweet, retweet: conversational aspects of retweeting on Twitter. In: Proceedings of the 43rd Hawaii international conference on system sciences (HICSS'10)

27. Lin N (1999) Social networks and status attainment. Annu Rev Sociol 25:467-487

28. Lin C, Salwen MB, Abdulla RA (2005) Uses and gratifications of online and offline news: new wine in an old bottle. In: Online news and the public, pp 221-236

29. Diddi A, LaRose R (2006) Getting hooked on news: uses and gratifications and the formation of news habits among college students in an Internet environment. J Broadcast Electron Media 50:193-210

30. Dunne A, Lawlor M, Rowley J (2010) Young people's use of online social networking sites - a uses and gratifications perspective. J Res Interact Mark 4:46-58

31. Chiu C, Hsu M, Wang E (2006) Understanding knowledge sharing in virtual communities: an integration of social capital and social cognitive theories. Decis Support Syst 42:1872-1888

32. Latane B (1981) The psychology of social impact. Am Psychol 36(4):343-356

33. Romero DM, Meeder B, Kleinberg J (2011) Differences in the mechanics of information diffusion across topics: idioms, political hashtags, and complex contagion on Twitter. In: Proceedings of the 20th international world wide web conference (WWW'11)

34. Lin YR, Margolin D, Keegan B, Baronchelli A (2013) # Bigbirds never die: understanding social dynamics of emergent hashtag. In: Proceedings of the 7th international AAAI conference on weblogs and social media (ICWSM'13)

35. Freeman S, Walker MR, Borden R, Latane B (1975) Diffusion of responsibility and restaurant tipping: cheaper by the bunch. Pers Soc Psychol Bull 1(4):584-587

36. Darley JM, Latane B (1968) Bystander intervention in emergencies: diffusion of responsibility. J Pers Soc Psychol 8(4p1):377

37. Stroud N (2011) Niche news. Westview Press, Boulder

38. http://thenextweb.com/twitter/2014/04/29/twitter-passes-255m-monthly-active-users-198m-mobile-users-sees-80-advertising-revenue-mobile/

39. http://twitter.com/#!/who_to_follow/interests/news

40. Quercia D, Askham H, Crowcroft J (2012) TweetLDA: supervised topic classification and link prediction in Twitter. In: Proceedings of the 4th annual ACM web science conference (WebSci'12)

41. Efron M (2004) The liberal media and right-wing conspiracies: using cocitation information to estimate political orientation in web documents. In: Proceedings of the 13th ACM international conference on information and knowledge management (CIKM'04)

42. Golbeck J, Hansen D (2011) Computing political preference among Twitter followers. In: Proceedings of the SIGCHI conference on human factors in computing systems (CHI'11)

43. Miller GA (1955) Note on the bias of information estimates. In: Information theory in psychology: problems and methods, pp 95-100

44. Munson S, Resnick P (2010) Presenting diverse political opinions: how and how much. In: Proceedings of the 28th ACM conference on human factors in computing systems (CHI'10)

45. Gelman A, Hill J (2006) Data analysis using regression and Multilevel/Hierarchical models. Cambridge University Press, Cambridge

46. Thelwall M, Buckley K, Paltoglou G (2011) Sentiment in Twitter events. J Am Soc Inf Sci Technol 62(2):1532-2882

47. Hansen LK, Arvidsson A, Nielsen FA, Colleoni E, Etter M (2011) Good friends, bad news - affect and virality in Twitter. In: Future information technology

48. Pfitzner R, Garas A, Schweitzer F (2012) Emotional divergence influences information spreading in Twitter. In: Proceedings of the 6th international AAAI conference on weblogs and social media (ICWSM'12)

49. Jenders M, Kasneci G, Naumann F (2013) Analyzing and predicting viral tweets. In: Proceedings of the 22nd international conference on world wide web companion (WWW'13 companion)

50. Sunstein CR (2001) Republic.com. Princeton University Press, Princeton

51. Nemeth CJ, Rogers J (1996) Dissent and the search for information. Br J Soc Psychol 35:67-76

52. Ross L, Lepper MR, Hubbard M (1975) Perseverance in self-perception and social perception: biased attributional processes in the debriefing paradigm. J Pers Soc Psychol 32(5):80-92

53. Sunstein CR (2009) On rumors: how falsehoods spread, why we believe them, what can be done. Farrar, Straus and Giroux, New York

54. Nyhan B, Reifler J (2010) When corrections fail: the persistence of political misperceptions. Polit Behav 32(2):303-330

55. Festinger L (1957) A theory of cognitive dissonance. Stanford University Press, Stanford

56. Sun E, Rosenn I, Marlow C, Lento TM (2009) Gesundheit! Modeling contagion through Facebook news feed. In: Proceedings of the 3rd international AAAI conference on weblogs and social media (ICWSM'09)

57. Yi JS, Melton R, Stasko J, Jacko JA (2005) Dust magnet: multivariate information visualization using a magnet metaphor. Inf Vis 4(4):239-256.

58. Hogan K (2004) The science of influence: how to get anyone to say "Yes" in 8 minutes or less! Wiley, Hoboken

59. Adams P (2011) Grouped: how small groups of friends are the key to influence on the social web. Pearson Education, Upper Saddle River

10

Predicting scientific success based on coauthorship networks

Emre Sarigöl, René Pfitzner*, Ingo Scholtes, Antonios Garas and Frank Schweitzer

*Correspondence: rpfitzner@ethz.ch
Chair of Systems Design, ETH
Zurich, Weinbergstrasse 56/58,
Zurich, 8004, Switzerland

Abstract

We address the question to what extent the success of scientific articles is due to social influence. Analyzing a data set of over 100,000 publications from the field of Computer Science, we study how centrality in the coauthorship network differs between authors who have highly cited papers and those who do not. We further show that a Machine Learning classifier, based only on coauthorship network centrality metrics measured at the time of publication, is able to predict with high precision whether an article will be highly cited five years after publication. By this we provide quantitative insight into the social dimension of scientific publishing – challenging the perception of citations as an objective, socially unbiased measure of scientific success.

Keywords: scientometrics; complex networks

1 Introduction

Quantitative measures are increasingly used to evaluate the performance of research institutions, departments, and individual scientists. Measures like the absolute or relative number of published research articles are frequently applied to quantify the *productivity* of scientists. To measure the *impact* of research, citation-based measures like the total number of citations, the number of citations per published article or the h-index [1], have been proposed. Proponents of such citation-based measures or rankings argue that they allow to quantitatively and objectively assess the *quality* of research, thus encouraging their use as simple proxies for the *success* of scientists, institutions or even whole research fields. The intriguing idea that by means of citation metrics the task of assessing research quality can be "outsourced" to the *collective intelligence* of the scientific community, has resulted in citation-based measures becoming increasingly popular among research administrations and governmental decision makers. As a result, such measures are used as one criterion in the evaluation of grant proposals and research institutes or in hiring committees for faculty positions. Considering the potential impact for the careers of – especially young – scientists, it is reasonable to take a step back and ask a simple question: To what extent do *social factors* influence the number of citations of their articles? Arguably, this question challenges the perception of science as a systematic pursuit for objective truth, which ideally should be free of personal beliefs, biases or social influence. On the other hand, quoting Werner Heisenberg [2], "*science is done by humans*", it would be surprising if specifically scientific activities were free from the influences of social aspects.

Whereas often the term "social influence" has a negative connotation, we don't think that social influence in science necessarily stems from malicious or unethical behavior, like e.g. nepotism, prejudicial judgments, discrimination or in-group favoritism. We rather suspect that, as a response to the increasing amount of published research articles and our limited ability to keep track of potentially relevant works, a growing importance of social factors in citation behavior is due to natural mechanisms of *social cognition* and *social information filtering*.

In this paper we address this issue by studying the influence of social structures on scholarly citation behavior. Using a data set comprising more than 100,000 scholarly publications by more than 160,000 authors, we extract time-evolving coauthorship networks and utilize them as a (simple) proxy for the evolving social (collaboration) network of the scientific discipline *computer science*. Based on the assumption that the centrality of scientists in the coauthorship network is indicative for the *visibility* of their work, we then study to what extent the "*success*" of research articles in terms of citations can be predicted using only knowledge about the embedding of authors in the coauthorship network *at the time of publication*. Our prediction method is based on a random forest classifier and utilizes a set of complementary network centrality measures. We find strong evidence for our hypothesis that authors whose papers are highly cited in the future have – on average – a significantly higher centrality in the coauthorship network at the time of publication. Remarkably, we are able to predict whether an article will belong to the 10% most cited articles with a precision of 60%. We argue that this result quantifies the existence of a *social bias*, manifesting itself in terms of visibility and attention, and influencing measurable citation "success" of researchers. The presence of such a social bias threatens the interpretation of citations as *objectively awarded esteem*, which is the justification for using citation-based measures as universal proxies of *quality* and *success*.

The remainder of this article is structured as follows: In Section 2 we review a number of works that have studied scientific collaboration structures as well as their relation to citation behavior. In Section 3 we describe our data set and provide details of how we construct time-evolving coauthorship networks. We further introduce a set of network-theoretical measures which we utilize to quantitatively assess the centrality and embedding of authors in the evolving coauthorship network. In Section 4 we introduce a number of hypotheses about the relations between the position of authors in the coauthorship network and the future success of their publications. We test these hypotheses and obtain a set of candidate measures which are the basis for our prediction method described in Section 5. We summarize and interpret our findings in Section 6 and discuss their implications for the application of citation-based measures in the quantitative assessment of research.

2 The complex character of citations

It is remarkable that, even though citation-based measures have been used to quantify research impact since almost sixty years [3], a complete *theory of citations* is still missing. In particular, researchers studying the social processes of science have long been arguing that citations have different, complex functions that go well beyond a mere attribution of credit [4]. For example, in [5] evidence was presented that papers, which have been publicly criticized via formal, published comments, are often highly cited. Furthermore, at the level of scientific articles, a citation can be interpreted as a "discursive relation", while at the level of authors citations have an additional meaning as expression of "professional relations" [4]. Additional interpretations have been identified at aggregate levels, like e.g. social groups, institutions, scientific communities or even countries citing each other. These findings suggest that citations are indeed a complex phenomenon which have both cognitive and a social dimension [4, 6]. The complex character of scholarly citations was further emphasized recently [7, 8]. Here, the authors argue that, apart from an attribution of scientific merit, references in scientific literature often serve as a tool to guide and orient the reader, to simplify scientific writing and to associate the work with a particular scientific community. Furthermore, they highlight that citation numbers of articles are crucially influenced not only by the popularity of a research topic and the size of the scientific community, but also by the number of authors as well as their prominence and visibility. These findings question an oversimplified interpretation of citation counts as objective quality indicator.

Facilitated by the wide-spread availability of scholarly citation databases, some advances in the understanding of the dynamics of citations have been made in the last years. For an interesting study of bibliometric indicators on the author level, see e.g. [9]. Generally, citation practices seem to differ significantly across different scientific disciplines, which complicates the definition of universal citation-based impact measures. However, the remarkable finding that – independent of discipline – citations follow a log-normal distribution which can be rescaled in such a way that citation numbers become comparable [10, 11], suggests that the mechanisms behind citation practices are universal across disciplines, and differences are mainly due to differing community sizes.

Additionally to investigations of the differences across scientific communities, the relations between citations and coauthorships were studied in recent works. Using data from a number of scientific journals, it was shown that the citation count of an article is correlated both with the number of authors and the number of institutions involved in its production [12, 13]. Studying data from eight highly ranked scientific journals, it was shown [14] that (a) single author publications consistently received the lowest number of citations and (b) publications with less than five coauthors received less citations than the average article. Studying citations between individuals rather than articles, in [15] it was observed that coauthors tend to cite each other sooner after the publication of a paper (compared to non-coauthors). Further, the authors showed that a strong tendency towards reciprocal citation patterns exists. These findings already indicate that social aspects influence citing behavior. In this work we are going to quantitatively reveal the extent of this influence.

Going beyond a mere study of direct coauthorship relations, first attempts to study *both* citation and coauthorship structures from a *network perspective* have been made recently. Aiming at a measure that captures both the *amount* as well as the *reach* of citations in a scientific community, a citation index that incorporates the distance of citing authors in the collaboration network was proposed [16]. Another recent study [17] used the topological distance between citing authors in the coauthorship network to extend the notion of self-citations. Interestingly, apart from direct self-citations, this study could not find a strong tendency to cite authors that are close in the coauthorship network.

Different from previous works, in this article we study correlations between the *centrality* of authors in collaboration networks and the *citation success* of their research articles. By this we particularly extend previous works that use a network perspective on coauthorship structures and citation patterns. Stressing the fact that *social relations* of authors play an important role for how much attention and recognition their research receives, we further contribute a quantitative view on previously hypothesized relations between the *visibility* of authors and citation patterns.

3 Time-evolving collaboration and citation networks

In this work we analyze a data set of scholarly citations and collaborations obtained from the Microsoft Academic Search (MSAS, http://academic.research.microsoft.com) service. The MSAS is a scholarly database containing more than 35 Million publication records from 15 scientific disciplines. Using the Application Programming Interface (API) of this service, we extracted a subset of more than 100,000 computer science articles, published between 1996 and 2008, in the following way: First, we retrieved unique numerical identifiers (IDs) of the 20,000 highest ranked authors in the field of *computer science*. This ranking is the result of an MSAS internal "field rating", taking into account several scholarly metrics of an author (number of publications, citations, h-index) and comparing them to the typical values of these metrics within a certain research field. In order to build coauthorship and citation networks of reasonable size, in a second step we chose 1,000 authors i.i.d. uniformly from the set of these 20,000 authors. In the third step, we obtained information on coauthors, publication date, as well as the list and publication date of citing works for all the publications authored by these 1,000 authors between 1996 and 2008. This results in a data set consisting of a total of 108,758 publications from the field of computer science, coauthored by a total of 160,891 researchers. Each publication record contains a list of author IDs, which, by means of disambiguation heuristics internally applied by the MSAS service, uniquely identify authors independent of name spelling variations. The absence of name ambiguities is one feature that sets this data set apart from other data sets on scholarly publications that are used frequently. Based on this data set we extracted a *coauthorship network*, where nodes represent authors and links represent coauthorship relations between authors. In addition, using the information about citing papers, we extracted *citation dynamics*, i.e. the time evolution of the number of citations of all publications in our data set. Similar to earlier works, we argue that the coauthorship network can be considered a first-order approximation of the complete scientific collaboration network [15]. Based on the publication date of an article, we additionally assign time stamps to the extracted coauthor links – thus obtaining time-evolving coauthorship networks.

We analyze the evolution of the coauthorship network using a sliding window of two years in which we aggregate all coauthorships occurring within that time. Starting with 1996, we slide this window in one year increments and obtain a total of 11 time slices representing the evolution of collaboration structures between 1996 and 2008. We use an extended time-window of two years to account for the continuing effect of a coauthorship in terms of awareness about the coauthors works. Although larger time windows are certainly possible (and their effects interesting to investigate), in this work we are less concerned with the optimal time-window size and consistently use the above described approach. However, consistency checks performed with varying time-window sizes suggest that our results are robust.

Table 1 summarizes the number of nodes and links in the coauthorship network, the number of publications in each time slice as well as the fractional size of the largest connected component (LCC). Note that the time-aggregated network (nearly) forms one giant connected component with only a minor fraction of isolated nodes. In contrast, some of the time slices fall apart in several larger disconnected components. Note also that the size of the largest connected component is increasing with time, which may indicate either a possible bias in the coverage of the MSAS database to favor newer articles, or an

Table 1 Number of papers and size of the collaboration network 2-year subgraphs between 1995-2008 used in our study.

Year	LCC fraction	Links	Nodes	Publications
1996-1997	0.18	61,046	2,845	1,160
1997-1998	0.37	130,938	6,381	3,070
1998-1999	0.45	153,412	8,470	4,054
1999-2000	0.50	186,318	10,413	5,320
2000-2001	0.60	358,188	13,451	6,561
2001-2002	0.63	413,846	15,309	7,026
2002-2003	0.74	542,912	20,238	9,193
2003-2004	0.77	653,224	23,624	10,608
2004-2005	0.79	745,352	26,258	11,430
2005-2006	0.83	889,996	29,886	12,919
2006-2007	0.84	914,614	32,412	13,568
2007-2008	0.86	858,554	35,255	14,214
Overall	0.99	5,324,330	160,891	108,758

increase of "collaborativeness" in science. As we are going to perform a social network analysis of the coauthorship time slices – and some measures (like eigenvector centrality) are not well-defined for unconnected graphs – we limit our following analysis on the largest connected component. For each network corresponding to one two-year time slice, we compute a number of node-level metrics that allow us to quantitatively monitor the evolution of network positions for all authors. In particular, we compute *degree centrality, eigenvector centrality, betweenness centrality* and *k-core centrality* of authors. For further details on the centrality measures used in this study, we refer the reader to the Supplementary Material (Additional file 1) or a standard network analysis textbook, e.g. [18]. Here we utilize implementations of these measures provided by the igraph package [19].

A major focus of our work is to assess the predictive power of an author's position in the coauthorship network for the citation success of her future articles. To do so we adopt a so-called *hindcasting approach*: For each publication p published in year t, we extract the list of coauthors as well as the LCC of the coauthorship network in the time slice $[t-2, t]$, and calculate the centrality measures. Based on the citation data, we furthermore calculate the number of citations c_p paper p gained within a time frame of *five years* after publication, i.e. in the time slice $[t, t+5]$.

In particular, we are interested in those publications that are among the most successful ones. Defining *success* is generally an ambiguous endeavor. As justified in the Introduction, here we take the (controversial) viewpoint that success is directly measurable in number of citations. We specifically focus on a simple notion of success in terms of having *highly cited papers* and, similar to [20], assume that a paper is *successful* if five years after publication it has more citations than 90% of all papers published in the same year. We refer to the set of successful papers published in year t as $P_\uparrow(t)$. The set of remaining papers, i.e. those published at time t that are cited less frequently than the top 10%, is denoted as $P_\downarrow(t)$.

4 Statistical dependence of coauthorship structures and citations

Having a large social network and "knowing the right people" often is a prerequisite for career success. However, science is often thought to be one of the few fields of human endeavor where success depends on the quality of an authors' work, rather than on her social connectedness. Given the time evolving coauthorship network, as well as the observed success (or lack thereof) of a publication, we investigate two research questions, aiming to quantify the aspect of social influence on citation success. First, we examine whether there is a general tendency of central authors in the coauthorship network to publish papers that are more successful than those of non-central authors. Second, we investigate the inverse effect and ask whether the success of a paper influences the future coauthorship centrality of its authors.

4.1 Effects of author centrality on citation success

To answer the first research question we test the following hypothesis.

Hypothesis 1 *At the time of publication, authors of papers in $P_\uparrow(t)$ are more central in the coauthorship network than authors of articles in $P_\downarrow(t)$.*

As papers often have more than one author, for each paper we only consider the coauthorship network centralities of the author with the highest coauthorship degree, and refer to this as the *coauthorship centrality of the paper*. This choice is motivated by the intuition that the centrality of the best connected coauthor should provide the major amount of (socially triggered) visibility for the publication. One might argue that this procedure introduces a centrality bias towards papers with a large number of authors. However, as the number of coauthors in our dataset is rather narrow with a mean of 3.95, a median of 3 and a standard deviation of 5.41 authors, a seizable bias cannot be expected. We test Hypothesis 1 by comparing coauthorship centrality distributions of papers in $P_\uparrow(t)$ and $P_\downarrow(t)$ for each year t. In order to compare the centrality distributions, we apply a *Wilcoxon-Mann-Whitney two-sample rank-sum-test* [21]. For each of the four centrality metrics we test the null hypothesis that coauthorship centrality distributions of papers in $P_\uparrow(t)$ and $P_\downarrow(t)$ are the same against the alternative hypothesis that the centrality distribution of papers in $P_\uparrow(t)$ is stochastically larger than that of papers in $P_\downarrow(t)$. The p-values of the tests as well as the corresponding averages and variances of the four considered centrality metrics in the two sets are shown in Table 2. Additionally, Figures 1, 2, 3 and 4 show kernel density estimates of these distributions. For all considered centrality metrics p-values are well below a significance level of 0.01. We can thus safely reject the null hypothesis, concluding that coauthorship centrality metrics of papers in $P_\uparrow(t)$ are stochastically larger than those of papers in $P_\downarrow(t)$. This result indicates that centrality metrics in the coauthorship network, at the time of publication of a paper, are indicative for future paper success. Note however, that this statistical dependency is more complicated than the linear Pearson or the more general Spearman correlation. Indeed, all the considered social network metrics are only weakly, if at all, correlated with citation numbers (see Supplementary Material (Additional file 1)). Table 3 summarizes to what extent citation success and coauthorship network centrality are statistically dependent. The left entry of each cell indicates

Table 2 p-values of one sided Wilcoxon-Mann-Whitney test. This quantifies whether the centrality distributions of authors of articles in $P_\uparrow$ are (in a statistical sense) larger than those of authors of articles in $P_\downarrow$. Also shown are the medians M and variances var of the centrality metrics in the two sets.

	p-value	$M(P_\downarrow)$	$M(P_\uparrow)$	var$P_\downarrow$	var$P_\uparrow$
k-core	1.28×10^{-115}	16	26	1.20×10^4	7.18×10^3
Eigenvector	2.52×10^{-34}	9.67×10^{-18}	2.08×10^{-17}	2.58×10^{-3}	5.40×10^{-4}
Betweenness	1.19×10^{-68}	19.38	11.4×10^4	4.19×10^{12}	1.58×10^{13}
Degree	5.63×10^{-125}	28	57	1.02×10^5	1.13×10^5

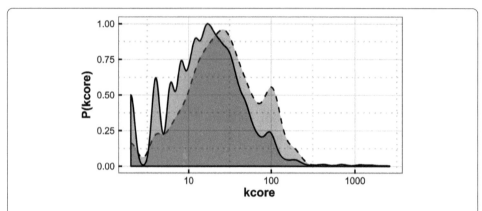

Figure 1 *k*-core centrality shift. Kernel density estimate of *k*-core coauthorship centrality of papers in $P_\downarrow$ (solid blue) and $P_\uparrow$ (dashed red).

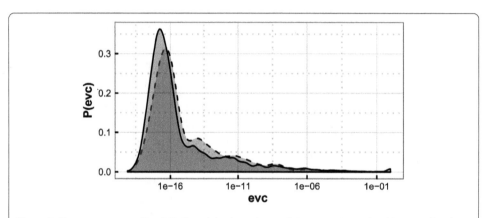

Figure 2 Eigenvector centrality shift. Kernel density estimate of eigenvector coauthorship centrality of papers in $P_\downarrow$ (solid blue) and $P_\uparrow$ (dashed red).

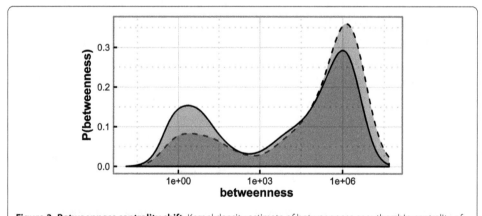

Figure 3 Betweenness centrality shift. Kernel density estimate of betweenness coauthorship centrality of papers in $P_\downarrow$ (solid blue) and $P_\uparrow$ (dashed red).

$P(\text{toppaper}|\text{topmetric})$, i.e. the fraction of papers belonging to the top $x\%$ successful papers, given that their authors have top $x\%$ centrality metrics. The right entry of each cell indicates $P(\text{topmetric}|\text{toppaper})$, i.e. the fraction of papers that have authors which are within the set of authors with top $x\%$ centrality metrics, given that the papers are within

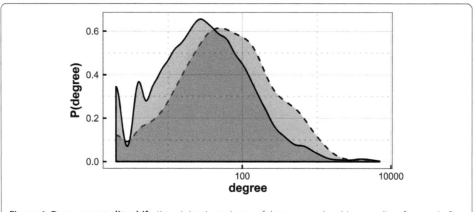

Figure 4 Degree centrality shift. Kernel density estimate of degree coauthorship centrality of papers in $P_\downarrow$ (solid blue) and $P_\uparrow$ (dashed red).

Table 3 The left entry of each cell indicates P(toppaper|topmetric), i.e. the fraction of papers belonging to the top x% successful papers, given that their authors have top x% centrality metrics. The right entry of each cell indicates P(topmetric|toppaper), i.e. the fraction of papers that have authors which are within the set of authors with top x% centrality metrics, given that the papers are within the top x% successful papers. Row *Intersection* indicates the intersection of all the above considered centrality metrics.

	Top 10%	Top 5%	Top 2%	Top 1%
k-core	0.22||0.21	0.17||0.16	0.07||0.07	0.01||0.01
Eigenvector	0.11||0.11	0.06||0.06	0.01||0.01	0.01||0.01
Betweenness	0.20||0.20	0.13||0.13	0.11||0.11	0.11||0.11
Degree	0.20||0.20	0.15||0.15	0.10||0.09	0.07||0.07
Intersection	0.36||0.15	0.27||0.11	0.17||0.06	0.12||0.04
# papers	3,700	1,844	730	362

the top x% successful papers. From these results, we conclude two observations: First, the probabilities in each cell are well below 1, indicating the absence of a simple linear (Pearson) correlation. Second, especially considering k-core centrality, knowing a paper is top 10% successful, the conditional probability that it was written by an author with top 10% k-core centrality, is P(topmetric|toppaper) = 0.21. Additionally, Table 3 shows that vice versa P(toppaper|topmetric) = 0.22 of all papers that are published by authors with top 10% k-core centrality, are among the most successful ones. In addition, we consider the intersection of all four centrality metrics. Here we even find that P(toppaper|topmetric) = 0.36 of all papers published authors with top 10% centrality w.r.t. *all four* centrality metrics, are among the top 10% most cited papers. We will use this observation as basis for a naive Bayes classifier in Section 5.

4.2 Coevolution of coauthorship and citation success

In the previous section we studied the question whether the centrality of authors in the coauthorship network is indicative for the success of publications in terms of citations. Our results suggested that centrality in coauthorship networks is indeed indicative for citation success. In the following we study the inverse relation and ask whether a shift in citation success of authors is indicative for their future position in the coauthorship network. To answer this question, we consider all authors who published an article both at time t and five years later at $t + 5$. We then categorize them based on the citation success of their articles published at time t and time $t + 5$. We introduce two sets of authors: Set $A_\searrow(t)$ is the set of authors who at time t had at least one publication in class $P_\uparrow(t)$, but who at time $t + 5$ did not have an article in class $P_\uparrow(t + 5)$ anymore. Set $A_\nearrow(t)$ contains all authors who at time t had no article in class $P_\uparrow(t)$ but who at time $t + 5$ published at least one article that falls in class $P_\uparrow(t + 5)$. In addition, we record the coauthorship centralities of authors in these two sets for two time windows $[t - 2, 2]$ and $[t + 3, t + 5]$. For authors in set $A_\nearrow$ we test the following hypothesis:

Hypothesis 2 *Authors that experience a positive shift in their citation success (i.e. authors in $A_\nearrow$) will become more central in the coauthorship network.*

Complementary to Hypothesis 2, for authors in set $A_\searrow$ we hypothesize:

Hypothesis 3 *Authors that experience a negative shift in their citation success (i.e. authors in $A_\searrow$) will become less central in the coauthorship network.*

In order to test for Hypothesis 2 and Hypothesis 3, we apply a *pairwise Wilcoxon-Mann-Whitney* test. To verify Hypothesis 2 we test if the centralities of authors have decreased in the case of a decrease in publication success from time t to $t + 5$. To verify Hypothesis 3 we test if the centralities of authors have increased in the case of an increase in publication success from time t to $t + 5$. Results of these hypotheses tests are presented in Table 4. Testing Hypothesis 2, for authors in $A_\nearrow$ we observe that p-values are much lower than the 0.01 significance threshold. We hence find evidence that authors in $A_\nearrow$ experience a significant *increase* in k-core, betweenness and degree centrality. Reversely, results for authors in $A_\searrow$ suggest a significant *decrease* in k-core, eigenvector and degree centrality. Based on these results we cannot reject Hypothesis 2 and Hypothesis 3, indicating that citation success significantly influences the future centrality of authors in the coauthorship network.

As an illustration of citation and coauthorship dynamics, Figures 5 and 6 show part of the coauthorship network. Color intensity of the nodes is scaled to their degree centrality, while node size is scaled to their betweenness centrality. A very strong community structure is clearly visible. Furthermore, we highlighted in red one particular author from the set $A_\nearrow(t)$ (2002), i.e. an author who did not have a paper in $P_\uparrow$ in 2002, but did so in 2007. In the considered five year span the highlighted author moved from a position in the periphery of the coauthorship network to a position in the center. Not only did the authors'

Table 4 *p*-values of Wilcoxon-Mann-Whitney test for different centrality metrics and alternative hypotheses. Column $A_\searrow$ presents *p*-values for authors in set $A_\searrow$, column $A_\nearrow$ presents *p*-values for authors in set $A_\nearrow$.

Centrality measure & alternative	$A_\searrow$	$A_\nearrow$
k-core$(t) >$ k-core$(t + 5)$	3.15×10^{-11}	1
k-core$(t) <$ k-core$(t + 5)$	1	3.04×10^{-55}
ev-centr$(t) >$ ev-centr$(t + 5)$	5.18×10^{-14}	0.86
ev-centr$(t) <$ ev-centr$(t + 5)$	1	0.14
bw-centr$(t) >$ bw-centr$(t + 5)$	0.23	1
bw-centr$(t) <$ bw-centr$(t + 5)$	0.77	7.29×10^{-30}
degree$(t) >$ degree$(t + 5)$	6.69×10^{-11}	1
degree$(t) <$ degree$(t + 5)$	1	7.72×10^{-62}
# authors	521	648

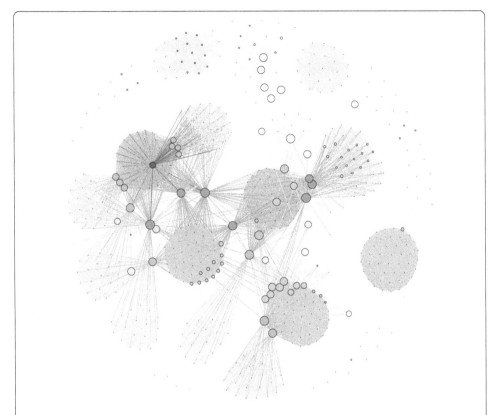

Figure 5 Citation success 2002. Illustration of correlation between citation success and centrality in the coauthorship network for year 2002. Color intensity of the nodes is scaled according to their degree centrality and size of nodes is scaled according to their betweenness centrality. Red node highlights one and the same author as in Figure 6.

degree centrality increase (see size of the node as well as joined red-colored links), but also the author's betweenness centrality largely increased.

Note that already in 2002 the author had comparatively high betweenness and degree centrality, which – according to our previous discussion – provided an ideal starting point for citation success in 2007.

5 Predicting successful publications

In the previous sections we presented evidence for the existence of statistical dependencies between authors' coauthorship centrality and the success of their publications. Results suggest that several coauthorship centrality metrics are indicative for citation success. However, we did not identify one single centrality metric whose magnitude is sufficient to predict whether the paper will become highly cited. In particular, we did not find that this would be true for the mere number of coauthors. Instead, we can guess that importance in the collaboration network is *multi-faceted* and thus influences by more than one network measure. In this section we thus develop a Machine Learning classifier which – taking into account several features of the authors position in the coauthorship network – is able to predict whether a publication will be highly cited.

Previous works have already attempted to predict citation success. For example in [22], the predictive power of the past h-index for the future h-index of a scientist was presented. Furthermore, in [23] additional indicators like, e.g. the length of the career or the

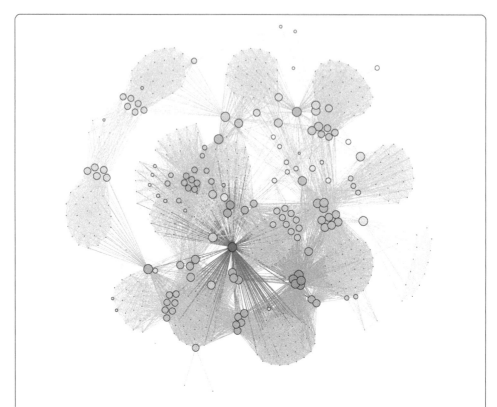

Figure 6 Citation success 2007. Illustration of correlation between citation success and centrality in the coauthorship network for year 2007. Color intensity of the nodes is scaled according to their degree centrality and size of nodes is scaled according to their betweenness centrality. Red node highlights one and the same author as in Figure 5.

number of articles in certain journals, have been integrated into a model to predict the future h-index of scientists. The authors of [20] compare the number of citations an article has received at a given point in time with the expected value in a preferential attachment model for the citation network. Deriving a z-score, the authors present a prediction of which papers will be highly cited in the future. Recently the authors reevaluate their earlier predictions and confirm the predictive power of their approach [24]. Whereas these three approaches attempt to predict success based on past citation dynamics, they do not investigate the underlying mechanisms that lead to citation success. Here we address this fundamental question and try to predict citation success merely based on centrality measures of authors in the coauthorship network. Clearly, many different factors will contribute to scientific success. In this work, however, we focus on the social component (based on the coauthorship network) in order to highlight the influence of social, and not necessarily merit-based, mechanisms on publication success.

In Section 4.1 we presented insights about the statistical dependency of citation success and several social network centrality measures (see Table 3). These results suggest that a naive Bayes predictor for citation success can already yield quite useful results, predicting whether or not a paper will be toppaper, given ex ante knowledge about topmetric of the authors. Using k-core centrality as a basis, we apply the following classification rule:

> *If a paper is authored by a top 10% k-core centrality author, then the paper will be among the top 10% most cited papers five years after publication.*

To evaluate the goodness of this prediction, we consider the error measures precision and recall (see Additional file 1 for a general definition of precision and recall). Observing that for k-core centrality in a 10% success scenario it is $P(\text{topmetric}|\text{toppaper}) = 0.21\%$ as well as $P(\text{toppaper}|\text{topmetric}) = 0.22\%$ and the fact that for a naive Bayes classifier recall $= P(\text{topmetric}|\text{toppaper})$ and precision $= P(\text{toppaper}|\text{topmetric})$ holds, one sees that a classifier with the above rule yields recall $= 21\%$ and precision $= 22\%$. Similarly, instead of k-core centrality other network measures presented in Table 3 can be used as basis for the above classification rule. As earlier works have tried to predict the success of papers based on the number of coauthors [14], using degree centrality as basis for the above classification rule directly extends these attempts, yielding a recall of 20% and a precision of 20%. Note, however, that degree centrality accumulates all coauthorships that have been established within the two-year sliding window of our analysis, not just the coauthorships of the paper under consideration.

We now ask whether a multi-dimensional naive Bayes classifier can improve this single metric classification result. Taking into account the intersection of all considered centrality metrics, we consider the following classification rule:

> *If a paper is authored by an author with a top 10% betweenness centrality, degree centrality, k-core centrality and eigenvector centrality, then the paper will be among the top 10% most cited papers five years after publication.*

Using this classifier, we achieve even better classification with a precision of 36%, however diminishing recall to 15%. Whereas these results already show that a naive Bayes classifier can yield interesting insights, in the following we will present a more sophisticated Machine Learning approach, taking multiple network centrality features into account and improving classification errors.

We first construct a feature vector for every publication as follows. For each publication appearing in year t, we extract all coauthors and compute the maximum and minimum of their centralities in the coauthorship network constructed based on the time window $[t-2, t]$. Then, for each publication we build a feature vector with ten features containing the maximum and minimum of the centrality metrics considered earlier (*degree, eigenvector, betweenness* and *k-core*), as well as the number of coauthors and the cumulative number of authors a paper has referenced. We then classify all publications regarding whether they fall in $P_\uparrow$ or $P_\downarrow$ according to the aforementioned publication classes, with $P_\uparrow$ defined as the set of the top 10% cited publications and $P_\downarrow$ as the remaining 90%.

The classification is done using a Random Forest classifier [25], extending the concept of classification trees (we use the R package *randomForest*, available at http://cran.r-project. org/web/packages/randomForest/). In general, the Random Forest classifier is known to yield accurate classifications for data with a large number of features [25]. Furthermore, it is a highly scalable classification algorithm, eliminating the need for separate cross validation and error estimation, as these procedures are part of the internal classification routine (for details on the procedure and the error estimates we refer to Additional file 1).

Table 5 summarizes precision, recall, and F-score of the resulting classification (see Supplementary Material (Additional file 1) for details on these measures). Comparing this result with the expectation from a random guess, which will correctly pick one of the top 10% publications only in 10% of the cases, the achieved precision of 60% is striking. In particular, by only considering positional features of authors in the coauthorship network,

Table 5 Error estimates of the Random Forest classifier to predict success of papers.

Nr. publications	Precision	Recall	F-score
36,000	0.6	0.18	0.28

we are able to achieve *an increase of factor six in predictive power* compared to a random guess. Also, we obtain a *recall* value of 18%, meaning that our classifier correctly identified about one fifth of all of the top 10% papers in a given research field. As a random guess would yield a recall of 10%, the Random Forest classifier *improves recall by 80%*.

This result allows for two conclusions: First, the fact that a high-dimensional random forest classifier performs better than a naive Bayes classifier, makes clear that social influence on scientific success cannot be measured by a single network metric and is instead a *multi-faceted* concept. Second, and most importantly, our result show that by *solely considering metrics of social influence*, such a classifier is able to predict scientific success with high precision.

Let us note that here we focused on the social influence on *success*. However, one might equally ask whether the complementary effect is true as well: can social factors predict whether a paper will be in the *bottom* 10% of all papers? We tested this hypothesis as well and found that, using the same procedure, with an achieved recall of 1.8% and a precision of 22.8%, whether a paper will be in the bottom 10% of all papers is *nearly unpredictable* using metrics of social influence only. Our interpretation of this finding is that even authors that are socially well connected will have papers that are not highly cited, simply because their content did not raise interest in the scientific community. This leads us to conclude that social factors are *necessary* factors for success, but are *not sufficient* – which is, in our opinion, a very easing result for the scientific community.

6 Discussion and conclusions

Using a data set on more than 100,000 scholarly publications authored by more than 160,000 authors in the field of computer science, in this article we studied the relation between the centrality of authors in the coauthorship network and the future success of their publications. Clearly, there are certain limitations to our approach, which we discuss in the following.

First of all, any data-driven study of social behavior in general and citation behavior in particular is limited by the completeness and correctness of the used data set. In our data set name ambiguities are automatically resolved by the Microsoft Academic Search (MSAS) database by sophisticated and validated disambiguation heuristics. This provides a clear advantage over simpler heuristics that have been used in similar studies. Although we did manual consistency checks of ambiguities for the top authors in our dataset, it is nevertheless not possible to exclude that there are some name ambiguities. However, since additionally author profiles in MSAS are to large parts manually edited by authors themselves, we are confident that name ambiguities are nearly negligible.

In order to rule out effects that are due to different citation patterns in different disciplines, we limited our study to computer science, for which we expect the coverage of MSAS to be particular good. While this limits the generalization of our results to other fields, our work nevertheless represents – to the best of our knowledge – the first large-scale case study of social factors in citation practices. As publication practices seem to vary widely across disciplines, it will be interesting to investigate whether our results hold for other research communities as well.

Clearly, any study that tries to evaluate the *importance* or *centrality* of actors in a social network needs to be concerned about the choice of suitable centrality measures. In order to not overemphasize one particular – out of the many – dimensions of centrality in networks, we chose to use *complementary centrality measures* that capture different aspects of importance at the same time. The results of our prediction highlight that the combination of different metrics is crucial – making clear that visibility and social influence are more complicated to capture than by a single centrality metric.

Finally, one may argue that our observation that authors with high centrality are cited more often is not a statement of a *direct causal relation* between centrality and citation numbers. After all, both centrality and citations could be secondary effects of, for instance, the scientific excellence of a particular researcher, which then translates into becoming central and highly cited at the same time. Clearly, we neither can – nor do we want – to rule out such possible explanations for our statistical findings. However, considering our finding of strong statistical dependence between social centrality and citation success, one could provocatively state the following: if citation-based measures were to be good proxies for scientific success, so should be measures of centrality in the social network. We assume that not many researchers would approve having the quality of their work be evaluated by means of such measures.

In summary, the contributions of our work are threefold:

1. We provide the, to the best of our knowledge, first large-scale study that analyses relations between the position of researchers in scientific collaboration networks and citation dynamics, using a set of complementary network-based centrality measures. A specific feature of our method is that we study *time-evolving* collaboration networks and citation numbers, thus allowing us to investigate possible mechanisms of social influence at a microscopic scale.

2. We show that – at least for the measures of centrality investigated in this paper – there is no *single* notion of centrality in social networks that could accurately predict the future citation success of an author. We expect this finding to be of interest for any general attempt to predict the success of actors based on their centrality in social networks.

3. Using modern Machine Learning techniques, we present a supervised classification method based on a Random Forest classifier, using a multidimensional feature vector of collaboration network centrality metrics. We show that this method allows for a remarkably precise prediction of the future citation success of a paper, solely based on the social embedding of its authors. With this, our method provides a clear indication for a strong statistical dependence between author centrality and citation success. Additionally, we show evidence that author centrality is more of a necessary condition for success than a sufficient one.

In conclusion, we provided evidence for a strong relation between the position of authors in scientific collaboration networks and their future success in terms of citations. We would like to emphasize that by this we *do not* want to join in the line of – sometimes remarkably uncritical – proponents of citation-based evaluation techniques. Instead, we hope to contribute to the discussion about the manifold influencing factors of citation measures and their explanatory power concerning scientific success. Especially, we *do not* see our contribution in the development of automated success prediction techniques, whose widespread adoption could possibly have devastating effects on the general scientific culture and attitude. Highlighting social influence mechanisms, we rather think that our findings are an important contribution to the ongoing debate about the meaningfulness and use of citation-based measures. We further hope that our work contributes to a better understanding of the multi-faceted, complex nature of citations and citation dynamics, which should be a prerequisite for any reasonable application of citation-based measures.

Competing interests

The authors declare that they have no competing interests.

Authors' contributions

All authors conceived and designed the research. ES and IS acquired the data. ES and RP analyzed the data. All authors discussed the research, wrote and approved the final version of the manuscript.

Acknowledgements

EM, IS and FS acknowledge funding by the Swiss National Science Foundation, grant no. CR31I1_140644/1. AG acknowledges funding by the EU FET project MULTIPLEX 317532. We especially thank Microsoft Research for granting unrestricted access to the Microsoft Academic Search service.

References

1. Hirsch JE (2005) An index to quantify an individual's scientific research output. Proc Natl Acad Sci USA 102(46):16569-16572. doi:10.1073/pnas.0507655102. http://www.pnas.org/content/102/46/16569.full.pdf+html
2. Heisenberg W (1969) Der Teil und Das Ganze: Gespräche Im Umkreis der Atomphysik. Piper und Co. Verlag, München
3. Garfield E (1955) Citation indexes for science: a new dimension in documentation through association of ideas. Science 122(3159):108-111. doi:10.1126/science.122.3159.108. http://www.sciencemag.org/content/122/3159/108.full.pdf
4. Leydesdorff L (1998) Theories of citation? Scientometrics 43(1):5-25. doi:10.1007/BF02458391
5. Radicchi F (2012) In science "there is no bad publicity": papers criticized in comments have high scientific impact. Sci Rep 2:815
6. Nicolaisen J (2003) The social act of citing: towards new horizons in citation theory. Proc Am Soc Inf Sci Technol 40(1):12-20. doi:10.1002/meet.1450400102
7. Laloë F, Mosseri R (2009) Bibliometric evaluation of individual researchers: not even right…not even wrong! Europhys News 40(5):26-29. doi:10.1051/epn/2009704
8. Bornmann L, Daniel H-D (2008) What do citation counts measure? A review of studies on citing behavior. J Doc 64(1):45-80
9. Radicchi F, Castellano C (2013) Analysis of bibliometric indicators for individual scholars in a large data set. Scientometrics 97(3):627-637
10. Radicchi F, Fortunato S, Castellano C (2008) Universality of citation distributions: toward an objective measure of scientific impact. Proc Natl Acad Sci USA 105(45):17268-17272
11. Stringer MJ, Sales-Pardo M, Amaral LAN (2010) Statistical validation of a global model for the distribution of the ultimate number of citations accrued by papers published in a scientific journal. J Am Soc Inf Sci Technol 61(7):1377-1385. doi:10.1002/asi.21335
12. Katz JS, Hicks D (1997) How much is a collaboration worth? A calibrated bibliometric model. Scientometrics 40(3):541-554. doi:10.1007/BF02459299
13. Figg WD, Dunn L, Liewehr DJ, Steinberg SM, Thurman PW, Barrett JC, Birkinshaw J (2006) Scientific collaboration results in higher citation rates of published articles. Pharmacotherapy 26(6):759-767. doi:10.1592/phco.26.6.759
14. Hsu J, Huang D (2011) Correlation between impact and collaboration. Scientometrics 86(2):317-324
15. Martin T, Ball B, Karrer B, Newman MEJ (2013) Coauthorship and citation in scientific publishing. arXiv:1304.0473
16. Bras-Amorós M, Domingo-Ferrer J, Torra V (2011) A bibliometric index based on the collaboration distance between cited and citing authors. J Informetr 5(2):248-264
17. Wallace ML, Lariviere V, Gingras Y (2012) A small world of citations? The influence of collaboration networks on citation practices. PLoS ONE 7(3):33339. doi:10.1371/journal.pone.0033339
18. Newman MEJ (2009) Networks: an introduction. Oxford University Press, New York
19. Csardi G, Nepusz T (2006) The igraph software package for complex network research. InterJournal:1695
20. Newman MEJ (2009) The first-mover advantage in scientific publication. Europhys Lett 86(6):68001
21. Mann HB, Whitney DB (1947) On a test of whether one of two random variables is stochastically larger than the other. Ann Math Stat 18(1):50-60. doi:10.1214/aoms/1177730491

22. Hirsch JE (2007) Does the *h* index have predictive power? Proc Natl Acad Sci USA 104(49):19193-19198. doi:10.1073/pnas.0707962104. http://www.pnas.org/content/104/49/19193.full.pdf+html

23. Acuna DE, Allesina S, Kording KP (2012) Future impact: predicting scientific success. Nature 489:201-202. doi:10.1038/489201a

24. Newman MEJ (2013) Prediction of highly cited papers. arXiv:1310.8220

25. Breiman L (2001) Random forests. Mach Learn 45(1):5-32

11

The dynamics of health behavior sentiments on a large online social network

Marcel Salathé[1,2,3]*, Duy Q Vu[4], Shashank Khandelwal[1,2] and David R Hunter[1,4]

*Correspondence: salathe@psu.edu
[1]Center for Infectious Disease Dynamics, Penn State University, University Park, PA, USA
[2]Department of Biology, Penn State University, University Park, PA, USA
Full list of author information is available at the end of the article

Abstract

Modifiable health behaviors, a leading cause of illness and death in many countries, are often driven by individual beliefs and sentiments about health and disease. Individual behaviors affecting health outcomes are increasingly modulated by social networks, for example through the associations of like-minded individuals - homophily - or through peer influence effects. Using a statistical approach to measure the individual temporal effects of a large number of variables pertaining to social network statistics, we investigate the spread of a health sentiment towards a new vaccine on Twitter, a large online social network. We find that the effects of neighborhood size and exposure intensity are qualitatively very different depending on the type of sentiment. Generally, we find that larger numbers of opinionated neighbors inhibit the expression of sentiments. We also find that exposure to negative sentiment is contagious - by which we merely mean predictive of future negative sentiment expression - while exposure to positive sentiments is generally not. In fact, exposure to positive sentiments can even predict increased negative sentiment expression. Our results suggest that the effects of peer influence and social contagion on the dynamics of behavioral spread on social networks are strongly content-dependent.

Keywords: social media; social network; diffusion; health behavior; contagion

Social networks play an important role in affecting the dynamics of health behaviors and the associated diseases [1–3], but identifying the main drivers of health behavior spread in social networks has been challenging. The observation that health behavior dynamics follow the patterns of social contacts - *e.g.* that behaviors are often clustered [4, 5] and positively assorted at the dyadic level [6, 7] - can be explained by multiple processes, the two most prominent being homophily and social influence. The homophily hypothesis posits that social contacts are a product of likemindedness, whereas the social influence hypothesis posits that likemindedness is a product of social contacts. Measuring and distinguishing between the effects of homophily and social influence can be difficult in observational studies [6, 8, 9], but is important for the development of health behavior intervention strategies. Vaccination behavior is a prime example of a health behavior shaping disease dynamics: outbreaks of vaccine preventable disease are more likely if overall vaccination rates decline [10], or if vaccination refusal is clustered in local communities [11, 12]. The continuously evolving public concern about vaccines despite the overwhelming scientific evidence on the safety of vaccines reflect the need for an increased understanding on how such sentiments spread over time [13].

Studying the dynamics of health behaviors on social networks can also be resource-intensive because social network data must often be inferred indirectly, and many health behaviors are complex and thus difficult to quantify. In recent years, online social media services have emerged as novel data sources where short messages are publicly shared, allowing for a detailed picture of the flow of information from person to person in large-scale networks. We have conducted a study to investigate the temporal dynamics of a readily quantifiable health sentiment - the intent to get vaccinated against a novel pandemic virus - on an online social network involving more than 100,000 people, and more than 4 million directed relationships among them. The health sentiment dynamics captured on this network are given by time-stamped messages published by the online social network users, retrospectively classified as expressing positive, neutral or negative sentiments about the intent to get immunized with pandemic influenza H1N1 vaccine [7]. Although not directly measuring the health behavior, the data were shown to explain a large fraction of the spatial variance in CDC-estimated influenza A H1N1 vaccination rates. Insofar as the dynamics of these sentiment have shaped the dynamics of the health behavior, we are interested in the factors affecting the spread of health sentiments in the social network.

The data were collected from the online social networking service Twitter (www.twitter.com), where users post short messages (so-called 'tweets') of up to 140 characters that are then broadcast to their followers. Follower relationships are directional - if user A chooses to follow user B, user A will receive messages from user B, but user B will not receive messages from user A. In this case, we call user A a follower of user B, and user B a followee of user A (although followees are sometimes referred to as 'friends' in the media, we prefer the term followee because it more clearly conveys the direction of the relationship). Nevertheless, user B may also choose to follow user A, in which case a bidirectional relationship is established, and both users will receive messages from each other. An application programming interface (API) provided by Twitter allows for the collection of tweets matching a given set of requirements (*e.g.*, containing a keyword), as well as the collection of follower and followee relationships among users. After data collection, machine learning algorithms were employed to label tweets as negative, positive or neutral with respect to the intent of getting vaccinated against influenza H1N1. Of the 477,768 collected tweets, 318,379 were classified as relevant to the influenza A(H1N1) vaccine. Of those, 255,828 were classified as neutral, 26,667 as negative, and 35,884 as positive. As our data collection efforts were whitelisted by Twitter (a practice that Twitter has now officially discontinued), we are confident that our data set represents the entirety of relevant content. We used an ensemble method combining a naive Bayes and a maximum entropy classifier with an accuracy of 84.29%. The full methodology is described in Salathé and Khandelwal 2011 [7].

In order to identify significant contributors to the likelihood that a user in the social network will express an opinionated (*i.e.*, positive or negative) sentiment in the future, we use an approach that estimates the individual effects of numerous covariates related to the past sentiment expression behavior of users and social contacts as well as the structure of their social network neighborhood (Figure 1). We associate two counting processes, $N_i^+(t)$ and $N_i^-(t)$, with each user i to count the number of positive and negative messages that the user has sent by time t [14]. This results in multivariate counting processes $N^+(t) = [N_i^+(t), \ldots, N_n^+(t)]$ and $N^-(t) = [N_i^-(t), \ldots, N_n^-(t)]$, where n is the number of users in the network. By a mathematical result called the Doob-Meyer theorem [14], each of these

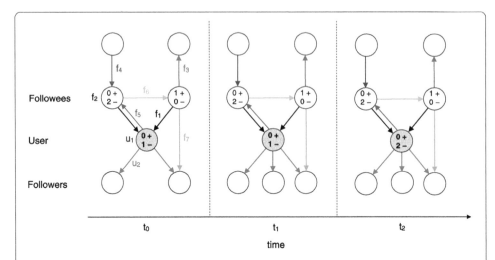

Figure 1 Illustration of covariates related to past sentiment expression behavior of users and social contacts as well as the structure of their social network neighborhood. Nodes represent users in the social network (the gray node represents the focal user), arrows represent the follower relationships, and numbers inside of nodes represent sentiment expression history (numbers of positive and negative sentiments expressed at given time; neutral sentiments are also counted, though we do not depict them here). The direction of the arrows represents the direction of information flow. Covariates f_1, f_2, and f_5 are explained in the article; the remaining covariates are explained in Additional file 1. For instance, the figure indicates that f_1 relates to the number of followees of the focal user and f_2 relates to the number of tweets these followees make, whereas f_5 counts reciprocated follower-followee relationships. Other covariates include information about the followers (as measured by u_2), the number of tweets made by the user (u_1), triangle-based covariates that measure certain types of clustering (f_6 and f_7), and numbers of follower and followees of the user's followees (f_3 and f_4). The figure illustrates that the values of these covariates may change with the advance of time (*e.g.* new tweets, new follower relationships, *etc.*).

(random) counting processes can be decomposed into an integrated conditional intensity process (the signal) and a random process called a martingale (the noise). We denote the conditional intensity functions for positive and negative tweeting events by user i as $\lambda^+(i,t|\beta^+,H_{t-})$ and $\lambda^-(i,t|\beta^-,H_{t-})$, where H_{t-} is the network right before time t, and β^+ and β^- are vectors of parameters.

Specifically, our models for the intensity functions $\lambda^+(i,t|\beta^+,H_{t-})$ and $\lambda^-(i,t|\beta^-,H_{t-})$ are Cox proportional hazards models [15], taking the form

$$\lambda^+\left(i,t|\beta^+,H_{t-}\right) = \lambda_0^+(t)\exp\left[\beta^+ \cdot s(i,H_{t-})\right] \tag{1}$$

(similarly for λ^-). Here, $s(i,H_{t-})$ is a vector of model-specific covariates, such as node degree and other network statistics deemed appropriate for explaining the intensity of events, which may depend on both the particular node i and the network history H_{t-} up to time t. In our model, each of the network covariates is multiplied by a corresponding element of one of the beta vectors, much like covariates in a regression model are multiplied by regression coefficients. Hence, the statistical significance of the estimated beta coefficients and their signs tell us how the corresponding covariates predict sentiment expression after correcting for all other covariate effects. Notably, the covariate vectors are not constant in time; this fact, in addition to the multivariate counting process response, distinguishes our approach from that of other studies of Twitter data such as that of Golder and Macy [16], who model multivariate continuous (not counting process) responses as functions of fixed predictor variables. Our choice of the Cox proportional hazards model in equation (1) is largely due to the wide use of this model not only in the case of independently sampled survival-time data for which it was originally developed but, more recently, in the counting process context where observations are not necessarily independent. This choice entails an assumption that the coefficients do not change over time and that the covariates influence the intensity function multiplicatively; alternatives such as the Aalen additive model, discussed below, use different assumptions.

We use exactly the same covariates in both models even though the coefficient vectors are different. The network covariates as summarized in Figure 1 capture a number of important aspects of network history H_{t_-} thought to be relevant for the dynamics of sentiment expression. A detailed description of all the covariates, along with a full list of the corresponding coefficient estimates and their p-values, is given in Additional file 1. Although we do not discuss them in the current paper, alternative methods for modeling $\lambda^+(i,t)$ exist. For instance, Vu et al. [17] discuss the so-called Aalen additive model for a similar situation, in which the effects of the covariates $s(i, H_{t_-})$ are additive, rather than multiplicative, and the coefficients β^+ and β^- may be assumed to change over time.

The coefficient vector β^+ in model given by equation (1), along with the vector β^- corresponding to the analogous model for negative tweeting intensity, is estimated using maximum partial likelihood. This is standard practice for Cox proportional hazards models, whose partial likelihood functions do not suffer from multi-modality due to the fact that the log-partial-likelihood is concave [18] with maximizers known to have desirable statistical properties [18, 19]. However, the computations are difficult in the present case because of the size of the dataset. Thus, we employ the computational innovations for caching the time series of network statistic updates outlined in Section 3.2 of Vu et al. [20]. Using standard statistical theory for the counting process approach to the Cox model [14, 19], we may also obtain confidence intervals for each coefficient. These confidence intervals do not take into account the error introduced by the possible misclassification of the sentiment expressed in each tweet by the automatic classifier we employ. Therefore, we do not base our statistical inferences on the single set of confidence intervals, but instead employ a series of random reclassifications of each tweet (the four categories being positive, negative, neutral, or unrelated to vaccination), based on a smaller set of test tweets used for calibration and using a method we detail in Additional file 1. In all, 200 different random reclassifications of every tweet are employed, and each such reclassification leads to a new realization of the network to which we apply our statistical estimation method. The resulting profile of 200 95% confidence intervals for every individual coefficient allows us to examine, in aggregate, the direction of each covariate's effect as well as its robustness against the misclassifications inherent in the automatic classification process. Examples of these sets of confidence intervals are presented in Figures 2 and 3 (with more given in Additional file 1).

We base our estimates on only the final 45 days of the data collection time period in order to ensure that they are based on a maximally accurate network representation. Network relationships could only be captured once a user had been identified as messaging about H1N1 vaccination, so cumulative network information improves toward the end of the data collection period. In particular, we have had to make the simplifying assumption that all users are in the network for the entire period on which estimates are to be based - as the exact time a user begins to follow other users' tweets is not observed - and we found this assumption to be suspect beyond 45 days from the end of the data collection period.

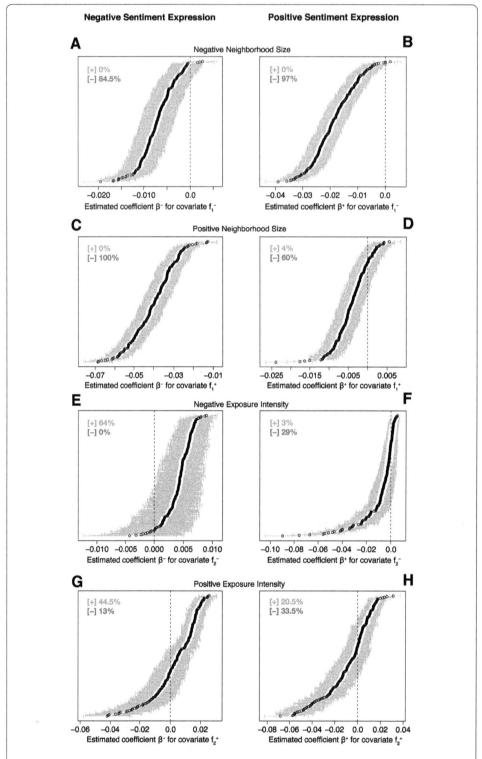

Figure 2 Estimated coefficients of covariates related to social contagion. Each panel shows the means (circle) and 95% confidence intervals (line) for 200 network realizations, stacked horizontally and ordered by increasing means for better readability. The left column (**A**, **C**, **E** and **G**) are estimated coefficients for the likelihood of negative sentiment expression, the right column (**B**, **D**, **F** and **H**) are estimated coefficients for the likelihood of positive sentiment expression. The vertical dotted line is positioned at an estimated coefficient of zero (*i.e.* no effect). The percentage numbers in the top left corner of each panel indicate what fraction of the network realizations yielded statistically significant positive (green) or negative (red) coefficient estimates.

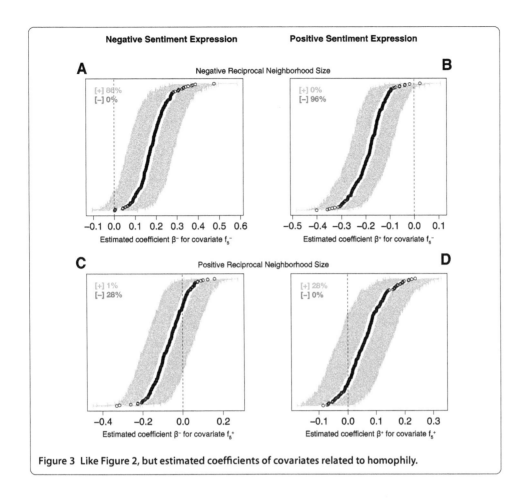

Figure 3 Like Figure 2, but estimated coefficients of covariates related to homophily.

For the time period of 45 days, 98,235 out of 101,853 nodes (96.4%), and 4,209,361 out of 4,858,985 edges (86.6%) are already observed. Therefore, our choice of 45 days represents a balance between the desire to minimize bias due to violations of our simplifying assumption and the desire to use as much data as possible to improve the precision of our estimates. We have verified that results based on a 30-day window were not qualitatively different (in terms of sign and statistical significance) than those based on a 45-day window, whereas a 60-day window appears to introduce bias due to violations of the simplifying assumption.

Because our main interest is in assessing the effects of homophily and social contagion on the health sentiment dynamics in the network, we would like to measure the effects of both how many opinionated people a user is connected to, as well as how many opinionated messages a user is exposed to. These two effects are often confounded because on average, the more people a user is connected to, the more messages a user is exposed to. We therefore define covariates that separate these two effects as much as possible. A further important consideration is that users cannot simply be classified as positive or negative in their overall opinions because over the course of time they might have expressed different sentiments in numerous tweets. To address this issue, each followee is weighted by the fraction of opinionated (positive or negative) tweets he or she makes. The following paragraph gives precise definitions of these three positive-sentiment covariates as employed by the vector $s(i, H_{t-})$ of the model given by equation (1). The three corresponding negative-sentiment covariates are defined similarly. The full set of covariates, of which there are 24 in our full model, is explained in Additional file 1.

In order to measure the extent to which a user is connected to people expressing positive or negative sentiments, we define the opinionated neighborhood size of a user to be the number of followees. The corresponding covariate, $f_1^+(i,t)$ as indicated in Figure 1, is defined as

$$f_1^+(i,t) = \sum_{j \in F(i,t)} \frac{N^+(j,t)}{N^a(j,t)}, \tag{2}$$

where $F(i,t)$ is the set of followees of i at time t and $N^+(j,t)$ and $N^a(j,t)$ are, respectively, the number of positive tweets and the total number of vaccination-related tweets (positive, negative, or neutral, but excluding any tweets not related to H1N1 vaccination) made by j before time t. We take the opinionated reciprocal neighborhood fraction of a user to be the proportion of followees that are reciprocal (*i.e.*, who are also followers), weighted by the positivity fraction. The corresponding covariate, $f_5^+(i,t)$ in Figure 1, is defined as

$$f_5^+(i,t) = \frac{1}{f_1^+(i,t)} \sum_{j \in F(i,t)} \frac{N^+(j,t)}{N^a(j,t)} Y_{ji}(t), \tag{3}$$

where $Y(t)$ is the adjacency matrix of the network at time t and thus $Y_{ji}(t)$ is the indicator that j follows i at time t. Finally, we define the average opinionated exposure intensity to be the weighted number of opinionated tweets by followees, normalized by the sum of the weights (to minimize the confounding with $f_1^+(i,t)$ as mentioned above). The corresponding covariate is

$$f_2^+(i,t) = \frac{1}{f_1^+(i,t)} \sum_{j \in F(i,t)} \frac{N^+(j,t)}{N^a(j,t)} N^+(j,t). \tag{4}$$

We focus our attention on the six coefficients corresponding to the covariates described above, *i.e.*, $f_1^+(i,t), f_2^+(i,t)$, and $f_5^+(i,t)$ and their corresponding negative-sentiment covariates. We do not study the remaining 18 coefficients in the model with the same level of detail, both for the sake of simplicity and because our interest lies primarily in those effects that relate directly to social contagion. However, it is important that the other statistics, all of which are explained in Additional file 1, are included in the model, since this means that the six coefficients we discuss are estimated after accounting for the effects of all of the other statistics. For instance, we account for possible triangle-based clustering effects by including terms for average number of shared followers (of followees) and average number of shared followees (of followees); as we mention below, these terms control for some types of homophily. Readers interested in statistics used in different applications might compare the statistics used in the citation network examples of Vu *et al.* [20] or the social network and email examples of Vu *et al.* [17] and Perry and Wolfe [18].

The results are summarized in Figures 2 and 3, which simultaneously account for two different types of uncertainty. Error due to selecting a random sample of individuals from a hypothetical infinite population of potential Twitter users, as represented by the model, is expressed by the 95% confidence intervals, whereas error due to misclassifying sentiments is captured by the 200 randomly reclassified samples. The percentages in green and red are therefore the proportion of times we could expect our dataset to result in rejecting the null hypothesis of no effect and concluding that a positive (green) or negative (red) effect exists; we may therefore understand these values as bootstrapped probabilities that our dataset will produce these two statistical results. Generally, larger opinionated neighborhood sizes have an inhibitory effect on the expression of opinionated sentiments (Figure 2A-D): While both larger positive and larger negative neighborhood sizes have the expected inhibitory effect on the expression of the opposite sentiments (*i.e.*, negative and positive, respectively), they also predict diminished expression of that same sentiment. If we look at the opinionated reciprocal neighborhood size (Figure 3), we see that the effects are content-dependent, *i.e.*, the effects are different for negative and positive sentiments. On one hand, larger positive reciprocal neighborhood sizes do not generally have a significant predictive effect on the rate of expressing opinionated sentiments. On the other hand, increasing negative reciprocal neighborhood size has the expected effect of increasing the likelihood of expressing a negative sentiment, and decreasing the likelihood of expressing a positive sentiment. Finally, the predictive effects of opinionated exposure intensity are also content-dependent (Figure 2E-H). While a range of outcomes are observed in the 200 network realizations obtained *via* reclassifying each tweet's sentiment (as explained earlier), there is a sizable fraction of outcomes that show unexpected effects. In particular, in a substantial fraction of cases, being exposed to an increased intensity of positive tweets is predictive of increased intensity of negative sentiment (Figure 2G), as well as decreased intensity of positive sentiment (Figure 2H). Finally, the past expression of a sentiment by an individual predicts an increased propensity for that individual to express that same sentiment again, a finding that is very consistent across all 200 network realizations (see Figure S1 in Additional file 1).

It is worthwhile to consider these results in the context of what the statistics are expected to measure. Our main interest is in identifying the extent to which social contagion and homophily drive sentiment dynamics within the social network. In an observational study like the present study, causality cannot be established. Furthermore, disentangling effects of homophily and contagion is notoriously hard [8] because they are often confounded. Our approach tries to minimize these issues as much as possible. We use the term social contagion to mean the extent to which exposure to a given sentiment is predictive of future expression of that sentiment. Previous studies have focused on binary outcomes such as the adoption (*vs.* non-adoption) of a service [6, 21], and have measured exposure as the number of social contacts that have adopted the service previously. Our methodology allows us to consider more complex measures of exposure: For instance, in the present analysis we measure both the number of social contacts expressing a given sentiment as well as the intensity with which the sentiment is expressed. Thus, both the opinionated neighborhood size as well as the average opinionated exposure intensity relate to social contagion as defined above. Homophily, on the other hand, is assessed by the opinionated reciprocal neighborhood size of a user, *i.e.*, the weighted number of reciprocal followees, or followees who are also followers of that user.

The finding that the opinionated neighborhood size generally has an inhibitory effect on the likelihood of expressing any opinionated sentiment (Figure 2A-D) is difficult to interpret in the context of a standard contagion framework, because contagion is normally associated with spread, rather than inhibition. For example, it makes intuitive sense that a larger number of negative followees should lead to a reduction in the expression of positive sentiments. The finding that it also leads to a reduction in the expression of negative sentiments is harder to interpret, but nevertheless agrees with the general pattern of inhibition. When looking at the average opinionated exposure intensity (Figure 2E-H), a different picture emerges. The results are rather sensitive to misclassification of the messages, but the most stable result (64% of all network realizations, Figure 2E) is that increased average negative exposure intensity does predict increased negative sentiment expression, in line with the expectation of social contagion. Surprisingly, the second most stable result (44.5% of all network realizations, Figure 2G) is that the average positive exposure intensity does also predict increased negative sentiment expression. Equally surprisingly, the third most stable result (33.5% of network realizations, Figure 2H) is that higher average positive exposure intensity predicts decreased positive sentiment expression. Taken together, the results suggest that exposure to negative sentiment is contagious - by which we merely mean predictive of future negative sentiment expression - while exposure to positive sentiments is generally not. They also suggest that exposure to increased intensity of opinionated sentiments has on balance led to increased negative sentiment expression and decreased positive sentiment expression, overall favoring the spread of negative vaccination sentiments.

The lack of detailed information about the users prohibits us from assessing manifest homophily, and our analysis is thus subject to the problem of latent homophily which is generally confounded with contagion [8]. We assess homophily with the opinionated reciprocal neighborhood size of a user, which is the weighted number of reciprocal followees (*i.e.*, followees who are also followers of that user). Bidirectional follower relationships mean that two users are interested in receiving messages from each other, which we assume to indicate that the users may share similar interests, which in turn suggests homophily. To further reduce the confounding effects of homophily and contagion, our model contains covariates for the number of shared followees and followers. These covariates are expected to control for latent homophily to a certain extent, since homophily is known to manifest itself in network clustering [8, 22]. Our findings suggest that the effects of homophily, insofar as we can measure it, are content-dependent: the positive reciprocal neighborhood size does generally not have significant effects (Figure 3C and D), while increasing negative reciprocal neighborhood size has the expected effects of predicting decreased positive and increased negative sentiment expression (Figure 3A and B). This finding further contributes to favoring the spread of negative vaccination sentiments.

Overall, the finding that the effects of various network covariates are strongly content-dependent suggests that a standard contagion framework might be too constrained to understand the health sentiment dynamics occurring on this network. By standard contagion framework, we mean the conceptual idea that increased exposure to any given agent (whether biological or social) will lead to an increased transmission - and predict an increased adoption - of that agent. In such a framework, the expectation is that there is a positive relationship between exposure and the consequent adoption of whatever it is individuals are exposed to. In our data, the only effect that corresponds to this pattern is that increased negative exposure intensity does predict increased negative sentiment expression. All the other results suggest that increased exposure predicts either a decrease of the same sentiment expression or an increase of the opposite sentiment expression.

From a public health perspective, the results raise some questions about the design of health behavior communication strategies. In particular, the notion that increased positive exposure intensity predicts increased negative sentiments could be of great concern if this turns out to be a consistent finding in future studies, since it would indicate that the level of positive messaging needs to be assessed carefully. Equally worrisome is the notion that the identified effects overall seem to favor the spread of negative sentiments, but not the spread of positive sentiments. This suggests that increased attention should be given to the prevention and control of negative sentiments (particularly if based on rumors, misinformation, misunderstandings, *etc.*). A recent study [23] has found that the popularity of documents shared on Twitter decreased significantly faster if the documents contained more words related to negative emotion, rather than to positive emotion. In general, the ability to measure the dynamics of sentiments on online networks generates opportunities to dramatically reduce the time lag between communication strategies and the assessment of the effects of those strategies.

The study framework has a number of limitations that need to be taken into account when assessing its applicability. First, our study design has been set up to catch expression of sentiments only (rather than actual vaccination behavior), but users might have been affected by exposure to sentiments from social contacts without ever expressing these sentiments themselves. For example, a user exposed to many negative messages may have been influenced and adopted a negative stance on H1N1 vaccination, but the user might not consequently have expressed that opinion in the network. Thus, a substantial fraction of actual contagion may have gone unnoticed. Conversely, peer pressure effects may have driven users to express a certain sentiment online even though they personally hold a different opinion (and behave differently from what one would expect based on the expressed sentiment), leading to false positives. Future research should address the question to what extent health sentiments expressed online overlap with actual health behaviors. Moreover, our study design ignores the possibility that follower relationships may have been established because users already share the same opinion on vaccination. While it is not unlikely that vaccination sentiments can be a contributor to establishing follower relationships, we believe that overall it had a small effect in the short period of time on which our analysis is based. Finally, the content of short messages like the ones studied here is subjective and open to interpretation by the reader of the message. Given the sometimes strong dependency of the effect on network realizations, this is an important problem that needs to be addressed in the future.

The dynamics of sentiments and behaviors on social networks is of great importance in many fields concerning human affairs [24], and particularly also in the health domain. There is an increased understanding that modifiable health behaviors are a key contributor to health outcomes [25], and that health behavior modification might be a key strategy to control major public health issues, both from the perspective of prevention (vaccination, smoking cessation, diet modification, *etc.*) and treatment (adherence to treatment plans, antibiotic overuse, *etc.*) strategies. The rapid worldwide adoption of online social network services means that an increasing fraction of (mis-)information diffusion is occurring on these networks. The methods and findings presented here are a small step towards an increased understanding of these dynamics, demonstrating both the promise and the challenges associated with these large and often unstructured data sets. In addition to online experiments [26, 27], analysis of large-scale, high-resolution observational data will provide a much better picture of the dynamics of health behavior diffusion on social networks.

Competing interests
The authors declare that they have no competing interests.

Authors' contributions
MS conceived and coordinated the project and collected original data. MS and DRH wrote the paper. DQV and DRH performed statistical analysis and wrote supplementary material. SK performed sentiment analysis. MS, DQV, SK and DRH discussed the results and implications and commented on the manuscript.

Author details
[1]Center for Infectious Disease Dynamics, Penn State University, University Park, PA, USA. [2]Department of Biology, Penn State University, University Park, PA, USA. [3]Department of Computer Sciences and Engineering, Penn State University, University Park, PA, USA. [4]Department of Statistics, Penn State University, University Park, PA, USA.

Acknowledgements
This work is supported by a Branco Weiss: Society in Science Fellowship to Marcel Salathé, and by the Office of Naval Research (ONR grant N00014-08-1-1015) and the National Institutes of Health (NIH grant 1R01GM083603) to DRH. Marcel Salathé gratefully acknowledges NIH RAPIDD support. This work was supported in part through instrumentation funded by the National Science Foundation through grant OCI-0821527.

References
1. Smith KP, Christakis NA (2008) Social networks and health. Annu Rev Sociol 34:405-429
2. Christakis NA, Fowler JH (2008) The collective dynamics of smoking in a large social network. N Engl J Med 358:2249-2258
3. Valente TW (2010) Social networks and health. Oxford University Press, Oxford
4. Christakis NA, Fowler JH (2007) The spread of obesity in a large social network over 32 years. N Engl J Med 357:370-379
5. Schuit AJ, van Loon AJM, Tijhuis M, Ocké M (2002) Clustering of lifestyle risk factors in a general adult population. Prev Med 35:219-224
6. Aral S, Muchnik L, Sundararajan A (2009) Distinguishing influence-based contagion from homophily-driven diffusion in dynamic networks. Proc Natl Acad Sci USA 106:21544-21549
7. Salathé M, Khandelwal S (2011) Assessing vaccination sentiments with online social media: implications for infectious disease dynamics and control. PLoS Comput Biol 7:e1002199
8. Shalizi CR, Thomas AC (2011) Homophily and contagion are generically confounded in observational social network studies. Sociol Methods Res 40:211-239
9. An W (2011) In: Scott J, Carrington PJ (eds) The SAGE handbook of social network analysis. Thousand Oaks, Sage, pp 514-532
10. Jansen VAA et al (2003) Measles outbreaks in a population with declining vaccine uptake. Science 301:804
11. Salathé M, Bonhoeffer S (2008) The effect of opinion clustering on disease outbreaks. J R Soc Interface 5:1505-1508
12. Omer SB, Enger KS, Moulton LH (2008) Geographic clustering of nonmedical exemptions to school immunization requirements and associations with geographic clustering of pertussis. Am J Epidemiol 168:1389-1396
13. Omer SB, Salmon DA, Orenstein WA, deHart MP, Halsey N (2009) Vaccine refusal, mandatory immunization, and the risks of vaccine-preventable diseases. N Engl J Med 360:1981-1988
14. Aalen OO, Borgan Ø, Gjessing HK (2008) Survival and event history analysis. Springer, Berlin
15. Cox DR (1972) Regression models and life-tables (with discussion). J R Stat Soc, Ser B, Stat Methodol 34:187-220
16. Golder SA, Macy MW (2011) Diurnal and seasonal mood vary with work, sleep, and daylength across diverse cultures. Science 333:1878-1881
17. Vu DQ, Asuncion AU, Hunter DR, Smyth P (2011) In: Proceedings of the 24th international conference on neural information processing systems (NIPS 2011), vol 24, pp 2492-2500
18. Perry PO, Wolfe PJ (2010) Point process modeling for directed interaction networks. arXiv:1011.1703
19. Andersen PK, Gill RD (1982) Cox's regression model for counting processes: a large sample study. Ann Stat 10:1100-1120
20. Vu DQ, Asuncion AU, Hunter DR, Smyth P (2011) In: Proceedings of 28th international conference on machine learning (ICML 2011), pp 857-864
21. Ugander J, Backstrom L, Marlow C, Kleinberg J (2012) Structural diversity in social contagion. Proc Natl Acad Sci USA 109:5962-5966
22. McPherson M, Smith-Lovin L, Cook JM (2001) Birds of a feather: homophily in social networks. Annu Rev Sociol 27:415-444
23. Wu S, Tan C, Kleinberg J, Macy M (2011) Does bad news go away faster. In: Proc. 5th international AAAI conference on weblogs and social media
24. Rogers EM (2003) Diffusion of innovations, 5th edn. Free Press, New York
25. Mokdad AH, Marks JS, Stroup DF, Gerberding JL (2004) Actual causes of death in the United States, 2000. JAMA J Am Med Assoc 291:1238-1245
26. Centola D (2010) The spread of behavior in an online social network experiment. Science 329:1194-1197
27. Centola D (2011) An experimental study of homophily in the adoption of health behavior. Science 334:1269-1272

12

Complex network analysis of teaching practices

Woon Peng Goh[1,2*], Dennis Kwek[3], David Hogan[4] and Siew Ann Cheong[2,5]

*Correspondence:
gohw0047@ntu.edu.sg
[1]Interdisciplinary Graduate School,
Nanyang Technological University,
50 Nanyang Avenue, Singapore,
639798, Singapore
Full list of author information is
available at the end of the article

Abstract

The application of functional analysis to infer networks in large datasets is potentially helpful to experimenters in various ?elds. In this paper, we develop a technique to construct networks of statistically signi?cant transitions between variable pairs from a high-dimensional and multiscale dataset of teaching practices observed in Grade 5 and Grade 9 Mathematics classes obtained by the National Institute of Education in Singapore. From the Minimum Spanning Trees (MST) and Planar Maximally Filtered Graphs (PMFG) of the transition networks, we establish that teaching knowledge as truth and teacher-dominated talking serve as hubs for teaching practices in Singapore. These practices re?ect a transmissionist model of teaching and learning. We also identify complex teacher-student-teacher-student interaction sequences of teaching practices that are over-represented in the data.

Keywords: complex networks; functional analysis; teaching practices; pedagogy theory

1 Introduction

In recent years, it has become popular to use networks to visualize and analyze the hierarchical structure within large datasets usually obtained from complex dynamical systems. Networks are especially useful for representing the extent and magnitude of interactions among the many components in complex systems. In such visualizations we show the important pair-wise relationships between variables. These relations may be directed transitions, causation, or activations, or undirected when we examine similarities or co-occurrences. Examples of such usage can be found in ?nance [1, 2], biology [3, 4], sociology [5], and language [6]. Even without any further quantitative analysis of the network structure, showing such pair-wise relationships on a network often gives us a powerful overview of the structures that exist within the data. Beyond such crude ?eyeballing? of the network, there exist tools to (i) ?lter out the most essential structure in the network [7? 9], (ii) identify important central nodes, (iii) quantify the hierarchical structure [10, 11], (iv) identify important patterns or paths in the network [4], and (v) identify clusters of nodes [12, 13].

Broadly speaking, there are two approaches to generate networks from data. First, some datasets such as air traffic data [14, 15] and World Wide Web connectivity data [16] contain explicit information about the network structure. In other cases, we often have to infer the interactions among various components or variables by performing functional analysis on the data [17]. Examples of this approach include the estimation of an undirected network of stocks based on the Pearson correlations of their daily returns [1], as well as the mapping of a directed functional network of brain regions from fMRI data using Granger causality as a directed measure [18]. In both examples, the resulting network provides us deeper insights into the system it represents - clustering of stocks in similar industries in the stock market, and a functional hierarchy in the brain. We believe there is great potential in applying functional analysis to infer networks in large datasets under-utilized by experimenters in various ?elds.

In 2010, the National Institute of Education (NIE) conducted a large-scale study of teaching practices in Singapore classrooms drawing on a representative national sample of schools. The study had the goal of investigating how teachers teach in Singapore, why they teach the way they do, and the effects of their teaching on student learning. The overall focus of the study was to map and model the logic of pedagogical instruction, the intellectual quality of knowledge work in classrooms, and the impact of instructional practice on student achievement while controlling for student and family characteristics. A total of 625 English and Mathematics lessons from Grades 5 and 9 classes were video-recorded and manually annotated for the presence of some 500 instructional indicators over the course of each lesson. These indicators focus on a broad range of organisational, instructional and interactional practices in the classroom, the knowledge and cognitive focus of teaching, the types of classroom talk and their knowledge content, how students respond, and the quality of the disciplinary knowledge of the subject-domain (English and Mathematics). The resulting data set is extremely high-dimensional (one dimension for each indicator) with greatly varying activities - some indicators are present up to 70% of the time while others appear only 0.001% of the time. Using commercial software such as SPSS to analyse the large dataset proved to be computationally intensive, as it explores the combinatorially large space of variables to ?nd statistically signi?cant transitions. In particular, such commercial software was unable to perform complex temporal analysis of classroom pedagogy, which remains a major methodological challenge for educational research [19].

In this paper, we describe a complex-network approach to the functional data collected in the NIE study. Our approach is both empirical and normative in that we focus, in the ?rst instance, on establishing statistically weighted relationships between instructional practice and, in the second, because we assume that not all instructional practices are equal and that from a normative perspective, there is a particular logic to instruction that teachers need to attend to if they are to optimise the intellectual quality of teaching and learning in the classroom. As such, teaching and learning activities do not follow a random sequence but follow a purposeful and deliberate sequence that teachers implement from their lesson plans, and simultaneously adapt in response to their monitoring of students? work. Effective teaching sequences, most often called learning progressions [20, 21], should lead to successful learning outcomes while ineffective sequences, perhaps due to structural weaknesses in the transition sequence, may not only have the opposite effect, but may disengage students from active learning in the long term. It follows that the resulting network of activity transitions should contain meaningful structures that correspond to actual teaching practices. The goals of this work are to (i) construct complex networks that typify activity transitions in the classroom, (ii) identify prevalent pairwise transitions and important practices, and (iii) extract sequences of transitions that frequently occur in the classroom. Since the focus of this paper is on the complex network methodology, we illustrate what the method is capable of discovering only for the data of Grade 5 and Grade 9 Mathematics.

2 Data

The data used in our analysis was obtained by the National Institute of Education through a comprehensive, large-scale, multi-dimensional, baseline study of descriptive and observational data on the state of instructional practices in Singapore classrooms. Known as the Core 2 Research Programme, it was a collaborative effort conducted by a team of over 35 research professors, research assistants and associates, and postdoctoral fellows and led by Professor David Hogan [22]. The Core 2 Programme utilized a nested design comprising three distinct, inter-related, and analytical lines of research, each designated a ?Panel? with speci?c foci ranging from teacher and student beliefs, attitudes, and motivations (using surveys), classroom instructional practices (using videographic observations and coding), and assessment practices (using artefactual analysis). The anonymized data used for this paper is drawn from the observational and coding panel which videotaped and collected data from English and Mathematics teachers in 15 Primary schools and 16 Secondary schools. Grades 5 (in Primary schools) and 9 (in Secondary schools) were selected as these were considered to be years crucial to the development of skills and knowledge needed for the high stakes national examinations for Primary schools (the Singapore Primary School Leaving Examination) and Secondary schools (the General Cambridge ?O? Level Examination). English and Mathematics were selected as key curriculum areas that have a signi?cant in?uence on student social mobility; literacy and numeracy skills are often seen as key leverages to opening up educational and career pathways. Data were collected from April through November 2010, resulting in 625 lessons (with 125-150 lessons per subject-level combination). Teachers selected for observation were asked to nominate a unit of work - a full sequence of lessons around a particular topic, theme or content area. Rather than discrete, random lessons for observation, the stipulation of a unit of work facilitates subsequent analyses that charts, models, and examines the developmental ebb and ?ow of knowledge and skills over time.

Within the lessons in the unit of work, an average lesson may have the following typical pedagogical activities. At the start of the lesson, about 35 students are seated in the classroom, with student tables arranged in rows of pairs. When the teacher enters the front of the classroom, students would stand up, bow and greet the teacher. She would then proceed to use the computer equipment and projector, or the white board, to deliver the topical content for the lesson. Students would pay attention to the teacher as she teaches from the front, engaged in learning what the teacher has to lecture to them. The teacher may vary the largely teacher-led pedagogical activity by introducing mathematical activities, usually in the form of mathematics problem-solving worksheets, for students to practice on. Such practice work is typically done by students individually or in pairs. Students may sometimes proceed to the white board to demonstrate their understanding of problem-solving to the rest of the class. The teacher will check the students? work by walking around the class, monitoring their mathematical practices and providing feedback when necessary. Upon ensuring that students are able to solve the problems in the worksheet, the teacher may proceed with teaching another, typically more procedurally complex, content, before getting students to practice again. This cycle of teacher lecture, student practice, teacher check and feedback, may continue until the teacher concludes the lesson with a short summary statement of what was taught for that lesson. Students would then rise, bow and thank the teacher for the lesson.

All lessons are video and audio recorded using two to three high-definition video cameras and up to four audio recorders, with the aim to capture all whole class interactions and the majority of pair or group work. Lesson recordings are then coded by subject specialists who are intensively trained in the use of the Singapore Pedagogy Coding Scheme 2 [23, 24]. Video recorded lessons, unlike in-situ classroom coding, afforded the detailed refinement of the coding scheme with the possibility of recoding to resolve any coding errors. Coded data are entered into Microsoft Excel and compiled in SPSS for statistical analyses. Each lesson is coded in three-minute "phases", with an average one hour lesson having 20 phases. In each phase, the states of more than 500 possible listed variables (we use variables as a more general term for instructional practices) are coded through manual annotation. See Additional file 1 for detailed descriptions of the variables as well as the decision to code in three-minute phases. Segmenting the lesson into phases allows for a temporal examination of instructional practices from the start to the end of a lesson, and across the unit of work. From these 500 variables, we selected roughly 160 which are believed to be most essential to the development of the intellectual quality of knowledge work for our network analysis.

The variables chosen extends current pedagogical research based on John Hattie's research on "Visible Learning" which describes effective pedagogical practices [25], by focusing on the nature of students doing disciplinary knowledge work in the classroom: the epistemic focus of instructional tasks; the nature of knowledge practices (including the generation, representation, communication and justification of knowledge claims); the epistemic classroom talk that helps makes these knowledge claims explicit, transparent and visible to students; and the cognitive complexity of the knowledge work undertaken in instructional tasks, recognising the contested nature of knowledge claims [26]. These selected variables are coded as either active (1) or inactive (0) for each lesson phase.

3 Methods

3.1 Defining transitions

The starting point of our analysis is to define what constitutes a transition from one variable to another and from this, develop a measure of transition frequency and significance. Previous work in network analysis tended to use measures like conditional probability [27], transfer entropy [28, 29], or Pearson correlation [1] to denote the relationship between variable pairs. The major shortcoming in these measures when applied to discrete binary signals is that they do not consider the characteristic event durations, i.e. a signal that is activated continuously across several phases are assumed to be distinct events at each phase and treated independently.

To formulate our definition of a transition from variable i to variable j, we assume: (i) the dynamics of the variables in our data set are well approximated by a lag-1 Markov process i.e. the states of the variables at phase $t + 1$ are solely conditioned on their states at phase t (see Figure 1(a) and (b)), and (ii) when a variable is active from phase t to $t + l$, but not present at $t − 1$, it is regarded as a single self-sustaining process first activated at phase t and lasting for duration l (see Figure 1(c)). For assumption (i) Figure 1(a) demonstrates that for a majority of variables, the ability to determine whether or not they are active at phase t is vastly improved by around one order of magnitude when we know the state of the

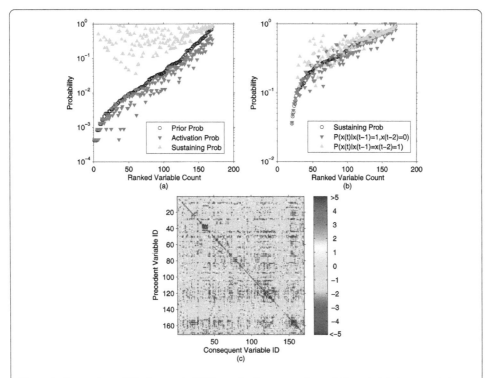

Figure 1 Comparison of Markov probabilities and colour map of correlations. In **(a)**, the open circles are the prior probabilities P_i (the probability of observing an active variable i at a given phase), the upwards pointing triangles are sustaining probabilities $P(x_i(t) = 1|x_i(t ? 1) = 1)$ (the probability of observing an active i given that i is already active at a preceding phase), and the downwards pointing triangles are the ? rst activation probabilities $P(x_i(t) = 1|x_i(t ? 1) = 0)$ (the probability of observing an active i given that i inactive at a preceding phase). We ranked the variables in increasing order of prior probabilities. We see clearly that a vast majority of the sustaining probabilities are at least an order of magnitude larger than their corresponding prior probabilities. These variables have the tendency to self-sustain which suggests that we should treat multiple-phase activation of these variables as a single event. In **(b)** we compare the lag-1 sustaining probabilities $P(x_i(t) = 1|x_i(t ? 1) = 1, x_i(t ? 2) = 0)$ and $P(x_i(t) = 1|x_i(t ? 1) = 1, x_i(t ? 2) = 1)$ (i.e. treating variables as a lag-2 dynamical process). Unlike in **(a)**, there is no clear increase in probability when the second preceding phase is accounted for. In **(c)** we show, on a colour map, the standard scores of observed conditional probabilities $P_{\text{observed}}(x_j(t) = 1|x_i(t ? 1) = 1)$ against their expected values if i and j were independent. If i and j were independent and characterized solely by their respective prior probabilities P_i and P_j, the expected conditional probabilities should be equal to the prior, i.e. $P_{\text{expected}}(x_j(t) = 1|x_i(t ? 1) = 1) = P_j$ and the distribution of conditional probabilities should have a standard deviation of $\sigma = \sqrt{P_j(1 ? P_j)/N_i}$. The standard score is obtained from $Z = (P_{\text{observed}}(x_j(t) = 1|x_i(t ? 1) = 1) ? P_j)/\sigma$. The colours on the map range from blue (lower than expected) to teal (equals expectation), and ? nally maroon (higher than expected). The dominant feature of this map is a diagonal of higher-than-expected conditional probabilities for self-transitions.

variables at $t ? 1$. We also see from Figure 1(b) that the additional knowledge of their state at $t ? 2$, however, did not improve signi? cantly our prediction capability. Thus, the lag-1 Markov process is sufficient and also efficient in modelling the dynamics of the variables in our data set. In Figure 1(c), we showed that for a variable i which is active from t to $t + l$, it is much more likely that the active state at $t + k$ where $1 \le k \le l$ is a self-transition from $t + k ? 1$ to $t + k$ rather than it being triggered by an external variable (assumption (ii)). Therefore, we search for inter-variable transitions only at the instances of ? rst activations. A transition is thus de? ned as an event whereby a consequent variable has been triggered (or ? rst activated) by the activity of the precedent. Formally, we say a transition from i to j occurs at time t if j is ? rst activated at time t with i active at $t ? 1$ (i.e. $i(t ? 1) = 1$, $j(t ? 1) = 0$,

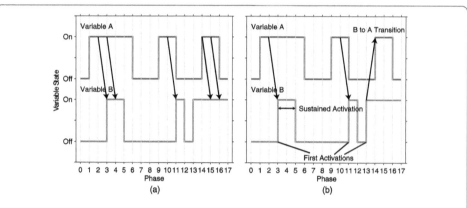

Figure 2 Method of counting transitions. If we count all active state to active state transitions between variable pairs as shown in **(a)**, there will be 5 transitions from variable *A* to *B*. This method assumes that every phase in which a variable is active is independent of its previous phase(s). If we assume that variables are activated in blocks, i.e. ?rst activated at a particular time and then self-sustained for a duration, then it becomes reasonable to count transition frequencies as shown in **(b)**. In **(b)**, transitions always result in a variable?s ?rst activation. We count two *A* to *B* transitions and one *B* to *A* transition.

$j(t) = 1$). The total number of transitions from variable i to j is therefore

$$N(j \leftarrow i) = \sum_{l=1}^{L} \sum_{t=1}^{T_l?1} x_i^l(t)\big(1 ? x_j^l(t)\big)x_j^l(t+1) \tag{1}$$

where $x_j^l(t)$ is the state of variable j at phase t of lesson l, L is the total number of lessons for a particular subject-level combination and T_l is the number of phases in lesson l. The procedure is illustrated in Figure 2.

3.2 Measuring signi?cance

For two variables that are frequently active, the number of mutual ?rst activations will also be large, even if they are causally unrelated. On the other hand, for two variables that are rarely active, even a small number of ?rst activations may indicate strong causal relation between them if this number is larger than expected by chance. To test a transition frequency for statistical signi?cance, we use the Monte Carlo sampling method described below.

Given a pair of variables i and j that we assume are uncorrelated, we can create synthetic signals of each variable with their lag-1 Markov models using the Monte Carlo sampling scheme explained in Table 1. This is our null model for the observed transitions from i to j. We generated $k = 10,000$ synthetic signals $\hat{x}_{i,h}^l(t)$, $h = 1,\ldots,k$ for variable i, and $\hat{x}_{j,h}^l(t)$, $h = 1,\ldots,k$ for variable j and computed the total number of transitions $\hat{N}_h$, $h = 1,\ldots,k$ as described in Equation (1) for each pair. The population of k transition frequencies form a distribution of $\hat{N}$.

Let p be the fraction of the population of $\hat{N}$ that is larger than or equal to the observed number of transitions $N_{\text{observed}}(j \leftarrow i)$. If $p \approx 0$ then N_{observed} is far above the mean of this distribution, there is a far greater number of observed transitions from i to j than expected from the null model which assumed the variables i and j were independent. If $p \approx 0.5$ then N_{observed} is close to the median of this distribution, and can be well explained by the null model. Finally, if $p \approx 1$ then there are much fewer transitions than expected from the null model.

Table 1 Monte Carlo sampling example

Phase	r	P(0)	x
1	?	?	0
2	0.52	$P(0|0) = 0.8$	0
3	0.86	$P(0|0) = 0.8$	1
4	0.67	$P(0|1) = 0.3$	1
5	0.23	$P(0|1) = 0.3$	0
6	0.91	$P(0|0) = 0.8$	1

Suppose $P(0|0) = 0.8$, $P(1|0) = 1 ? P(0|0) = 0.2$, $P(0|1) = 0.3$, $P(1|1) = 1 ? P(0|1) = 0.7$, and we start with $x(1) = 0$. Then to generate a sequence using these transition probabilities, we draw 5 random numbers $r = (0.52, 0.86, 0.67, 0.23, 0.91)$ uniformly from the interval $[0, 1)$ and allow $x(t) = 0$ when $r < P(0|0)$, $x(t? 1) = 0$ and $x(t) = 0$ when $r < P(0|1)$, $x(t? 1) = 1$. Since $x(1) = 0$, to obtain $x(2)$ we look at $P(0|0)$. Since $r(2) < P(0|0)$, $x(2) = 0$. However, $r(3) > P(0|0)$, giving $x(3) = 1$. Iterating further, since $x(3) = 1$, we look at $P(0|1)$ and $r(4) > P(0|1)$, $x(4) = 1$. Then $r(5) < P(0|1)$, $x(5) = 0$. Finally, $r(6) > P(0|0)$, and $x(6) = 1$. The sequence we get is therefore $x = (0, 0, 1, 1, 0, 1)$.

We take the signi?cance value to be $s = 1 ? 2p$. By rescaling in this manner, $s \approx 0, 1$, or $?1$ if the observed transition frequency $N_{observed}$ is, respectively, approximately the same as, greater than, or less than the value expect from the null model. We can then compute the signi?cance-weighted transition frequencies by multiplying each transition frequency with its signi?cance. The weighting procedure diminishes insigni?cant frequencies and makes lower-than-expected frequencies negative. The weighted scores are

$$N_{\text{weighted}}(i \leftarrow j) = sN(i \leftarrow j). \tag{2}$$

For our analysis, we admit only edges where the signi?cance $s > 0.5$, i.e. $p < 0.25$ and thus there is 75% con?dence that the transition is not spurious.

3.3 Network visualization and ?ltering

We then visualize the weighted transition frequencies N_{weighted} on two complex directed networks (one for Grade 5 Mathematics and one for Grade 9 Mathematics) where each node on the network represents a variable and the directed edges between nodes denote transitions. If we show all the edges in these networks without any ?ltering, we get ?fur balls? like that shown in Figure3. The network is too densely interconnected and the important structures are obscured. Therefore it is essential to apply ?ltering schemes that remove less important edges and highlight the more important ones. We employ two popular techniques widely used in complex network analysis. They are the Minimal Spanning Tree (MST) [30] and the Planar Maximally Filtered Graph (PMFG) [7]. Since we seek to identify transitional motifs (paths) in this work, it is important to choose a method that preserves connectedness. We selected the MST and PMFG ?ltering methods because they guarantee connectedness in the resulting network (at least in the undirected sense). Other popular complex network ?ltering schemes, such as threshold ?ltering and disparity ?l-tering [8] do not satisfy this condition

For a network with N nodes, the MST is a subgraph where the N nodes are connected by the $N ? 1$ most important edges. As its name implies, the MST is a tree, and therefore it can have no loops. It is constructed using Kruskal?s algorithm β1] as follows: (i) the edges of the network are ranked in decreasing order of weight, (ii) populate the MST with all nodes in the existing graph, (iii) starting from the edge with the largest weight, add an edge to the MST provided the edge added does not result in a closed loop, (iv) repeat (iii) until all nodes in the MST are connected. An example of the construction of a MST is shown in Figure 4(a).

Figure 3 Unfiltered network of significant transitions. Here, we show the network of all significant ($s > 0.5$) transitions between variables from the data of Grade 5 Mathematics. The network is drawn with the following features: (i) node diameters are proportionate to the prior probability P_i of their corresponding variables, (ii) arrowheads of the edges point in the direction from the precedent to the consequent, (iii) edges thicknesses are proportionate to the weighted frequency with thick lines denoting high weighted transition frequencies, and (iv) the placement of the nodes are determined by a multilevel force algorithm [32] that was included in the graphing software. This algorithm assigns attractive and repulsive forces among nodes according to their connectedness and allows the graph to dynamically relax into a

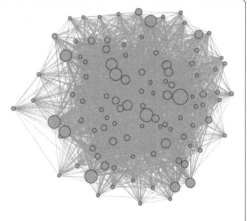

configuration of low energy. The multilevel treatment ensures that the graph relaxes into the global minimum energy configuration instead of being trapped in a local minimum. In this scheme, the distances between nodes are *roughly inversely* proportionate to the score between them i.e. a pair of nodes with high score will be placed closed together in the network. For this unfiltered network, the density of edges is so great that it is very difficult to discern any meaningful structure from it.

Figure 4 Construction of MST and PMFG graphs. The solid lines in **(a)** show a MST graph built from decreasing order of edge weights i.e. the edges with the highest weights are included first. The edges represented by dashed lines with weights 8, 4, and 1 are not included since they will result in loops in the network. **(b)**, **(c)**, and **(d)** shows the properties of the PMFG. Even though the edges in **(b)** intersect, the graph is planar. This is because the lines can easily be redrawn such that they do not intersect like in **(c)**. However, if the new blue edge is added to the graph **(d)** there is no way to redraw the edges or rearrange the nodes such that the links never intersect. Therefore the graph in **(d)** is not planar.

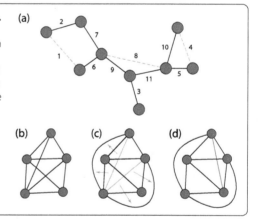

The PMFG filtering scheme, similar to the MST, admits edges in decreasing order of strength starting from the strongest link as long as the graph remains planar. Without elaborating on mathematical details, a planar graph is a graph that can in principle be embedded on a planar surface without any crossing of links (see Figure 4(b)-(d)). The PMFG retains more information ($3(N - 2)$ links) while conserving all the hierarchical structure associated with the MST.

More importantly, whereas the MST allows only a single possible undirected path between any pair of nodes (i.e. only the dominant pathways are preserved), the resulting PMFG is less restrictive and preserves several alternate paths that can be taken from one node to another. In Section 4.2, it was shown that many transitions taken in the most prevalent motifs are captured in alternate pathways preserved the PMFG but not in the MST. The fact that several important pedagogical transitions happen not along the dominant paths but the alternate paths suggests that the MST filtering is overly restrictive. Thus, in Figures 6(a) and 6(b), we chose to display the PMFG graphs and highlight their respective MST backbone.

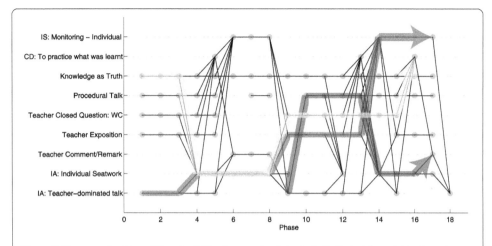

Figure 5 Time-resolved transition chart. The time-resolved chart of a limited set for variables for a chosen lesson. Diagonal lines in the chart represent signi?cant ($s > 0.5$) transitions de?ned in Section 3.1. There are several paths in the chart which involves two or more transitions (three or more variables) and some of these paths are highlighted. For each path on the time-resolved chart there is a corresponding path in the time-integrated transition network.

3.4 Dynamical motifs

Beyond recognizing just the pairwise transitions between lesson variables, we also wish to identify important sequences of two or more signi?cant transitions which we call dynamical motifs. These sequences enables us to track the progression of practices across many phases spanning a longer duration of a lesson. To do so, we return to the annotated data of individual lessons and search for frequently occurring sequences of signi?cant transitions. This procedure is illustrated in a form of a time-resolved chart shown in Figure 5. Dynamical motifs identi?ed are sequences that were repeated frequently over many lessons.

4 Results
4.1 Prevalent transitions in teaching practices

In Figures 6(a) and 6(b), the ?ltered graphs of weighted transition frequencies are shown for Grade 5 Mathematics and Grade 9 Mathematics respectively. We can observe that across both grade levels, teaching practices are organised around source (outgoing) hubs that correspond to *Knowledge as Truth* and *Instructional Activity (IA): Teacher-Dominated Talk*. These source hubs are characterized by a large concentration of signi?cant outgoing transitions. Although these hubs also tend to be the most frequent practices, the frequency alone does not account for the large number of signi?cant outgoing transitions. This suggests strongly that *Knowledge as Truth* and *Instructional Activity (IA): Teacher-Dominated Talk* are indeed important hubs that drive the initiation of teaching sequences.

For Grade 5 (Figure 6(a)), *IA: Teacher-Dominated Talk* is an especially generative node which leads to nodes such as *Knowledge as Truth* (via *Supervisory Monitoring*, where teachers monitor students? behaviour in class),*To Practice What Was Learnt* (where students practice what teachers taught them), *Procedural Talk* (classroom talk about procedural knowledge), and *Doing Mathematics Activity* (students doing a mathematics task in a disciplinary manner). An attendant observation is that teacher responses during *Doing Mathematics Activity* tend to be short (one or two word responses such as ?yes?, ?good?,

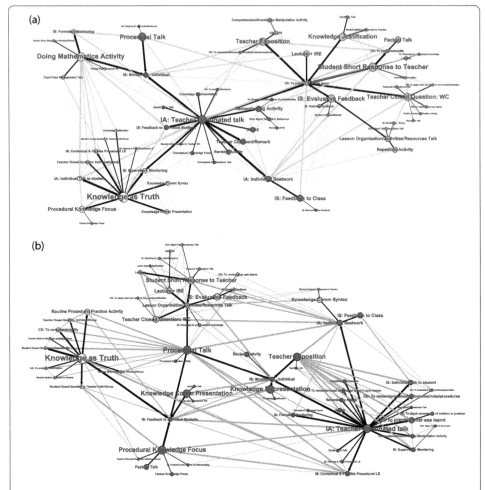

Figure 6 Transition networks of teaching practices during Mathematics lessons. The PMFG-?ltered networks for **(a)** Grade 5 Mathematics and **(b)** Grade 9 Mathematics are drawn with features (i), (ii), and (iii) as described in Figure 3. We use dark edges to highlight the MST backbone of the PMFG network. The node placement was determined by the same multilevel force algorithm [32] in Figure 3 acted on the MST edges. We also indicate the community of the nodes in the graph by their colour. They are detected with a community-detection algorithm [13] that was built into the graphing software based on its MST backbone as well. The detection process, not guided by any pedagogy theory, nevertheless produced communities of variables that are in general agreement in pedagogy theory.

?well done?, etc.). But while*Doing Mathematics Activity* is a generative node in Grade 5, it all but disappears by Grade 9 (Figure 6(b)). We also note the presence of sink (incoming) hubs such as *CD: To Practice What Was Learnt, IA: Individual Seatwork,* and *IS: Monitoring - Individual* which attracts several signi?cant incoming transitions. Unlike the source hubs, sink hubs are practices that occur much less frequently and are harder to detect. The network analysis methodology uniquely discerns these hubs with their special role.

At Grade 9, *Knowledge as Truth* and *IA: Teacher-Dominated Talk* are still present as large hubs, but additional hubs have appeared: *Procedural Talk, Procedural Knowledge Focus, Knowledge Communication Presentation* and *Knowledge Representation.* The latter two hubs refer to how students present and communicate mathematical ideas (typically when asked by the teacher to present a problem solution on the white board in front of the classroom), and to how students represent mathematical ideas using different representational forms (typically abstract forms, rather than concrete or pictorial), respectively.

Here, we find that while *IA: Individual Seatwork* and *IS: Monitoring - Individual* remain as prominent sink hubs for Grade 9, *IS: Feedback to Individual Students* has replaced *CD: To Practice What Was Learnt* in its role.

4.2 Motifs of teaching practices

The most common length-3 and length-4 motifs for Grade 5 and Grade 9 Mathematics are shown in Figure 7. A motif is said to be length-*n* if it consists of *n* − 1 successive significant transitions, but is not followed by an *n*th transition that is statistically significant. Some of the length-4 motifs contain a length-3 stem that branches out into more than one statistically significant fourth transition.

As we can see, Grade 5 motifs typically show a common ?cycle? of teaching: The teacher starts talking about content (*IA: Teacher-Dominated Talk, Knowledge as Truth, Procedural Talk*); next, students are often given individual practice work (*IA: Individual Seatwork*); then, the teacher provides some feedback (*Comment/Remark*), returns to lengthy talk (*IA: Teacher-Dominated Talk, Exposition*), or asks the whole class a closed question which typically has one correct answer (*Teacher Closed Question: WC*). Sometimes, the sequences carry on with more practice work (*CD: To Practice What Was Learnt, IA: Individual Seatwork*) as well as the teacher?s monitoring of the student learning (*S: Monitoring - Individual, IS: Formative Monitoring, IS: Supervisory Monitoring*) or providing individual feedback (*IS: Feedback to Individual Students, IA: Individual Talk to Student*).

The Grade 9 motifs are largely similar to those in Grade 5, but with a greater focus on *Procedural Knowledge Focus* in the middle of the common motifs. Also, some Grade 9 lessons tend to end with the teacher providing a closing exposition (*Teacher Exposition*), lecture, and IRE (a form of talk where the teacher Initiates, the student Responds, and the teacher Evaluates) (*Lecture, Lecture + IRE*).

Interestingly, there are motif links such as *IA: Individual Seatwork* to *Teacher Exposition* for Grade 5, *Procedural Talk* to *IA: Individual Seatwork* for Grade 5, and *Procedural Knowledge Focus* to *IS: Monitoring - Individual* for Grade 9 which are present in the collection of common motifs in Figure 7 while not appearing in their respective PMFG-?ltered networks in Figure 6. The PMFG ?ltering scheme picks edges in descending order of statistical signi?cance. However, because the statistical signi?cances are time-integrated, there is no guarantee that successive transitions in the PMFG appear one after the other during actual lessons. These time-integrated transitions may be part of two motifs, one ending at the node that the other starts at. This is why a time-resolved analysis must also be carried out to identify dynamical motifs consisting of successive transitions that are statistically signi?cant.

5 Discussion

The transmissionist model of teaching views teaching as a straightforward and unproblematic process of transferring information (knowledge) from the mind of the teacher to the mind of the student [33?35]. In this model, knowledge is a collection of facts about the world and procedures to solve problems; knowledge is objective, ?xed, and external and learning is something akin to accumulating goods - but goods in the form of propositional knowledge, whether factual or conceptual; the goal of schooling is to transmit these facts and procedures from the teacher to the student; teachers know these facts and procedures, and their job is to transmit them to students; learning is an intra-subjective process

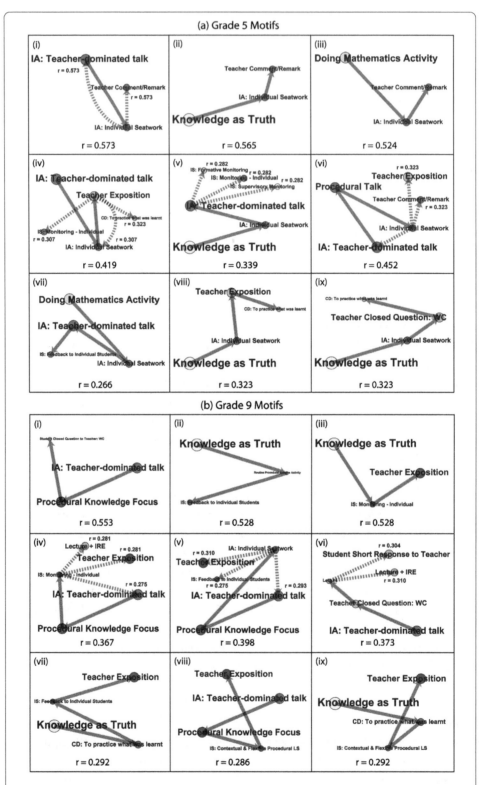

Figure 7 Common lesson motifs. The most common motifs for both grades are listed here. For each grade, the ?rst row lists the most common length-3 motifs that do not signi?cantly extend to other variables and prevalence *r* gives the fraction of lessons in which the paths are present. The second and third rows present length-4 motifs. Motifs with broken arrows indicate the possible terminations of a common stem of three indicators. For these motifs we show *r* for each possible ending adjacent to the ?nal node together with the total prevalence of all alternatives.

that goes on inside students? minds as knowledge is transferred or transmitted from the teacher to the student; simpler facts and procedures should be learned ?rst, followed by progressively more complex facts and procedures; the way to determine the success of schooling is to test students to see how many of these facts and procedures they have acquired through well-established assessment procedures. In the transition networks of both Grade 5 and Grade 9 Mathematics, *Knowledge as Truth* and *Instructional Activity (IA): Teacher-Dominated Talk* are seen as dominant hubs. *Knowledge as Truth* means that the knowledge that is presented in the lesson is viewed as non-contestable, non-negotiable and objectively valid. As an *Instructional Activity (IA), Teacher-Dominated Talk* means simply that the teacher does most of the talking in the classroom. These practices operate most effectively in the transmissionist model of teaching, since knowledge is unproblematic and non-contestable, and teachers need only to ensure that they cover the curriculum. Not the least of the opportunity costs for *Teacher-Dominated Talk* however, is that when students are not given the opportunity to engage in extended and productive discussions during lessons, misconceptions often go undetected, existing conceptual schemas can go unchallenged, students might become disengaged with the learning process, and over time, because they have less agency in the class to speak up, and lose motivation to become good students.

However, as Ball [36] points out, mathematics instruction ought to involve a lot more than the transmission of facts and procedures. Above all, mathematics instruction should provide students with rich opportunities to engage in authentic, domain-speci?c mathematical practices. ?Mathematics practices? she goes on, ?focus on the mathematical know-how, beyond content knowledge, that constitutes expertise in learning and using mathematics [such as] justifying claims, using symbolic notation efficiently, de?ning terms precisely, and making generalisations are examples of mathematical practices.? Thus, the transmissionist model is insufficient as a teaching and learning model for mathematics. In Grade 5, the strong presence of *Doing Mathematics Activity* is an important practice that we hoped to see in mathematics classrooms. *Doing Mathematics Activity* is inherently disciplinary in nature, and students need to acquire the mathematics-speci?c disciplinary skills, knowledge and disposition to understand mathematics deeply, debate, and discuss mathematical procedures and concepts, and appreciate the importance and relevance of mathematics. It captures the idea that mathematics learning does not consist purely of learning algorithmic procedures (captured in *Procedural Talk* and *Procedural Knowledge Focus*) and content (captured in *Factual Talk* and *Factual Knowledge Focus*), but requires students to perform discipline-speci?c knowledge practices as outlined by Ball. Similarly, Stein and Lane [37] characterize ?doing mathematics? as ?The use of complex, non-algorithmic thinking to solve a task in which there is not a predictable, well-rehearsed approach or pathway explicitly suggested by the task, task instructions, or a worked out example. ?Doing mathematics? processes are often likened to the processes in which mathematicians engage when solving problems.? These activities are the most demanding of all activities, since they require the students to draw upon a range of mathematical knowledge and procedures/skills to complete some work that has no well-rehearsed way of completing the task. Instead, students are likely to be asked to design, test and justify a new procedure to ?t a new kind of problem.

The disappearance of *Doing Mathematics Activity* as a hub in Grade 9 suggests that at this level, the focus on what we consider to be a highly-valued disciplinary understanding of mathematics has been replaced by a focus on procedural knowledge (*Procedural Knowledge Focus*) as an effective and efficient means to present such knowledge, such as efficient problem solving methods. Yet, we believe that it is precisely because of this pedagogical approach focused on a highly proceduralised and efficient form of learning abstract mathematics that has made Singapore one of the top performing countries in international assessments that measure students? ability in mathematics. Our observation con?rms the PISA 2012 ?ndings on Singapore Mathematics [38] which shows that there is a strong relationship between the teaching of Formal Mathematics (as opposed to Applied Mathematics or Word Problems) and student mathematical performance in the PISA tests.

Finally, teaching and learning must be understood as a process. Christie [39] talks of the prototypical classroom lesson having a beginning, middle and end pattern. The beginning comprises some form of teacher direction (Curriculum Initiation), followed by the teacher and students? sharing of direction (Curriculum Collaboration/Negotiation) and ending with students? independent activity (Curriculum Closure). In the motifs we identi?ed for Grade 5 and Grade 9, the didactic of teacher-student-teacher as well as teacher-student-teacher-student sequences highlights the complex interaction cycles that occur in mathematics classrooms. Almost all lessons begin, as described above, with a teacher-led initiation (*Knowledge as Truth, Instructional Activity (IA): Teacher-Dominated Talk, Procedural Talk, Procedural Knowledge Focus*). Often, these motifs lead immediately to individual practice work (*IA: Individual Seatwork*), seemingly replacing the middle phase of Christie?s pattern with student?s independent activity. Some motifs then terminate with feedback from the teacher in the form of lengthy talk (*Teacher Comment/Remark, IA: Teacher-Dominated Talk, Teacher Exposition*) following student?s practice work. These motifs suggest a teacher-dominated closure in the teaching pattern. However, in other motifs, we discovered a fourth movement which is a return to more practice work (*CD: To Practice What Was Learnt*) coupled with teacher?s monitoring of such practice work (*IS: Monitoring - Individual, IS: Formative Monitoring, IS: Supervisory Monitoring*).

In Grade 9, the greater focus on *Procedural Knowledge Focus* is in line with the high stakes environment that Grade 9 teachers and students are entrenched in, requiring students to learn - at least a year early from the Grade 10 national examinations - procedures and practice skills that are necessary to perform well in the high stakes mathematics examination. Interestingly, when the focus is on *Procedural Knowledge Focus*, it is often followed by a more personalised approach where the teacher may provide individualised, speci?c, feedback (*IS: Feedback to Individual Students*) or learning support (*IS: Contextual & Flexible Procedural LS*). Such feedback and support are positive signs that rather than a summative exposition at the end (which does occur nevertheless), teachers and students have the opportunity to provide some feedback to one another. Expositions do end in about half of the motifs, likely due to the need to ensure that the important content and skills are reiterated and summarised, a necessary conclusion to the transmissionist model.

6 Conclusion

In this work, we presented a technique of constructing transition networks from high-dimensional and multiscale data to allow for highly simpli?ed analysis of interdependence and correlation. We applied the technique on teaching practices data obtained by the National Institute of Education in Singapore. We were able to identify and verify the dominant transitions between instructional practices and also pick out motifs of sequences of several practices and activities that are common in many lessons. We established that teaching practices of both Grade 5 and Grade 9 Mathematics lessons are organized around *Knowledge as Truth* and *Instructional Activity (IA): Teacher-Dominated Talk* hubs which exemplify the transmissionist model of teaching. In addition, a *Doing Mathematics Activity* hub is present in the Grade 5 transition network. This suggests that teaching practices at this level have incorporated exploratory elements into the pedagogy, a positive sign towards the goal of 21st century learning. In contrast, in Grade 9, disciplinary understanding of mathematics has been replaced by a focus on procedural knowledge, which nevertheless accounts for Singapore?s strong performance in international benchmarks. The motifs we extracted from the network highlight cycles of complex teacher-student-teacher-student sequences with great similarity between Grade 5 and Grade 9. In future work, this methodology will be employed and modi?ed for more in-depth study of the transitions data. This includes using knowledge of the topology of the transition network to formulate strategies that can direct the ?ow of teaching activities towards a desired outcome.

Additional material

Additional ?le 1: Singapore Pedagogy Coding Scheme 2

Competing interests
The authors declare that they have no competing interests.

Authors? contributions
DH and DK provided the functionally coded data set, and the pedagogical conceptual framework for this study. They also jointly framed and interpreted the results of the data analysis. SAC and WPG developed the complex transitions network methodologies and tests for statistical signi?cances, while WPG performed the data analysis. WPG, DK, SAC were principally responsible for writing the manuscript while DH reviewed and rewrote sections of the penultimate draft of the manuscript.

Author details
[1]Interdisciplinary Graduate School, Nanyang Technological University, 50 Nanyang Avenue, Singapore, 639798, Singapore. [2]Complexity Institute, Nanyang Technological University, 60 Nanyang View, Singapore, 639673, Singapore. [3]Office of Education Research, National Institute of Education, 1 Nanyang Walk, Singapore, 637616, Singapore. [4]School of Education, Faculty of Humanities and Social Sciences, University of Queensland, Brisbane, QLD 4072, Australia. [5]School of Physical & Mathematical Sciences, Nanyang Technological University, 21 Nanyang Link, Singapore, 637371, Singapore.

Acknowledgements
The data is drawn from a National Institute of Education project OER 20/09DH, Core 2 Research Programme (Panel 3), funded by the Office of Education Research, National Institute of Education. The project?s principal investigator is Professor David Hogan, and the co-principal investigators are Dr Phillip Towndrow and Dr Dennis Kwek. Data were collected and coded by over 15 research assistants and associates, led by Professor David Hogan, Dr Phillip Towndrow, Dr Dennis Kwek, and Dr Ridzuan Rahim.

References
1. Mantegna RN (1999) Hierarchical structure in ?nancial markets. Eur Phys J B 11(1):193-197
2. Tumminello M, Lillo F, Mantegna RN (2010) Correlation, hierarchies, and networks in ?nancial markets. J Econ Behav Organ 75(1):40-58
3. Jeong H, Mason SP, Barab?si A-L, Oltvai ZN (2001) Lethality and centrality in protein networks. Nature 411(6833):41-42
4. Milo R, Shen-Orr S, Itzkovitz S, Kashtan N, Chklovskii D, Alon U (2002) Network motifs: simple building blocks of complex networks. Science 298(5594):824-827
5. Potterat JJ, Phillips-Plummer L, Muth SQ, Rothenberg RB, Woodhouse DE, Maldonado-Long TS, Zimmerman HP, Muth JB (2002) Risk network structure in the early epidemic phase of HIV transmission in Colorado Springs. Sex Transm Infect 78(Suppl 1):i159-i163
6. Sol? RV, Corominas-Murtra B, Valverde S, Steels L (2010) Language networks: their structure, function, and evolution. Complexity 15(6):20-26
7. Tumminello M, Aste T, Di Matteo T, Mantegna RN (2005) A tool for ?ltering information in complex systems. Proc Natl Acad Sci USA 102(30):10421-10426
8. Serrano M?, Bogu?? M, Vespignani A (2009) Extracting the multiscale backbone of complex weighted networks. Proc Natl Acad Sci USA 106(16):6483-6488

9. Radicchi F, Ramasco JJ, Fortunato S (2011) Information ?ltering in complex weighted networks. Phys Rev E 83(4):046101

10. Newman ME (2003) The structure and function of complex networks. SIAM Rev 45(2):167-256

11. Trusina A, Maslov S, Minnhagen P, Sneppen K (2004) Hierarchy measures in complex networks. Phys Rev Lett 92(17):178702

12. Clauset A, Newman ME, Moore C (2004) Finding community structure in very large networks. Phys Rev E 70(6):066111

13. Blondel VD, Guillaume J-L, Lambiotte R, Lefebvre E (2008) Fast unfolding of communities in large networks. J Stat Mech Theory Exp 2008(10):P10008

14. Watts DJ, Strogatz SH (1998) Collective dynamics of ?small-world? networks. Nature 393(6684):440-442

15. Amaral LAN, Scala A, Barthelemy M, Stanley HE (2000) Classes of small-world networks. Proc Natl Acad Sci USA 97(21):11149-11152

16. Albert R, Jeong H, Barab?si A-L (1999) Internet: diameter of the world-wide web. Nature 401(6749):130-131

17. Bullmore E, Sporns O (2009) Complex brain networks: graph theoretical analysis of structural and functional systems. Nat Rev Neurosci 10(3):186-198

18. Roebroeck A, Formisano E, Goebel R (2005) Mapping directed in?uence over the brain using Granger causality and fMRI. NeuroImage 25(1):230-242

19. Mercer N (2008) The seeds of time: why classroom dialogue needs a temporal analysis. J Learn Sci 17(1):33-59

20. Duschl R, Maeng S, Sezen A (2011) Learning progressions and teaching sequences: a review and analysis. Stud Sci Educ 47(2):123-182

21. Popham WJ (2011) Transformative assessment in action: an inside look at applying the process. ASCD, Alexandria

22. Hogan D, Towndrow P, Kwek D, Chan M (2013) Final report of the Core 2 research programme. Technical report, National Institute of Education

23. Luke A, Freebody P, Cazden C, Lin A (2004) Singapore Pedagogy Coding Scheme. Technical report, National Institute of Education

24. Luke A, Cazden C, Lin A, Freebody P (2004) The Singapore classroom coding system. Technical report, National Institute of Education

25. Hattie J (2013) Visible learning: a synthesis of over 800 meta-analyses relating to achievement. Routledge, London

26. Hogan D, Kwek D, Towndrow P, Rahim RA, Tan TK, Yang HJ, Chan M (2013) Visible learning and the enacted curriculum in Singapore. In: Deng Z, Gopinathan S, Lee CK-E (eds) Globalization and the Singapore curriculum: from policy to classroom. Springer, Singapore, pp 121-150

27. Heckerman D, Geiger D, Chickering DM (1995) Learning Bayesian networks: the combination of knowledge and statistical data. Mach Learn 20(3):197-243

28. Kwon O, Yang J-S (2008) Information ?ow between stock indices. Europhys Lett 82(6):68003

29. Honey CJ, K?tter R, Breakspear M, Sporns O (2007) Network structure of cerebral cortex shapes functional connectivity on multiple time scales. Proc Natl Acad Sci USA 104(24):10240-10245

30. West DB et al (2001) Introduction to graph theory, vol 2. Prentice Hall, Upper Saddle River

31. Kruskal JB (1956) On the shortest spanning subtree of a graph and the traveling salesman problem. Proc Am Math Soc 7(1):48-50

32. Hu Y (2005) Efficient, high-quality force-directed graph drawing. Mathematica J 10(1):37-71

33. Olson DR, Torrance N (ed) (1996) The handbook of education and human development: new models of learning, teaching and schooling. Blackwell, Cambridge, pp 9-27

34. Richardson V (1996) The role of attitudes and beliefs in learning to teach. In: Handbook of research on teacher education, 2nd edn, pp 102-119

35. Sawyer RK (2008) Introduction. In: Sawyer RK (ed) The Cambridge handbook of the learning sciences, vol 2. Cambridge University Press, New York

36. Ball DL et al (2003) Mathematical pro?ciency for all students: toward a strategic research and development program in mathematics education. RAND Corporation, Santa Monica

37. Stein MK, Lane S (1996) Instructional tasks and the development of student capacity to think and reason: an analysis of the relationship between teaching and learning in a reform mathematics project. Educ Res Eval 2(1):50-80

38. OECD (2013) PISA 2012 assessment and analytical framework. doi:10.1787/9789264190511-en

39. Christie F (2005) Classroom discourse analysis: a functional perspective. Bloomsbury Publishing, London

13

Sentiment cascades in the 15M movement

Raquel Alvarez[1], David Garcia[2*], Yamir Moreno[1] and Frank Schweitzer[2]

*Correspondence: dgarcia@ethz.ch
[2]Chair of Systems Design, ETH Zurich, Weinbergstrasse 56/58, Zurich, 8092, Switzerland
Full list of author information is available at the end of the article

Abstract

Recent grassroots movements have suggested that online social networks might play a key role in their organization, as adherents have a fast, many-to-many, communication channel to help coordinate their mobilization. The structure and dynamics of the networks constructed from the digital traces of protesters have been analyzed to some extent recently. However, less effort has been devoted to the analysis of the semantic content of messages exchanged during the protest. Using the data obtained from a microblogging service during the brewing and active phases of the 15M movement in Spain, we perform the first large scale test of theories on collective emotions and social interaction in collective actions. Our findings show that activity and information cascades in the movement are larger in the presence of negative collective emotions and when users express themselves in terms related to social content. At the level of individual participants, our results show that their social integration in the movement, as measured through social network metrics, increases with their level of engagement and of expression of negativity. Our findings show that non-rational factors play a role in the formation and activity of social movements through online media, having important consequences for viral spreading.

Keywords: emotions; activity cascades; group action

1 Introduction

The Occupy and 15M movements are recent examples of self-organized social movements that appeared in developed countries in response to a widespread perception of social and economical inequality [1, 2]. While these movements address a wide range of problems in different countries, they share a common factor, their usage of social media to communicate, organize, and deliberate about the purpose of the movement and its actions [3, 4]. Social media allow the participants of these movements to circumvent their lack of influence on state- and private-owned mass media [5], creating an emergent structure without a central actor or decision group. As a side effect, these movements leave public digital traces of their activity, which allows us to analyze their formation, behavior, and organization up to unprecedented scales and resolutions.

Collective actions pose a classical paradox of the tragedy of the commons [6]: A purely rational individual would choose not to participate in a movement it agrees with, as it would receive its collective benefits without the associated costs and risks of taking part on it. Thus, the existence of collective actions and social movements requires considerations beyond rational decisions, including emotions [7] and social influence [8] between the participants of a social movement. In this article, we present a detailed quantitative analysis of the digital traces of the 15M movement, the Spanish precursor of Occupy movements across Europe and America [2]. This decentralized movement emerged in Spain in the aftermath of the so-called Arab Spring as a reaction to public spending cuts and the economic crisis. It was mainly nucleated in online social networks before massive offline demonstrations ended up in several camp sites in many city squares. From that point on, the movement consolidated and lasted for months. Even today the foundations of the 15M movement drives the political agenda of some new parties and associations in Spain.

Our analysis covers its online social structure and the content of the public messages exchanged in `Twitter`, the main online medium used by the movement. `Twitter` users create directed links to follow the messages of other users and communicate through short public messages called *tweets*. We analyze the content of a large set of tweets about the 15M movement, extracting sentiment values and semantic content related to social and cognitive processes. Our aim is to explore the role of social emotions in group activity and collective action. We address how emotional interaction supports the creation of social movements and how emotional expressions lead to the involvement of the participants of the movement.

According to the theory of collective identity of Emile Durkheim, group gatherings contribute to the creation of collective identity by means of rituals and symbols that produce an atmosphere of emotional synchrony [9]. These rituals are often emotionally charged and show an inverse relation between emotional intensity and frequency [10]. The emotions experienced by the participants of these gatherings contribute to social inclusion and identification with the collective, as empirically shown in a variety of experiments [11]. This also holds for the 15M movement, for which survey results show that participants of the large demonstrations across Spain in 2011 felt a stronger emotional communion with the movement, in comparison to those participants who did not attend to the demonstration [12]. In this article, we provide a quantitative analysis of how collective identity and action emerged in the 15M movement, through the analysis of the digital traces of its participants in the `Twitter` social network. We pay special attention to emotional expression in tweets, social inclusion in the follower network of the participants of the movement, and sentiment polarization in the creation and social response to the movement.

Online media offer large datasets to explore political activity at a large scale, to find out about popularity and mobilization in political campaigns [13], and political alignment based on public messages [14, 15]. Analyzing online social networks, for example by means of the k-core decomposition method, can also reveal relevant information about the role of influential individuals [16, 17] and the social resilience of an online community [18]. Users of online social networks communicate through public messages that provide the breeding ground for collective emotional states, which have the potential to create the identity and mobilization of the movement. Previous states of collective emotional persistence were detected in the short messages of IRC chats [19] and spread through social networks as cascades of emotions [20], forming patterns in which happy individuals are likely to be connected to other happy ones [21].

In our analysis we follow a top-down approach, from the collective level of the movement to the actions of its individuals and their relations. We start by analyzing the dynamic aspect of the 15M movement, identifying cascades of tweets as in previous research [17]. We measure the size of these cascades in terms of the amount of participants communicating in the cascade (spreaders), and the amount of participants exposed to the cascade (listeners). We analyze how cascade sizes depend on collective emotions and the use of terms related to cognitive and social processes. Finally, we zoom into the microscopic level of individuals and their interactions, creating an additional dataset of tweets of each participant of the 15M movement. We relate their expression of emotions, cognitive, and social processes to their activity and social integration in the movement, as quantified by their k-core centrality within the social network.

2 Results

2.1 Sentiment analysis in Spanish

Our adaptation of SentiStrength to the Spanish language [22], explained in the Materials and Methods section, reaches accuracy values above 0.6 for two test datasets (see Table II in Additional file 1). These results are comparable to state of the art unsupervised techniques of sentiment analysis for the Spanish language [23]. Furthermore, the quality of the sentiment analysis tool does not differ for tweets related to politics and economics (see Table III in Additional file 1). This result shows that our application of SentiStrength is valid, as 15M tweets appear in a context of political protests related to economic measures.

2.2 Activity and information cascades

Previous research has shown a positive relation between retweeting and emotional content [24]. Here, we go beyond a plain retweeting behavior and analyze cascades associated with the 15M topic. We quantify emotions in the tweets related to the 15M movement through sentiment analysis on a dataset of tweets selected by the hashtags related to the 15M movement, as explained in the Materials and Methods section. We focus on the analysis of tweet cascades, also defined in Materials and Methods, to detect how the content of tweets influences both the activity and the volume of information perceived by the participants of the movement.

We define the size of an activity cascade as the number of unique `Twitter` users that produce a tweet in the cascade, also known as the number of spreaders, n_{sp}. The associated size of an information cascade corresponds to the amount of unique users who receive some tweet of the cascade in their tweet feeds. This concept, commonly known as exposure of the tweets in the cascade, is the sum of the amount of participants who follow at least one spreader, denoted as n_c.

We characterize the collective emotions in a cascade, c, using the ratios of positive, neutral, and negative tweets:

$$r_p(c) = \sum_{m \in T(c)} \frac{\Theta(e_m == 1)}{N(c)}, \qquad r_u(c) = \sum_{m \in T(c)} \frac{\Theta(e_m == 0)}{N(c)},$$

$$r_n(c) = \sum_{m \in T(c)} \frac{\Theta(e_m == -1)}{N(c)}, \tag{1}$$

where $T(c)$ is the set of tweets on cascade c, e_m is the emotional content of tweet m as given by the sentiment analysis tool, and $N(c)$ is the total amount of tweets related to the 15M movement comprising cascade c. The collective emotions expressed by the participants of a cascade have the potential to activate additional participants, influencing its activity size and information spreading. To test this possibility, we classify cascades according to their

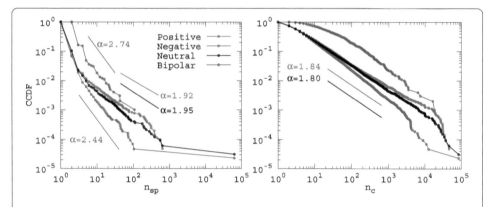

Figure 1 Complementary cumulative density function for activity cascade sizes (left) and information cascade sizes (right). In this case, cascades have been classified according to their aggregate sentiment into positive, negative, neutral and bipolar.

ratios of positive, $r_p(c)$, and negative, $r_n(c)$, tweets and compare these with the total ratios of positive tweets, μ_p, and negative tweets, μ_n. If both $r_p(c) \leq \mu_p$ and $r_n(c) \leq \mu_n$, we label the cascade as *neutral*. If $r_p(c) > \mu_p$ and $r_n(c) \leq \mu_n$, we label it as *positive*, and if $r_n(c) > \mu_n$ and $r_p(c) \leq \mu_p$, we label it as *negative*. When both $r_p(c) > \mu_p$ and $r_n(c) > \mu_n$, we label it as *bipolar*. From the total of 96,065 cascades we analyzed, 43,415 are positive (45.19%), 20,989 are negative (21.85%), 30,664 are neutral (31.92%), and 997 are bipolar (1.04%).

Figure 1 shows the complementary cumulative density function (CCDF) of activity cascade sizes, $P(x > n_{sp})$, and of information cascade sizes, $P(x > n_c)$. Bipolar cascades are likely to be larger than positive, negative, and neutral, but we do not observe extremely large bipolar cascades, since they are less frequent in general. We apply the Kolmogorov-Smirnov test (KS) with a tail correction factor, as explained in [25], to test the equality of information and activity cascades across emotion classes. The KS tests validate the observation that cascade sizes (both n_{sp} and n_c) in bipolar cascades are different from in any of the other three classes (details in Additional file 1, Table V). Furthermore, the test rejects the null hypothesis that positive cascade sizes are distributed as their negative and neutral counterparts, and only fails to reject the null hypothesis for the case of negative versus neutral information cascades.

To further compare these cascades classes, we fit power law distributions of the form $p(x) \sim x^{-\alpha}$ for $x \geq x_{min}$, to the empirical distributions of n_{sp} and n_c. The power law distribution is characterized by a skewed right tail that starts at a minimum value of x_{min} and scales with exponent α. The estimated value of α can reveal important properties of how the mean and variance of the distribution scale with system size, which in our case is the amount of users in the network. For example, $\alpha \leq 2$ implies that both the mean and the variance of x increase with the size of the sample [26], and thus the expected cascade size would increase for larger movements. Power law distributions were fitted using the Python package *powerlaw* [27]. Power law fits reveal that n_{sp} for positive cascades decays with an exponent $\alpha = 2.44 \pm 0.07$ (see Table VI in Additional file 1 for details). This means that the distribution of n_{sp} decreases faster than negative and neutral cascades, with exponents $\alpha = 1.92 \pm 0.07$ and $\alpha = 1.95 \pm 0.09$ respectively, but slower than bipolar ones, which are best fitted with an exponent of $\alpha = 2.74 \pm 0.32$. The exponents of positive and bipolar activity cascade sizes, right above 2, imply that their expected size does not scale with system size, i.e. they do not become larger with larger populations. This is not the case for negative and neutral activity cascades, with exponents too close to 2 to arrive at any conclusion.

We also investigate the goodness of the fits by comparing them to fits to other distributions. In this way we are able to identify if a power law behavior is a good description of our data. Specifically, we calculate the likelihood ratio, R (see Table VI in Additional file 1), between the power law and a lognormal distribution, and the corresponding p-value indicating the significance for the observed likelihood direction. Positive values of R suggest that the most likely model is a power law distribution. However, when these values are obtained in combination with high p-values ($p > 0.05$), the evidence of a power law versus a lognormal distribution is moderated [27].

For the case of information cascades, the distributions of negative and neutral cascade sizes are similar (KS p-value 0.285), but the null hypothesis that they have the same size as the positive ones could be rejected. The fit of power-law distributions reveals that the scaling of positive and bipolar cascade sizes are similar, $\alpha = 2.01 \pm 0.02$ and $\alpha = 1.99 \pm 0.08$ respectively, while negative and neutral information cascade size distributions decay with $\alpha = 1.80 \pm 0.01$ and $\alpha = 1.84 \pm 0.01$ (see Table VI in Additional file 1 for details). The exponents below 2 imply that the expected size of the audience of negative and neutral cascades increases with system size, while bipolar and positive have exponents too close to 2 to arrive to any conclusion. Furthermore, the log-likelihood analysis indicates that data is better described by a log-normal distribution for positive and bipolar cascades. Although this evidence is moderated (p-values 0.34 and 0.67 respectively), it suggests that positive and bipolar information cascades are more likely to follow a lognormal distribution than a power law distribution and thus do not scale with system size.

The above results highlight the role of emotional expression inside a social movement: cascades with positive emotions (including bipolar ones) do not seem to trigger more activity nor spread more information than those with more objective and negative expression. This difference for distinct collective emotions opens the question of the role of the first tweet in the cascade. To test if this effect is due to the sentiment of the first tweet in the cascade, we extend our analysis to compare the distributions of cascades sizes for cascades that started with a positive, negative, or a neutral tweet (Section IV in Additional file 1). We find no consistent differences on cascade sizes depending on the emotions expressed in the first tweet of the cascade. This highlights the role of collective emotions in spreading processes: it is not the emotion of the tweet that triggers the cascade what matters, it is the overall sentiment of all the people involved in the cascade.

In addition to the sentiment, the semantic content of tweets can be analyzed with respect to social and cognitive content through psycholinguistic methods (see Section 4). In particular, the content of tweets in relation to social and cognitive processes have the potential to determine the success or failure of the spreading process. To check this we perform an analogous analysis of the distribution of the cascade size for different cascades types. In particular, we apply the same method as in the previous section to classify the collective emotions in cascades, comparing their ratios of social and cognitive terms to the mean values of the whole dataset. This way, each cascade is classified having either high social content or a low social content, and having either a high cognitive content or a low cognitive content.

The influence of social processes becomes evident when analyzing the distributions of cascade sizes depending on their social content, shown in Figure 2. The distributions of

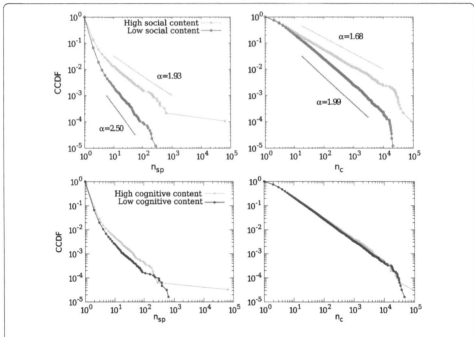

Figure 2 CCDF of activity (left) and information (right) cascade sizes for cascades of high and low social content (top) and high and low cognitive content (bottom). Dashed lines show the result of power-law fits.

both information and activity cascade sizes are different for high and low social content, as validated by a KS test (see Table IX in Additional file 1). Power-law fits indicate that the distribution of the size of activity cascades with high social content have an exponent of $\alpha = 1.87 \pm 0.09$, while the distribution for low social content has an exponent of 2.33 ± 0.07. This difference highlights the role of social processes in cascades during the formation of the 15M movement. Cascades with social expression had an expected size that scaled with the size of the movement, while those that did not include such language were subcritical. For the case of information cascades, the same result seems to hold. In this case, however, information cascades with high social content exhibit a power-law behavior with exponent $\alpha = 1.66 \pm 0.01$, which indicates that the expected size scales with the system size. The outcome is not so clear for low social content information cascades, for which $\alpha = 1.98 \pm 0.02$ is compatible with 2. However, the latter are best described by a log-normal distribution, as suggested by the log-likelihood ratio R, and the expected size of the audience does not scale with the system size (details on these fits can be found in Additional file 1, Table X).

The above results indicate that the behavior of cascades (both of activity and information) having high social content is different from those where the social content is lower. On the contrary, words associated with cognitive processes did not play such an important role in cascade sizes. The lower panel of Figure 2 shows the CCDF of cascade sizes classified depending on their cognitive content. The cognitive content of the tweets in an information cascade does not make it larger, as validated with a KS test (see Additional file 1). For the case of activity cascade sizes, a KS test rejects the hypothesis that they are the same, indicating that high cognitive content have a slightly larger likelihood of involving more spreaders, but not more listeners. Power-law fits show that the exponents of both types of cascades are above 2; while both exponents of information cascades are below 2.

Table 1 Linear regression results for individual activity level and integration in the movement

	$n(u)$	$k_c(u)$	$k_{in}(u)$	$k_{out}(u)$	pos(u)	neg(u)	soc(u)	cog(u)	R^2
$n(u)$		0.193***	0.015**	0.032***	0.010*	0.026***	−0.022***	−0.005	0.048
$k_c(u)$	0.094***		0.676***	0.090***	0.005	0.012***	−0.012***	−0.003	0.537

***$p < 0.001$, **$p < 0.01$, *$p < 0.05$.

2.3 The movement at the local level

The above analysis shows how expression related to social processes and emotions leads to spreading of activity and information through the social network of 15M. The cascades present in the movement are not just large groups of tweets; participants contribute repeatedly in these, and show heterogeneous levels of engagement in the movement.

In this section, we test the principle of Durkheim's theory that social integration in a movement leads to higher levels of participation, followed by feelings of emotional synchrony with other participants in group actions. The main group actions of 15M were physical meetings in the center of towns, demonstrations, and assemblies. But other kind of group activities took place in the online medium. Tweet cascades created pockets of interaction within `Twitter`, such that participants were aware of the large attention that the movement was receiving online. To quantify the social activity of each participant, we compute a vector of user features that quantifies the integration in the movement, its level of activity, and its expressed emotions and levels of social and cognitive content. We estimate participant integration in the movement in terms of the follower/following network, i.e., a network in which a link from user u to user v is created when the latter follows the former. Thus, the direction of links goes from a user to its followers, indicating the direction in which information flows. We measure the k-core centrality of a user, $k_c(u)$ (explained in Materials and Methods), where the higher k_c, the better integrated the user is. We also control for its amount of followers, $k_{out}(u)$, and the amount of participants followed by u, $k_{in}(u)$. The level of engagement in the movement is approximated by the total amount of tweets about 15M created by the participant, $n(u)$. We measure the expression of emotions by means of the ratios of positive, pos(u), and negative tweets, neg(u), and the ratios of words related to social processes, soc(u), and cognitive processes, cog(u).

We analyze the correlations between normalized versions of the variables using a series of linear regressions. Table 1 shows the results only for the regression of $n(u)$ and $k_c(u)$, the rest is reported in Additional file 1, Table XI. As proposed by Durkheim, the level of engagement in the movement increases with social integration, estimated through the coreness of the user. Other metrics, such as in- and out-degree, are also positively related to the activity of a user, but with weight much smaller than the weight of coreness. The right panel of Figure 3 shows the CCDF of $n(u)$ for different participants by their coreness. Integration in the movement is correlated with activity, showing that participants with higher integration in the movement are clearly more active. It must be noted that this analysis does not test the causal nature of this relation, but clearly rejects the null hypothesis of the independence between activity and integration.

As visible in the left panel of Figure 3, positive expression has no significant effect on engagement. Participants with different $k_c(u)$ do not have significantly different ratios of positive tweets about 15M. Negative expression has a positive but small weight in both activity and coreness, as reported in Table 1. We can reject the hypotheses that negative expression is uncorrelated or negatively correlated with integration in the movement, but

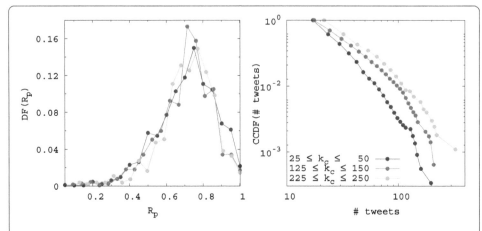

Figure 3 Positivity and engagement for three ranges of integration in the movement. Left: probability density function of the ratio of positive tweets of participants, for three ranges of k_c. Right: CCDF of the engagement of participants, measured by their amount of tweets about 15M, for three intervals of k_c. Participants with higher integration in the movement are more engaged and active in the online medium.

the size effect of negative expression in both integration and engagement is very low, as shown by the weight in Table 1.

We do not find any significant relation between coreness and cognitive expression. But we find a significant negative weight of social expression in relation to both activity and coreness. This is consistent with our finding that cascades with higher social content activate larger amounts of participants. These cascades potentially start in the core and reach participants with lower integration in the movement. Tweets about topics less related to social processes do not reach the periphery of the movement. In conclusion, less integrated users appear to be driven more by social processes.

An alternative condition for the emotions and the ratios of social and cognitive terms of each participant is the assortativity with other participants. Members of the 15M movement might be more emotional due to the emotional expression of their immediate neighbors, in addition to their social integration within the movement as a whole. To test this, we measure Pearson's correlation coefficient of the ratios of positive, negative, neutral, social, and cognitive tweet ratios of the participants, with the same ratio calculated over the set of users that each participant follows inside the movement. We replicate this analysis for two datasets, one based only on the tweets about 15M, and the other using an independent sample of 200 tweets per participant (detailed in Materials and Methods). To test the significance of our results against spurious correlations due to the network topology, we also computed correlation coefficients in 1000 shuffled datasets in which the emotion, cognitive, and social scores were permuted [28].

Table 2 reports the correlation coefficients for each dataset. All correlations are significant and positive, indicating that the emotions and semantic content expressed by a participant are correlated with its first neighbors, and thus emotions and psycholinguistic content are shared along social links within the movement. It should be noted that the correlation coefficients for the 15M data are much weaker than for the 200 tweets from each individual, indicating that the latter sample has more power to reveal correlations in psycholinguistic analysis. While the 15M data is sparser and noisier, the conclusions of the analysis of 15M data are consistent with the analysis of 200 tweets per individual, and robust with respect to the shuffled datasets. Furthermore, these results are in line with

Table 2 Pearson coefficients of neighborhood correlations and means and two standard deviations of 1000 shuffled datasets

Dataset	pos (u)	neg (u)	neu (u)	soc (u)	cog (u)
15M	0.063	0.068	0.065	0.035	0.128
15M shuffled	0.00002 (0.008)	−0.0001 (0.007)	0.0001 (0.007)	−0.0002 (0.008)	−0.0002 (0.007)
individuals	0.261	0.364	0.315	0.336	0.358
ind. shuffled	0.029 (0.01)	0.014 (0.009)	0.017 (0.009)	0.028 (0.009)	0.022 (0.009)

All coefficients have $p < 10^{-10}$ in the empirical data.

previous research [21] on emotional expression of subjective well-being, and extend the analysis with the presence of correlations for social and cognitive terms beyond emotional expression in `Twitter`.

3 Discussion

The present work analyzes the evolution of the 15M movement through sentiment and linguistic analysis of the participants' communication in the `Twitter` social network. Using a dataset of tweets related to the 15M movement, we track the activity of 84,698 `Twitter` users. Our analysis includes 556,334 tweets during a period of 32 days, providing an illustration of the structure of the movement in two ways: (i) at the dynamic aspect of cascades in the discussion between connected users, and (ii) at the individual level of social integration and participation of each user.

We combine psycholiguistics, sentiment analysis, and dynamic cascade analysis, to understand the role of tweet content in the size and reach of collective discussions in `Twitter`. In line with previous works in social psychology [29], we assess the role of emotions in social interaction and collective action. We test the hypothesis that collective emotions fuel social interaction by analyzing cascades according to their emotional, cognitive, and social content. We find that the sentiment expressed in the first tweet of a cascade does not significantly impact the size of the cascade. Instead, the collective emotions in the cascade are responsible for its size in terms of spreaders and listeners. In particular, cascades without positive content tend to be larger, and their size follows a qualitatively different distribution. The cognitive content of the tweets of a cascade play no role in their spread. On the other hand, our analysis of social content in the cascades reveals a clear pattern: cascades with large ratios of social-related terms have distributions of listener and spreader sizes that scale with system size, in contrast with cascades with low ratios of social-related terms, which follow distributions that have bounded means.

Our analysis at the individual level reveals that users are more integrated in the movement, measured by their k-core centrality, if they exhibit higher levels of engagement and express stronger negativity, in line with the overall negative context of the movement (indignants). Our analysis also reveals that highly integrated and influential users have a lower tendency to express social content in tweets. This indicates that social activation became salient in the periphery of the movement rather than in its core. We emphasize that our findings are consistent with theories in sociology and social psychology and confirm their statements by quantifying, for the first time, social and psychological influence in collective action at large scale.

Our results have implications for research on social movements. The differentiation between social and cognitive processes is evident when analyzing the size of cascades. Larger cascades have higher amounts of social terms, invoking the participation of other users.

This is also consistent with our findings at the individual level: social integration is clearly related to activity levels, showing the relevance of nonrational factors in collective action. The members of a movement are not deterministically defined by their demographic background and income. Instead, the amount of social connections they have in the movement and their synchrony with the emotions expressed by the movement as a whole are predictors of their involvement.

Our findings show the added value of including additional psycholinguistic classes into our analysis, i.e. the consideration of social and cognitive terms beyond sentiment analysis. Furthermore, our sentiment analysis adaptation to Spanish demonstrates the relevance of sentiment analysis in languages other than English, offering new opportunities to compare collective phenomena in a wide variety of societies and political systems.

Beyond social movement analysis, our work has implications for studying other online phenomena, such as memes or viral marketing campaigns. Our findings on cascade sizes for different psycholinguistic classes suggest that words related to social processes lead to larger collective responses in `Twitter`, pushing the virality of content above a critical threshold that produces qualitatively different cascading behavior.

4 Materials and methods

4.1 15M tweets and network

Our dataset comprises activity from `Twitter` related to the 15M movement in Spain, which brewed for some time in several online social media, and mainly rised with the launch of the digital platform *Democracia Real Ya* (*Real Democracy Now*). Twitter and Facebook were utilized to organize a series of protests that took off on the 15th of May, 2011, when demonstrators camped in several cities [30, 31]. From that moment on, camps, demonstrations and protests spread throughout the country, and the 15M became a grassroots movement for additional citizen platforms and organizations. As many of the adherents are online social media users, the growth and stabilization of the movement was closely reflected in time-stamped data of twitter messages. Some of these tweets were extracted from the `Twitter` API according to a set of pre-selected keywords (see Table I in Additional file 1), and the collection comprises messages exchanged from the 25th of April at 00:03:26 to the 26th of May at 23:59:55, 2011. The sample of tweets was filtered by the Spanish startup company *Cierzo Development LTd.*, which exploits its own private SMMART (Social Media Marketing Analysis and Reporting Tool) platform, and therefore no further details are available. According to previous reports, the SMMART platform collects 1/3 of the total `Twitter` traffic. From the sample of tweets we obtained, the follower/following network is extracted: for the active users, i.e. those who posted at least one tweet in the sample collected, the set of followers is retrieved, and the resulting network is filtered to include only the active followers. The resulting network is composed of nodes that represent users, and edges with directionality corresponding to the information flow in `Twitter`. This way, if a user u is a follower of user v, there will be a directed link from v to u in the network.

4.2 Sentiment analysis

To detect the sentiment expressed in each tweet, we apply the Spanish adaptation of `SentiStrength` [15], a state-of-the-art sentiment analysis tool for short, informal messages from social media [22]. `SentiStrength` is used in a wide variety of applications, from the sentiment analysis of stock markets [32], to reactions to political campaigns [13], and interaction in different social networks [22]. We tailored SentiStrength to the Spanish language based on a sentiment corpus of more than 60,000 tweets and evaluated it on an independent corpus of more than 7,000 human-annotated tweets [23]. More details about our application of SentiStrength and the results of this evaluation can be found in the Supplementary Information. After sentiment detection, for each tweet m, we have an emotion value e_m associated with the tweet. $e_m = 1$ if the tweet is positive with respect to its emotional charge, $e_m = 0$ if the tweet is neutral, and $e_m = -1$ if the tweet is negative. We abbreviate these as *positive*, *neutral* and *negative* tweets, always referring to their emotional charge.

4.3 Linguistic content analysis

We analyze the content of tweets based on frequencies of terms from the Linguistic Inquiry and Word Count lexicon (LIWC) [33]. This lexicon is a standard technique for psycholinguistics, including terms associated to affect, cognition, and social processes. LIWC has been used to predict suicides [34], and to analyze collective mood fluctuations [35]. For each tweet, we apply a simple dictionary detection technique based on the lemmas of the lexicon, stemming the tweets and detecting the use of terms in the LIWC classes of social and cognitive processes. This way, for each tweet m we have two counts of social, soc_m, and cognitive, cog_m, terms as well as the amount of words, w_m, in the tweet.

4.4 Cascade detection

Cascades in online networks may be defined in several ways with respect to the variety of online platforms, discussion topics, or interaction means between users. Here we adopt the definition first described in [31] which is based on *time-constrained* cascades. Time is discretized according to a window width, and tweets posted at consecutive time windows are considered to be part of the same piece of information if users emitting them show a follower/following relationship. Specifically, user u_j posting the tweet at time t_1 must follow user u_i sending the tweet at time t_0. Previous works showed the robustness of cascade statistics for different time windows [30, 31]. Here we choose a 24 hours-window to minimize the eventual correlations due to the effect of circadian activity in human online behavior. The content being sent is not required to be the same. This is motivated by three main facts: first, our sample, i.e., the set of tweets, has been previously filtered by topic, allowing us to safely assume that the information circulating is limited to a restricted topic, the 15M movement. Second, the 15M movement is a deliberative process, characterized by discussions and debates about the political and social situation of the country, the organization of protests and demonstrations, and conversations about the strategies to follow. Finally, Twitter is considered to be both a micro-blogging service and a message interchange service, as suggested by the high values of link reciprocity $\rho \sim 0.49$ and the mention functionality. Time-constrained cascades allow to take into account these frequent situations in which people discuss about particular topics using their own words to express their ideas, rather than forwarding a restricted piece of information.

A cascade is then an ordered set of consecutive activities of a set of users having follower relations. This way we know who started the cascade and when, and the seed tweet triggering the cascade. We can additionally distinguish between activity cascades and information cascades. The first ones involve only the set of active users, i.e. those responding to the message, whereas information cascades also comprise listeners, i.e. users receiving the message but not participating in the discussion. We want to first investigate if the initial tweet determines the size of the cascade. For instance, one could argue that positive messages can trigger larger cascades, or vice versa, negative messages trigger a debate that can last over several time windows.

4.5 *k*-core centrality

The *k*-core value is an individual measure of importance based on the core structure of the network. A *k*-core is defined as the largest subnetwork comprising nodes of degree at least *k*. Note that to compute this measure we consider the undirected network, i.e., we consider every link as if it was undirected, and therefore a node of degree *k* is a node whose total degree is $k = k_{in} + k_{out}$. The *k*-core decomposition method assigns an integer number to every node in the network, obtained by a recursive pruning of their links. The procedure starts with isolated nodes, which are assigned a *k*-core value $k_c = 0$. Then, nodes with degree $k = 1$ are removed along with their links, and assigned $k_c = 1$. If any of the remaining nodes is left with $k = 1$ connections it is also removed and contained in the $k_c = 1$ core. The process continues with $k_c = 2, 3, \ldots$ until every node has been assigned to a k_c shell. This metric goes beyond degree, as it takes into account the centrality of the neighbors to define the centrality of a node.

4.6 200 tweet timeline data

An extended dataset of tweets from the participants was also extracted. It comprises the last 200 tweets (if available) posted by the set of active users. It consists of a sample of 15,411,025 tweets (see Table IV in Additional file 1) retrieved the 20th of October, 2013.

Additional material

> **Additional file 1: Supplementary information.**

Competing interests
The authors declare that they have no competing interests.

Authors' contributions
RA and YM gathered data; RA and DG analyzed the data; RA, DG, YM, FS designed research and wrote the article.

Author details
[1]Institute for Biocomputation and Physics of Complex Systems, University of Zaragoza, Campus Rio Ebro, Zaragoza, 50018, Spain. [2]Chair of Systems Design, ETH Zurich, Weinbergstrasse 56/58, Zurich, 8092, Switzerland.

Acknowledgements
DG and FS acknowledge financial support by the Swiss National Science Foundation (CR21I1_146499). RA, FS, and YM acknowledge financial support by EU-FET project MULTIPLEX 317532.

References
1. Hughes N (2011) Young people took to the streets and all of a sudden all of the political parties got old: the 15M movement in Spain. Soc Mov Stud 10(4):407-413. doi:10.1080/14742837.2011.614109
2. Castañeda E (2012) The indignados of Spain: a precedent to occupy wall street. Soc Mov Stud 11(3–4):309-319. doi:10.1080/14742837.2012.708830
3. Zuckerman E (2014) New media, new civics? Policy Internet. 6(2):151-168. doi:10.1002/1944-2866.POI360
4. Tufekci Z (2014) The medium and the movement: digital tools, social movement politics, and the end of the free rider problem. Policy Internet. 6(2):202-208. doi:10.1002/1944-2866.POI362
5. Herman ES, Chomsky N (2008) Manufacturing consent: the political economy of the mass media. Random House, London

6. Olson M (2009) The logic of collective action: public goods and the theory of groups, vol 124. Harvard University Press, Cambridge

7. Garcia D, Zanetti MS, Schweitzer F (2013) The role of emotions in contributors activity: a case study of the gentoo community. In: International conference on social computing and its applications. doi:10.1109/CGC.2013.71

8. Mavrodiev P, Tessone CJ, Schweitzer F (2013) Quantifying the effects of social influence. Sci Rep 3:1360. doi:10.1038/srep01360

9. Durkheim E (1915) The elementary forms of the religious life. George Allen & Unwin, London

10. Atkinson QD, Whitehouse H (2011) The cultural morphospace of ritual form: examining modes of religiosity cross-culturally. Evol Hum Behav 32(1):50-62

11. Páez D, Rimé B (2013) Collective emotional gatherings: their impact upon identity fusion, shared beliefs, and social integration. In: Von Scheve C, Salmela M (eds) Collective emotions. Oxford University Press, Oxford

12. Páez D, Javaloy F, Wlodarczyk A, Espelt E, Rimé B (2013) The 15-M movement: actions as rituals, social sharing, beliefs, values and emotions. Rev Psicol Soc 28(1):19-33

13. Garcia D, Mendez F, Serdült U, Schweitzer F (2012) Political polarization and popularity in online participatory media: an integrated approach. In: Proceedings of the first edition workshop on politics, elections and data - PLEAD '12, pp 3-10. doi:10.1145/2389661.2389665

14. Conover MD, Gonçalves B, Ratkiewicz J, Flammini A, Menczer F (2011) Predicting the political alignment of twitter users. In: Privacy, security, risk and trust (passat), 2011 IEEE third international conference on and 2011 IEEE third international conference on social computing (socialcom), pp 192-199. IEEE

15. Garcia D, Thelwall M (2013) Political alignment and emotional expression in Spanish Tweets. In: Workshop on sentiment analysis at SEPLN, pp 151-159

16. Kitsak M, Gallos LK, Havlin S, Liljeros F, Muchnik L, Stanley HE, Makse HA (2010) Identification of influential spreaders in complex networks. Nat Phys 6(11):888-893

17. Baños R, Borge-Holthoefer J, Moreno Y (2013) The role of hidden influentials in the diffusion of online information cascades. EPJ Data Sci 2:6. doi:10.1140/epjds18

18. Garcia D, Mavrodiev P, Schweitzer F (2013) Social resilience in online communities: the autopsy of Friendster. In: 1st ACM conference in online social networks (COSN'13), pp 39-50. doi:10.1145/2512938.2512946

19. Garas A, Garcia D, Skowron M, Schweitzer F (2012) Emotional persistence in online chatting communities. Sci Rep 2:402. doi:10.1038/srep00402

20. Šuvakov M, Mitrović M, Gligorijević V, Tadić B (2013) How the online social networks are used: dialogues-based structure of MySpace. J R Soc Interface 10:79. doi:10.1098/rsif.2012.0819

21. Bollen J, Gonçalves B, Ruan G, Mao H (2011) Happiness is assortative in online social networks. Artif Life 17(3):237-251

22. Thelwall M, Buckley K, Paltoglou G, Skowron M, Garcia D, Gobron S, Ahn J, Kappas A, Kuster D, Janusz A (2013) Damping sentiment analysis in online communication: discussions, monologs and dialogs. In: Computational linguistics and intelligent text processing. Lecture notes in computer science, vol 7817. Springer, Berlin, pp 1-12

23. Díaz Esteban A, Alegría I, Villena Román J (2013) Proceedings of the TASS workshop at SEPLN 2013. Actas del XXIX Congreso de la Sociedad Española de Procesamiento de Lenguaje Natural. IV Congreso Español de Informática. SEPLN. http://www.congresocedi.es/images/site/actas/ActasSEPLN.pdf

24. Pfitzner R, Garas A, Schweitzer F (2012) Emotional divergence influences information spreading in Twitter. In: The 6th international AAAI conference on weblogs and social media. AAAI Press, Menlo Park, pp 2-5. http://www.aaai.org/ocs/index.php/ICWSM/ICWSM12/paper/view/4596

25. Clauset A, Shalizi CR, Newman ME (2009) Power-law distributions in empirical data. SIAM Rev 51(4):661-703

26. Newman M (2005) Power laws, Pareto distributions and Zipf's law. Contemp Phys 46(5):323-351. doi:10.1080/00107510500052444

27. Alstott J, Bullmore E, Plenz D (2014) Powerlaw: a Python package for analysis of heavy-tailed distributions. PLoS ONE 9(4):e95816

28. Fowler JH, Christakis NA et al (2008) Dynamic spread of happiness in a large social network: longitudinal analysis over 20 years in the Framingham Heart Study. Br Med J 337:a2338

29. Christophe V, Rimé B (1997) Exposure to the social sharing of emotion: emotional impact, listener responses and secondary social sharing. Eur J Soc Psychol 27(1):37-54

30. González-Bailón S, Borge-Holthoefer J, Rivero A, Moreno Y (2011) The dynamics of protest recruitment through an online network. Sci Rep 1:197

31. Borge-Holthoefer J, Rivero A, Moreno Y (2012) Locating priviledged spreaders on an online social network. Phys Rev E 85:066123

32. Zheludev I, Smith R, Aste T (2014) When can social media lead financial markets? Sci Rep 4:4213

33. Chung CK, Pennebaker JW (2011) Linguistic inquiry and word count (LIWC): pronounced "Luke,"... and other useful facts. In: Applied natural language processing and content analysis: advances in identification, investigation and resolution, p 206

34. Stirman SW, Pennebaker JW (2001) Word use in the poetry of suicidal and nonsuicidal poets. Psychosom Med 63(4):517-522

35. Golder SA, Macy MW (2011) Diurnal and seasonal mood vary with work, sleep, and daylength across diverse cultures. Science 333(6051):1878-1881

14

Fast filtering and animation of large dynamic networks

Przemyslaw A Grabowicz[1,2]*, Luca Maria Aiello[3] and Filippo Menczer[4]

*Correspondence:
pms@mpi-sws.org
[1] Max Planck Institute for Software Systems, Saarland University, Saarbrucken, Germany
[2] Institute for Cross-Disciplinary Physics and Complex Systems, University of Balearic Islands, Palma de Mallorca, Spain
Full list of author information is available at the end of the article

Abstract

Detecting and visualizing what are the most relevant changes in an evolving network is an open challenge in several domains. We present a fast algorithm that filters subsets of the strongest nodes and edges representing an evolving weighted graph and visualize it by either creating a movie, or by streaming it to an interactive network visualization tool. The algorithm is an approximation of exponential sliding time-window that scales linearly with the number of interactions. We compare the algorithm against rectangular and exponential sliding time-window methods. Our network filtering algorithm: (i) captures persistent trends in the structure of dynamic weighted networks, (ii) smoothens transitions between the snapshots of dynamic network, and (iii) uses limited memory and processor time. The algorithm is publicly available as open-source software.

1 Introduction

Network visualization is widely adopted to make sense of, and gain insight from, complex and large interaction data. These visualizations are typically static, and incapable to deal with quickly changing networks. Dynamic graphs, where nodes and edges churn and change over time, can be effective means of visualizing evolving networked systems such as social media, similarity graphs, or interaction networks between real world entities. The recent availability of live data streams from online social media motivated the development of interfaces to process and visualize evolving graphs. Dynamic visualization is supported by several tools [1–4]. In particular, Gephi [3] supports graph streaming with a dedicated API based on JSON events and enables the association of timestamps to each graph component.

While there is some literature on dynamic layout of graphs [5–7], not much work has been done so far about developing information filtering techniques for dynamic visualization of large and quickly changing networks. Yet, for large networks in which the rate of structural changes in time could be very high, the task of determining the nodes and edges that can represent and transmit the salient structural properties of the network at a certain time is crucial to produce meaningful visualizations of the graph evolution.

We contribute to filling this gap by presenting a new graph filtering and visualization tool called `fastviz` that processes a chronological sequence of weighted interactions between the graph nodes and dynamically filters the most relevant parts of the network to visualize. Our algorithm:

- captures persistent trends in structural properties of dynamic networks, while removing no longer relevant portions of the networks and emphasizing old nodes and links that show fresh activity;
- smoothens transitions between the snapshots of a dynamic network by leveraging short-term and long-term node activity;
- uses limited memory and processor time and is fast enough to be applied to large live data streams and visualize their representation in the form of a network.

The reminder of this paper is structured as follows. First, we introduce related studies in Section 2. Next, we introduce the `fastviz` filtering method for dynamic networks in Section 3. We compare this method against rectangular and exponential sliding time-window approaches and show what are the advantages of our method. Finally, we present visualizations created with our filtering methods for four different real datasets in Section 4, and conclude the study.

2 Related work

Graph drawing [8, 9] is a branch of information visualization that has acquired great importance in complex systems analysis. A good pictorial representation of a graph can highlight its most important structural components, logically partition its different regions, and point out the most central nodes and the edges on which the information flows more frequently or quickly. The rapid development of computer-aided visualization tools and the refinement of graph layout algorithms [10–13] allowed increasingly higher-quality visualizations of large graphs [14]. As a result, many open tools for static graph analysis and visualization have been developed in the last decade. Among the best known we mention Walrus [15], Pajek [16, 17], Visone [18], GUESS [19], Networkbench [20], NodeXL [21], and Tulip [22]. Studies about comparisons of different tools have also been published recently [23].

The interest in depicting the shape of online social networks [24, 25] and the availability of live data streams from online social media motivated the development of tools for animated visualizations of *dynamic graphs* [26], in *offline* contexts, where temporal graph evolution is known in advance, as well as in *online* scenarios, where the graph updates are received in a streaming fashion [5]. Several tools supporting dynamics visualization emerged, including GraphAEL [1] (http://graphael.cs.arizona.edu/), GleamViz (www.gleamviz.org), Gephi [3] (gephi.org), and GraphStream [4] (graphstream-project. org). Despite static visualizations based on time-windows [23], alluvial diagrams [27], or matrices [28–30] have been explored as solutions to capture the graph evolution, dynamic graph drawing remains the technique that has attracted more interest in the research community so far. Compared to static visualizations, dynamic animations present additional challenges: user studies have shown that they can be perceived as harder to parse visually, even though they have the potential to be more informative and engaging [31].

As a result, a large corpus of work about the theoretical concepts on good visualization practices, especially for dynamic graphs, has been produced in the last two decades. Besides the work done in defining efficient update operations on graphs [32, 33], several principles about good graph visualizations have been proposed and explored in different studies. Friedrich and Eades [34] defined high-level guidelines for a good visualization of graph evolution with animations, including uniform, smooth and symmetrical movement of graph elements, with minimization of edge crossings and overviewing some techniques that make the visualization more enjoyable, such as fadeout deletion of nodes. Graph *readability* has been measured in user studies in relation to several tasks [35–37]; the experimental findings highlight the importance of visualization criteria such as minimizing bends and edge crossings and maximizing cluster separation in facilitating the viewer's interpretation and understanding of the graph. A general concept that has been studied for long in relation to the quality of dynamic graph visualization is the *mental map* [38–40] that the viewer has of the graph structure. In practical terms, the placement of existing nodes and edges should change as little as possible when a change is made to the graph [41], under the hypothesis that if the mental map is preserved the parsing of the visual information is faster and more accurate. More recent work [42] has reappraised the importance of the mental map in the comprehension of a dynamic graph series, while identifying some cases in which it may help [43, 44] (e.g., memorability of the graph evolution, following long paths, recognition of recurrent patterns, tracking a large number of moving objects).

More in general, there are several open fronts in empirical research in graph visualization to identify the impact of certain factors on the quality of the animation (e.g., speed [45], interactivity [46]). An extensive overview of this aspect has been conducted recently by Kriglstein *et al.* [47]. Methods to preserve the stability of nodes and the consistency of the network structure leveraging hierarchical organization on nodes have been proposed [48–51]. User studies have shown that hierarchical approaches that collapse several nodes in larger meta-nodes can improve graph readability in cases of high edge density [52]. The graph layout also has a significant impact on the readability of graphs [53]. Some work has been done to adapt spectral and force-directed graph layouts [54] to *incremental layouts* that recompute the position of nodes at time t based on the previous positions at time $t-1$ minimizing displacement of vertices [5, 55–57] or to propose new "stress-minimization" strategies to map the changes in the graph [7].

Although much exploration has been done in the visualization principles to achieve highly-readable animations, two aspects have been overlooked so far.

First, not many techniques to extract and visualize the most relevant information from *very large* graphs have been studied yet. Graph decomposition has been used in a static context to increase the readability of the network by splitting it into modules to be visualized separately [58], while sliding time-windows have been employed to discard older nodes and edges in visualization of graph evolution [59]. A hierarchical organization of nodes according to some authority or centrality measure allows to visualize the graph at different levels of details, eliminating the need to display all nodes and edges at once [60]. Some work has been done about interactive exploration by blending different visualization paradigms [61] and time-varying clustering [62]. Indices to measure the relevance of events in a dynamic graph at both node and community level have also been proposed [63], even if they have not been applied to any graph animation task. Yet, none of these techniques has been tested on very large data and none of the modern visualization tools provide features for the detection of the most relevant components of a graph at a given time. On the other hand, quantitative studies on the characterization of temporal networks [64–66] have been conducted, but with no direct connection with the dynamic visualization task.

Last, the visualization of large graphs in an online scenario, where node and edge updates are received in a live stream, and the related practical implications of dynamic visualizations, have rarely been considered. In this context, just some exploratory work has been carried out about information selection techniques for dynamic graph visualization, including solutions based on temporal decay of nodes and edges [59], node clustering [58], and centrality indices [60, 63].

3 Network filtering

We introduce the `fastviz` algorithm that takes in input a chronological stream of interactions between nodes (i.e., network edges) and converts it into a set of graph updates that account only for the most relevant part of the network. The algorithm has two stages: buffering of filtered network and generation of differential updates for the visualization (see Figure 1). The algorithm stores and visualizes the nodes with the highest strengths, i.e., the highest sum of weights of their connections.

3.1 Input

The data taken as input is an ordered chronological sequence of interactions between nodes. The interactions can be either pairwise or cliques of interacting nodes. For instance, the following input:

$$\langle t_i, n_1, \ldots, n_m, w_i \rangle$$

represents the occurrence of interactions between nodes $n_1, \ldots, n_m$ of weight w_i at epoch time t_i. Entries with more than two nodes are interpreted as interactions happening between each pair of members of the clique with the respective weight. Multiple interactions

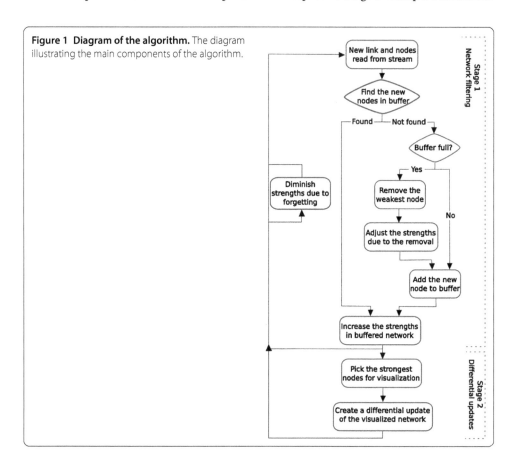

Figure 1 Diagram of the algorithm. The diagram illustrating the main components of the algorithm.

between the same pair of nodes sum up by adding up their corresponding weights. The advantage of the clique-wise format over the pairwise format is that the size of input files is smaller.

3.2 Filtering criterion

In the first stage of the algorithm, at most N_b nodes with the highest strengths are saved in the buffer together with the interactions among them. The strength S_i of a node i is a sum of weights of all connections of that node, i.e., $S_i = \sum_j w_{ij}$, where w_{ij} is the weight of an undirected connection between nodes i and j. Whenever a new node, which does not appear in the buffer yet, is read from the input, it replaces the node in the buffer with the lowest value of the strength. If an incoming input involves a node that is already in the buffer, then the strength of the node is increased by the weight of the incoming connection. To emphasize the most recent events and penalize stale ones, a forgetting mechanism that decreases the strengths of all nodes and weights of all edges is run periodically every time period T_f by multiplying their current values by a forgetting factor $0 \leq C_f < 1$. This process leads to the removal of old inactive nodes having low strength and storage of old nodes with fresh activity and high strength.

Note that the forgetting mechanism corresponds to a sliding time-window with exponential decay. The decay determines the weighting of the past interactions in the sliding time-window aggregation of a dynamic network. Standard rectangular sliding time-window aggregates all past events within the width T_{tw} of the time-window weighting them equally. In contrast, in `fastviz` and in the sliding time-window with an exponential decay the weighting decreases exponentially (see Figure 2). (Under a set of assumptions one can calculate how much time will a given node stay in the buffered network. Let us assume that at the time t_n the strength of a node n is $S_n(t_n)$, that this strength will not be increased after time t_n, that the next forgetting will happen in T_f time, and that the strength of the weakest buffered node $S_w < S_n(t_n)$ is constant over time. Under these assumptions, the node n will stay buffered for time $t - t_n > \frac{\log(S_w/S_n(t_n))}{\log(C_f)} T_f$.) Such exponential decay has two advantages over a standard rectangular sliding time-window approach. First, it gives more importance both to the most recent and to the oldest connections, while giving less importance to the middle-aged interactions. Second, it produces a dynamic network in

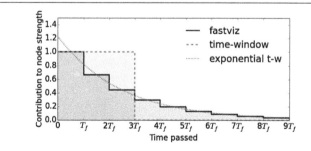

Figure 2 The aggregating curves of dynamic network filtering methods. The aggregating curves for `fastviz` (black line), rectangular sliding time-window (green dashed), and exponential time-window (blue dotted). The steps of the `fastviz` method correspond to consecutive multiplications by the forgetting factor $C_f = 2/3$ performed after each forgetting period T_f. The rectangular time-window width is set to $T_{tw} = 3\,T_f$. The exponent of the exponentially decaying time-window corresponds to the forgetting factor of `fastviz`. For these values of the parameters, areas under the aggregating curves of both methods are approximately equal, according to Equation 1.

which changes are smoother due to the balanced weighting of old and new connections. Finally, instead of using the sliding time-window with exponential decay, we introduced the `fastviz` algorithm to limit the computational complexity of network filtering. In principle, time-window methods do not introduce such a bound. We explore and confirm these points in the following subsections using real dynamic networks.

3.3 Filtering criterion versus rectangular and exponential sliding time-windows

Comparison of structural properties of networks produced with different filtering methods is not straightforward. First, since the networks are dynamic, one needs to compare the structural properties of the static snapshots of the networks produced by the two methods at the same time. Second, parameters of the methods, i.e., forgetting factor C_f and time-window width T_{tw}, influence the algorithms, so one needs to draw an equivalency between them to compare the methods under the same conditions. A natural condition to consider is the one of equal areas under the curves from Figure 2, representing the contribution of an interaction event to the representation of a node over time. Note that under this condition a node with constant non-zero activity in time will have the same strength in networks created with each method. For `fastviz`, the area A_{fv} under the aggregation curve is equal to the sum of a geometric progression. Assuming an infinite geometric progression, we get the approximate $A_{fv} = T_f/(1 - C_f)$. The area under the aggregation curve of the rectangular time-window is simply $A_{tw} = T_{tw}$. By demanding the areas to be equal, we obtain the relation between the parameters of the two methods

$$T_{tw} = \frac{T_f}{1 - C_f}. \tag{1}$$

In general, the forgetting period T_f is fixed, therefore there is only one free parameter controlling the filtering, e.g., the forgetting factor C_f, which we assign according to the dynamic network, i.e., the faster the network densifies in time, the more aggressive forgetting we use (see Appendix B for more details about the values of parameters). In the following paragraphs, we analyze the dynamics of several structural properties of the networks produced with `fastviz`, rectangular, and exponential sliding time-window methods having equal aggregating areas.

To highlight the differences between the three filtering methods, we apply them to two real dynamic networks from Twitter characterized by high changeability and measure the structural properties of resulting networks (Figure 3). The networks represent interactions in Twitter during two widely popular events: the 2013 Super Bowl and the announcement of Osama bin Laden's death. Further description and properties of these datasets are provided in the next section.

Due to this fact the computational complexity of sliding-time window methods increases in time, whereas it is bounded in `fastviz`. Since network structural properties such as average degree and clustering depend on the size of the network, we calculate these properties for the subgraphs of equal size, i.e., for the N_b strongest nodes of the full network produced by each of the sliding time-window methods (Figures 3C-J). For simplicity, we refer to these subgraphs of N_b nodes as the buffered networks.

Second, we find that the networks produced with our filtering method do not experience drastic fluctuations of the global and local clustering coefficients and degree assortativity, which are especially evident for the rectangular time-window (Figures 3E, G, H,

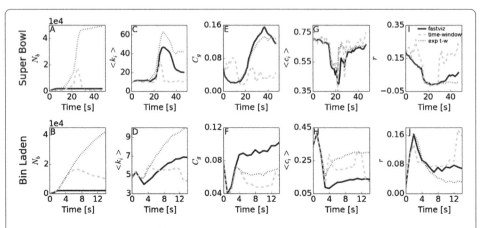

Figure 3 Structural properties of filtered dynamic networks. Structural properties of filtered dynamic networks representing user interactions surrounding the 2013 Super Bowl or the announcement of Osama bin Laden's death. The values of the properties are plotted as a function of time for the `fastviz` filtering (black line), rectangular sliding time-window of matching width (green dashed), or exponential sliding time-window (blue dotted). The following network properties are plotted from the left-most to the right-most column: the total number of nodes N_b, the average degree $\langle k_i \rangle$, the global clustering coefficient C_g, the average local clustering coefficient $\langle c_i \rangle$, and the degree assortativity r.

and I). We conclude that the `fastviz` filtering produces smoother transitions between network snapshots than rectangular sliding time-window. This property of our method may improve readability of visualizations of such dynamic networks.

Finally, `fastviz` captures persistent trends in the values of the properties by leveraging the short-term and long-term node activity. For instance, it captures the trends in degree, clustering coefficients, and assortativity that are less visible with the rectangular time-window, while they are well-visible with the exponential time-window (Figures 3C-F, I, and J). Note that high average degree obtained for networks produced with exponential time-window corresponds to the nodes that are active over a prolonged time-span, whose activity is aggregated over unbounded aggregation period, and the number of nodes is unbounded as well. On the contrary, rectangular sliding time-window shows the degree aggregated over a finite time-window, while `fastviz` limits the number of tracked nodes, leading to lower reported average degree.

To measure the similarity of sets of nodes filtered with different methods we calculate Jaccard similarity coefficient. Specifically, we measure the Jaccard coefficient J of the sets of N_b strongest nodes filtered with `fastviz` and each of the time-window methods (Figures 4A and B). The value of the coefficient varies in time and among datasets. However, the similarity between `fastviz` and exponential time-window is significantly higher than between `fastviz` and rectangular time-window. For the Super Bowl dataset, the similarity between `fastviz` and exponential time-window is close to 1 most of the time and has a drop in the middle. The drop corresponds to the period of the game characterized by the intense turnout of nodes and edges in the buffered network. Hence, the similarity is not equal to 1 for the two methods because the weakest nodes are often forgotten and interchanged with new incoming nodes in `fastviz`, while in exponential time-window method they are not forgotten and can slowly become stronger over time. In the next subsection we show that this similarity is close to 1 at all times for the subsets of strongest nodes selected for visualization.

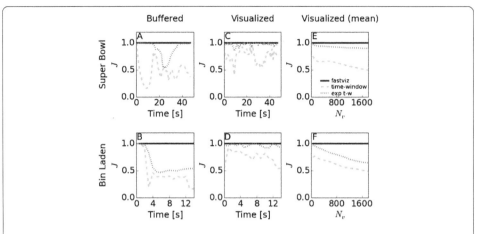

Figure 4 Jaccard similarity of networks produced with various methods. Jaccard similarity coefficient J between sets of nodes obtained with `fastviz` and rectangular sliding time-window (green dashed) or exponential sliding time-window (blue dotted). The nodes belong to either buffered or visualized networks representing Twitter interactions during the Super Bowl or Osama bin Laden's death. Specifically: **(A-D)** the Jaccard coefficient as a function of time; **(E-F)** the Jaccard coefficient averaged over time as a function of the number of nodes in the visualized network.

3.4 Network updates for visualization

In the second stage, for the purpose of visualization, the algorithm selects $N_v < N_b$ nodes with the highest strength and creates a differential update to the visualized network consisting of these nodes and the connections between them. Each such differential update is meant to be visualized in the resulting animation of the network, e.g., as a frame of a movie.

We compare the visualized networks generated by each of the filtering methods. Each of the visualized networks consists of $N_v = 50$ strongest nodes and all connections existing between them in the buffered network. The similarity of the nodes visualized by the `fastviz` and exponential time-window methods, measured as Jaccard coefficient J, is 1 or close to 1 (Figures 4C and D). The visualized networks of the two methods are almost identical. The structural properties of the networks created with the two methods yield almost the same values at each point in time (Figures 5A-J). This result is to be expected, since the forgetting mechanism of `fastviz` corresponds closely to the exponential decay of connection weights. The advantage of our method over exponential time-window consists of the limited computational complexity, which makes the `fastviz` filtering feasible even for the largest datasets of pairwise interactions. Naturally, the similarity between visualized networks created with the two methods decreases with the size of the visualized network N_v (Figures 4E and F). More specifically, the similarity decreases with the ratio N_v/N_b, as we keep in our experiments a constant value of $N_b = 2,000$. Hence, to visualize larger networks one can choose to buffer more nodes.

The comparison of the evolution of structural properties of the corresponding buffered and visualized networks shows that these networks differ significantly for each of the filtering methods (compare Figure 3 vs. Figure 5). This difference is the most salient in the case of rectangular time-window, which yields considerably larger fluctuations of structural properties than the other methods. In the cases of `fastviz` and exponential time-window some structural properties show evolution that is qualitatively similar for buffered and visualized networks, e.g., the average degree and the global clustering coefficient (Fig-

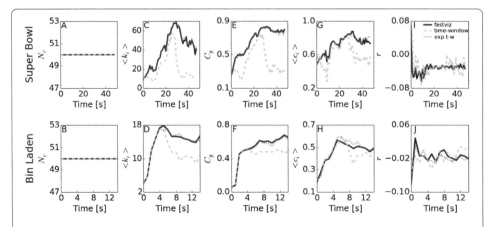

Figure 5 Structural properties of visualized dynamic networks. Structural properties of the visualized dynamic networks representing Twitter interactions during the Super Bowl or Osama bin Laden's death. The values of the properties are plotted as a function of time for the `fastviz` filtering (black line), rectangular sliding time-window (green dashed), or exponential sliding time-window (blue dotted). The following network properties are plotted from the left-most to the right-most column: the total number of visualized nodes N_v, the average degree $\langle k_i \rangle$, the global clustering coefficient C_g, the average local clustering coefficient $\langle c_i \rangle$, and the degree assortativity r.

ures 3C-F vs. Figures 5C-F). We conclude that the structure of visualized network differs significantly from the structure of buffered network, although this difference is smaller for `fastviz` than for rectangular sliding time-window.

3.5 Computational complexity

The computational complexity of the buffering stage of the algorithm is $\mathcal{O}(EN_b)$, where E is the total number of the pairwise interactions read (the cliques are made of multiple pairwise interactions). Each time when an interaction includes a node that is not yet stored in the buffered graph the adjacency matrix of the graph needs to be updated. Specifically, the weakest node is replaced with the new node, so N_b entries in the adjacency matrix are zeroed, which corresponds to $\mathcal{O}(EN_b)$. The memory usage scales as $\mathcal{O}(N_b^2)$, accounting for the adjacency matrix of the buffered graph. (For certain real dynamic networks, the buffered graph is sparse. In such cases, one can propose more optimized implementations of `fastviz`. Here, we focus on limiting the time complexity so that it scales linearly with the number of interactions and describe the generic implementation that achieves it.) The second, update-generating, stage has computational complexity of $\mathcal{O}(UN_b \log(N_b))$, where U is the total number of differential updates, which is a fraction of E and commonly it is many times smaller than E. (Typically, a large number of interactions is aggregated to create one differential update to the visualized network. In the examples that we show in the next section, one update aggregates from 400 to 2 million interactions. Therefore, U is from 400 to 2 million times smaller than E.) This term corresponds to the fact that the strengths of all buffered nodes are sorted each time an update to the visualized network is prepared. The memory trace of this stage is very low and scales as $\mathcal{O}(N_v)$. We conclude that our method has computational complexity that scales linearly with the number of interactions. It is therefore fast, that is, able to deal with extremely large dynamic networks efficiently.

4 Visualization

In this section, we describe animations of exemplary dynamic graphs filtered with `fastviz`. Principally, the sequence of graph updates can be converted into image frames that are combined into a movie depicting the network evolution. We implement this visualizing technique and create with it the network animations described below. Alternatively, the updates can be fed directly to the Gephi Streaming API to produce an interactive visualization of the evolving network. The Gephi Streaming API allows graph streaming from a client to a server where Gephi is running. In such a case, the graphs are streamed directly from our filtering system to the Gephi server without any third-party modules. In Appendix A, we introduce implementation details of both approaches. Finally, corresponding animations can be created by other visualization tools fed with the `fastviz` updates; we highly encourage their development.

4.1 Datasets

We test the `fastviz` filtering and our visualizing technique on four datasets very different from each other in nature, size, and time span (see Table 1). The datasets and movies produced from each dataset are described in the following subsections (see Figure 6). In Appendix A, we present the source code of both tools with their documentation, four dynamic graph datasets, and instructions to recreate the visualizations introduced in this

Table 1 Statistics of the experimental datasets

Dataset	Time period	Nodes	Edges	Nodes drawn
Super Bowl	2 days	49k	1.1M	577
Osama bin Laden's death	2 hours	95k	198k	279
IMDB movie keywords	6 years	1k	220M	301
US patent title words	34 years	414k	90M	106

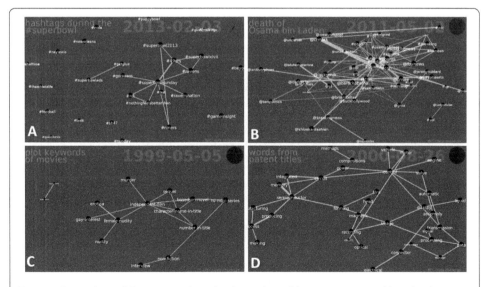

Figure 6 Screenshots of the generated movies. Screenshots of the movies generated from the datasets: **(A)** Super Bowl (full animation is available at http://youtu.be/N1wmJG3dVhs), **(B)** Osama bin Laden's death (http://youtu.be/gk03CJDAp_w), **(C)** IMDB keywords (http://youtu.be/JxWGjMdLUdQ), **(D)** US Patents (http://youtu.be/Q7p-bRY7_n0).

section. In Appendix B, we provide and describe the values of the parameters of the algo-rithm and the visualizing tool used for these datasets.

4.2 Twitter

We use data obtained through the Twitter *gardenhose* streaming API, which covers around 10% of the tweet volume. We focus on two events: the announcement of Osama bin Laden's death and the 2013 Super Bowl. We consider user mentions and hashtags as entities and their co-occurrence in the same tweet as interactions between them.

The first video (Figure 2A) shows how the anticipation for the Super Bowl steadily grows on early Sunday morning and afternoon, and how it explodes when the game is about to start. Hashtags related to #commercials and concerts (e.g., #beyonce) are evident. Later, the impact of the #blackout is clearly visible. The interest about the event drops rapidly after the game is over and stays low during the next day.

The video about the announcement of Osama bin Laden's death (Figure 2B) shows the initial burst caused by @keithurbahn and how the breaking news was spread by users @brianstelter and @jacksonjk. The video shows that the news appears later via #cnn and is announced by @obama. The breaking of this event on Twitter is described in detail by Lotan [67].

4.3 IMDB movies

We use a dataset from IMDB of all movies, their year of release and all the keywords as-signed to them (from imdb.to/11SZD). We create a network of keywords that are assigned to the same movies. Our video (Figure 2C) shows interesting evolution of the keywords from "character-name-in-title" and "based-on-novel" (first half of 20th century), through "martial-arts" (70s and 80s) to "independent-film" (90s and later), "anime" and "surreal-ism" (2000s).

4.4 Patents

We use a set of US patents issued between 1976 and 2010 [68]. We analyze the appearance of words in their titles. Whenever two or more words appear in a title of a patent we create a link between them at the moment when the patent was issued. To improve readability we filter out stopwords and the generic frequent words: "method," "device" and "apparatus." Our video (Figure 2D) shows that at the beginning of the period techniques related to "en-gine" and "combustion" were popular, and later start to cluster together with "motor" and "vehicle." Another cluster is sparked by patents about "magnetic" "recording" and "image" "processing." It merges with a cluster of words related to "semiconductor" and "liquid" "crystal" to form the largest cluster of connected keywords at the end of the period.

4.5 Other visualizations

Other than these experimental datasets, on-demand animations of Twitter hashtag co-occurrence and diffusion (retweet and mention) networks can be generated with our tool via the Truthy service (truthy.indiana.edu/movies). Hundreds of videos have al-ready been generated by the users of the platform and are available to view on YouTube (youtube.com/user/truthyatindiana/videos).

4.6 Summary

The datasets in our case studies are fairly diverse in topicality, time span, and size, as shown in Table 1. Nevertheless, our method is able to narrow down the visualization to meaningful small subgraphs with less than 600 distinct nodes in all cases. The high performance of the algorithm makes it viable for real-time visualizations of live and large data streams. On a desktop machine the algorithm producing differential updates of the network took several minutes to finish for the US patents and less than two minutes for the other datasets. Given such a performance, it is possible to visualize in real-time highly popular events such as the Super Bowl, which produced up to 4,500 tweets per second.

5 Conclusions

Tools for dynamic graph visualization developed so far do not provide specialized ways to dynamically select the most important portions of large evolving graphs. We contribute to filling this gap by proposing an algorithm to filter nodes and edges that best represent the network structure at a given time. Our method captures trends and smoothens the dynamics of structural properties of weighted networks by leveraging the short-term and long-term node activity. Furthermore, our filtering method uses limited memory and processor time making it viable for large live data streams. We implemented our filtering algorithm in open source tools that take in input a stream of interaction data and output a movie of the network evolution or a live Gephi animation. As future work, we wish to improve our algorithm by means of further optimization and to enhance the tools by providing a standalone module for live visualization of graph evolution.

Appendix A: Implementation details and source code

We have implemented two independent tools described in the manuscript. The first tool is the `fastviz` algorithm. The second tool converts the sequence of updates into image frames that are combined into a movie depicting the network evolution. We release the source code of both tools (see the project website github.com/WICI/fastviz). Here, we describe the two tools in more detail.

The first tool is the `fastviz` algorithm. It takes in input a chronological stream of interactions between nodes and converts it into a set of graph updates that account only for the most relevant part of the network in the JSON format. In the network filtering stage, the algorithm stores a buffered network of size N_b, limiting the computational complexity and memory usage of the algorithm. In the second stage, for the purpose of visualization, the algorithm selects $N_v < N_b$ nodes with the highest strength and all edges between these nodes with the highest strength and all edges between these nodes that have weight above a certain threshold w^{min}. The subgraph induced by the N_v nodes is compared with the subgraph in the previous state and a differential update is created. The updates are created per every time interval that is determined with the time contraction parameter T_c. A value of 10 for this parameter means that the time will flow in the visualization 10 times faster than in the data given as the input (see Appendix B). The differential updates are written in output in the form of a JSON file formatted according to the Gephi Streaming API [69]. We choose JSON format specifically due to the compatibility with Gephi Streaming API. In short, each line of the JSON file corresponds to one update of the graph structure and contains a sequence of JSON objects that specify the addition/deletion/attribute change of nodes and edges. We also introduced a new type of object to deal with labels on the screen, for example, to write the date and time on the screen.

The second tool converts the sequence of updates into image frames that are combined into a movie depicting the network evolution. To this end, the sequence of updates produced by the filtering algorithm is fed to a python module that builds a representation of a *dynamic graph*, namely an object that handles each of the updates and reflects the changes to its current structure. The transition between the structural states of the graph determined by the received updates is depicted by a sequence of image frames. Each differential update correspond to one visualization frame, i.e., one frame of an animation. In its initial state, the nodes in the network are arranged according to the Fruchterman Reingold graph layout algorithm [11]. The choice of the layout is arbitrary and other layouts can be used and compared. However, due to the focus of this study on the filtering method, rather than the quality of the visualization, we do not explore any other layout algorithms. For each new incoming event, a new layout is computed by running N iterations of the layout algorithm, using the previous layout as a seed. Intermediate layouts are produced at each iteration of the algorithm. Every intermediate layout is converted to a png frame that is combined through the *mencoder* tool [70] to produce a movie that shows a smooth transition between different states. The movie is encoded with the frequency of 30 frames per second. To avoid nodes and edges to appear or disappear abruptly in the movie, we use animations that smoothly collapse dying nodes and expand new ones. A configuration file allows to modify the default movie appearance (e.g, resolution, colors) and layout parameters (see the project website).

We release the source code of both tools with the documentation under the GNU General Public License (see the project website github.com/WICI/fastviz). Together with the tools we release the datasets used in this paper and instructions on how to recreate all the examples of animations presented in this manuscript. Additionally, the updates created with `fastviz` can be fed directly to the Gephi Streaming API to produce an interactive visualization of the evolving network. Respective instructions can be found at the website of the project.

Appendix B: Algorithm parameters

The exact behavior of the `fastviz` filtering depends on the parameters introduced in the manuscript. We present the values of the parameters used in the case studies and their default values in Table 2. The default values of the parameters are meant to be universal and give reasonably good visualizations for most datasets. Overall, three parameters require adjustment to the input data, namely time contraction T_c, edge width threshold w^{min}, and

Table 2 Values of the parameters of the `fastviz` algorithm for the introduced case studies

Dataset	T_c	w^{min}	C_f
Super Bowl	3,600	10	0.8
Osama bin Laden's death	500	0.95	0.9
IMDB movie keywords	$3,600 \times 24 \times 1,095$	10	0.75
US patent title words	$3,600 \times 24 \times 400$	20	0.65
Default	3,600	0.95	0.75

The last row contains the default values of the corresponding parameters of the algorithm. Remaining parameters of the algorithm are set to their default values, i.e., $T_f = 10$ frames, $N_b = 2,000$, $N_v = 50$.

forgetting factor C_f. We provide exemplary values of these parameters for the introduced datasets in Table 2 and describe these parameters in detail below.

The time contraction T_c corresponds to the number of seconds in data time scale that are going to be contracted to one second of the visualization. The larger the time span of the dataset, the larger should be this parameter in order to keep the length of visualization fixed. For instance, if the timespan of the network is 10 hours, and one wants to see its evolution in a 10-second-long animation, then T_c should be set to 3,600. It is crucial to provide a desired value for this parameter, because providing a value that is too large will create just a few network updates and a very short animation, while providing a value that is too small will create a large number of updates making the JSON file very big and the animation very long.

The minimal edge weight w^{min} is a threshold above which edges appear in the visualization. Low value of this parameter may results in many edges of low weight appearing in the animation, while high value of the parameter may prevent any edges from being visualized. In case a user does not have any information about the visualized network, we recommend leaving this parameter at its default value of 0.95, which will visualize all edges of standard weight 1 or higher.

The forgetting factor C_f decides how fast older interactions among nodes are forgotten in comparison with more recent interactions. This parameter can be tuned individually for the purpose of the visualization. In general, the faster the network densifies in time, the more aggressive should be the forgetting, i.e., the lower should be the forgetting factor C_f. In general, keeping the default value of this parameter is safe, although its adjustment will improve the quality of visualization.

Competing interests
The authors declare that they have no competing interests.

Authors' contributions
All authors designed the research. PAG wrote the source code of the algorithm and LMA wrote the source code of the visualization tool. All authors deployed the tools. PAG and LMA analyzed the data. All authors wrote, reviewed and approved the manuscript.

Author details
[1] Max Planck Institute for Software Systems, Saarland University, Saarbrucken, Germany. [2] Institute for Cross-Disciplinary Physics and Complex Systems, University of Balearic Islands, Palma de Mallorca, Spain. [3] Yahoo! Research, Barcelona, Spain. [4] Center for Complex Networks and Systems Research, Indiana University, Bloomington, USA.

Acknowledgements
We are grateful to André Panisson for inspiration and to Jacob Ratkiewicz, Bruno Gonçalves, Mark Meiss, and other members of the Truthy project (cnets.indiana.edu/groups/nan/truthy) for helpful discussions and suggestions. PAG acknowledges funding from the JAE-Predoc program of CSIC and partial financial support from the MINECO under project MODASS (FIS2011-24785). This work is supported in part by the NSF (ICES award CCF-1101743) and the James S. McDonnell Foundation and by the SocialSensor FP7 project, partially funded by the EC under contract number 287975.

References
1. Erten C, Harding P, Kobourov S, Wampler K, Yee G (2004) GraphAEL: graph animations with evolving layouts. In: Liotta G (ed) Graph drawing. Lecture notes in computer science, vol 2912. Springer, Berlin
2. Broeck W, Gioannini C, Goncalves B, Quaggiotto M, Colizza V, Vespignani A (2011) The GLEaMviz computational tool, a publicly available software to explore realistic epidemic spreading scenarios at the global scale. BMC Infect Dis 11:37
3. Bastian M, Heymann S, Jacomy M (2009) Gephi: an open source software for exploring and manipulating networks. In: ICWSM'09: proceedings of the international AAAI conference on weblogs and social media. AAAI Press, Menlo Park
4. Dutot A, Guinand F, Olivier D, Pigné Y (2007) GraphStream: a tool for bridging the gap between complex systems and dynamic graphs. In: EPNACS: emergent properties in natural and artificial complex systems
5. Brandes U, Fleischer D, Puppe T (2005) Dynamic spectral layout of small worlds. In: GD'05: proceedings of the 13th international symposium on graph drawing. Springer, Berlin

6. Brandes U, Fleischer D, Puppe T (2007) Dynamic spectral layout with an application to small worlds. J Graph Algorithms Appl 11(2):325-343
7. Brandes U, Indlekofer N, Mader M (2012) Visualization methods for longitudinal social networks and stochastic actor-oriented modeling. Soc Netw 34(3):291-308
8. Kamada T (1989) Visualizing abstract objects and relations. World Scientific, Singapore
9. Tollis IG, Di Battista G, Eades P, Tamassia R (1999) Graph drawing: algorithms for the visualization of graphs. Prentice Hall, New York
10. Kamada T, Kawai S (1989) An algorithm for drawing general undirected graphs. Inf Process Lett 31:7-15
11. Fruchterman TMJ, Reingold EM (1991) Graph drawing by force-directed placement. Softw Pract Exp 21(11):1129-1164. doi:10.1002/spe.4380211102
12. Gansner ER, North SC (1998) Improved force-directed layouts. In: GD'98: proceedings of the 6th international symposium on graph drawing. Springer, London
13. Hu YF (2005) Efficient and high quality force-directed graph drawing. The Mathematica J 10:37-71
14. Herman I, Melançon G, Marshall MS (2000) Graph visualization and navigation in information visualization: a survey. IEEE Trans Vis Comput Graph 6:24-43. doi:10.1109/2945.841119
15. Munzner TM (2000) Interactive visualization of large graphs and networks. PhD thesis, Stanford University, Stanford
16. Batagelj V, Mrvar A (2002) Pajek—analysis and visualization of large networks. In: Mutzel P, Junger M, Leipert S (eds) Graph drawing. Lecture notes in computer science, vol 2265. Springer, Berlin
17. De Nooy W, Mrvar A, Batagelj V (2005) Exploratory social network analysis with Pajek. Cambridge University Press, Cambridge
18. Brandes U, Wagner D (2003) Visone—analysis and visualization of social networks. In: Graph drawing software. Springer, Berlin
19. Adar E (2006) GUESS: a language and interface for graph exploration. In: Proceedings of the SIGCHI conference on human factors in computing systems, CHI'06. ACM, New York
20. Network workbench tool, Indiana University, Northeastern University, and University of Michigan. http://nwb.cns.iu.edu. Accessed 13 Mar 2014
21. Smith MA, Shneiderman B, Milic-Frayling N, Mendes Rodrigues E, Barash V, Dunne C, Capone T, Perer A, Gleave E (2009) Analyzing (social media) networks with NodeXL. In: C&T'09: proceedings of the fourth international conference on communities and technologies. ACM, New York
22. Auber D, Archambault D, Lambert RBA, Mathiaut M, Mary P, Delest M, Dubois J, Melancon G (2012) The tulip 3 framework: a scalable software library for information visualization applications based on relational data. Technical report 7860, INRIA
23. Ahn JW, Taieb-Maimon M, Sopan A, Plaisant C, Shneiderman B (2011) Temporal visualization of social network dynamics: prototypes for nation of neighbors. In: SBP'11: proceedings of the 4th international conference on social computing, behavioral-cultural modeling and prediction. Springer, Berlin
24. Heer J, Vizster BD (2005) Visualizing online social networks. In: InfoVis'05: proceedings of the IEEE symposium on information visualization. IEEE Computer Society, Washington
25. Falkowski T, Bartelheimer J, Spiliopoulou M (2006) Mining and visualizing the evolution of subgroups in social networks. In: WI'06: proceedings of the 2006 IEEE/WIC/ACM international conference on web intelligence. IEEE Computer Society, Washington
26. Demetrescu C, Eppstein D, Galil Z, Italiano GF (2010) Dynamic graph algorithms. In: Atallah MJ, Blanton M (eds) Algorithms and theory of computation handbook. Chapman & Hall/CRC, Boca Raton
27. Rosvall M, Bergstrom CT (2010) Mapping change in large networks. PLoS ONE 5:e8694. doi:10.1371/journal.pone.0008694
28. Yi JS, Elmqvist N Lee S (2010) TimeMatrix: analyzing temporal social networks using interactive matrix-based visualizations. Int J Hum-Comput Interact 26:11-12
29. Stein K, Wegener R, Schlieder C (2010) Pixel-oriented visualization of change in social networks. In: ASONAM'10: proceedings of the international conference on advances in social networks analysis and mining. IEEE Computer Society, Washington
30. Gove R, Gramsky N, Kirby R, Sefer E, Sopan A, Dunne C, Shneiderman B, Taieb-Maimon M (2011) NetVisia: heat map & matrix visualization of dynamic social network statistics & content. In: SocialCom'11: proceedings of the 3rd IEEE international conference on social computing. IEEE Computer Society, Washington
31. Farrugia M, Quigley A (2011) Effective temporal graph layout: a comparative study of animation versus static display methods. Inf Vis 10:47-64. doi:10.1057/ivs.2010.10
32. Ramalingam G, Reps T (1996) On the computational complexity of dynamic graph problems. Theor Comput Sci 158:233-277
33. Henzinger MR, King V (1999) Randomized fully dynamic graph algorithms with polylogarithmic time per operation. J ACM 46:502-516
34. Friedrich C, Houle ME (2002) Graph drawing in motion II. In: Mutzel P, Junger M, Leipert S (eds) Graph drawing. Lecture notes in computer science, vol 2265. Springer, Berlin, pp 220-231. doi:10.1007/3-540-45848-4_18
35. Purchase HC (1997) Which aesthetic has the greatest effect on human understanding? In: GD'97: proceedings of the 5th international symposium on graph drawing. Springer, London, pp 248-261. http://dl.acm.org/citation.cfm?id=647549.728779
36. Huang W, Hong SH, Eades P (2006) How people read sociograms: a questionnaire study. In: APVis'06: proceedings of the 2006 Asia-Pacific symposium on information visualisation—volume 60. Australian Computer Society, Darlinghurst, pp 199-206. http://dl.acm.org/citation.cfm?id=1151903.1151932
37. Huang W, Eades P, Hong SH (2008) Beyond time and error: a cognitive approach to the evaluation of graph drawings. In: Proceedings of the 2008 workshop on BEyond time and errors: novel evaLuation methods for Information Visualization, BELIV'08, vol 3. ACM, New York, pp 1-8. http://doi.acm.org/10.1145/1377966.1377970
38. Eades PWL, Misue K, Sugiyama K (1991) Preserving the mental map of a diagram. In: Compugraphics, pp 24-33
39. Misue K, Eades P, Lai W, Sugiyama K (1995) Layout adjustment and the mental map. J Vis Lang Comput 6(2):183-210
40. Freire M, Rodríguez P (2006) Preserving the mental map in interactive graph interfaces. In: AVI'06: proceedings of the working conference on advanced visual interfaces. ACM, New York

41. Coleman MK, Parker DS (1996) Aesthetics-based graph layout for human consumption. Softw Pract Exp 26(12):1415-1438. doi:10.1002/(SICI)1097-024X(199612)26:12<1415::AID-SPE69>3.0.CO;2-P

42. Archambault D, Purchase HC (2013) The "Map" in the mental map: experimental results in dynamic graph drawing. Int J Hum-Comput Stud 71(11):1044-1055. http://www.sciencedirect.com/science/article/pii/S107158191300102X

43. Archambault D, Purchase H (2012) The mental map and memorability in dynamic graphs. In: 2012 IEEE Pacific visualization symposium (PacificVis), pp 89-96

44. Archambault D, Purchase H (2013) Mental map preservation helps user orientation in dynamic graphs. In: Didimo W, Patrignani M (eds) Graph drawing. Lecture notes in computer science, vol 7704. Springer, Berlin, pp 475-486. doi:10.1007/978-3-642-36763-2_42

45. Ghani S, Elmqvist N, Yi JS (2012) Perception of animated node-link diagrams for dynamic graphs. Comput Graph Forum 31(3):1205-1214. doi:10.1111/j.1467-8659.2012.03113.x

46. Archambault D, Munzner T, Auber D (2008) GrouseFlocks: steerable exploration of graph hierarchy space. IEEE Trans Vis Comput Graph 14(4):900-913. doi:10.1109/TVCG.2008.34

47. Kriglstein S, Pohl M, Stachl C (2012) Animation for time-oriented data: an overview of empirical research. In: 16th international conference on information visualisation, pp 30-35

48. North SC (1996) Incremental layout in DynaDAG. In: GD'95: proceedings of the symposium on graph drawing. Springer, London

49. North SC, Woodhull G (2002) Online hierarchical graph drawing. In: GD'01: revised papers from the 9th international symposium on graph drawing. Springer, London

50. Archambault D, Munzner T, Auber D (2007) TopoLayout: multilevel graph layout by topological features. IEEE Trans Vis Comput Graph 13(2):305-317

51. Archambault D (2009) Structural differences between two graphs through hierarchies. In: GI'09: proceedings of graphics interface. Canadian Information Processing Society, Toronto

52. Archambault D, Purchase H, Pinaud B (2010) The readability of path-preserving clusterings of graphs. Comput Graph Forum 29(3):1173-1182. http://hal.inria.fr/inria-00471432

53. Blythe J, McGrath C, Krackhardt D (1996) The effect of graph layout on inference from social network data. In: GD'95: proceedings of the symposium on graph drawing. Springer, London, pp 40-51. http://dl.acm.org/citation.cfm?id=647547.728581

54. Brandes U (2001) Drawing on physical analogies. In: Kaufmann M, Wagner D (eds) Drawing graphs. Springer, London

55. Branke J (2001) Dynamic graph drawing. In: Kaufmann M, Wagner D (eds) Drawing graphs. Springer, London

56. Diehl S, Gorg C (2002) Graphs, they are changing. In: Goodrich M, Kobourov S (eds) Graph drawing. Lecture notes in computer science, vol 2528. Springer, Berlin

57. Frishman Y, Tal A (2008) Online dynamic graph drawing. IEEE Trans Vis Comput Graph 14:727-740

58. Rodrigues EM, Milic-Frayling N, Smith M, Shneiderman B, Hansen D (2011) Group-in-a-box layout for multi-faceted analysis of communities. In: SocialCom'11: proceedings of the 3rd IEEE international conference on social computing. IEEE Computer Society, Washington

59. Dynes SBC, Gloor PA, Gloor PA, Gloor PA, Laubacher R, Laubacher R, Zhao Y, Zhao Y, Dynes S (2004) Temporal visualization and analysis of social networks. In: NAACSOS'04: conference of North American Association for Computational Social and Organizational Science

60. Kumar G, Garland M (2006) Visual exploration of complex time-varying graphs. IEEE Trans Vis Comput Graph 12:805-812

61. Hadlak S, Schulz HJ, Schumann H (2011) In situ exploration of large dynamic networks. IEEE Trans Vis Comput Graph 17(12):2334-2343. http://dblp.uni-trier.de/db/journals/tvcg/tvcg17.html#HadlakSS11

62. Sallaberry A, Muelder C, Ma KL (2013) Clustering, visualizing, and navigating for large dynamic graphs. In: GD'12: proceedings of the 20th international conference on graph drawing. Springer, Berlin, pp 487-498. http://dx.doi.org/10.1007/978-3-642-36763-2_43

63. Asur S, Parthasarathy S, Ucar D (2007) An event-based framework for characterizing the evolutionary behavior of interaction graphs. In: KDD'07: proceedings of the 13th ACM SIGKDD international conference on knowledge discovery and data mining. ACM, New York

64. Clauset AEN (2007) Persistence and periodicity in a dynamic proximity network. In: DIMACS workshop on computational methods for dynamic interaction networks

65. Cattuto C, Van den Broeck W, Barrat A, Colizza V, Pinton JF, Vespignani A (2010) Dynamics of person-to-person interactions from distributed RFID sensor networks. PLoS ONE 5(7):e11596. doi:10.1371/journal.pone.0011596

66. Krings G, Karsai M, Bernhardsson S, Blondel V, Saramaki J (2012) Effects of time window size and placement on the structure of an aggregated communication network. EPJ Data Sci 1:4. http://www.epjdatascience.com/content/1/1/4

67. Lotan G (2011) Breaking bin Laden: a closer look. http://blog.socialflow.com/post/5454638896/breaking-bin-laden-a-closer-look. Accessed 13 Mar 2014

68. LaRowe G, Ambre S, Burgoon J, Ke W, Börner K (2009) The scholarly database and its utility for scientometrics research. Scientometrics 79(2):219-234

69. Graph Streaming API documentation. http://wiki.gephi.org/index.php/Specification_-_GSoC_Graph_Streaming_API. Accessed 13 Mar 2014

70. Mencoder tool documentation. http://www.mplayerhq.hu/design7/documentation.html. Accessed 13 Mar 2014

15

The emergence of roles in large-scale networks of communication

Sandra González-Bailón[1*], Ning Wang[2] and Javier Borge-Holthoefer[3*]

*Correspondence:
sgonzalezbailon@asc.upenn.edu;
jborge@qf.org.qa
[1] Annenberg School for
Communication, University of
Pennsylvania, Philadelphia, USA
[3] Qatar Computing Research
Institute, Qatar Foundation, Doha,
Qatar
Full list of author information is
available at the end of the article

Abstract

Communication through social media mediates coordination and information diffusion across a range of social settings. However, online networks are large and complex, and their analysis requires new methods to summarize their structure and identify nodes holding relevant positions. We propose a method that generalizes the sociological theory of brokerage, originally devised on the basis of local transitivity and paths of length two, to make it applicable to larger, more complex structures. Our method makes use of the modular structure of networks to define brokerage at the local and global levels. We test the method with two different data sets. The findings show that our approach is better at capturing role differences than alternative approaches that only consider local or global network features.

Keywords: modularity; bridges; structural holes; structural similarity; online networks

1 Introduction

Networks of inter-personal communication have grown larger and more complex with the emergence of digital technologies [1]. Methods that summarize this intricacy help identify the building blocks that explain network dynamics like diffusion. Much research has been conducted in the last two decades to assess how the structure of networks correlates with their dynamics. Several methods have been developed to reduce the complexity of networks through the identification of their characteristic features, which involves determining the differences between observed and expected patterns under a null model of random connections. Reduction techniques like community detection or backbone extraction belong to this tradition; both techniques use the distribution of edges as the basis from where to identify the inner structure of a network [2, 3].

Blockmodels and structural equivalence offer an alternative approach, shifting attention from the edges to the nodes and to how similar they are as assessed by their connections to other nodes in the network [4–6]. The notion of structural equivalence has a long history in the analysis of social networks and the definition of roles, but it has recently been extended to make it less strict in its technical definition, more scalable, and applicable to other complex (non-social) networks [7]. Devising methods for role identification is important for network science because roles offer a scheme for network reduction and the construction of simplified maps of the original structure; but also, and significantly, because they offer a criterion to group nodes in categories that might be associated with similar behavior. We follow this prior research and propose a new method for the identification of roles in large networks.

The main assumption of our work is that roles respond to a division of labor that reflects different functions, or behavior, within the network. Detecting structurally similar positions depends on the network features emphasized by the method. Our goal is to compare different methods and assess which structural features are more successful at identifying relevant nodes. We use two different empirical data sets for that endeavor: the first, collected from Twitter, tracks patterns of communication around a political protest organized in May of 2012. The second, smaller and collected manually, is the classic (and renowned) Zachary's Karate club network [8], which we use mostly as a robustness test for our method. We analyze these data with two aims: to determine whether users that shared similar network positions (according to alternative methods) behaved similarly in the exchange of information; and to identify the roles that were more significant in that exchange.

On a theoretical level, we want to add a mesoscopic dimension to classic theories of brokerage in social networks, which have traditionally focused on local information flows [9–12]. As the proponents of this previous work, we sustain that roles are theoretically important because they are independent of the specific network under analysis: roles help us draw a typology of actors that transcends the composition of a given network. Unlike that previous research, however, we also contend that large networks require identifying roles on a coarse-grained level of analysis that takes the entire network structure into account; the relevant source of actor heterogeneity is otherwise lost in the detail of local positions. This is particularly important in the study of collective phenomena like protest coordination via social media: these communication networks tend to be large and complex, with distinct local affiliations, a small core of highly active actors, and a large periphery of lowly committed users [13–16]. The ability to broker information in such networks does not arise from local connectivity alone.

The rest of the paper proceeds as follows. First, we revise previous work on roles in social networks and defend the need to follow a more mesoscopic approach to role identification. Then we discuss our data and methods, emphasizing that we can generalize our analytical strategy to other data sets and case studies. The presentation of findings considers whether actors that are classified as structurally similar exhibit also similar behavior. We compare three approaches to the identification of roles, and we evaluate their performance when it comes to capturing differences in communication activity. The findings show that our method, which defines structural similarity in terms of local and global brokerage, is better able to capture differences in communication dynamics. A summary and discussion of the main findings closes the paper.

2 Roles in social networks

Sociologists have long characterized individual actors by the roles they play in social systems [17]. Roles refer to a set of expectations and patterns of behavior associated to positions in a social structure. The network translation of this idea usually relies on the notion of structural equivalence and its looser version, structural similarity: actors playing similar roles will have similar patterns of connections with other actors in a network [6, 18–20]. Two structurally similar actors have comparable ties to each other and to the other actors in the network. Roles offer an abstraction of these similarities: they provide categories that reduce networks to comparable building blocks.

Traditionally, research on social networks has assumed that network structure mirrors preexisting roles: being a professor at a university or a director in a company translates into having a set of similar ties with the other actors in the network (i.e. students and faculty, or other directors). Networks reflect, in this sense, formal roles that are defined within the parameters of shared institutions and mutual expectations. But roles can also emerge spontaneously from interactions in networks: some actors are able to play a differential role because of their structural position, for instance as when brokers emerge in informal networks of communication [10, 11]. According to this idea, ties do not reflect preexisting roles; instead, they allow actors to play certain functions - for instance, broker information. Actors playing a brokering role share a common trait: they span structural holes in a network by building bridges across sub-graphs that would be unconnected in their absence. This position gives them the possibility to control information flows, a role they share with other brokers in the network.

Although the idea of structural similarity requires taking into account connections at the level of the overall network, most network measures of roles (and brokerage in particular) still rely on local patterns. The identification of brokers in social networks is based either on structural constraint [10], which roughly measures transitivity in personal networks; or on the betweenness of actors in paths of length two [11], that is, on being the vertex in an open triad through which the two unconnected nodes interact. In addition to using only local information, these definitions of social roles are purely structural - that is, they capture the potential for brokerage given the absence of alternative routes through which information can flow, but they do not assess the extent to which information actually flows [21, 22]. In other words, roles are defined in terms of positions in a structure, and they are rarely validated in terms of behavior or action.

In spite of these acknowledged limitations, the local approach has still proved fruitful to identify general roles and analyze their association with the performance of organizations and elites [9–12, 23]. Gould and Fernandez [9], for instance, offer a typology of brokers on the basis of how actors mediate communication across pre-defined groups. Their typology (GF from now on) is depicted in Figure 1, panel A. According to this classification, when all nodes in a path of length two (or open triad) are part of the same group, the actor brokering the connection acts as a coordinator; when all nodes belong to different groups, the broker fulfills a liaison role; she acts as a gatekeeper or a representative depending

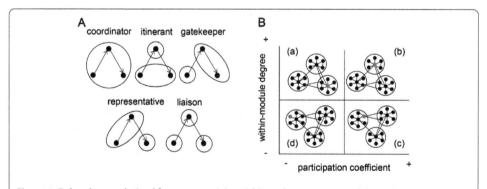

Figure 1 Role schemes derived from connectivity within and across groups. Schematic representation of role classifications derived from two methods. The method illustrated in panel **A** uses a local measure of brokerage [9]. The method illustrated in panel **B** uses the modular structure of a network to define within module degree and the diversity of connections to other modules [6].

on whether she belongs to the same group as the recipient of the information or as the source; and she plays an itinerant role when she belongs to a group distinct from the other two nodes in the triad. Differentiating these roles is important because they highlight the empirical possibility that the effects of brokerage, or its value, change across scenarios - a possibility that is more likely if nodes affiliated to different groups manage different types of information.

In larger networks, using paths of length two as the main criterion to identify structurally similar positions does not offer much space for discrimination - these local configurations abound and most nodes will be part of many of them. This is one of the reasons why a more scalable criterion to identify roles in complex networks was proposed recently by Guimerà and Amaral (GA from now on, [6]). As with the GF typology, the GA method requires a partition of the network in groups, often drawn from the topology itself using community detection methods [2]. Once this partition is generated, nodes are classified in a two-dimensional space that measures their intra-module centrality (i.e. the number of connections with other nodes classified in the same group) and their participation coefficient (i.e. the propensity to connect to nodes that are classified in other groups). This two-dimensional space is then fragmented in regions according to some heuristic derived from how nodes distribute in the space. In general, though, there are four main types of nodes, summarized in Figure 1, panel B: (a) provincial hubs, or nodes that are highly connected with other nodes in their module, but poorly connected to other modules; (b) connector hubs, or nodes that are highly connected to other nodes in their module and are also well connected to other groups; (c) non-hub connectors, or nodes that are poorly connected to their module but well connected to other modules; and (d) peripheral nodes, or nodes that are poorly connected to both their module and other groups.

The two role schemes summarized in Figure 1 overlap to some extent: brokers classified as coordinators are more likely to appear in categories (a) or (d), whereas brokers playing a liaison role are more likely to appear in categories (b) and (c). There are two important differences between the two schemes, however. The first is that the GA approach allows us to make a global definition of what counts as a structural hole based on the relative absence of ties across groups (as identified by community detection methods); this is more discriminatory than the local definition of holes based on paths of length two. In doing so, though, the GA method disregards the importance of local connections: it is personal networks that help us identify the role that actors play in their immediate social environments; the ability to broker connections on that level of analysis can also be consequential in emergent group dynamics [10, 17]. The second difference is that the GA method disregards the directionality of connections, but directionality is crucial in communication networks - and well captured by the GF schema. In the following section, we propose a third hybrid method that integrates the two schemes (HM from here on), and we assess its relative performance for the identification of similarly behaving nodes.

3 Data and methods

We use two data sets to compare the three role detection methods. The first was collected from Twitter for the period April 30 to May 30 2012 using the platform's search API. We applied filtering parameters to select messages that contained hashtags related to the Occupy and 'indignados' movements, retrieving about 445,000 messages. The filtering parameters and observation window were selected with the goal of analyzing communication dynamics around an international call for action, a political protest that took place in May 12. Using the unique author identifiers contained in the messages, we run further queries to reconstruct the network of following/followers. This one-step snowball crawl returned a network of more than 38 million users; of these, we only retained users that had sent at least one message during the observation period, as well as their connections to other users that were also involved in protest-related communication. In addition, we parsed the messages to identify re-tweets (RTs) and mentions (@), which allowed us to reconstruct direct interactions and explicit channels of information flow amongst users. More information about the data can be found in [24], and a discussion of the sampling procedure in [25].

Sampling choices and defining the boundaries for data collection are always important parameters in any research design. On the basis of prior work assessing the bias in samples of Twitter networks [25] we believe that we are probably underestimating the number of users in the sparser parts of the network (i.e. the periphery) and, as a consequence, also the centrality of the most central users: they get many of their connections from peripheral users (whose individual contributions are small, but statistically large when aggregated). An important aspect of the data for our purposes is that it captures a topology of connections (the follower structure) and a more dynamic layer of actual communication and information exchange (via mentions and RTs). This information is difficult to obtain from other sources of data - including our second data set.

The second network we analyze was collected in the context of anthropological research on conflict dynamics in small groups [8]. This network, which tracks communication among the members of a Karate club, is a well-known benchmark in community detection research because it can be characterized by the existence of two large groups or communities - the two factions that ended up splitting and resulted in the foundation of a new club. This network is small ($N = 34$) and because of that - and the anthropological research providing contextual information - it offers a more intuitive validity test for role detection methods. We use this data to examine the extent to which our method can be generalized across data sources and social settings.

The first step in our analyses involved finding out the modular structure of the two networks (follower structure for the Twitter data). We did so applying the fast greedy community detection method [26], as implemented in the open-source library *igraph* [27]. The method seeks the optimization of modularity Q defined as

$$Q = \frac{1}{2m} \sum_{i,j} [A_{i,j} - P_{i,j}]\delta_{C_i C_j} = \frac{1}{2m} \sum_{i,j} \left[A_{ij} - \frac{k_i k_j}{2m}\right]\delta_{C_i C_j}, \tag{1}$$

where the graph is represented as a matrix with cells $A_{i,j}$, which are valued 1 if a link exists between i and j, 0 otherwise; the second term corresponds to the configuration model, that is, the expected counts under the assumption of random connections between the nodes; finally, Kronecker delta $\delta_{C_i C_j}$ has a value 1 if nodes i and j belong to the same community C, and 0 otherwise.

The fast greedy approach to graph optimal partitioning relies on a recursive agglomerative scheme. As such, all nodes belong to their own community at start time ($M = N$); then the algorithm attempts to merge communities into larger ones. If the resulting partition improves the previous Q value, the merge is accepted and the algorithm advances towards further attempted mergers. Compared to other algorithms to optimize Q (and detect some sort of modular structure), the greedy approach is efficient and reliable: it can handle very large networks and it typically yields a number of modules $M \ll N$, which fits well the nature of our data.

Applied to our networks, this method yielded a partition with 123 groups and modularity coefficient $Q \sim 0.55$ for the Twitter data; and 4 groups and modularity coefficient $Q \sim 0.42$ for the Zachary's Karate club data. For the Twitter data, most nodes (96%) are contained in the three largest communities: community 1 is formed by $\sim$48,000 nodes; community 2 is formed by $\sim$6,000 nodes; and community 3 is formed by $\sim$67,000 nodes. The two largest communities correspond, largely, to the two social movements considered (i.e. Occupy and 'indignados'). For the Zachary data, most nodes are contained in the two largest communities that correspond to the two factions: community 1 is formed by 12 nodes, and community 2 is formed by 11 nodes. The other two smaller communities (sizes 6 and 5) are subgraphs where some of the nodes are not directly connected to the leaders of each faction and rely on the mediation of another node. This falls in line with the insights gained from the ethnographic observations: "Not all individuals in the network were solidly members of one faction or the other. Some vacillated between the two ideological positions, and others were simply satisfied not to take sides" [8]. The algorithmic community partition identifies both the two factions and the indecisive club members. Figure 2 shows the community partition for the two networks.

We are aware that the fast greedy approach and the partition it yields may not be the most resolved or the most stable in terms of different criteria, for instance persistence [28, 29] or stability [30, 31]. Determining the stability or persistence of the method is beyond the scope of the current work. Instead, we settle for a partition that we know yields meaningful results and is coherent with a substantive interpretation of the data. The fast greedy approach is also just one of the many methods we could have employed to identify communities in the networks; however, its validity is supported by the fact that the resulting partitions are aligned with contextual information about the data: for the Zachary network, the communities identified are consistent with the ethnographic narrative of the original study [8]; for the Twitter data, the outputs reflect the divide between 'indignados' and Occupy users, and we know that different community detection methods yield

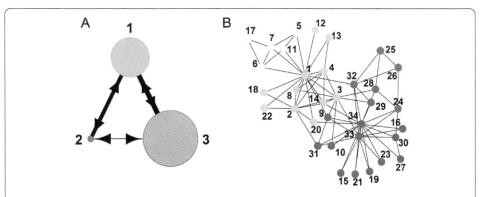

Figure 2 Community partition for the Twitter and Zachary's networks. Panel **A** shows the three largest communities of the Twitter network, and follower-following connections across them; panel **B** shows the full Zachary's network color-coded by community membership and visualized according to the Fruchterman-Reingold layout algorithm.

qualitatively similar results [24]. Because of this, we are confident that the communities identified by the fast greedy approach have empirical validity.

Finally, we consciously chose a method for the identification of non-overlapping communities because the three role schemes we test required us to do so - different theoretical goals or empirical settings might benefit from a role scheme that allows overlapping membership. However, prior research has established that disjoint communities apply important constraints to dynamics on networks, specifically to dynamics of information diffusion (see, for instance [32]). It remains an empirical question whether allowing for overlapping membership (where it makes substantive sense) can improve the modeling and explanation of those dynamics.

Once obtained, we used the community partition to determine vertex roles as defined in both the GF and the GA schemes. For the Twitter data, we first compiled the contribution matrices C^{in} and C^{out} of N nodes to M modules, where the rows of in- and out-C correspond to nodes and the columns correspond to modules. The elements of $C_{i\alpha}$ are the number of links that node i dedicates to (or receives from) module α, and can be easily obtained by multiplying the adjacency matrix of the network A_{ij} and the partition matrix S [33]. For the Zachary data, we adapted these computations to take into account that ties are undirected. These matrices summarize the tie contributions necessary to apply the GF and GA classification schemes.

The GA scheme exploits the modular information to measure the importance of a node within its community and as assessed by its inter-community bridging capability. The within-module relevance of a node is quantified through a standardized measure of the number of links the node devotes to its own community:

$$z_i = \frac{\kappa_i - \overline{\kappa}_{s_i}}{\sigma_{\kappa_{s_i}}}, \tag{2}$$

where κ_i is the number of links of node i to other nodes in the same module s_i, $\overline{\kappa}_{s_i}$ is the average of κ within module s_i, and $\sigma_{\kappa_{s_i}}$ is the standard deviation of κ in module s_i.

In other words, this score measures how many standard deviations away nodes are from the mean of their communities - the extent to which they are outliers in their own groups.

The inter-modular connectivity, on the other hand, is quantified with the participation coefficient:

$$P_i = 1 - \sum_{s=1}^{N_M} \left(\frac{\kappa_{is}}{k_i} \right)^2, \tag{3}$$

where κ_{is} is the number of links of node i to nodes in modules s, and k_i is the total degree of node i. This coefficient is closer to 1 if the links are uniformly distributed among all modules and 0 if all links are within the same module.

Although the GA method has proved fruitful in the study of metabolic networks [34] and in other areas [7, 35], it is far from ideal when analyzing directed networks, where a node might have a prominent role because of its out-degree but a modest one when it comes to in-degree. In communication networks this difference matters: it amounts to differentiating sources of information from spreaders. In the context of online networks, and Twitter in particular, this difference is especially relevant since a user can follow a potentially unlimited amount of accounts, thus critically biasing the validity of the measures on which the GA roles are defined. Throughout this work we report on GA roles as obtained from the C^{out} contribution matrix. We chose to report the results for out-going links following the intuition that the role as an information producer is more relevant than the role as a receiver - admittedly an arbitrary decision, which ought to be interpreted as an additional reason for us to develop a method that integrates in- and out-connectivity in a more meaningful way.

The hybrid method for role detection we propose (HM) is based on both the GF and GA schemes. We employ two different metrics to define the two-dimensional space from where role regions are drawn. Compared to the GA method (summarized in Figure 1, panel B) we don't use node degree to define the vertical axis, but instead a local measure of brokerage base on paths of length two, similar to the notion of structural constraint [8]:

$$C_i = \sum_j \left(a_{ij} + \sum_k a_{ik} a_{kj} \right)^2 . \tag{4}$$

As originally defined, the constraint of a node i can reach a maximum of k^3 and a minimum of k. A low constraint C_i indicates that node i has open triads in its personal network or, to put it differently, that it participates in paths of length two as those captured by the GF method (summarized in Figure 1, panel A). Low constraint indicates that a node has a high brokerage potential. To ease the comparison with the GA scheme, we normalize C_i so that it falls into the $[0,1]$ interval; and we invert it $(1 - C_i)$ so that higher values indicate higher brokerage scores. Also, we scale the resulting quantity by k to ensure that nodes that fill many topological gaps are placed higher in the ranking. In the end, the new score reads

$$C_i' = k \left(1 - \frac{C_i - k_i}{k_i^3 - k_i} \right) . \tag{5}$$

We define the horizontal axis of the two-dimensional space with a module-dependent measure that captures brokerage on a mesoscale. Our approach to this relies, again, on the GF scheme (Figure 1, panel A) but we depart from the original proposal in that we obtain the group partition using the network structure itself (as opposed to some exogenous node attribute). Using the in- and out-contribution matrices C_{in} and C_{out}, we measure the frequency with which a node is involved in each of the 5 role categories as defined by GF. We keep these counts in a vector g.

To project vector g onto single scalar, we weight it according to the following logic: because we are interested in the extent of extra-modular connections (which help us identify brokerage opportunities on a meso-level), we sort the GF role categories in the following order, from low to high: (1) coordinator; (2) gatekeeper; (3) representative; (4) itinerant; and (5) liaison. We then weighted each of the vector g's components by their position in the ranking, such that

$$s = 1c + 2g + 3r + 4i + 5l. \tag{6}$$

The idea behind this operationalization is that higher ranked brokers play a more important role in building global bridges, given the modular structure of the network and our choice to use modules as the group partition. A node playing the liaison role, for instance,

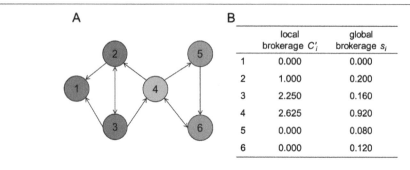

Figure 3 Local and global brokerage in an example network with three groups. This toy network illustrates our measures of local and global brokerage. Node color represents group affiliation or community. Node 4 has high local and global brokerage scores because it spans several communities and it sits on several paths of length two. Node 6 is highly constrained on the local level, but it spans a hole across communities, hence its higher global score.

bridges more structural holes at the mesolevel (i.e. it creates ties across communities) than a node playing a coordinating role (i.e. where ties span holes that are internal to the same community). Gatekeepers are lower ranked than representatives because we assume them to have a more passive role in information exchange - although arguably this depends on the actual dynamics of communication. Since we want s to lie in the interval $[0,1]$, we normalize the sum by the maximum possible count of the liaison role l in vector g, i.e. the score s^* that an ideal super-connector node would display in the network under study, i.e. $s^* = 5k_{max}$.

Figure 3 illustrates how these two measures of brokerage operate. Panel A depicts an example network with nodes classified in three groups (coded by different colors); panel B shows the node scores for the local and global measures of brokerage. The scores indicate that node 4 is both a local and a global broker - in the sense that it controls paths linking nodes classified in different groups; node 6, on the other hand, is a broker in the global sense, but it is highly constrained on the individual level. These two measures are thus not necessarily correlated and they help identify network positions that might be functional for different reasons.

4 Findings

There are two main questions we want to answer with the methods introduced above: Do nodes that share similar network positions behave similarly in the exchange of information? And which nodes are more significant in allowing information to diffuse? To answer these questions, we first apply and compare the three methods, and then assess their definition of structural similarity through the lens of actual node behavior.

4.1 Distribution of roles

Figure 4 plots the frequency counts for each of the roles defined by the GF, the GA, and the HM methods. The upper panels summarize the Twitter data, the lower panels summarize Zachary's data (note that the gatekeeping and representative roles are indistinguishable because this network is undirected). In all three methods, we are using the same network topology and the same group partition, drawn from the modularity maximization applied to the follower network (in the Twitter case) and the face-to-face communication network (in the Zachary's data case). In all cases, the role regions are also divided using the 95%

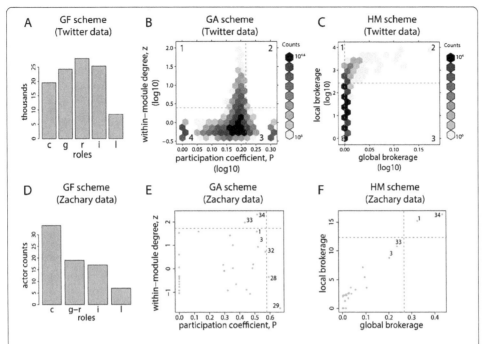

Figure 4 Distribution of roles according to the three methods. Panel **A** plots the frequency counts for the five GF roles, that is, the number of nodes that predominantly play each role. Panels **B** and **C** show the binned scatterplots mapping the distribution of nodes on the two-dimensional space defined by the degree-based method (GA) and the brokerage-based method (HM). The GA method is more restrictive in the definition of global connectors (region 2), with no nodes in that region. The lower panels summarize Zachary's data. Because this network is undirected, the gatekeeping and representative roles are indistinguishable. The HM sets two nodes clearly apart from the rest; these nodes are the leaders of the two factions identified in the original ethnographic study.

percentile of the distributions as a threshold. What changes across row panels is how roles are defined: using only local information (GF); using only global information (GA); and using both global and local information (HM). In region 1 of panel B, for instance, we have the 'provincial hubs', that is, nodes that are very well connected compared to the average of their communities but who do not connect well with other groups; in region 1 of panel C, on the other hand, we have nodes that have high brokerage scores in their local, personal networks, but who do not broker connections with nodes in other communities.

These alternative definitions of roles respond to different theoretical intuitions of why connectivity in networks matters. The first (GF) assumes that nodes that directly mediate communication between pairs that would be disconnected otherwise can benefit from that close arbitration; however, this definition does not tell us much about the larger network structure, and how central or significant brokers are in the overall picture. The second method (GA) presumes that relative centrality and the diversity of connections determine the relevance of a node: it relies on identifying the most prominent nodes within and across groups. Finally, the third method (HM) undermines the relevance of centrality and highlights, instead, the importance of mediation both at the local and global levels. These operationalizations result in substantially different classification of nodes - in the context of our data, for instance, the GA schema turns out to be very restrictive in the definition of region 2 ('connector hubs'), where no nodes can be found in either of the two datasets.

Most nodes in the Twitter network play (predominantly) a representative role (GF scheme); most are peripheral: they have a low within-module degree and low participa-

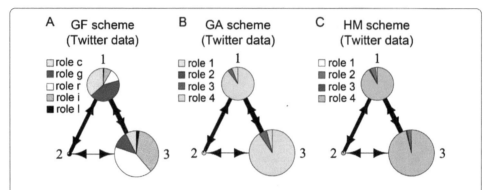

Figure 5 Distribution of roles by community in the Twitter network. Pie charts across panels correspond to the three largest communities in the following-follower Twitter network; the slices are proportional to the number of nodes playing the given role. The GA and HM schemes are more homogeneous in the distribution than the GF scheme.

tion coefficient (GA scheme); and most have low brokerage scores, both at the global and local levels (HM scheme). In the Zachary network, the HM scheme sets two nodes clearly apart from the rest - these nodes are the leaders of the two factions identified in the original ethnographic study [8], and the centers of the two largest communities identified in Figure 2, panel B. The GF method fails to identify the relevant leaders because all actors are predominantly coordinators, and it only identified a small elite of 7 actors of which the two leaders form part. The GA method, on the other hand, gives more prominence to actors that are central in the smaller communities and hides the instigators of the split. Only the HM role classification clearly sets these two pivotal actors apart.

For the Twitter data, results on this descriptive level are not that intuitive: the network is too large to be able to identify relevant identities, and we lack the ethnographic work that Zachary did. On the aggregate level, as Figure 5 shows, we can see how roles distribute by community across methods. The GF scheme, for instance, shows that community 1 (where most users communicate about Occupy) is mostly formed by coordinators and gatekeepers, whereas community 3 (with a majority of 'indignados' users) is mostly formed by representatives and itinerants. Most liaison roles are in the smaller community 2. The GA and HM schemes are, by comparison, more homogeneous: the three communities are mostly populated by peripheral users, and users with low brokerage scores.

Overall, these roles are defined on the basis of network topology only: they tell us that there are little opportunities for communication across communities, and that the vast majority of users don't control many direct diffusion channels - either because they are not well connected, or because their connections are redundant. The following section considers if this distribution of roles is associated with actual communication dynamics - which is what Zachary couldn't test with his data since his definition of ties implied face-to-face communication.

4.2 Association of roles with activity

The relevance of role schemes relies on their ability to sort out similar behavior. In the context of Twitter data, the expectation is that users with structurally similar positions will behave similarly in the exchange of information. We make use of RTs and mentions as a way to assess communication dynamics. We separate RTs from mentions because they allow information to flow in opposite directions and respond to different logics: RTs are

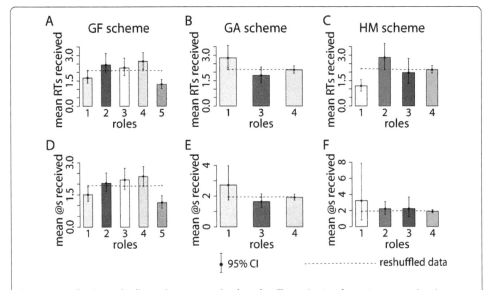

Figure 6 Authority and salience in conversation by roles. The authority of users is measured as the number of RTs received; salience is measured as the number of mentions received. The random benchmark is based on 1,000 permutations randomizing role assignment. The 95% confidence intervals are based on bootstrapped percentiles. Only the HM scheme is able to differentiate roles that are significantly associated to higher authority and salience in conversation.

about diffusing information; mentions are about raising awareness or engaging in conversation.

The bar plots in Figure 6 assess the authority and salience of users classified by roles. Authority is measured as the number of RTs received: the assumption is that a higher number of re-tweets signals higher prominence as a source of information. Salience, on the other hand, is measured as the number of mentions received: more mentions indicates that a user is better recognized and more acknowledged by other users engaging in conversation. Although the number of RTs received could also be interpreted as a measure of 'salience', we differentiate it from 'authority' to emphasize that users become prominent in the exchange of information for different reasons: RTs are about retransmission; mentions are about engaging in conversation.

To have a benchmark for comparison, we reshuffled the roles variable for each of the schemes (1,000 permutations), and calculated the mean number of RTs and mentions for the randomized data. To further assess the significance of the comparisons, we also calculated the confidence intervals for the mean values associated to each role (95% level based on bootstrapped percentiles). In panels A and D, for instance, we see that the users who predominantly engage in coordination or liaison roles are less central and visible than users acting as gatekeepers, itinerants, and - most significantly - representatives. Panels B and E suggest, on the other hand, that 'provincial hubs' (nodes with high within-module degree but low participation coefficient) are both more central and salient, although these differences are not significant.

The HM scheme uncovers differences that the other two methods fail to capture: the most re-tweeted users are those playing the role of local and global brokers; but the most salient users are brokers only on the local level (panels C and F). This suggests two things: first, that users with role 2 are essential conduits for global flows of information: they not only have more brokering ties across communities, they are also re-tweeted more often,

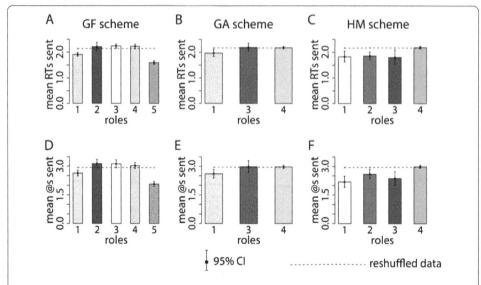

Figure 7 Retransmission and outreach efforts by roles. Retransmission efforts are measured as number of RTs made; outreach is measured as number of mentions made. The HM scheme sets role 4 apart as the source of most of the communication efforts.

which is a precondition for information cascades; and two, the findings also reveal that there is an organic division of labor in the network: users acting as authorities are different (and have different network positions) than users that become the target of conversation more often. The HM scheme identifies this division of labor more clearly than the other two methods.

Figure 7 provides additional evidence on how roles distribute in the network, this time tracking retransmission and outreach efforts (measured as the number of RTs and mentions made, as opposed to received). Activity levels according to the GF scheme do not vary much compared to those depicted in Figure 6; this suggests that this scheme is not very useful to distinguish nodes that are relevant because they receive attention versus those that are relevant because they produce the attention. Both the GA and HM schemes suggest that most of the messages are generated by peripheral roles (i.e. the less significant nodes in terms of authority and salience). Only the HM method, however, clearly sets apart the group of nodes that produce most of the RTs and mentions: they are the users with low brokerage scores both at the local and global levels.

5 Discussion

Role schemes aim to identify network features that make nodes structurally similar. The assumption is that nodes that are similar in their connections will exhibit a similar behavior or fulfill a comparable function within the system the network maps. The three methods we compare here use the modular structure of the network to define roles, but they differ on how they capture the heterogeneity of individual positions: the GF approach makes use of local features (i.e. mediation in paths on length two); the GA approach focuses on the distribution of degree centrality, and the number of ties that link to different communities, measures both that require global knowledge of the network; and the HM approach, which combines the previous two by assessing brokerage at the local (i.e. personal network) and global (i.e. inter-community ties) levels.

This focus on different network features results in alternative role classifications that, as the findings reported show, capture with more or less success differences in behavior. On the basis of our data, we can conclude that the hybrid model combining local and global measures of brokerage is able to better characterize significant behavior. In the Zachary network, it helps identify the leaders of the two opposing factions; in the context of the Twitter network, it helps identify the division of labor that emerges in the orchestration of political action: on the one hand, users playing role 2 (local and global brokers) act as sources of information, but the most visible users play role 1 (they are the local brokers); on the other hand, most of the messages sending those RTs and mentions are generated by users playing role 4. This allocation of roles not only helps uncover an organic division of labor (organic for unplanned); it also allows inferring the logic that lies behind communication dynamics. If RTs are used to disseminate information from a source to an audience, mentions are used to try to gain the attention of other users or engage in direct conversation. It is not coincidental that users receiving many RTs have more global networks than users receiving many mentions.

There are many other alternative schemes that could possibly shed light on communication behavior; and many of the parameters we fixed in our operationalizations could also be modified. For instance, applying an alternative community detection method would have yielded a different partition; or we could have employed a partition completely independent of network topology, based on some node attribute like membership or affiliation to specific organizations. We think, however, that the modular structure of networks contains significant information about how social systems self-organize, and so we advocate for the topological approach to the classification of nodes (unlike the GF scheme as originally formulated). The two datasets we use exhibit a clear modular structure that responds to identifiable social factors (i.e. conflict dynamics, membership to social movements). This makes the use of our partition substantively meaningful - it reflects well the groups that operate within the network - but the method might yield uninterpretable results if the forces driving the formation of modules in networks are unknown.

Thus, before generalizing our approach and making it applicable to other settings, careful consideration should be given to how the partition is generated and whether it makes sense for the empirical data under analysis. A relevant aspect to take into account in this respect is that in some scenarios overlapping communities might be more meaningful. The three schemes we consider here are based on the assumption that communities are exclusive, but future research should address the effects that multiple memberships would have on the definition of roles.

The second parameter that could be modified is the threshold we use to delineate role regions. We used the 95% percentile, which is arguably an *ad hoc* heuristic. This threshold was chosen to give prominence to the tail of distributions that are skewed, but future work should also assess changes in the performance of role schemes with shifts in this threshold. The sensitivity of role classification to different heuristics is, ultimately, an empirical question: for some data structures, some divisions will yield more informative classifications than others.

On a theoretical level, we argue that a role scheme based on brokerage is more discriminating than a scheme based on degree. The findings show that roles based on brokerage result in a reduction of the network that is more informative about the functions that nodes play. The reason, we sustain, is that the analysis of brokerage allows integrating more levels of analysis (from local bridges in open triads to ties linking modules), and it thus offers a more informative definition of structural similarity.

6 Conclusion

This paper extends previous sociological research on the importance of brokerage to the analysis of large networks of communication. Our goal was twofold: to determine whether users that share similar network positions behave similarly; and to identify the roles that are more significant for information diffusion. Our findings confirm the expectation that nodes creating bridges within and across communities (role 2 in the HM scheme) are more likely to be used as sources of information: they are the leaders in the Zachary network and the users receiving a higher number of RTs in the Twitter network. This suggests that these users are crucial in the global exchange of information. For the Twitter data, we also found that roles reveal a division of labor in how communication takes place: users that act as authorities are not the most visible; and the most central or visible are not the most active. Overall, the relative performance of different role schemes depends on the empirical data; but the methods to define structural similarity can be generalized beyond the specificities of particular data sets. Improving our definitions of structural similarity is important because they offer a method to model and simplify complex structures - an exercise that is increasingly necessary to make sense of large-scale digital networks and the communication they facilitate.

Competing interests
The authors declare that they have no competing interests.

Authors' contributions
SGB and JGH designed research, performed analyses, and wrote the paper. NW collected the data and performed preliminary analyses.

Author details
[1] Annenberg School for Communication, University of Pennsylvania, Philadelphia, USA. [2] Oxford Internet Institute, University of Oxford, Oxford, UK. [3] Qatar Computing Research Institute, Qatar Foundation, Doha, Qatar.

References
1. Rainie L, Wellman B (2012) Networked. The new social operating system. MIT Press, Cambridge
2. Newman MEJ (2012) Communities, modules and large-scale structure in networks. Nat Phys 8:25-31
3. Serrano MÁ, Boguñá M, Vespignani A (2009) Extracting the multiscale backbone of complex weighted networks. Proc Natl Acad Sci USA 106:6483-6488
4. Harrison CW, Boorman SA, Breiger RL (1976) Social structure from multiple networks. I. Blockmodels of roles and positions. Am J Sociol 81:730-780
5. Boorman SA, Harrison CW (1976) Social structure from multiple networks. II. Role structures. Am J Sociol 81:1384-1446
6. Lorrain F, White HC (1971) Structural equivalence of individuals in social networks. J Math Sociol 1:49-80
7. Guimera R, Nunes Amaral LA (2005) Functional cartography of complex metabolic networks. Nature 433:895-900
8. Zachary WW (1977) An information flow model for conflict and fission in small groups. J Anthropol Res 33:452-473
9. Burt RS (2005) Brokerage and closure. An introduction to social capital. Oxford University Press, Oxford
10. Burt RS (1992) Structural holes. The social structure of competition. Harvard University Press, Cambridge
11. Gould RV, Fernandez RM (1989) Structures of mediation: a formal approach to brokerage in transaction networks. Sociol Method 19:89-126
12. Gould RV (1989) Power and social structure in community elites. Soc Forces 68:531-552
13. Baños R, Borge-Holthoefer J, Wang N, Moreno Y, González-Bailón S (2013) Diffusion dynamics with changing network composition. Entropy 15:4553-4568
14. González-Bailón S, Borge-Holthoefer J, Rivero A, Moreno Y (2011) The dynamics of protest recruitment through an online network. Sci Rep 1:197
15. Conover MD, Davis C, Ferrara E, McKelvey K, Menczer F, Flammini A (2013) The geospatial characteristics of a social movement communication network. PLoS ONE 8:e55957
16. Conover MD, Ferrara E, Menczer F, Flammini A (2013) The digital evolution of Occupy Wall Street. PLoS ONE 8:e64679
17. Merton RK (1957) Social theory and social structure. Free Press, New York

18. Burt RS (1982) Toward a structural theory of action: network models of social structure, perception and action. Academic Press, New York
19. Burt RS (1976) Positions in networks. Soc Forces 55:93-122
20. Burt RS (1978) Cohesion versus structural equivalence as a basis for network subgroups. Sociol Methods Res 7:189-212
21. Aral S, Van Alstyne M (2011) The diversity-bandwidth trade-off. Am J Sociol 117:90-171
22. Spiro ES, Acton RM, Butts CT (2013) Extended structures of mediation: re-examining brokerage in dynamic networks. Soc Netw 35:130-143
23. Burt RS (2004) Structural holes and good ideas. Am J Sociol 110:349-399
24. González-Bailón S, Wang N (2013) Networked Discontent: The Anatomy of Protest Campaigns in Social Media SSRN: http://ssrn.com/abstract=2268165
25. González-Bailón S, Wang N, Rivero A, Borge-Holthoefer J, Moreno Y (2014) Assessing the bias in samples of large online networks. Soc Netw 38:16-27
26. Newman MEJ (2006) Finding community structure in networks using the eigenvectors of matrices. Phys Rev E 74:036104
27. Csárdi G, Nepusz T (2006) The igraph software package for complex network research. InterJournal:1965
28. Arenas A, Fernández A, Gómez S (2008) Analysis of the structure of complex networks at different resolution levels. New J Phys 10:053039
29. Arenas A, Fernández A, Gómez S (2008) A complex network approach to the determination of functional groups in the neural system of *C. elegans*. In: Liò P, Yoneki E, Crowcroft J, Verma D (eds) Bio-inspired computing and communication, vol 5151. Springer, Berlin, pp 9-18
30. Le Martelot E, Hankin C (2012) Multi-scale community detection using stability optimisation. Int J Web Based Communities 9:323-348
31. Le Martelot E, Hankin C (2013) Fast multi-scale detection of relevant communities in large-scale networks. Comput J 56:1136-1150
32. Weng L, Menczer F, Ahn Y-Y (2013) Virality prediction and community structure in social networks. Sci Rep 3:2522
33. Arenas A, Borge-Holthoefer J, Gómez S, Zamora-López G (2010) Optimal map of the modular structure of complex networks. New J Phys 12:053009
34. Baños R, Borge-Holthoefer J, Moreno Y (2013) The role of hidden influentials in the diffusion of online information cascades. EPJ Data Sci 2:6
35. Olesen JM, Bascompte J, Dupont YL, Jordano P (2007) The modularity of pollination networks. Proc Natl Acad Sci USA 104:19891-19896

16

Partisan asymmetries in online political activity

Michael D Conover[1], Bruno Gonçalves[2*], Alessandro Flammini[1] and Filippo Menczer[1]

*Correspondence:
b.goncalves@neu.edu
[2]College of Computer and Information Sciences, Northeastern University, Boston, MA 02115, USA
Full list of author information is available at the end of the article

Abstract

We examine partisan differences in the behavior, communication patterns and social interactions of more than 18,000 politically-active Twitter users to produce evidence that points to changing levels of partisan engagement with the American online political landscape. Analysis of a network defined by the communication activity of these users in proximity to the 2010 midterm congressional elections reveals a highly segregated, well clustered, partisan community structure. Using cluster membership as a high-fidelity (87% accuracy) proxy for political affiliation, we characterize a wide range of differences in the behavior, communication and social connectivity of left- and right-leaning Twitter users. We find that in contrast to the online political dynamics of the 2008 campaign, right-leaning Twitter users exhibit greater levels of political activity, a more tightly interconnected social structure, and a communication network topology that facilitates the rapid and broad dissemination of political information.

1 Introduction

Digitally-mediated communication has become an integral part of the American political landscape, providing citizens access to an unprecedented wealth of information and organizational resources for political activity. So pervasive is the influence of digital communication on the political process that almost one quarter (24%) of American adults got the majority of their news about the 2010 midterm congressional elections from online sources, a figure that has increased three-fold since the Pew Research Center began monitoring the statistic during the 2002 campaign [1]. Relax the constraint that a majority of a person's political news and information must come from online sources and the figure jumps to include the 54% of adult Americans who went online in 2010 to get political information. Critically, this activity precipitates tangible changes in the beliefs and behaviors of voters, with 35% of Internet users who voted in 2010 reporting that political information they saw or read online made them decide to vote for or against a particular candidate [1].

Within this ecosystem of digital information resources, social media platforms play an especially important role in facilitating the spread of information by connecting and giving voice to the voting public [2–4]. Networked and unmoderated, social media are characterized by the large-scale creation and exchange of user-generated content [5], a production and consumption model that stands in stark contrast to the centralized editorial and distribution processes typical of traditional media outlets [6, 7].

In terms of political organization and engagement, the benefits of social media use are many. For voters, social media make it easier to share political information, draw attention to ideological issues, and facilitate the formation of advocacy groups with low barriers to entry and participation [8, 9]. The ease with which individual voters can connect with one another directly also makes it easier to aggregate small-scale acts, as in the case of online petitions, fundraising, or web-based phone banking [10]. Together, these features contribute to the widespread use of social media for political purposes among the voting public, with as many as 21% of online adults using social networking sites to engage with the 2010 congressional midterm elections [11]. Moreover, a survey by the Pew Internet and American Life Project finds that online political activity is correlated with more traditional forms of political participation, with individuals who use blogs or social networking sites as a vehicle for civic engagement being more likely to join a political or civic group, compared to other Internet users [12].

Likewise, candidates and traditional political organizations benefit from a constituency that is actively engaged with social media, finding it easier to raise money, organize volunteers and communicate directly with voters who use social media platforms [13]. Social media also facilitate the rapid dissemination of political frames, making it easy for key talking points to be communicated directly to a large number of constituents, rather than having to subject messages to the traditional media filter.

Considered in this light, it becomes clear why social media were argued to have played such an important role in the political success of the Democratic party in the 2008 presidential and congressional elections [14–16]. Survey data from the Pew Research Center showed that, along the seven dimensions used to measure online political activity, Obama voters were substantially more likely to use the Internet as an outlet for political activity [17]. In particular, Obama voters were more likely than McCain voters to create and share political content, and to engage politically on an online social network [17]. Moreover, a 2009 Edelman report found that in addition to a thirteen million member e-mail list, the Obama campaign enjoyed twice as much web traffic, had four times as many YouTube viewers and five times more Facebook friends compared to the McCain campaign [13]. While the direct effect of any one media strategy on the success of a campaign is difficult to assess and quantify, the data show that Obama campaign had a clear advantage in terms of online voter engagement.

Motivated by the connection between the widely reported advantage in on-line mobilization and the result of the 2008 presidential election, we seek to understand structural shifts in the American political landscape with respect to partisan asymmetries in online political engagement. We work toward this goal by examining partisan differences in the behavior, communication patterns and social interactions of more than 18,000 politically-active users of Twitter, a social networking platform that allows individuals to create and share brief 140-character messages. Among all social media services, Twitter makes an appealing analytical target for a number of reasons: the public nature of its content, the accessibility of the data through APIs, a strong focus on news and information sharing, and its prominence as a platform for political discourse in America and abroad [18, 19]. These features make a compelling case for using this platform to study partisan political activity.

For this analysis we build on the findings of a previous study which established the macroscopic structure of US domestic political communication on Twitter. In that work we employed clustering techniques and qualitative content analysis to demonstrate that the network of political retweets exhibits a highly segregated, partisan structure [20]. Despite this segregation, we found that politically left- and right-leaning individuals engage in interaction across the partisan divide using mentions, a behavior strongly correlated with a type of cross-ideological provocation we term 'content injection.'

Having established the large-scale structure of these communication networks, in this study we employ a variety of methods to provide a more detailed picture of domestic political communication on Twitter. We characterize a wide range of differences in the behavior, communication, geography and social connectivity of thousands of politically left- and right-leaning users. Specifically, we demonstrate that right-leaning Twitter users exhibit greater levels of political activity, tighter social bonds, and a communication network topology that facilitates the rapid and broad dissemination of political information, a finding that stands in stark contrast to the online political dynamics of the 2008 campaign.

With respect to individual-level behaviors, we find that right-leaning Twitter users produce more than 50% more total political content and devote a greater proportion of their time to political discourse. Right-leaning users are also more likely to use hyperlinks to share and refer to external content, and are almost twice as likely than left-leaning users to self-identify their political alignment in their profile biographies. At the individual level, these behavioral factors paint a picture of a right-leaning constituency comprised of highly-active, politically-engaged social media users, a trend we see reflected in the communication and social networks in which these individuals participate.

Regarding connectivity patterns among users in these two communities we report findings related to three different networks, described by the set of explicitly declared follower/followee relationships, mentions, and retweets. Casting the declared follower network as the social substrate over which political information is most likely to spread, we find that right-leaning users exhibit a greater propensity for mutually-affirmed social ties, and that right-leaning users tend to form connections with a greater number of individuals in total compared to those on the left. With respect to the way in which information actually propagates over this substrate in the form of retweets, right-leaning users enjoy a network structure that is more likely to facilitate the rapid and broad dissemination of political information. Additionally, right-leaning users exhibit a higher probability to rebroadcast content from and to be rebroadcast by a large number of users, and are more likely to be members of high-order retweet network k-cores and k-cliques, structural features that are associated with the efficient spreading of information and adoption of political behavior and opinions. Pointing definitively to a vocal, socially engaged, densely interconnected constituency of right-leaning users, these topological and behavioral features provide a significantly more nuanced perspective on political communication on this important social media platform. Moreover, through its use of digital trace data to illuminate a complex sociological phenomenon, this article illustrates the explanatory power of data science techniques and underscores the potential of this burgeoning scientific epistemology.

2 Platform and data

2.1 The Twitter platform

Twitter is a popular social networking and microblogging site where users can post 140-character messages containing text and hyperlinks, called *tweets*, and interact with one another in a variety of ways. In the present section we describe four of the platform's key features: follow relationships, retweets, mentions, and hashtags.

Twitter allows each user to broadcast tweets to an audience of users who have elected to subscribe to the stream of content he or she produces. The act of subscribing to a user's tweets is known as *following*, and represents a directed, non-reciprocal social link between two users. From a content consumption perspective, each user can sample tweets from a variety of content streams, including the stream of tweets produced by the users he or she follows, as well as the set of tweets containing specific keywords known as hashtags.

A hashtag is a tokens prepended with a pound sign (e.g., #token) which, when displayed, functions as a hyperlink to the stream of recent tweets containing the specified tag [21]. While they can be used to specify the topic of a tweet (e.g., #oil or #taxes), when used in political communication hashtags are commonly employed to identify one or more intended audiences, as in the case of the most popular political hashtags, #tcot and #p2, acronyms for 'Top Conservative on Twitter' and 'Progressives 2.0', respectively. In this way, hashtags function to broaden the audience of a tweet, extending its visibility beyond a person's immediate followers to include all users who seek out content associated with the tag's topic or audience. For this reason, as outlined in Section 3.1, we restrict our analysis to the set of tweets containing political hashtags, ensuring that the content under study is broadly public and expressly political in nature.

In addition to broadcasting tweets to the public at large, Twitter users can interact directly with one another in two primary ways: retweets and mentions. Retweets often act as a form of endorsement, allowing individuals to rebroadcast content generated by other users, thus raising the content's visibility [22]. Mentions allow someone to address a specific user directly through the public feed, or, to a lesser extent, refer to an individual in the third person. In this study, we differentiate between mentions that occur in the body of the tweet and those that occur at the beginning of a tweet, as they correspond to distinct modes of interaction. Mentions located at the beginning of a tweet are known as 'replies', and typically represent actual engagement, while mentions in the body of a tweet typically constitute a third-person reference [23]. Together, retweets and mentions act as the primary mechanisms for explicit, public user-user interaction on Twitter.

2.2 Data

The analysis described in this article relies on data collected from the Twitter 'gardenhose' streaming API[a] between September 1st and January 7th, 2011 - the eighteen week period surrounding the November 4th United States congressional midterm elections. The gardenhose provides a sample of approximately 10% of the entire Twitter corpus in a machine-readable format. Each tweet entry is composed of several fields, including a unique identifier, the content of the tweet (including hashtags and hyperlinks), the time it was produced, the username of the account that produced the tweet, and in the case of retweets or mentions, the account names of the other users associated with the tweet.

From this eighteen week period we collected data on 6,747 right-leaning users and 10,741 left-leaning users, responsible for producing a total of 1,390,528 and 2,420,370 tweets, respectively. It's useful to note that we evaluate all gardenhose tweets associated with each user, rather than just those containing political hashtags, in order to facilitate comparisons between the two groups in terms of relative proportions of attention allocated to political communication.

3 Methodology

In order to examine differences in the behavior and connectivity of left- and right-leaning Twitter users we rely on the political hashtags and partisan cluster membership labels established in a previous study on political polarization. In addition to reviewing the approach used to establish these features, we show that the networks and communities under study are representative of domestic political communication on Twitter in general.

3.1 Identifying political content

As outlined in Section 2.1, hashtags are used to specify the topic or intended audience of a tweet, and allow a user to engage a much larger potential audience than just his or her immediate followers. We define the set of pertinent political communication as any tweet containing at least one political hashtag. While an individual can engage in political communication without including a hashtag, the potential audience for such content is limited primarily to his or her immediate followers. Moreover, restricting our analysis to tweets which have been expressly identified as political in nature allows us to define a high-fidelity corpus, avoiding the risk of introducing undue noise through the use of topic detection strategies [24, 25].

To isolate a representative set of political hashtags and to avoid introducing bias into the dataset we performed a simple algorithmic hashtag discovery procedure. We began by seeding our sample with the two most popular political hashtags, #p2 ('Progressives 2.0') and #tcot ('Top Conservatives on Twitter'). For each seed we identified the set of hashtags with which it co-occurred in at least one tweet, and ranked the results using the Jaccard coefficient. For a set of tweets S containing a seed hashtag, and a set of tweets T containing a second hashtag, the Jaccard coefficient between S and T is

$$\sigma(S, T) = \frac{|S \cap T|}{|S \cup T|}. \tag{1}$$

Thus, when the tweets in which both seed and the second hashtag occur make up a large portion of the tweets in which either occurs, the two are deemed to be related. Using a similarity threshold of 0.005 we identified sixty-six unique hashtags (Table 1), eleven of which were excluded due to overly-broad or ambiguous meanings (Table 2). While it is a common practice among spammers to contribute content to popular hashtag streams, we do not believe this phenomenon plays a substantial role in a shaping the structure of the sample data. During a previous study we found that of 1,000 manually-inspected accounts identified by this methodology fewer than 3% corresponded to foreign language or spam activity [20].

3.2 Representativeness

Using the technique outlined above we identified many high-profile political hashtags, and with them the majority of tweets and users associated with domestic political communication on Twitter. Supporting this claim, Figure 1 shows a roughly exponential decay in hashtag popularity as measured in terms of number of users or tweets associated with the hashtag. This sharp decay in the tag popularity indicates that the inclusion of additional political hashtags is not likely to substantially increase the size or alter the structure of the corpus.

Table 1 Political hashtags related to #p2 **and** #tcot **(acronyms for 'Progressives 2.0' and 'Top Conservatives on Twitter')**

Just #p2	#casen #dadt #dc10210 #democrats #du1 #fem2 #gotv #kysen #lgf #ofa #onenation #p2b #pledge #rebelleft #truthout #vote #vote2010 #whyimvotingdemocrat #youcut
Both	#cspj #dem #dems #desen #gop #hcr #nvsen #obama #ocra #p2 #p21 #phnm #politics #sgp #tcot #teaparty #tlot #topprog #tpp #twisters #votedem
Just #tcot	#912 #ampat #ftrs #glennbeck #hhrs #iamthemob #ma04 #mapoli #palin #palin12 #spwbt #tsot #tweetcongress #ucot #wethepeople

Tweets containing any of these were included in our sample.

Table 2 Hashtags excluded from the analysis due to ambiguous or overly broad meaning

Excluded from #p2	#economy #gay #glbt #us #wc #lgbt
Excluded from both	#israel #rs
Excluded from #tcot	#news #qsn #politicalhumor

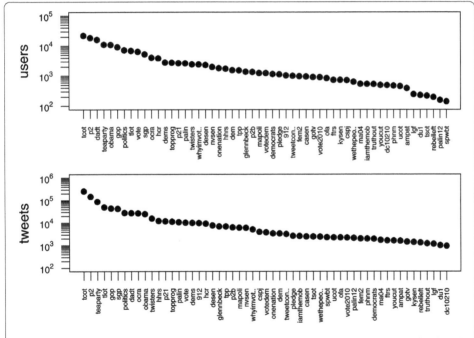

Figure 1 Hashtag popularity decay in terms of total number of tweets and users associated with each tag. On the horizontal axis tags have been ordered according to one of the two popularity measures: number of tweets (bottom) and users (top). The roughly exponential decay indicates that the inclusion of additional hashtags is unlikely to result in a substantial increase in the size of the corpus.

This claim is also supported by Figure 2, which shows that there is a strong effect of diminishing returns with respect to the observed number of unique users and tweets as the number of hashtags included in our analysis increases. This effect is due to the fact that many tweets are annotated with multiple hashtags, and many users utilize several different hashtags over the course of the study period. As a result, the inclusion of a single hashtag may result in the inclusion of many tweets and users also redundantly associated with other hashtags.

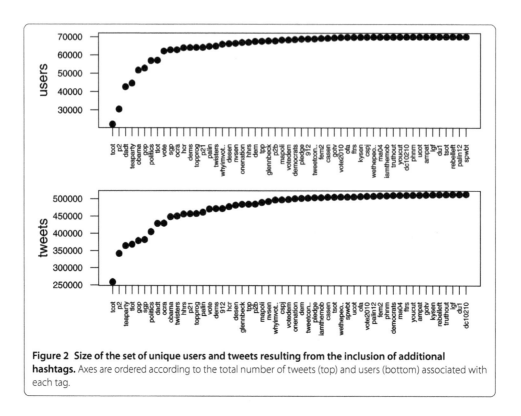

Figure 2 Size of the set of unique users and tweets resulting from the inclusion of additional hashtags. Axes are ordered according to the total number of tweets (top) and users (bottom) associated with each tag.

To further support the claim that sampling based on this set of hashtags produces a representative set of political tweets, we selected all the tweets in the gardenhose from the study period that included any one of 2,500 hand-selected political keywords related to the 2010 elections [26]. We considered only the 312,560 tweets in this set containing a hashtag because we use this characteristic to define public political communication on Twitter. We found that 26.4% of these tweets are covered by our target set of hashtags. Furthermore, among the ten most popular hashtags not included in our target set (#2010memories, #2010disappointments, #ff, #p2000, #2010, #business, #uk, #newsjp, #asia, #sports), only one is explicitly political and its volume accounts for less than 2% of public political communication. This coverage confirms that we have isolated a substantial and representative sample of political communication on Twitter.

3.3 Inferring political identities from communication networks

In a previous study we used the set of political tweets from the six weeks preceding the 2010 midterm election to build a network representing political retweet interactions among Twitter users. In this network an edge runs from a node representing user A to a node representing user B if B retweets content originally broadcast by A, indicating that information has propagated from A to B. This network consists of 23,766 non-isolate nodes among a total of 45,365, with 18,470 nodes in its largest connected component and 102 nodes in the next-largest component. We describe the construction of an analogous network of political mentions in Section 5.3.

Using a combination of network clustering algorithms and manually-annotated data we determined that the network of political retweets neatly divides the population of users in the largest connected component into two distinct communities (Figure 3) [20]. In brief, we used Rhaghavan's label propagation method seeded with node labels determined by

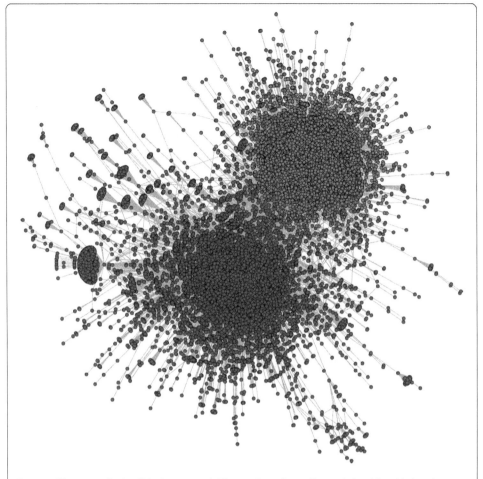

Figure 3 The network of political retweets, laid out using a force-directed algorithm. Node colors reflect cluster assignments, which correspond to politically homogeneous communities of left- and right-leaning users with 87% accuracy. (See Section 3.3.)

Newman's leading eigenvector modularity maximization method to assign cluster membership to each node [27, 28]. The final community assignments are consistent and robust to fluctuations in starting conditions [20]. To determine whether these communities were composed of users from the political left and right, respectively, we used qualitative content analysis to evaluate the tweets produced by 1,000 random users appearing in the intersection of the mention and retweet networks [29, 30].

To establish the reproducibility of these results we had two authors, working independently, determine whether the content of a user's tweets express a 'left', 'right' or 'undecidable' political identity according to the coding rubric developed in a previous study [20]. These annotations were compared against the work of an independent non-author judge, and using a well-established measure of inter-annotator agreement we report 'nearly perfect' inter-annotator agreement between author and non-author annotations for the 'left' and 'right' classes (Cohen's Kappa values of 0.80 and 0.82, respectively) and 'fair to moderate' agreement for the 'undecidable' category (Cohen's Kappa value of 0.42) [29, 30]. From these high levels of inter-annotator agreement we conclude that an objective outside party would be able to reproduce our class assignments for most users.

Table 3 Partisan composition of retweet cluster communities as determined through manual annotation of 1, 000 random users. (See Section 3.3)

Cluster	Left	Right	Undecidable	# Nodes
A (Top)	1.19%	93.4%	5.36%	7,115
B (Bottom)	80.1%	8.71%	11.1%	11,355

Based on this content analysis, we determined that the retweet network communities are highly politically homogeneous, consisting of 80.1% left- and 93.4% right-leaning users, respectively (Table 3) [20]. In this study we use network community membership as a proxy for the political identities of all 18,470 users in the largest connected component of the retweet network, and hereafter focus on the behavior of these users. Based on the relative proportions of right- and left-leaning users identified during the qualitative content analysis stage, this mechanism results in correct predictions for 87.3% of users in the largest connected component of the retweet network [31].

In the following sections we leverage these data to explore, in detail, how users from the political left and right utilize this important social media platform for political activity in different ways.

4 Behavior: individual-level political activity

Before examining structural differences in the social and communication networks of left- and right-leaning Twitter users, we first focus on political activity at the individual level. In this section we compare users in the left- and right-leaning communities in terms of their relative rates of content production, the amount of attention they allot to political communication, their respective rates of political self-identification, and their propensity for sharing information resources in the form of hyperlinks.

Right-leaning users are substantially more active and politically engaged with this social media platform. Specifically, our analysis shows that left-leaning users produce less total political content, allocate proportionally less time to creating political content, are less likely to reveal their political ideology in their profile biography, and are less likely to share resources in the form of hyperlinks. All of these findings stand in stark contrast to survey data and media reportage of the 2008 online political dynamics, and provide evidence in support of the notion that right-leaning voters are becoming more politically engaged online.

4.1 Political communication

From the perspective of leveraging social media for political organization, the baseline level of activity among a constituency is one of the most important characteristics of a population. Figure 4 shows that while left- and right-leaning users produce approximately the same number of tweets per user, right-leaning individuals actually produce 54% more total political content despite comprising fewer users altogether. This trend is the result of divergent priorities among left- and right-leaning users, as right-leaning users devote a substantially larger portion of their activity on Twitter to political communication. In fact, right-leaning users were almost twice as likely to create political content, with 22% of all tweets produced by right-leaning users containing one or more of the political hashtags under study, compared to only 12% for left-leaning users.

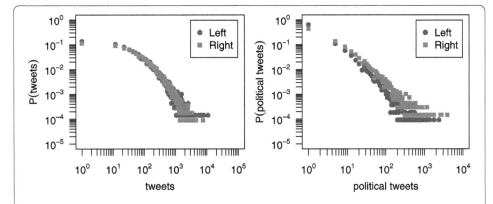

Figure 4 Total number of tweets produced by right- and left-leaning users (left) compared to the total number of political tweets produced by users in each group. While both groups produce a comparable amount of content in general, right-leaning users produce a much larger number of political tweets despite comprising fewer users in total. We observe that users' behavior tends to be broadly distributed, with many individuals creating relatively few tweets, while a few individuals produce substantially larger volumes of content. Note, however, that this sample includes only users who produced at least one political hashtag, rather than a random sample among all Twitter users, a feature likely responsible for the low number of users who produce few total tweets.

4.2 Partisan self-identification

In addition to devoting a larger proportion of tweets to political content, right-leaning users are much more likely to use their 140-character profile 'biography' to explicitly self-identify their political alignment. A survey of the biographies of 400 random users from the set of individuals selected for qualitative content analysis (Section 3.3) reveals that 38.7% of right-leaning users included reference to their political alignment in this valuable space, as compared with only 24.6% of users in the left-leaning community. Taken together, this analysis demonstrates that right-leaning users are much more likely to use Twitter as an outlet for political communication, and are substantially more inclined to view the Twitter platform as an explicitly political space.

4.3 Resource sharing

One of the key functions of the Twitter platform is to serve as a medium for sharing information in the form of hyperlinks to external content [22]. Given the constraints of the 140-character format, hyperlinking activity is especially important to the dissemination of detailed political information among members of a constituency.

With respect to this aspect of online political engagement, too, we see that right-leaning users are more active then those individuals in the left-leaning community. Among all tweets produced by users in the right-leaning community, 43.4% contained a hyperlink, compared with 36.5% of all tweets from left-leaning users. This trend is even more pronounced if we consider only resource sharing within the set of political tweets, with left-leaning users including a hyperlink in 50.8% of political tweets, as compared to right-leaning users, who include hyperlinks 62.5% of the time. From these observations we conclude that right-leaning users are more inclined to treat Twitter as a platform for aggregating and sharing links to web-based resources, an activity crucial to the efficient spread of political information on the Twitter platform.

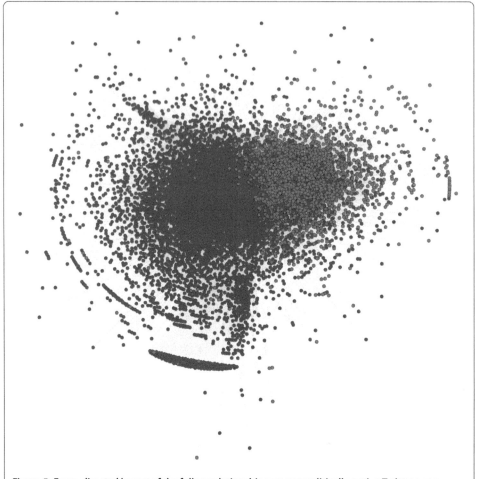

Figure 5 Force-directed layout of the follow relationships among politically-active Twitter users.
Nodes are colored according to political identity, connections to users who did not engage political
communication on Twitter are not included.

5 Connectivity: global-level political activity

Next, we turn our attention to structural differences in social interaction and communication networks of left- and right-leaning users.

5.1 Follower network

We begin with an analysis of the network defined by the follower/followee relationships shared among members of these two groups (Figure 5). Encoding the fact that a user subscribes to the content produced by another, the follower network is best understood as describing the social substrate over which information is likely to flow between political actors on Twitter. Specifically, though not all connections in the follower network encode equally meaningful social relationships [32], content is broadcast equally along all edges in this network.

We examine the differences in the follower subgraphs induced by considering only connections between users of the same political affiliation. For the purposes of this analysis, a directed edge is drawn from user A to user B if A is a follower of B. Basic statistics about these two subgraphs, including average degree, undirected clustering coefficient, and proportion of reciprocal links are presented in Table 4. We see that along all dimensions, users

Table 4 Follower network statistics for the subgraphs induced by the set of edges among users of the same political affiliation

Community	Nodes	Edges	Average degree	Clustering coefficient	Reciprocity
Left	9,941	803,329	80.80	0.134	42.8%
Right	6,426	1,503,417	233.95	0.221	64.8%

Reciprocity is defined as $\frac{D_R}{D}$, where D_R is the number of dyads with an edge in each direction and D is the total number of dyads with at least one edge. Follower data was only available for a subset of the study population, owing to private or deleted accounts.

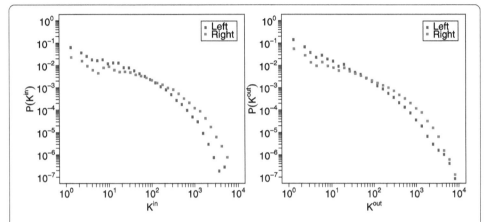

Figure 6 Log binned in- and out-degree distributions of the internal follower network at left, and right, respectively. As a result of considering only follower relationships among politically-active users we observe strong cutoffs in both distributions that make curve-fitting unreliable. However, comparing the two distributions it's clear that the right-leaning community has a much greater proportion of users with many followers (Kolmogorov-Smirnov $p < 10^{-3}$), despite being comprised of fewer users in total. Understood as an information diffusion substrate, the proliferation of high-profile hubs gives a natural advantage to the right-leaning community.

in the right-leaning community are much more tightly interconnected, with a substantially higher average clustering coefficient and greater average degree. Additionally, we observe a higher proportion of reciprocal links between right-leaning users, indicating the presence of stronger, mutually-affirmed interest among individuals in this community. All of these factors indicate that right-leaning users are more tightly interconnected, resulting in a basic structural advantage with respect to the challenge of efficiently spreading political information on the Twitter platform.

Using the Kolmogorov-Smirnov two-sample test to measure the degree of similarity between the in- and out-degree distribution for left- and right-leaning users we find a significant difference between the in-degree distributions of left- and right-leaning users, but only a marginal difference between the corresponding out-degree distributions (Figure 6). We interpret this to mean that a right-leaning user is more likely to have a large audience of followers who may potentially rebroadcast his or her call to action or piece of political information. For example, left-leaning users are roughly twice as likely as right-leaning users to have in-degree one, while users that are associated with the right are almost four times more likely to have in-degree 1,000 than users associated with the left. Additionally, users in the left-leaning community are more likely to be only peripherally connected into the network, as evidenced by the distribution of the k-core shell indices of users in each community (Figure 7). For a given network, the k-core is the maximal subgraph whose nodes (as members of the subgraph) have at least degree k, or, in other words, have at

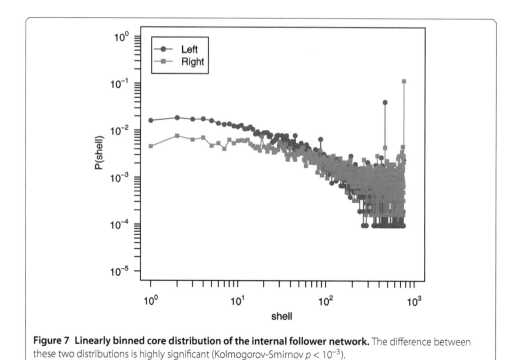

Figure 7 Linearly binned core distribution of the internal follower network. The difference between these two distributions is highly significant (Kolmogorov-Smirnov $p < 10^{-3}$).

least k neighbors in the k-core itself. The shell index, c, of a node refers to the coreness (k) of the highest-order k-core of which the node is a member [33].

These observations lead us to conclude that there are substantial structural differences in the fundamental patterns of social connectivity among politically left- and right-leaning Twitter users, a finding supported by the seminal work of Adamic and Glance [34] on the connectivity patterns of high-profile partisan bloggers. Specifically, the right-leaning community is much more densely interconnected, with more users tightly integrated into the right-leaning social network. In contrast, the network of follower/followee relations among left-leaning users exhibits a much more decentralized, loosely-interconnected structure, with far fewer mutually-affirmed social connections.

5.2 Retweet network

Next we consider the structure of the network of political retweets in order to understand how information actually spreads on the social substrate characterized in Section 5.1. While each link in the follower network represents a potential pathway along which information may flow, edges in the retweet network correspond to real information propagation events. Specifically, when user A rebroadcasts a tweet produced by user B, she explicitly signifies receipt of the content in question, and thus we draw an edge from user B to user A indicating the direction of information flow. Consequently, the structure of the retweet network reveals much about how information actually spreads within these two communities. Visualized previously in Figure 3, basic statistics describing the networks induced by retweets containing at least one political hashtag between users of the same partisan affiliation are show in Table 5.

In practice, the tightly-interconnected structure of the retweet network confers communication advantages to the right-leaning community of users. Examining the in- and out-degree distributions for these two communities we find that though the power-law

Table 5 Retweet network statistics for the subgraphs induced by the set of edges among users of the same political affiliation

Community	Nodes	Edges	Average degree	Clustering coefficient	Reciprocity
Left	11,353	32,772	2.88	0.032	13.5%
Right	7,115	39,713	5.58	0.045	12.1%

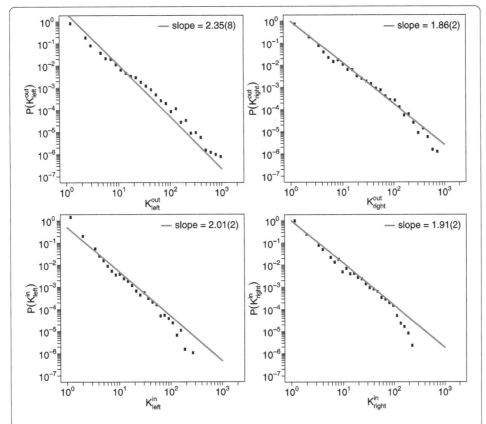

Figure 8 Log binned in- and out-degree distributions for the left- and right-leaning retweet network communities. Slopes and standard errors were inferred using the maximum likelihood estimation method described by Clauset, Shalizi and Newman [38]. The rapid decay of the left-leaning degree distribution indicates that right-leaning users are retweeted by and retweet content from a larger number of users than those on the left.

exponents are similar, the difference between them is statistically significant at the 95% level (Figure 8). The faster decay in the degree distribution of the left-leaning community implies that right-leaning users are rebroadcast by and rebroadcast content from a larger number of individuals than users on the left. That right-leaning users pay attention to more information sources compared to left-leaning individuals is indicative of a higher degree of engagement with the Twitter platform itself. Similarly, an individual wishing to rapidly reach a wide audience has a natural advantage given the structure of the right-leaning retweet network.

With respect to the number of users in high-order k-cores, too, we see that the right-leaning community enjoys structural advantages, with a greater proportion of highly active users connected to other highly active users (Figure 9). This difference could lead to consequences in the spread of information through these networks. Work by Kitsak et al. indicates that it is individuals with high shell index, rather than those who are most cen-

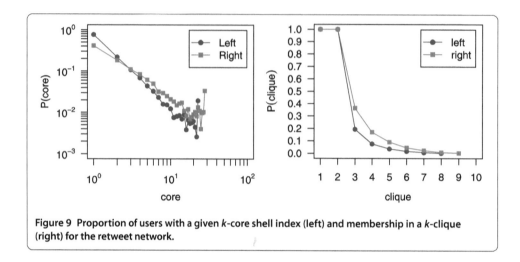

Figure 9 Proportion of users with a given *k*-core shell index (left) and membership in a *k*-clique (right) for the retweet network.

Table 6 Mention network statistics for the subgraphs induced by the set of edges among users of the same political affiliation

Community	Nodes	Edges	Average degree	Clustering coefficient	Reciprocity
Left	11,353	50,273	4.42	0.053	20.8%
Right	7,115	64,993	9.13	0.078	24.5%

tral or well connected, who are the most effective spreaders of information under a simple SIR-based information diffusion model [35]. Users on the right therefore, are more likely than those on the left to be wired into the political communication network in such a way that they are able to facilitate the broad and rapid dissemination of political information.

We also find that a substantially higher proportion of right-leaning user participate in fully-connected subgraphs of size *k*, known as *k*-cliques. This result is especially important in the context of the complex contagion hypothesis, which posits that repeated exposures to controversial behaviors are essential to the adoption of these behaviors. Work by Romero, Meeder and Kleinberg focused specifically on online social networks indicates that this effect is particularly pronounced for political discourse on Twitter [36]. With fewer users in high-order *k*-cores, individuals in the left-leaning community will be less likely to encounter multiple users discussing the same partisan talking points or calls to action, exactly the kind of contentious content whose propagation is most likely to benefit from repeated exposure.

5.3 Mention network

Mentions are most strongly associated with direct, conversational engagement when the target username appears at the beginning of a tweet, as opposed to appearing in the body text. Among the mentions in our sample, the overwhelming majority (94.5%) take this form, providing strong evidence that connectivity among and between users in these two groups represents actual political discourse rather than simply third-person references. In Table 6 we report descriptive statistics on the topology of the left- and right-leaning mention networks, where an edge from *A* to *B* is drawn between two users of the same political affiliation if *A* mentions *B* in a tweet containing at least one political hashtag. Though the two networks exhibit very similar degree distributions, one important distinction is the fact that a greater proportion of mention relationships in the right-leaning community are reciprocal. Compared to the number of reciprocal mentions observed in degree-preserving reshufflings of the left- and right-leaning mention networks, the right-leaning community exhibits 7.5 times as many reciprocal mention interactions than is expected by chance alone, compared to a 5.6 times as many reciprocal links in the left-leaning community. Reciprocal interactions suggest the presence of more meaningful social connections, manifest in conversational dialogue, rather than, for example, unidirectional commentary on the content of another user's tweets [32]. Here too, we find that users on the political right are more engaged with one another on Twitter, indicating that they are likely to benefit from a richer dialogue and hence more opportunities for frame-making and consensus building with respect to political topics.

6 Political geography

In addition to characterizing differences in behavior and connectivity, we can also examine the geographic distribution of individuals in these two communities. Here we present a cartogram in which the color of each state has been scaled to correspond to the degree to which, in that state, the observed number of tweets originating from the left-leaning community exceeds what we should expect by chance alone.

Because fewer than one percent of Twitter users provide precise geolocation data, we instead rely on the self-declared 'location' field of each user's profile to enable geographic analysis of data at the scale of this study. As a free-text field, users are able to enter in arbitrary data, and non-location responses such as 'the moon' do appear in the results. Complicating this analysis further, some users do not report any location data, though we do not report a partisan bias in terms of non-entries. Despite these caveats, a large number of users do report actual locations, and using the Yahoo Maps Web Service API,[b] we are able to make a best-guess estimate about the state with which a user most strongly identifies.

Thus, for each state in which we observe N total tweets, and the relative proportion of tweets originating from left-leaning users (P_l), we can treat the arrival of partisan tweets as a Bernoulli process, and compute the number of tweets we should expect to see from left-leaning users as NP_l. Likewise, we can compute the extent to which the observed number of tweets associated with left-leaning users (T_l) is above or below the expected number, measured in terms of standard deviations, as $\frac{T_l - NP_l}{\sqrt{NP_l \cdot (1 - P_l)}}$. Figure 10 uses color to encode these deviations for each state, with states in which the volume of activity far exceeds what should be expected by chance shown in deep red, and those in which the observed volume is far below what should be expected by chance shown in light yellow.

Initial inspection of this figure reveals that the geographic distribution of individuals from the left-leaning network community corresponds strongly to the traditional political geography of the United States. We see that left-leaning individuals feature prominently on the coasts and North East, and tend to be underrepresented in the midwest and plains states.

Looking more closely, however, we find that there are some places in which the partisan makeup of tweets is quite different from what might be hypothesized intuitively. For example, Utah, a traditionally conservative state which at the time of this writing had two Republican senators, exhibits a dramatically higher volume of left-leaning content than should be expected by chance alone. One possible explanation for this observation could be that individuals in some states with an ideologically homogeneous population turn to

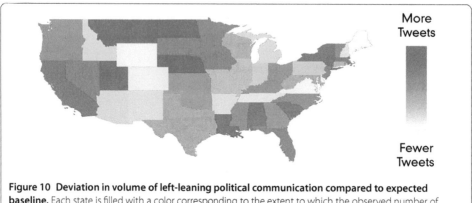

Figure 10 Deviation in volume of left-leaning political communication compared to expected baseline. Each state is filled with a color corresponding to the extent to which the observed number of tweets is above or below what should be expected in the case where each state has traffic volume proportional to that observed across all Twitter traffic.

social media as an outlet for political expression. While this is but one possible explanation among many, and a more rigorous analysis is required to support any definitive claim, this example illustrates the ways in which novel hypotheses can derive from data-driven analyses of political and sociological phenomena.

7 Conclusion

In this study we have described a series of techniques and analyses that indicate a shifting landscape with respect to partisan asymmetries in online political engagement. We find that, in contrast to what might be expected given the online political dynamics of the 2008 campaign, right-leaning Twitter users exhibit greater levels of political activity, tighter social bonds, and a communication network topology that facilitates the rapid and broad dissemination of political information.

In terms of individual behavior, politically right-leaning Twitter users not only produce more political content and devote a greater proportion of their time to political discourse, but are also more likely to view the Twitter platform as an explicitly political space and identify their political leanings in their profiles. With respect to social interactions, the right-leaning community exhibits a higher proportion of reciprocal social and mention relationships, are more likely to rebroadcast content from a large number of sources, and are more likely to be members of high-order retweet network k-cores and k-cliques. Such structural features are directly associated with the efficient spreading of information and adoption of political behavior. Taken together, these features are indicative of a highly-active, densely-interconnected constituency of right-leaning users using this important social media platform to further their political views.

This study is characteristic of an emerging mode of inquiry in the political and social sciences, whereby large-scale behavioral data are aggregated and analyzed to shed quantitative light on questions whose scale was previously considered outside the realm of tractable analysis [37]. Using structural features of a digital communication network one can make high-fidelity inferences about the political identities of thousands of individuals. Such data provide a deeper understanding of the changing landscape of American online political activity. Looking forward, techniques such as these are likely to become increasingly important as the political and social sciences rely in greater measure on large-scale digital trace data describing human opinion and behavior.

Competing interests
The authors declare that they have no competing interests.

Author's contributions
MDC and BG collected the data and performed the analysis. MDC, BG, AF and FM conceived the experiments and wrote the manuscript.

Author details
[1]Center for Complex Networks and Systems Research, School of Informatics and Computing, Indiana University, Bloomington, IN 47408, USA. [2]College of Computer and Information Sciences, Northeastern University, Boston, MA 02115, USA.

Endnotes
[a] http://dev.twitter.com/pages/streaming_api/.
[b] http://developer.yahoo.com/maps/rest/V1/geocode.html.

References
1. Pew Internet and American Life Project (2010) The Internet and Campaign 2010. Technical report, Pew Research Center
2. Bennett L (2003) New media power: The Internet and global activism. In: Couldry N, Curran J (eds) Contesting media power: Alternative media in a networked world. Rowman and Littlefield, Totowa, pp 17-37
3. Aday S, Farrel H, Lynch M, Sides J, Kelly J, Zuckerman E (2010) Blogs and bullets: new media in contentious politics. Technical report, U.S. Institute of Peace
4. Farrell H, Drezner D (2008) The power and politics of blogs. Public Choice 134:15-30
5. Kaplan A, Haenlein M (2010) Users of the world, unite! The challenges and opportunities of Social Media. Bus Horiz 53:59-68
6. Benkler Y (2006) The wealth of networks: how social production transforms markets and freedom. Yale University Press, New Haven
7. Sunstein CR (2007) Republic.com 2.0. Princeton University Press, Princeton
8. Tolbert C, McNeal R (2003) Unraveling the effects of the Internet on political participation? Polit Res Q 56(2):175
9. Garrett R (2006) Protest in an information society: A review of literature on social movements and new ICTs. Information, Communication & Society 9(2):202-224
10. Land M (2009) Networked activism. Harv Hum Rights J 22:205
11. Pew Internet and American Life Project (2010) Social media and politics in 2010 campaign. Technical report, Pew Research Center
12. Pew Internet and American Life Project (2010) The Internet and civic engagement. Technical report, Pew Research Center
13. Lutz M (2009) The social pulpit: Barack Obama's social media toolkit. Technical report, Edelman
14. Carr D (2008) How Obama tapped into social networks' power. The New York Times
15. Creamer M (2008) Obama wins! ... Ad age's marketer of the year. Advertising Age
16. Holahan C (2008) John McCain is way behind online. Bloomberg Businessweek
17. Pew Internet and American Life Project (2008) Social networking and online videos take off: Internet's broader role in campaign 2008. Technical report, Pew Research Center. http://people-press.org/reports/display.php3?ReportID=384
18. Kwak H, Lee C, Park H, Moon S (2010) What is Twitter, a social network or a news media. In: Proceedings of the 19th international conference on World wide web. ACM, New York, pp 591-600
19. Howard P, Duffy A, Freelon D, Hussain M, Marai W, Mazaid M (2011) Opening closed regimes, what was the role of social media during the Arab Spring? Project on Information Technology Political Islam 1-30
20. Conover M, Ratkiewicz J, Francisco M, Gonçalves B, Flammini A, Menczer F (2011) Political polarization on Twitter. In: Fifth international AAAI conference on weblogs and social media, p 89
21. Java A, Song X, Finin T, Tseng B (2007) Why we Twitter: understanding microblogging usage and communities. In: Proc. of the 9th WebKDD and 1st SNA-KDD 2007 workshop on Web mining and social network analysis
22. Boyd D, Golder S, Lotan G (2008) Tweet, tweet, retweet: conversational aspects of retweeting on Twitter. In: Proc. Hawaii intl. conf. on systems sciences, pp 1-10
23. Honeycutt C, Herring SC (2008) Beyond microblogging: conversation and collaboration via Twitter. In: Proc. 42nd Hawaii intl conf. on system sciences
24. Landauer T, Foltz P, Laham D (1998) An introduction to latent semantic analysis. Discourse Process 25(2):259-284
25. Blei D, Ng A, Jordan M (2003) Latent Dirichlet allocation. J Mach Learn Res 3:993-1022
26. Ratkiewicz J, Conover M, Meiss M, Gonçalves B, Patil S, Flammini A, Menczer F (2011) Truthy: mapping the spread of astroturf in microblog streams. In: Proc. 20th intl. World Wide Web conf. (WWW)
27. Newman MEJ (2006) Finding community structure in networks using the eigenvectors of matrices. Phys Rev E, Stat Nonlinear Soft Matter Phys 74(3):036104
28. Raghavan UN, Albert R, Kumara S (2007) Near linear time algorithm to detect community structures in large-scale networks. Phys Rev E, Stat Nonlinear Soft Matter Phys 76(3):036106
29. Krippendorff K (ed) (2004) Content analysis: an introduction to its methodology. Sage, Thousand Oaks
30. Kolbe RH (1991) Content analysis research: an examination of applications with directives for improving research reliability and objectivity. J Consum Res 18(2):243-250
31. Conover M, Ratkiewicz J, Gonçalves B, Haff J, Flammini A, Menczer F (2011) Predicting the political alignment of Twitter users. In: Proceedings of 3rd IEEE conference on social computing (SocialCom)
32. Huberman B, Romero D, Wu F (2009) Social networks that matter: Twitter under the microscope. First Monday 14:8

33. Barrat A, Barthlemy M, Vespignani A (2008) Dynamical processes on complex networks. Cambridge University Press, Cambridge

34. Adamic L, Glance N (2005) The Political Blogosphere and the 2004 U.S. Election: Divided They Blog. In: Proc. 3rd intl. workshop on link discovery (LinkKDD), pp 36-43

35. Kitsak M, Gallos L, Havlin S, Liljeros F, Muchnik L, Stanley H, Makse H (2010) Identifying influential spreaders in complex networks. Nat Phys 6:888-893

36. Romero D, Meeder B, Kleinberg J (2011) Differences in the mechanics of information diffusion across topics: idioms, political hashtags, and complex contagion on twitter. In: Proceedings of the 20th international conference on World Wide Web. ACM, New York, pp 695-704

37. Lazer D, Pentland A, Adamic L, Aral S, Barabasi A, Brewer D, Christakis N, Contractor N, Fowler J, Gutmann M et al (2009) Life in the network: the coming age of computational social science. Science 323(5915):721

38. Clauset A, Shalizi C, Newman M (2009) Power-law distributions in empirical data. SIAM Rev 51:661

Permissions

List of Contributors

Chunyan Wang
Department of Applied Physics, Stanford University, Stanford, CA, USA

Bernardo A Huberman
Social Computing Lab, HP Labs, Palo Alto, California, USA

John Bryden
School of Biological Sciences, Royal Holloway, University of London, Egham, TW20 0EX, UK

Sebastian Funk
Department of Ecology and Evolutionary Biology, Princeton University, Princeton, NJ 08544, USA
London School of Hygiene & Tropical Medicine, Keppel Street, London, WC1E 7HT, UK

Vincent AA Jansen
School of Biological Sciences, Royal Holloway, University of London, Egham, TW20 0EX, UK

Vsevolod Salnikov
naXys, University of Namur, Rempart de la Vierge 8, Namur, 5000, Belgium

Daniel Schien
Department of Computer Science, University of Bristol, Merchant Venturers Building, Woodland Road, Bristol, BS8 1UB, UK

Hyejin Youn
Santa Fe Institute, 1399 Hyde Park Road, Santa Fe, NM 87501, USA
Institute for New Economic Thinking, Oxford Martin School, Walton Well Rd, Oxford, OX2 6ED, UK
Mathematical Institute, University of Oxford, Oxford, UK

Renaud Lambiotte
naXys, University of Namur, Rempart de la Vierge 8, Namur, 5000, Belgium

Michael T Gastner
Department of Engineering Mathematics, University of Bristol, Merchant Venturers Building, Woodland Road, Bristol, BS8 1UB, UK
Institute of Technical Physics and Materials Science, Research Centre for Natural Sciences, Hungarian Academy of Sciences, P.O. Box 49, Budapest, 1525, Hungary

Luca Maria Aiello
Department of Computer Science, University of Torino, Torino, Italy

Alain Barrat
Centre de Physique Theorique, Aix-Marseille Universite et Universite du Sud Toulon Var, CNRS UMR 6207, Marseille, France.
Data Science Laboratory, ISI Foundation, Torino, Italy

Ciro Cattuto
Data Science Laboratory, ISI Foundation, Torino, Italy

Rossano Schifanella
Department of Computer Science, University of Torino, Torino, Italy

Giancarlo Ruffo
Department of Computer Science, University of Torino, Torino, Italy

Alexander V Mantzaris
Department of Mathematics and Statistics, University of Strathclyde, 26 Richmond Street, Glasgow, G1 1XH, UK

Alexander Amini
SENSEable City Laboratory, Massachusetts Institute of Technology, 77 Massachusetts Avenue, Cambridge, 02139, USA

Kevin Kung
SENSEable City Laboratory, Massachusetts Institute of Technology, 77 Massachusetts Avenue, Cambridge, 02139, USA

Chaogui Kang
SENSEable City Laboratory, Massachusetts Institute of Technology, 77 Massachusetts Avenue, Cambridge, 02139, USA

Stanislav Sobolevsky
SENSEable City Laboratory, Massachusetts Institute of Technology, 77 Massachusetts Avenue, Cambridge, 02139, USA

Carlo Ratti
SENSEable City Laboratory, Massachusetts Institute of Technology, 77 Massachusetts Avenue, Cambridge, 02139, USA

Carmen Vaca Ruiz
Politecnico di Milano, Piazza Leonardo Da Vinci, 32, Milan, Italy FIEC, Escuela Superior Politecnica del Litoral, Campus Gustavo Galindo, Km 30.5 via Perimetral, Guayaquil, Ecuador

Luca Maria Aiello
Yahoo Labs, Av. Diagonal 177, 08018, Barcelona, Spain

Alejandro Jaimes
Yahoo Labs, Av. Diagonal 177, 08018, Barcelona, Spain

Sears Merritt
Department of Computer Science, University of Colorado, Boulder, CO 80309, USA

Aaron Clauset
Department of Computer Science, University of Colorado, Boulder, CO 80309, USA
BioFrontiers Institute, University of Colorado, Boulder, CO 80303, USA
Santa Fe Institute, 1399 Hyde Park Rd., Santa Fe, NM 87501, USA

Jisun An
Qatar Computing Research Institute, Majlis Al Taawon Street, Doha, Qatar

Daniele Quercia
Yahoo Labs, Avinguda Diagonal 177, Barcelona, Spain

Meeyoung Cha
Graduate School of Culture Technology, KAIST, 291 Daehak-ro, Daejeon, Republic of Korea

Krishna Gummadi
Max Plank Institute for Software Systems, Campus E1 5, Saarbrücken, Germany

Jon Crowcroft
Computer Laboratory, University of Cambridge, 15 JJ Thomson Avenue, Cambridge, UK

Emre Sarigöl
Chair of Systems Design, ETH Zurich, Weinbergstrasse 56/58, Zurich, 8004, Switzerland

René Pfitzner
Chair of Systems Design, ETH Zurich, Weinbergstrasse 56/58, Zurich, 8004, Switzerland

Ingo Scholtes
Chair of Systems Design, ETH Zurich, Weinbergstrasse 56/58, Zurich, 8004, Switzerland

Antonios Garas
Chair of Systems Design, ETH Zurich, Weinbergstrasse 56/58, Zurich, 8004, Switzerland

Frank Schweitzer
Chair of Systems Design, ETH Zurich, Weinbergstrasse 56/58, Zurich, 8004, Switzerland

Marcel Salathé
Center for Infectious Disease Dynamics, Penn State University, University Park, PA, USA
Department of Biology, Penn State University, University Park, PA, USA
Department of Computer Sciences and Engineering, Penn State University, University Park, PA, USA

Duy Q Vu
Department of Statistics, Penn State University, University Park, PA, USA

Shashank Khandelwal
Center for Infectious Disease Dynamics, Penn State University, University Park, PA, USA
Department of Biology, Penn State University, University Park, PA, USA

David R Hunter
Center for Infectious Disease Dynamics, Penn State University, University Park, PA, USA
Department of Statistics, Penn State University, University Park, PA, USA

Woon Peng Goh
Interdisciplinary Graduate School, Nanyang Technological University, 50 Nanyang Avenue, Singapore, 639798, Singapore Complexity Institute, Nanyang Technological University, 60 Nanyang View, Singapore, 639673, Singapore

Dennis Kwek
Office of Education Research, National Institute of Education, 1 Nanyang Walk, Singapore, 637616, Singapore

David Hogan
School of Education, Faculty of Humanities and Social Sciences, University of Queensland, Brisbane, QLD 4072, Australia

Siew Ann Cheong
Complexity Institute, Nanyang Technological University, 60 Nanyang View, Singapore, 639673, Singapore
School of Physical & Mathematical Sciences, Nanyang Technological University, 21 Nanyang Link, Singapore, 637371, Singapore

Raquel Alvarez
Institute for Biocomputation and Physics of Complex Systems, University of Zaragoza, Campus Rio Ebro, Zaragoza, 50018, Spain

David Garcia
Chair of Systems Design, ETH Zurich, Weinbergstrasse 56/58, Zurich, 8092, Switzerland

Yamir Moreno
Institute for Biocomputation and Physics of Complex Systems, University of Zaragoza, Campus Rio Ebro, Zaragoza, 50018, Spain

Frank Schweitzer
Chair of Systems Design, ETH Zurich, Weinbergstrasse 56/58, Zurich, 8092, Switzerland

Przemyslaw A Grabowicz
Max Planck Institute for Software Systems, Saarland University, Saarbrucken, Germany
Institute for Cross-Disciplinary Physics and Complex Systems, University of Balearic Islands, Palma de Mallorca, Spain

Luca Maria Aiello
Yahoo! Research, Barcelona, Spain

Filippo Menczer
Center for Complex Networks and Systems Research, Indiana University, Bloomington, USA

Sandra González-Bailón
Annenberg School for Communication, University of Pennsylvania, Philadelphia, USA

NingWang
Oxford Internet Institute, University of Oxford, Oxford, UK

Javier Borge-Holthoefer
Qatar Computing Research Institute, Qatar Foundation, Doha, Qatar

Michael D Conover
Center for Complex Networks and Systems Research, School of Informatics and Computing, Indiana University, Bloomington, IN 47408, USA

Bruno Gonçalves
College of Computer and Information Sciences, Northeastern University, Boston, MA 02115, USA

Alessandro Flammini
Center for Complex Networks and Systems Research, School of Informatics and Computing, Indiana University, Bloomington, IN 47408, USA

Filippo Menczer
Center for Complex Networks and Systems Research, School of Informatics and Computing, Indiana University, Bloomington, IN 47408, USA

Printed in the USA
CPSIA information can be obtained
at www.ICGtesting.com
JSHW051429221024
72173JS00006B/1413

9 781682 852989